Project Risk Management

Second Edition

Project Risk Management

Processes, Techniques and Insights

Second edition

Chris Chapman and Stephen Ward

School of Management, University of Southampton, UK

John Wiley & Sons, Ltd

This publication is designed to provide accurate and authoritative information in regard to
the subject matter covered. It is sold on the understanding that the Publisher is not engaged
in rendering professional services. If professional advice or other expert assistance is
required, the services of a competent professional should be sought.

Other Wiley Editorial Offices

John Wiley & Sons Inc., 111 River Street, Hoboken, NJ 07030, USA

Jossey-Bass, 989 Market Street, San Francisco, CA 94103-1741, USA

Wiley-VCH Verlag GmbH, Boschstr. 12, D-69469 Weinheim, Germany

John Wiley & Sons Australia Ltd, 33 Park Road, Milton, Queensland 4064, Australia

John Wiley & Sons (Asia) Pte Ltd, 2 Clementi Loop #02-01, Jin Xing Distripark, Singapore 129809

John Wiley & Sons Canada Ltd, 22 Worcester Road, Etobicoke, Ontario, Canada M9W 1L1

Wiley also publishes its books in a variety of electronic formats. Some content that appears
in print may not be available in electronic books.

British Library Cataloguing in Publication Data

A catalogue record for this book is available from the British Library

ISBN-13: 978-0-470-85355-9 (H/B)

Project management by Originator, Gt Yarmouth, Norfolk (typeset in 10/12pt Garamond)
Printed and bound in Great Britain by Antony Rowe Ltd, Chippenham, Wiltshire
This book is printed on acid-free paper responsibly manufactured from sustainable forestry
in which at least two trees are planted for each one used for paper production.

Contents

Foreword to the first edition

All projects involve risk—the zero risk project is not worth pursuing. This is not purely intuitive but also a recognition that acceptance of some risk is likely to yield a more desirable and appropriate level of benefit in return for the resources committed to the venture. Risk involves both threat and opportunity. Organizations that better understand the nature of the risks and can manage them more effectively cannot only avoid unforeseen disasters but can work with tighter margins and less contingency, freeing resources for other endeavours, and seizing opportunities for advantageous investment that might otherwise be rejected as 'too risky'.

Risk is present in every aspect of our lives; thus risk management is universal but in most circumstances an unstructured activity, based on common sense, relevant knowledge, experience and instinct. Project management has evolved over recent years into a fully-fledged professional discipline characterized by a formalized body of knowledge and the definition of systematic processes for the execution of a project. Yet project risk management has, until recently, generally been considered as an 'add-on' instead of being integral to the effective practice of project management.

This book provides a framework for integrating risk management into the management of projects. It explains how to do this through the definition of generic risk management processes and shows how these processes can be mapped onto the stages of the project life cycle. As the disciplines of formal project management are being applied ever more widely (e.g., to the management of change within organizations) so the generic project risk management processes set out here will readily find use in diverse areas of application.

The main emphasis is on processes rather than analytical techniques, which are already well documented. The danger in formalized processes is that they can become orthodox, bureaucratic, burdened with procedures, so that the practitioner loses sight of the real aims. This book provides the reader with a fundamental understanding of project risk management processes but avoids being overprescriptive in the description of the execution of these processes. Instead, there is positive encouragement to use these generic processes as a starting point for elaboration and adaptation to suit the circumstances of a particular application, to innovate and experiment, to simplify and streamline the practical implementation of the generic processes to achieve cost-effective and efficient risk management.

The notion of risk efficiency is central to the theme. All risk management processes consume valuable resources and can themselves constitute a risk to the project that must be effectively managed. The level of investment in risk management within projects must be challenged and justified on the level of expected benefit to the overall project. Chris Chapman and Steve Ward document numerous examples drawn from real project experience to substantiate the benefits of a formal process-oriented approach. Ultimately, project risk management is about people making decisions to try to optimize the outcome, being proactive in evaluating risk and the possible responses, using this information to best effect, demonstrating the need for changes in project plans, taking the necessary action and monitoring the effects. Balancing risk and expectation is one of the most challenging aspects of project management. It can also be exciting and offer great satisfaction, provided the project manager is able to operate in a climate of understanding and openness about project risk. The cultural change required in organizations to achieve this can be difficult and lengthy, but there is no doubt that it will be easier to accomplish if risk management processes are better understood and integrated into the practice of project management.

This book is a welcome and timely addition to the literature on risk management and will be of interest to all involved in project management as well as offering new insights to the project risk analyst.

Peter Wakeling
Director of Procurement Policy (Project Management)
Ministry of Defence (Procurement Executive)

Foreword to the second edition

The analysis of risk and the development of risk management processes have come a long way over the last 10 years, even since the late 1990s. Hence the need for a second edition of Chapman and Ward's *Project Risk Management*, first published in 1997.

They not only continue to push back the boundaries, Chapman has also been involved in the development of work aimed at practitioners—PRAM (Association for Project Management) and RAMP (Institution of Civil Engineers and Faculty/Institute of Actuaries). They importantly make comparisons between their work and both PRAM and RAMP, as well as with the Project Management Institute's PMBOK 2000. They have developed and named the generic framework SHAMPU (Shape, Harness, and Manage Project Uncertainty) process and compare it with PRAM, RAMP, and PBOK 2000. I suggest that the authors of these three will want to use SHAMPU as a challenge to their own further thinking.

Chapman and Ward say that their book is largely about how to achieve effective and efficient risk management in the context of a single project. Determining what can be simplified, and what it is appropriate to simplify, is not a simple matter! In their final chapter they adopt a corporate perspective on project risk management processes. Thus they mirror the work already under way by the ICE/Actuaries team who have embarked on the development of STRATrisk, designed to enable prime decision makers to deal more systematically with the most important opportunities and threats to their business.

They quote Walsham who has suggested a management framework which views organizational change as a jointly analytical, educational and political process where important interacting dimensions are the context, content and process of the change. They conclude by stating that 'most project risk is generated by the way different people perceive issues and react to them.' Those of us who have driven such projects as the Hong Kong Mass Transit Railway (very successfully) and the Channel Tunnel (less so) will say 'hear, hear' to all of that.

Professor Tony M. Ridley
Imperial College London
Past President, Institution of Civil Engineers

Preface

Projects motivating this book

The projects that motivated initial development of many of the ideas in this book were primarily large engineering projects in the energy sector: large-scale Arctic pipelines in the far north of North America in the mid-1970s, BP's North Sea projects from the mid-1970s to the early 1980s, and a range of Canadian and US energy projects in the early 1980s. In this period the initial focus was 'the project' in engineering and technical terms, although the questions addressed ranged from effective planning and unbiased cost estimation to effective contractual and insurance arrangements and appropriate technical choices in relation to the management of environmental issues and related approval processes.

The projects that motivated evolution of these ideas from the mid-1980s to the present (August 2003) involved considerable diversification: defence projects (naval platforms, weapon systems, and information systems), civil information systems, nuclear power station decommissioning, nuclear waste disposal, deep mining, water supply system security, commodity trading (coffee and chocolate), property management, research and development management, civil engineering construction management systems, electric utility long-term and medium-term corporate planning, electric utility generation unit construction and installation or enhancement, commercial aircraft construction, the construction of Channel Tunnel rolling stock, and the risk and benefit management of a major branch banking information systems project, to mention a few that are used directly or indirectly as examples in this book. In this period the focus was on what aspects of project risk management are portable, in the sense that they apply to garden sheds and nuclear power stations, and in what way do ideas have to be tailored to the circumstances, in the sense that garden sheds and nuclear power stations require some clear differences in approach.

The reader may be concerned with projects with features well beyond our experience, but we believe that most of what we have to say is still directly relevant, provided the projects of concern involve enough uncertainty to make formal consideration of that uncertainty and associated risk worthwhile. Even if this condition is not satisfied, informal or intuitive project risk management will benefit indirectly from some of the insights offered.

What this book is about

This book makes no attempt to cover all aspects of project management. However, it addresses project risk management as a process that is an 'add-in' to the project management process as a whole, rather than an 'add-on'. The need to integrate these processes is central to the argument and to the basic position adopted by this book.

The need to start to understand project risk management by understanding processes is also central to our case. The details of models or techniques or computer software are important, but they are not of direct concern here.

Senior managers who want to make intelligent use of risk management processes without depending on their risk analysts need to understand most of this book (the exceptions are signposted). Those who wish to participate effectively in risk management processes also need to understand most of this book. Those who wish to lead risk management processes need to understand this book in depth and a wide range of additional literature on technique, model and method design, and computer software.

A very important message emphasized here is that project risk management in the context of any particular project can be viewed as a project in its own right, as part of a multiproject environment concerned with all other aspects of project management, such as planning resources, building teams, quality management, and so on. An immediate implication of this view is a need to 'plan the risk management process' as part of a process of 'planning the project planning process'. In the absence of another source of quality audit for project management, this also implies using the risk management process to make sure all other desirable aspects of project management are in place. A more subtle and far-reaching implication is that everything we know about project management in general, and multiproject management in particular, applies to the project risk management process itself.

There is an inevitable circularity in the ideal structure for such a book, largely because of the iterative nature of risk management processes. The authors have restructured it several times to avoid approaches that overtly failed. We believe the present structure works, but the reader will have to be the judge. A range of different approaches to this book might be suggested, from 'work your way through each chapter in detail before going on to the next', to 'skim the whole book and then go back to the bits of most interest'. We leave the readers to judge what best suits their inclinations, with a few hints we hope are useful.

The layout of this book

The book is in three parts. Part I sets the scene and introduces a generic risk management process. Part II examines each phase of this process in detail. Part

III addresses assumptions used in Part II and considers modifications to the generic process in order to achieve efficiency as well as effectiveness, 'closing the loop'.

Part I   Setting the scene (Chapters 1–4)

Chapter 1 identifies the need for a broad approach to project risk management. One feature of this breadth is addressing opportunities as well as threats. Another is addressing uncertainty, including ambiguity, wherever it matters. A third is a concern for the roots of uncertainty in terms of a project's six *W*s: the *who* (parties), *why* (motives), *what* (design), *whichway* (activities), *wherewithal* (resources), and *when* (timing) questions.

Chapter 2 considers the implications of the Project Life Cycle (PLC), using an eight-stage framework. This helps to clarify the context in which risk management operates and a range of project management issues that risk management needs to address. For example, the nature of the process used to manage project risk should be driven by *when* in the PLC it is used.

Chapter 3 describes the key motives for formal Risk Management Processes (RMPs). These include the benefits of documentation, the value of quantitative analysis that facilitates distinguishing between targets, expectations, and commitments, the pursuit of risk efficient ways of carrying out a project, and related culture changes. Effective exploitation of risk efficiency implies highly proactive risk management that takes an integrated and holistic approach to opportunity and threat management with respect to all six *W*s.

Chapter 4 outlines the nine-phase generic process framework employed to discuss RMPs. This framework is compared with a number of other published frameworks, as a basis for understanding the transferable nature of the concepts developed in the rest of this book for users of alternative RMP frameworks and as a basis for understanding the choices available when developing RMP frameworks for particular organizations.

Part II   Elaborating the generic process (Chapters 5–13)

Part II elaborates the nine-phase generic process of Chapter 4, one chapter per phase. The elaborations are a distillation of processes we have found effective and efficient in practice. This is 'theory grounded in practice', in the sense that it is an attempt to provide a systematic and ordered description of what has to be done in what order to achieve the deliverables each phase should produce. It is a model of an idealized process, intended to provide an understanding of the nature of risk management processes. This model needs to be adapted to the specific terrain of specific studies to be useful. Examples are provided to help link the idealized process back to the practice they are based on, to facilitate their application in practice.

Much of what most experienced professional risk analysts do is craft, based on craft skills learned the hard way by experience. Part II is an attempt to explain systematically as much as we can in a particular generic process context, indicating along the way areas where craft skills are particularly important. Some specific technique is also provided, but technique in terms of the 'nuts and bolts' or mechanics of processes is not the focus of this book.

Part III   Closing the loop (Chapters 14–17)

Part II makes a number of assumptions about application context to facilitate a description of the nine-phase generic framework outlined in Chapter 4. Part III addresses relaxing these assumptions. However, other 'unfinished business' also has to be addressed, concerned with designing and operating efficient and effective risk management processes.

Chapter 14 explores the implications of initiating a risk management process at different stages in a project's life cycle.

Chapter 15 considers making risk management processes *efficient* as well as *effective*, providing two extended examples to illustrate what is involved in practice.

Chapter 16 addresses uncertainty and risk ownership issues, considering a contractor's perspective, and the need to align client and contractor motivation.

Chapter 17 takes a corporate perspective of project risk management processes and considers what is involved in establishing and sustaining an organizational project risk management capability.

As its title suggests, the emphasis of this book is processes, in terms of the insight necessary to use risk management processes effectively and develop efficiency in doing so. It uses examples to focus on very specific lessons provided by practice. These examples may be viewed as the basis for, or evidence of, 'theory grounded in practice', or they may be viewed as 'war stories with a moral', depending on the reader's preferences.

Changes for the second edition

The basic structure for the second edition in terms of chapters is the same as for the first edition, except that the contents of Chapters 15 and 16 have been reversed. However, the text has been substantially revised throughout, and there has been some rearrangement of material between chapters. An important aspect of these revisions has been to take an uncertainty management perspective that addresses uncertainty associated with ambiguity in a wide variety of forms and considers opportunity management as well as threat management.

This is necessary for the achievement of really effective risk management and reflects recent developments in best practice.

Chapters 1, 3, 4 and 15 contain new material. Chapter 1 has been extended with new sections on the nature of uncertainty in projects. Chapter 3 now includes an extended explanation of the nature of risk efficiency and an associated operational definition of 'risk'. Chapter 4 is largely new material. After introducing a particular generic risk management process framework, a historical perspective is provided to clarify the origins of this framework. Subsequent new sections compare this process framework with other published frameworks including those adopted by the US Project Management Institute (PMI) and the UK Association for Project Management (APM). Chapter 15 is a recasting of Chapter 16 of the first edition with a focus on making risk management processes efficient as well as effective. Most of the chapter is new material in the form of two extended examples to illustrate what is involved when adapting generic processes to specific applications when efficiency as well as effectiveness needs to be addressed.

Acknowledgements

Part of the motivation for the first edition of this book was our awareness of a growing interest in project risk management guidelines for specific industries and in more general standards, in the UK and elsewhere. Chapman considerably developed his thinking interacting with other specialists in project risk management (e.g., see Charette, 1989) while working on the CCTA (The Government Centre for Information Systems) publication *Management of Project Risk* (CCTA, 1995b) and while working with AEA Technology on their project risk management guidelines. Both authors developed their thinking while working with the Association of Project Managers (APM) Specific Interest Group (SIG) on Project Risk Management, to the extent that the chapter structure of the first edition of this book was changed more than half way through writing it to reflect the SIG's agreed process description in the *Project Risk Analysis and Management (PRAM) Guide* (APM, 1997).

The *PRAM Guide* complements this book. Both books have a very similar generic process chapter (outlined in Chapter 4 of this book, Chapter 3 in the *PRAM Guide*, both drafted by Chapman), describing the generic process in terms of nine phases, a characterization that we believe works well in conceptual and practical operational terms. The support of that characterization by the organizations represented by more than a hundred people active in the APM SIG on Project Risk Management was the basis of this belief, but the nine-phase structure has worked well when developing this book and in practical applications since the first edition. If readers prefer other structures, the nine phases used here will map onto all those the authors are aware of, with two specific examples of such mapping discussed in Chapter 4.

Members of the APM SIG on Project Risk Management who were involved in the working party that contributed to the generic process definition described in Chapter 4 (and their organizations at that time) are: Paul Best (Frazer-Nash), Adrian Cowderoy (City University, Business Computing), Valerie Evans (MoD-PE), Ron Gerdes (BMT Reliability Consultants Ltd), Keith Gray (British Aerospace (Dynamics)), Steve Grey (ICL), Heather Groom (British Aerospace (Dynamics)), Ross Hayes (University of Birmingham, Civil Engineering), David Hillson (HVR Consulting Services Ltd), Paul Jobling (Mouchel Management Ltd), Mark Latham

(BAeSEMA), Martin Mays (CORDA, BAeSEMA), Ken Newland (Quintec Associates Ltd), Catriona Norris (TBV Schal), Grahame Owen (IBM (UK) Ltd), Philip Rawlings (Eurolog), Francis Scarff (CCTA), Peter Simon (PMP), Martin Thomas (4D Management Consultancy), and David Vose (DVRA). We would particularly like to thank Peter Simon (chair of the working party) and his co-editors of the *PRAM Guide*, David Hillson and Ken Newland.

The second edition of this book has also benefited from Chapman's involvement in *Risk Analysis and Management for Projects (RAMP) Guide* (Simon, 1998 and Lewin, 2002). Chris Lewin (Unilever plc), Mike Nichols (The Nichols Group), and Luke Watts (Strategic Thought) deserve particular thanks in this context. The *RAMP Guide* also complements this book, although the generic processes are somewhat different, as described in Chapter 4.

Most of Chapter 2 is reprinted from the *International Journal of Project Management*, Volume 13, S. C. Ward and C. B. Chapman, 'A risk management perspective on the project life cycle, pages 145–149, Copyright (1995), with kind permission from Elsevier, PO Box 800, Oxford OX5 1GB, UK.

Chapter 15 uses material reprinted from the *International Journal of Project Management*, Volume 18, C. B. Chapman and S. C. Ward, 'Estimation and evaluation of uncertainty: A minimalist first pass approach', pages 369–383; with kind permission from Elsevier, PO Box 800, Oxford OX5 IGB, UK. It also uses material from a forthcoming paper in the *Journal of the Operational Research Society*, C. B. Chapman and S. C. Ward, 'Constructively simple estimating: A project management example', Copyright (2003), with kind permission from Palgrave, Brunel Road, Basingstoke RG21 6XS, UK.

Chapter 16 uses material reprinted from the *International Journal of Project Management*, Volume 12, S. C. Ward and C. B. Chapman, 'Choosing contractor payment terms', pages 216–221, Copyright (1994); Volume 9, S. C. Ward, C. B. Chapman, and B. Curtis, 'On the allocation of risk in construction projects', pages 140–147, Copyright (1991); and Volume 9, S. C. Ward and C. B. Chapman, 'Extending the use of risk analysis in project management', pages 117–123, Copyright (1991), with kind permission from Elsevier, PO Box 800, Oxford OX5 1GB, UK.

Figures 8.2, 11.5 and 11.6 are reproduced from C. B. Chapman, D. F. Cooper and M. J. Page, *Management for Engineers*, John Wiley & Sons. Figures 8.3 and 14.1 are reproduced by permission of the Operational Research Society, Seymour House, 12 Edward Street, Birmingham B1 2RX, UK.

The authors would like to acknowledge the contributions of a large number of colleagues we have worked for and with over a number of years. It would be inappropriate to list them and their contributions, but we would like to express our gratitude. We would also like to thank referees who suggested changes to the first edition: Martin Hopkinson (HVR Consulting Services Ltd), Ken Newland (Quintec Associates Ltd), Professor Mike Pidd (University of Lancaster), Philip Rawlings (Euro Log Ltd) and Alan Walker (Prime Minister's Office of Public Service Reforms). We apologize to them for failing to take any advice we should have. Only the errors and omissions are entirely our own.

Part I
Setting the scene

Part I (Chapters 1–4) sets the scene, introducing concepts used throughout the rest of the book.

Chapter 1 identifies the need for a broad approach to project risk management. One feature of this breadth is addressing opportunities as well as threats. Another is addressing uncertainty, including ambiguity, wherever it matters. A third is a concern for the roots of uncertainty in terms of a project's six *W*s: the *who* (parties), *why* (motives), *what* (design), *whichway* (activities), *wherewithal* (resources), and *when* (timing) questions.

Chapter 2 considers the implications of the project life cycle (PLC), using an eight stage framework. This helps to clarify the context in which risk management operates and a range of project management issues that risk management needs to address. For example, the nature of the process used to manage project risk should be driven by *when* in the PLC it is used.

Chapter 3 describes the key motives for formal risk management processes (RMPs). These include the benefits of documentation, the value of quantitative analysis that facilitates distinguishing between targets, expectations, and commitments, the pursuit of risk efficient ways of carrying out a project, and related culture changes. Effective exploitation of risk efficiency implies highly proactive risk management that takes an integrated and holistic approach to opportunity and threat management with respect to all six *W*s.

Chapter 4 outlines the nine phase generic process framework employed to discuss RMPs. This framework is compared with a number of other published frameworks, as a basis for understanding the transferable nature of the concepts developed in the rest of this book for users of alternative RMP frameworks and as a basis for understanding the choices available when developing RMP frameworks for particular organizations.

1 Uncertainty, risk, and their management

I keep six honest serving men, they taught me all I knew; their names are what and why and when and how and where and who.—Rudyard Kipling

Uncertainty as a central feature of effective project management

The need to manage uncertainty is inherent in most projects that require formal project management, using 'uncertainty' in the plain English 'lack of certainty' sense. Consider the following illustrative definition of a project:

> *an endeavour in which human, material and financial resources are organised in a novel way, to undertake a unique scope of work of given specification, within constraints of cost and time, so as to achieve unitary, beneficial change, through the delivery of quantified and qualitative objectives*—Turner (1992).

This definition highlights the change-inducing nature of projects, the need to organize a variety of resources under significant constraints, and the central role of objectives in project definition. It also suggests inherent uncertainty related to novel organization and a unique scope of work, which requires attention as a central part of effective project management.

Much good project management practice can be thought of as effective uncertainty management. For example, good practice in planning, co-ordination, setting milestones, and change control procedures seeks to manage uncertainty directly. However, most texts on project management do not consider the way uncertainty management should be integrated with project management more generally, in terms of a wide view of what a co-ordinated approach to proactive and reactive uncertainty management can achieve.

Threats and opportunities

A simplistic focus on project success and uncertainty about achieving it can lead to uncertainty and risk being defined in terms of 'threats to success' in a purely negative sense. For example, suppose success for a project is measured solely in terms of realized cost relative to some target or commitment. Then both 'uncertainty' and 'risk' might be defined in terms of the threat to success posed by a given plan in terms of the size of possible cost overruns and their likelihood. From this perspective it can be a natural step to regard risk management as essentially about removing or reducing the possibility of underperformance. This is extremely unfortunate, because it results in a very limited appreciation of project uncertainty and the potential benefits of project risk management. Often it can be just as important to appreciate the positive side of uncertainty, which may present opportunities rather than threats. Two examples may help to illustrate this point.

Example 1.1   Capturing the benefits of 'fair weather'

North Sea offshore pipe laying involves significant uncertainty associated with weather. Relative to expected (average) performance, long periods of bad weather can have significant sustained impact. It is important to recognize and deal with this 'threat'. It is also very important to recognize that the weather may be exceptionally kind, providing a counterbalancing opportunity. Making sure supplies of pipe can cope with very rapid pipe laying is essential, for obvious reasons. Also important is the need to shift following activities forward, if possible, if the whole pipeline is finished early. If this is not done, 'swings and roundabouts' are just 'swings': the bad luck is accumulated, but the good luck is wasted, a ratchet effect inducing significant unanticipated delay as a project progresses.

Example 1.2   A threat resolved creates an opportunity

The team responsible for a UK combined cycle gas turbine electricity project were concerned about the threat to their project's completion time associated with various approvals processes that involved important novel issues. Gas was to be provided on a take-or-pay contract in which gas supply would be guaranteed from an agreed date, but gas not required from that date would have to be paid for anyway. This made any delay relative to the commitment operating date very expensive, the cost of such unused gas being in effect a project cost. The only response identified was to move the whole project forward three months in time (starting three months earlier and finishing three months earlier) and arrange for standard British Gas supplies for testing purposes if the project actually finished three months early. Using British Gas supplies for testing was a non-trivial change, because its gas composition was different, requiring different testing procedures and gas turbine contract differences. This response would deal with planning delays, the motivation for first suggesting it, but it would also deal with any other reasons for delay, including those not identified. Further, it provided a very high degree of confidence that the combined cycle gas turbine plant would be operational very shortly after the main gas supply initiation date. But, of special importance here, this response made it practical to maintain the strategy of using British Gas supplies for testing, but move the whole project (this time including the main gas supply availability date) back in time (starting and finishing later) in order to time the take-or-pay contract date to coincide directly with the beginning of the peak winter demand period, improving the corporate cash flow position. The opportunity to improve the cash flow position in this way, while maintaining confidence with respect to the take-or-pay contract for gas, was deemed to be a key impact of the risk management process. The search for a way to resolve a threat was extended to the identification of a related but separate opportunity, and the opportunity was the key benefit of the process.

These two examples illustrate the importance of opportunities as well as threats, the first in cost terms at an activity level, the second in cost and revenue terms at a project level. In the first example, if the implications of good luck are not seized and only bad luck is captured, the accumulated effect is reasonably obvious once the mechanism is understood, and it should be clear that this applies to all activities in all projects. The second example illustrates the benefits of creative, positive thinking, which looks beyond merely overcoming or neutralizing a problem to associated opportunities. This aspect of problem solving is more subtle and is not widely understood, but it can be very important, in direct terms and from a morale point of view. High morale is as central to good risk management as it is to the management of teams in general. If a project team becomes immersed in nothing but attempting to neutralize threats, the ensuing doom and gloom can destroy the project. Systematic searches for opportunities, and a management team willing to respond to opportunities identified by those working for them at all levels (which may have implications well beyond the remit of the discoverer), can provide the basis for systematic building of morale.

In any given decision situation both threats and opportunities are usually involved, and both should be managed. A focus on one should never be allowed to eliminate concern for the other. Moreover, opportunities and threats can sometimes be treated separately, but they are seldom independent, just as two sides of the same coin can only be examined one at a time, but they are not independent when it comes to tossing the coin. Courses of action are often available that reduce or neutralize potential threats and simultaneously offer opportunities for positive improvements in performance. It is rarely advisable to concentrate on reducing threats without considering associated opportunities, just as it is inadvisable to pursue opportunities without regard for the associated threats.

Recognizing this, guides published by the US Project Management Institute (PMI) and the UK Association for Project Management (APM) have adopted a broad view of risk in terms of threats and opportunities. Their definitions of risk are very similar, as follows:

> *Risk—an uncertain event or condition that, if it occurs, has a positive or negative effect on a project objective*—PMI (2000, p. 127).

> *Risk—an uncertain event or set of circumstances that, should it occur, will have an effect on the achievement of the project's objectives*—APM (1997, p. 16).

These widely used definitions embrace both welcome upside and unwelcome downside effects. In spite of this, there is still a tendency for practitioners to think of risk management in largely downside, threat management terms (a tendency that the authors are not always able to resist). It is important to keep 'beating the drum' to remind ourselves that we are dealing with the upside as well as the downside of uncertainty, with a balance appropriate to context. Even in a safety-critical context, when the downside has clear priority, it is a serious mistake to forget about the upside. Hillson (2002a) explores alternative definitions of risk with a focus on this issue, and Hillson (2002b) explores the trend toward a greater focus on opportunity management.

Uncertainty about anything that matters as a starting point

While we warmly endorsed the PMI and APM definitions with respect to their breadth in terms of threats and opportunities, we strongly resist the very restricted and limiting focus on 'events', 'conditions,' or 'circumstances', which cause effects on the achievement of project objectives. Rather than a focus on the occurrence or not of an event, condition, or set of circumstances, it is important to take uncertainty about anything that matters as the starting point for risk management purposes, defining uncertainty in a simple 'lack of certainty' sense. Uncertainty management is not just about managing perceived threats, opportunities, and their implications; it is about identifying and managing all the many sources of uncertainty that give rise to and shape our perceptions of threats and opportunities. It implies exploring and understanding the origins of project uncertainty before seeking to manage it, with no preconceptions about what is desirable or undesirable. Key concerns are understanding where and why uncertainty is important in a given project context, and where it is not. This is a significant change in emphasis compared with most project risk management processes.

It could be argued that this starting point means we are talking about 'risk and uncertainty management' or just 'uncertainty management' (including risk management), not 'risk management'. That is the direction we are taking (Chapman and Ward, 2002; Ward and Chapman, 2003), but the term 'project risk management' is too well established to be replaced widely in the near term and is retained for this book. Our publisher was understandably reluctant to change the title of a second edition while the first edition (Chapman and Ward, 1997) had sales that were very healthy and stable, one example of the inertia involved. But increasing the emphasis on opportunity management in an uncertainty management context is a key feature of this edition relative to the first.

Uncertainty in projects

The scope for uncertainty in any project is considerable, and most project management activities are concerned with managing uncertainty from the earliest stages of the Project Life Cycle (PLC), clarifying what can be done, deciding what is to be done, and ensuring that it gets done. Uncertainty is in part about 'variability' in relation to performance measures like cost, duration, or 'quality'. It is also about 'ambiguity' associated with lack of clarity because of the behaviour of relevant project players, lack of data, lack of detail, lack of structure to consider issues, working and framing assumptions being used to consider the issues, known and unknown sources of bias, and ignorance about how much effort it is worth expending to clarify the situation.

In a project context these aspects of uncertainty can be present throughout the PLC, but they are particularly evident in the pre-execution stages, when they contribute to uncertainty in five areas:

1. variability associated with estimates;
2. uncertainty about the basis of estimates;
3. uncertainty about design and logistics;
4. uncertainty about objectives and priorities;
5. uncertainty about fundamental relationships between project parties.

All these areas of uncertainty are important, but generally they become more fundamentally important to project performance as we go down the list. Potential for variability is the dominant issue at the top of the list, but ambiguity becomes the dominant underlying issue toward the bottom of the list. Uncertainty about variability associated with estimates involves the other four areas: each of them involving dependencies on later areas in this list.

Variability associated with estimates

An obvious area of uncertainty is the size of project parameters such as time, cost, and quality related to particular activities. For example, we may not know how much time and effort will be required to complete a particular activity. The causes of this uncertainty might include one or more of the following:

- lack of a clear specification of what is required;
- novelty or lack of experience of this particular activity;
- complexity in terms of the number of influencing factors and the number of interdependencies;
- limited analysis of the processes involved in the activity;
- possible occurrence of particular events or conditions that might affect the activity.

Only the last of these items is directly related to specific events or conditions as referred to in the PMI (2000) and APM (1997) definitions of 'risk'. The other sources of uncertainty arise from a lack of understanding of what is involved. Because they are less obviously described as threats or opportunities, they may be missed unless a broad view of uncertainty management is adopted.

Uncertainty about the basis of estimates

The quality of estimates depends on: who produced them, what form they are in; why, how, and when they were produced; from what resources and experience base; and what assumptions underpin them. The need to note assumptions about resources, choices, and methods of working is well understood if not always fully operationalized. Most of the time estimates ignore, or assume away, the existence of uncertainty that relates to three basic sources: 'known unknowns', 'unknown unknowns', and 'bias' (Chapman and Ward, 2002). All three of these sources of uncertainty can have a very substantial impact on estimates, and this needs to be recognized and managed.

Uncertainty about design and logistics

In the conception stage of the PLC the nature of the project deliverable and the process for producing it are fundamental uncertainties. In principle, much of this uncertainty is removed in pre-execution stages of the PLC by attempting to specify what is to be done, how, when, and by whom, and at what cost. In practice, a significant amount of this uncertainty may remain unresolved through much of the PLC. The nature of design and logistics assumptions and associated uncertainty may drive some of the uncertainty about the basis of estimates.

Uncertainty about objectives and priorities

Major difficulties arise in projects if there is uncertainty about project objectives, the relative priorities between objectives, and acceptable trade-offs. These difficulties are compounded if this uncertainty extends to the objectives and motives of the different project parties and the trade-offs parties are prepared to make between their objectives. A key issue is: 'do all parties understand their responsibilities and the expectations of other parties in clearly defined terms, which link objectives to planned activities?' 'Value management' has been introduced to encompass this (Green, 2001). The need to do so is perhaps indicative of a perceived failure of risk management practices. However approached, risk management and value management need joint integration into project management.

Uncertainty about fundamental relationships between project parties

The relationships between the various parties may be complex, even if they look quite simple. The involvement of multiple parties in a project introduces uncertainty arising from ambiguity in respect of (Ward, 1999):

- specification of responsibilities;
- perceptions of roles and responsibilities;
- communication across interfaces;
- the capability of parties;
- formal contractual conditions and their effects;
- informal understandings on top of, or instead of, formal contracts;
- mechanisms for co-ordination and control.

Ambiguity about roles and responsibilities for bearing and managing project-related uncertainty can be crucial. This ambiguity ought to be systematically addressed in any project, not just in those involving formal contracts between different organizations. Contractor organizations are often more aware of this source of ambiguity than their clients, although the full scope of the threats and opportunities that this ambiguity generates for each party in any contract (e.g., via claims) may not always be fully appreciated until rather late in the day. For example, interpretations of risk apportionment implied by standard contract clauses may differ between contracting parties (Hartman and Snelgrove, 1996; Hartman et al., 1997). The nature of assumptions about contractual relationships and associated uncertainty may drive uncertainty about objectives and priorities with further knock-on effects. If a 'fair weather partnership' cracks when the going gets tough, everything else comes apart, and lost opportunities may be the biggest casualty.

The six *W*s framework for the roots of uncertainty

In the authors' experience the initial motivation for applying formal risk management usually arises because of concerns about design and logistics issues in
major projects that involve the large-scale use of new and untried technology.
However, the most important issues that risk management helps to resolve are
usually related to objectives and relationships between project parties. For
example, a common issue in most projects is: 'do we know what we are
trying to achieve in clearly defined terms, which link objectives to planned
activities?' It is important to understand why this situation arises and to
respond effectively in *any* project context.

A convenient starting point is consideration of the project definition process
portrayed in Figure 1.1. There are six basic questions that need to be addressed:

1. *who*   who are the parties ultimately involved?   (parties);
2. *why*   what do the parties want to achieve?   (motives);
3. *what*   what is it the parties are interested in?   (design);
4. *whichway*   how is it to be done?   (activities);
5. *wherewithal*   what resources are required?   (resources);
6. *when*   when does it have to be done?   (timetable).

For convenience we refer to these question areas as 'the six *W*s', using the
designations in parentheses as well as the W labels for clarity when appropriate.
While somewhat contrived, this terminology helps to remind us of the need to
consider all six aspects of a project, reinforced by the Rudyard Kipling quote
used to open this chapter.

The flow lines in Figure 1.1 show the influences on project definition that are
the roots of uncertainty. In the context of roots of uncertainty, these arrows can
be interpreted as indicating the knock-on effects of uncertainty in each entity. As
Figure 1.1 shows, the roots of uncertainty may extend back to the basic purpose
of the project and even the identity of the relevant parties. Any uncertainty
associated with entities earlier in the cycles portrayed by the diagram are of
fundamental importance later. In the earliest stage of a project, during conception, uncertainty is at its greatest. The purpose for which the project is required
and the parties who will be involved may not be clear.

As indicated in Figure 1.1, 'project initiators' are a subset of the *who*, the
'project parties ultimately involved'. Project initiators kick the whole process
off. One or more project initiators first identify the basic purpose of the
project, or intended benefit from it, the *why* or motives for the project. These
motives will usually include profit, involving revenue and cost, along with 'other
motives'. Initially, the nature of these motives will be defined, but they will not
be quantified as objectives. That is, in terms of the mission–goals–objectives
hierarchy often used to move from an overall mission statement to quantified

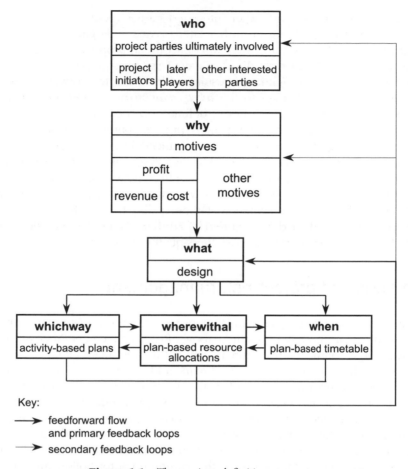

Figure 1.1—The project definition process

objectives, the initial focus of the *why* may be on mission and broadly defined goals.

Why, in terms of the initial conception of purpose, drives the initial *what*, the design. The design—be it a building, other physical product, service, or process—drives the initial activity-based plans, associated plan-based resource allocations, and plan-based timetable, the initial *whichway*, *wherewithal*, and *when*. Subsequently, there is significant feedforward and feedback along the *whichway–wherewithal–when* dimensions and some feedback to the *what*. The *whichway–wherewithal–when* entities then feed back into quantification of cost, possibly revenue and other motives, and *why* in terms of a more developed, measured definition. These considerations may relate to capital cost only or more complex, through-life performance criteria. This can involve related feedback to the *who*, with changes of a still more fundamental nature involving the project initiators, 'later players', and 'other interested parties'. As the project evolves it may be appropriate to bring in further later players, enlarging the *who* (e.g., to banks for resource reasons). It may also become appropriate to consider other interested parties who are not direct players (e.g., regulators).

In each case the feedback loops result in subsequent feedforward, which may result in fundamental changes to the *what, whichway, wherewithal,* or *when.*

This brief description of the project definition process in terms of the six *W*s involved is an oversimplification for many projects, but it is sufficiently complex to highlight the nature of important roots of uncertainty in projects. In particular, if we recognize that the *what, whichway,* and *wherewithal* together describe the quality of a project and ignore revenue and other motives, then the lower part of Figure 1.1 corresponds to the well-known cost–time–quality triad. The limited perspective inherent in the simple cost–time–quality triad is then apparent from the expansion of this triad by Figure 1.1. Further, Figure 1.1 provides a useful operational basis for addressing cost–time–quality trade-offs.

The scope of project risk management

Efficient and effective project management requires appropriate management of all the sources of uncertainty outlined above. Risk Management Processes (RMPs) that adopt a simplistic focus on threats will not address many of these sources of uncertainty. RMPs concerned with threats and opportunities using the APM (1997) or PMI (2000) definitions of 'risk' will do better, but will still tend to be focused on uncertain *events, conditions,* or *circumstances.* This does not facilitate consideration of aspects of variability that are driven by underlying ambiguity. To address uncertainty in both variability and ambiguity terms we need to adopt a more explicit focus on uncertainty management. Uncertainty about anything that matters has to be the starting point for holistic and integrated project risk management.

To this end it is useful to define 'risk' as an *uncertain effect* on project performance rather than as a *cause of an (uncertain) effect* on project perform-ance. Such a definition of project 'risk' is '*the implications of uncertainty about the level of project performance achievable*'. However, this definition on its own is not an effective operational alternative to those provided by the PMI or APM. We provide it here as a short form of a more complete operational definition provided in Chapter 3. What this short-form definition attempts to clarify now is that managing project risk must start with managing sources of project uncer-tainty about achievable performance that matter. Opportunities and threats are part of the sources of uncertainty that matter, but they are not risk *per se* in our terms. Similarly, uncertain events, conditions, or circumstances that may have an effect (positive or negative) on project objectives are part of the sources of uncertainty that matter, but they are not risk *per se* in our terms. Why uncertainty matters is not a simple issue, but Chapter 3 outlines key aspects of what is involved; the rest of this book illustrates what is involved in more detail, and Chapman and Ward (2002) elaborate further.

To realize in practical terms the advantages of this wider perspective, it is essential to see project risk management as an important extension of conventional project planning, with the potential to influence project design as well as activity-based plans on a routine basis, occasionally influencing very basic issues like the nature of the project parties and their objectives for the project. There are many ways to classify 'plans'. In general we will associate 'plans' with all six *W*s, sometimes identifying 'activity-based plans', 'plan-based resource allocations', and so on, as indicated in Figure 1.1. For the present purposes it is useful to distinguish 'base' plans and 'contingency' plans.

'Base plans' are target scenarios, a portrayal of how we would like a project to go, incorporating proactive responses to uncertainty identified by proactive RMP planning. Base plans provide a basis for project preparation, execution, and control. Underlying the base plan in activity terms is a design, which may be worth identifying as a 'base design' if changes are anticipated. Base plans in activity terms imply base plans in resource allocation terms and associated base plan timetables. It may be useful to associate the *who* and *why* with base plans explicitly too, if changes are anticipated.

Control involves responding to threats and opportunities, and revising performance targets where appropriate. 'Contingency plans' are a second level of plan, a portrayal of how we would like to respond to threats or opportunities associated with a base plan, incorporating reactive responses to uncertainty identified by proactive RMP planning. Where uncertainty presents potential future threats or opportunities, risk management seeks to modify the future incidence and quality of threats or opportunities and their possible impact on project performance via proactive planning in terms of base plans and contingency plans. This does not mean that reactive planning will not be necessary or that all possible out-turns will have been predicted. It means that proactive planning will have been carried out to an extent that allows reactive planning to cope without nasty surprises most of the time. Reactive risk management, responding to the control function, sometimes without contingency plans in place, should be reasonably panic-free, without a need for crisis management most of the time. A degree of crisis management may be essential even in the context of very effective and comprehensive risk management, but relatively few crises should come totally 'out of the blue'. To illustrate these points, consider another example, building on Example 1.1.

Example 1.3 Effective contingency planning for a pipe-laying problem

Offshore oil or gas pipe laying in the North Sea in the 1970s involved a number of serious sources of uncertainty. If no proactive planning had been undertaken, the potential for overwhelming crisis management was obvious.

The pipes laid in the North Sea at this time were constructed from sections of rigid steel pipe coated with concrete, welded to the pipeline on the lay barge, then eased over the stern of the barge by taking up the tension on sets of bow anchors, maintaining a smooth S shape of pipe between the barge and the ocean floor. As bow anchors approached the lay barge, they were picked up by tugs, carried ahead, and reset. Improperly controlled lowering of new pipeline sections could result in a pipe buckle—a key pipe-laying threat. Excessive waves greatly increased this threat. Barges were classified or designated to indicate maximum safe wave heights for working (e.g., 3 metre or 1.6 metre). In the face of excessive wave heights the operators would put a 'cap' on the open end of the pipe and lower it to the ocean floor, retrieving it when the waves reduced. These lowering and lifting operations could themselves lead to buckles.

The base plan for laying pipe assumed no major sources of uncertainty (opportunities or threats) would be realized, only minor day-to-day variations in performance that could be expected to average out.

The potential opportunity provided by unusually good weather and the potential threat posed by unusually bad weather were assessed by direct reference to historical weather records. Control was exercised by monitoring progress relative to the base plan, aggregating all reasons for being early or late, until a significant departure from the base plan was identified. A control response could be triggered by an accumulation of minor difficulties or the realization of a major threat like a pipe buckle. Once the need for a control response had been identified and an appropriate response selected reflecting the nature of the realized threats or opportunities, the associated response became part of the revised base plan.

Effective comprehensive contingency planning ensured that the most crucial prior actions necessary to implement the preferred revisions to the base plan would be in place if it was cost-effective to put them in place. The implications of not putting them in place were understood when making a decision not to do so.

Should a pipe buckle occur, there would be a potential need for additional pipe. This had to be ordered well in advance of starting the pipe laying if a delay associated with awaiting delivery were to be avoided. Effective contingency planning needed to ensure that enough pipe was available most of the time. However, it would not have been cost-effective to ensure buckles never led to a shortage of pipe. Nor would it have been cost-effective to undertake detailed planning to deal with all the knock-on effects of a pipe buckle.

Proactive risk management needs to be embedded in both base plans and contingency plans. Further, proactive and reactive planning are not alternatives, they are complementary aspects of planning as a whole, with proactive contingency planning supporting reactive contingency planning when this is cost-effective. Similarly, crisis management is not an alternative to risk management; it is a consequence of risk management failure. Nevertheless, even the most effective risk management must fail on occasions if it is to remain cost-effective on the average. Only if risk management fails completely, or is simply not addressed, will crisis management become the dominant management mode.

Project risk management is usually associated with the development and evaluation of contingency plans supporting activity-based plans, but effective project risk management will be instrumental in the development of base plans and contingency plans for all six Ws. Really effective risk management will strongly influence design and may significantly influence motives and parties. It will certainly influence basic timing and resource allocation plans. Planning and risk management in this sense are integrated and holistic.

Treating project management and project risk management as closely coupled processes is central to the approach taken in this book. In practice, some separation may be essential because different people and organizations may be involved, and other differences are important. However, the separability should be limited, to avoid imposing constraints that can prove very expensive. This is another key aspect of an integrated and holistic approach.

2   The project life cycle

The moving finger writes; and, having writ, moves on: nor all thy piety nor wit shall lure it back to cancel half a line, nor all thy tears wash out a word of it.—Edward Fitzgerald

Introduction

An appreciation of the potential for risk management in projects has to be grounded on a clear understanding of the nature and scope of decision making involved in project management. A natural framework for examining these decisions is the project life cycle (PLC). A structured view of the PLC is also important to provide a framework for looking ahead for sources of uncertainty that are seeded earlier and for understanding how the risk management process (RMP) ought to change as the PLC unfolds. In order to focus on the structure of the PLC, much of this chapter will consider a single project in isolation, but it ends with a short discussion of the implications of a multiproject environment.

Eight stages

The PLC is a convenient way of conceptualizing the generic structure of projects over time. It is often described in terms of four *phases*, using terms like conceptualization, planning, execution, and termination (Adams and Barndt, 1988). Alternative phraseology may be used, such as formation, build-up, main programme, and phase-out (Thamhain and Wileman, 1975), but the underlying phases identified are essentially the same. These phases are commonly described in a manner emphasizing the extent to which they differ in terms of the level of resources employed (Adams and Barndt, 1988), the degree of definition, the level of conflict (Thamhain and Wileman, 1975), the rate of expenditure, and so on. This can help to show how management attention to the factor being considered needs to vary over the life of the project. Useful recent references to the PLC literature include Bonnai et al. (2002) and Tummala and Burchett (1999).

A similar argument applies to sources of uncertainty and their management. However, an appreciation of the scope for risk management and how to approach it requires consideration of the differences between phases of the PLC in a greater level of detail than the typical four phase structure. Table 2.1

Table 2.1—Phases, stages, and steps in the project life cycle (PLC)

Phases	Stages	Steps
conceptualization	**conceive** the product	trigger event concept capture clarification of purpose concept elaboration concept evaluation
planning	**design** the product strategically	basic design development of performance criteria design development design evaluation
	plan the execution strategically	basic activity and resource-based plans development of targets and milestones plan development plan evaluation
	allocate resources tactically	basic design and activity-based plan detail development of resource allocation criteria allocation development allocation evaluation
execution	**execute** production	co-ordinate and control monitor progress modification of targets and milestones allocation modification control evaluation
termination	**deliver** the product	basic deliverable verification deliverable modification modification of performance criteria deliver evaluation
	review the process	basic review review development review evaluation
	support the product	basic maintenance and liability perception development of support criteria support perception development support evaluation

breaks down the typical four *phase* characterization of the PLC into eight *stages*. We use the term 'stage' rather than 'phase' to emphasize the difference and to reserve the word 'phase' for the decomposition of the RMP. Table 2.1 also breaks each *stage* into *steps*. The breakdown into eight stages goes some way toward highlighting sources of uncertainty and facilitating their management. However, the still more detailed description of the PLC provided by steps is useful to underline where particular sources of uncertainty arise in the PLC and how risk management might be most effective. In the early stages these steps imply a process of gradually increasing detail and a focus on the nature of a product or service deliverable, as distinct from the later focus on its delivery and then its operation.

The conceive stage

It is useful to think of the conceive stage as part of an innovation process and draw on ideas from Lemaitre and Stenier's description of the innovation process (Lemaitre and Stenier, 1988), although the scope of our conceive stage is somewhat different. The conceive stage involves identifying a deliverable to be produced and the benefits expected from the deliverable. It begins with a 'trigger event' (Lyles, 1981), when a member of an initiating organization perceives an opportunity or need. At this point the project deliverable may be only a vague idea, and some initial development may be associated with the 'concept capture' step. 'Clarification of purpose' involving the identification of relevant performance objectives and their relative importance is another key step in the conceive stage. This step may be problematic to the extent that different views about the appropriate objectives are held by influential stakeholders who try to negotiate mutually acceptable objectives. Objectives at this stage are likely to be ill defined or developed as aspirational constraints (e.g., latest completion date, minimum levels of functionality, maximum cost, and so on). Before the concept can be developed further, in a 'concept elaboration' step, sufficient political support for the idea must be obtained and resources allocated to allow the idea to be refined and made more explicit. Other individuals, organizations, or potential stakeholders may become involved. Support at this stage may be passive, merely allowing conceptualization to proceed, rather than an expression of positive approval of the project. The focus of this stage is early cycles through the six Ws's framework of Figure 1.1.

Eventually, an evaluation of the project concept and objectives as defined to date becomes necessary—the 'concept evaluation' step in Table 2.1. Evaluation here (and later) is not simply a *go/no-go* decision, but a *go/no-go/maybe* decision. A *go* decision takes the process into the the next stage. A *no-go* decision causes it to stop. A *maybe* decision involves iteration through one or more previous steps. The basic process threat in this stage is moving on to design before the project concept and objectives have crystallized, and before effective concept evaluation. Underlying this threat is a failure to foresee 'concept killer' threats that reveal themselves later in the process and 'concept maker' opportunities that may be lost without trace. The basic process opportunity in this stage is finding all the concept maker opportunities for the projects that otherwise might not be proceeded with and all the concept killer threats for projects best rejected.

The design stage

A *go* decision in the conceive stage initiates a 'basic design' at a strategic level in the first step of the design stage, giving form to the deliverable of the project. The focus of this stage is giving substance to the *what* entity, although loops through the other five *W*s will be involved. This usually requires a step increase in the effort or resources involved. 'Development of performance criteria' builds on the basic design and project objectives. For many projects this involves refining project objectives, but it may involve the identification of additional objectives and further negotiation where pluralistic views persist. This step influences 'design development', which leads to 'design evaluation' using the developed performance criteria to assess the current design in *go/no-go/maybe* terms. As in the concept stage, *no-go* will end the process. A *maybe* evaluation is most likely to lead to iteration through one or more development steps, but if fundamental difficulties not anticipated in the concept stage are encountered, the loop may go back to the concept stage. *Go* takes the process on to the plan stage. The basic process threat at this stage is moving on to the plan stage before effective design development and evaluation at a strategic level is complete. Underlying this risk is a failure to foresee 'design breaker' threats that might be designed out and that reveal themselves later in the process, and 'design maker' opportunities that may be lost and never found. The basic process opportunity in this stage is finding and resolving all the design breaker threats and finding and capturing all the design maker opportunities. Decomposition of the Table 2.1 'planning phase' into design, plan, and allocate stages serves to focus the management of this and related subsequent threats and opportunities.

The plan stage

A *go* decision in the design stage initiates formal capture and development of basic activity and resource based plans at a strategic level, indicating how the design will be executed (*whichway*), what resources are required in broad terms (*wherewithal*), and how long it will take (*when*). The focus of this stage is these three *W*s, but loops through the other three will be involved. Yet more individuals and organizations may become involved. 'Development of targets and milestones' involves determining specific targets for producing the project deliverable, typically in terms of cost and time, but sometimes in terms of resource usage or other considerations as well. 'Plan development' follows and leads to 'plan evaluation' in *go/no-go/maybe* terms. A *maybe* decision may require further development of targets and milestones within the plan stage, but more fundamental difficulties may take the process back to design development or even concept elaboration. The basic process threat at this stage is moving on to the allocate stage before effective development and evaluation of the plans in terms of all six *W*s at a strategic level, and both 'maker' and 'breaker' threats at a strategic planning level underlie this. The basic process opportunity is avoiding the breakers and capturing the makers.

The allocate stage

A *go* decision in the plan stage takes the process on to the allocate stage and a detailed allocation of internal resources and contracts to achieve the plan. The allocate stage is a significant task involving decisions about project organization, identification of appropriate participants, and allocation of tasks between them. Resource allocation with a view to project implementation requires much more detail than earlier stages needed. The detail of the *what* (design) drives the detail of the *whichway* (activities), which drives the detail of the *wherewithal* (resources), which drives the detail of the *when* (timing), with iterative, interactive loops. The *who* may also require redefinition.

Either implicitly or explicitly the allocation stage involves the allocation of execution uncertainty and risk between participants. Risk and uncertainty allocation is an important source of process uncertainty because it can significantly influence the behaviour of participants and hence impact on project performance, and how best to do it is itself very uncertain. In particular, allocation of execution and termination phase uncertainty influences the extent and manner in which such uncertainties are managed. This warrants careful consideration of the basis for allocating tasks, uncertainty, and risk in the 'development of resource allocation criteria' step.

'Allocation development' necessarily involves revising detailed design and planning in order to allocate tasks unless this whole stage is contracted out along with the balance of the project. Contracts and subcontractual structures may require development. Again, the nature of the issues changes with the change of stage, and the level of effort may escalate. As in the earlier project stages, development during this stage is followed by 'allocation evaluation'. A *maybe* decision that goes back to the plan, design, or even conceive stage is extremely unwelcome, and a *no-go* decision will be seen as a serious disaster in many cases. If the 'devil is in the detail', earlier evaluation steps will be seen to have failed at this stage. The basic process threats and opportunities revolve around augmenting effective strategic plans with the detail essential to make execution a success.

The rationale for separate design, plan, and allocate stages

Possible arguments against decomposition of the Table 2.1 'planning phase' into design, plan, and allocate stages is their interdependent nature and the need to iterate within this phase. We believe that the importance of this dependence and the process threats and opportunities it generates is highlighted by their separation. Quite different tasks are involved, with different end products at different levels of detail in some cases, and different sources of process uncertainty are involved. The decisions to move from design to plan to allocate are very important. This makes it important to treat them as separable, recognizing their important interdependencies.

There is a related question about the focus on *whichway, wherewithal* and *when* in the plan stage, and the subsequent detailed treatment of these same three Ws plus design in the allocate stage. Why not separate them to yield still more stages? In this case the interdependence is too strong to make separability useful for present purposes. However, Figure 1.1 clearly suggests it will be important to distinguish these Ws in each of these two stages for some purposes.

More generally, the decomposition of the Table 2.1 'planning phase' into three stages is useful because it captures useful separability, but further formal decomposition is not useful at the level of generality of concern here. Figure 2.1 emphasizes the interstage feedback loop structure of the conceive–design–plan–allocate stages and following stages. 'Primary feedback loops' are 'primary' in the interstage sense, ignoring the more fundamental feedback

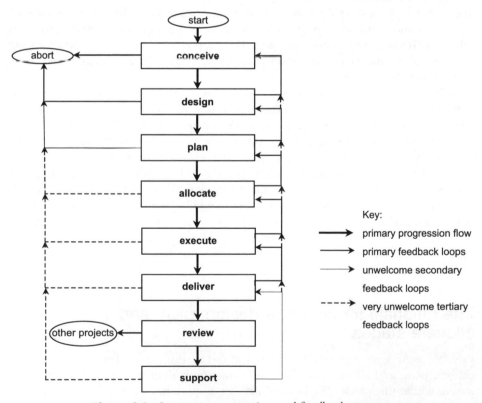

Figure 2.1—Interstage progression and feedback structure

loops within each stage. Primary feedback involves costs, but should be cost-effective if limited and therefore welcome. 'Secondary' and 'tertiary' feedback loops indicate more costly feedback, to be avoided if possible.

The execute stage

A *go* decision in the allocate stage initiates the main body of the project—the execute stage. The start of this stage signals the start of order-of-magnitude increases in effort and expenditure. The planning is over; the action begins. During execution, the essential process threat is that co-ordination and control procedures prove inadequate. A common perceived threat in the execute stage is the introduction of design changes, but these may be earlier sources of uncertainty coming home to roost, including opportunities that should have been spotted earlier to take full advantage of them. Consequent adjustments to production plans, costs, and payments to affected contractors ought to be based on an assessment of how project uncertainty is affected by the changes and the extent to which revised risk management plans are needed.

For most projects, repeated iteration will be necessary through the steps within the execute stage. Exceptionally, loops back to earlier stages may be necessary. Big surprises, including major opportunities missed earlier, could take some aspects of the project right back to the concept stage or lead to a *no-go* decision, including project abortion. Both nasty and pleasant surprises are realized sources of uncertainty from earlier stages that were not identified, indicating a failure of the risk management process in earlier stages.

The rationale for separate deliver, review, and support stages

The project 'termination phase' of Table 2.1 involves three distinct aspects, captured in the deliver, review, and support stages, each encompassing different risk management concerns. The rationale for their separation, and no further separation, has the same form as the argument for separation of the design, plan, and allocate stages. However, arguably the case for separation is even stronger in terms of the very different nature of these stages.

The deliver stage

The deliver stage involves commissioning and handover. Again the issues are different from previous stages. The 'basic deliverable verification' step involves verifying what the product of the project will do in practice—its actual performance as distinct from its designed performance. An important threat is that the deliverable fails to meet expected performance criteria. Modification of product performance may be achievable, but modification of performance criteria or influencing stakeholder expectations and perceptions may be necessary. However, unless they were explicitly anticipated these are not sources of process uncertainty in this stage, they are a realization of earlier unmanaged sources of uncertainty. 'Delivery evaluation' focuses on the need for quality assessment and modification loops, including compensating for unanticipated weaknesses by developing unanticipated strengths. Loops back to the concept stage or a *no-go* abort decision are still possible. The basic process threat is being unable to 'make the best of a bad job'. The basic process opportunity is making the best of 'delighting the customer'.

The review stage

The review stage involves a documented audit of the project management process after delivery of the product. Some lessons will be obvious—the 'basic review' starting point. But allocating resources to systematic study to draw out lessons that were not obvious—'review development'—is important. Missing important lessons means the same mistakes will be made again—the key source of process uncertainty in this stage. Not having such a stage explicitly identified almost guarantees the realization of this source of uncertainty. Hindsight may suggest some actions were successful, or not, for unanticipated reasons. Such occurrences ought to be noted for future reference. An important aspect of the review should be documentation of the manner in which performance and other criteria relevant to each project stage developed—in particular the rationale for any changes. 'Review evaluation' involves evaluating the likely relevance and usefulness of review data for informing future project management practice. Unlike evaluation steps in previous stages, the review stage as conceived here is not concerned with the possibility of aborting the project or loops back to earlier stages. As indicated in Figure 2.1, the purpose of review evaluation is to inform practice on other projects. A positive, 'opportunity management' approach to the review stage is important, with the emphasis on capturing good practice and rewarding the deserving, not highlighting bad practice and punishing the guilty.

The support stage

The support stage involves living with the product—the ongoing legacy of apparent project 'completion', possibly in a passive 'endure' mode—until the product of the project is discarded, decommissioned, or otherwise disposed of. 'Basic maintenance and liability perception' is the starting point when the project is complete in the handover sense, noting that handover may be an internal matter in organizational terms. 'Development of support criteria' and associated 'support perception development' leads to 'support evaluation', which may be repeated periodically. The focus of this evaluation may be a within-stage loop back to development of perceptions or a limited loop back to the deliver stage. Exceptionally, the outcome could be a *no-go* decision involving product withdrawal or other explicit withdrawal of support for the project's product. Again, surprises are not sources of uncertainty inherent in this stage, but sources of process uncertainty in earlier stages realized in this stage.

Elaborations to the eight stage framework

Despite the number of steps in Table 2.1, and the possibility of iteration at each evaluation step, our description of the PLC is still a simple one by comparison with the complexities of real projects. Nevertheless, it is a useful basic framework that can be built on in various ways, illustrated by the following elaborations.

Separable project dimensions

In practice, projects are planned and executed in several dimensions that are separable to some extent: physical scope, functionality, technology, location, timing, economics, financing, environmental, and so on. This means that each step in Table 2.1 could be viewed as multidimensional, with each step considering each dimension in parallel or in an iterative sequence. In this latter case, the PLC might be visualized as a spiral of activities moving forward through time, where each completed circle of the spiral represents one step in Table 2.1 completed and each spiral represents sequential consideration of the various project dimensions. Charette (1993) uses similar notions in a related context.

Parallel components

Many projects, especially large ones, may be managed as a set of component projects running in parallel. The steps in Table 2.1 can still be used to describe the progress of each component project, although there is no necessity for the component life cycles to remain in phase at all times. 'Fast-tracking' is a simple example of this, where completion of the parent project can be expedited by overlapping project design, plan, allocate, and execute stages. This implies that some components of the parent project can be designed and planned, and allocation and execution commenced for these components, before designing and planning is complete for other components. As is widely recognized, such staggered execution is only low risk to the extent that the design of components first executed is not dependent on the design of subsequent components. Plans that involve an element of 'fast tracking' should be supported by an appropriate RMP, with a focus on feedback from more advanced components into the life cycle steps of following components.

Objectives not easily defined

For many projects objectives and related performance criteria can be refined progressively through the conceive, design, plan, and allocate stages of the PLC. However, in some projects (e.g., information systems or software development projects), it may not be practicable to ensure that all project objectives are well defined or crystallized prior to the execute stage. This becomes apparent in earlier stages, where *go* decisions acknowledge the situation. In this scenario 'control evaluation', undertaken each time a milestone is achieved, ought to include a 'configuration review' (Turner, 1992; Turner and Cochrane, 1993) of objectives currently achievable with the project. If these are unsatisfactory, further stages of design and plan may be necessary.

Contracting

When allocation of tasks in the allocate stage involves the employment of contractors, the tendering and subsequent production work of the contractor can be regarded as a component project in its own right. For the contractor, all the steps in Table 2.1 are passed through on becoming involved in the parent project. What the client regards as the allocate stage is regarded by the contractor as the conceive, design, plan, and allocate stages. In the case where the contractor has a major responsibility for design (as in turnkey or design-and-build contracts), the client will move quickly through the conceive, design, and plan stages, perhaps considering these stages only in general outline terms. Then the contractor carries out more detailed work corresponding to these stages. For the contractor's project, the 'trigger' involves both a need and an opportunity to tender for work, usually managed at a high level in the contracting organization. The conceive stage corresponds to a preliminary assessment of the bidding opportunity and a decision to tender or not (Ward and Chapman, 1988). This is followed by costing design specifications and plans provided in more or less detail by the client, perhaps some additional design-and-plan development, evaluation of the tendering opportunity, price setting, and submission of a bid. For the contractor's project, the allocate stage involves further allocation of tasks, perhaps via subcontracting, detailed design work and production scheduling as indicated above.

Incomplete definition of methods

In some projects, such as product development projects, it may not be practicable to define completely the nature or sequence of activities required prior to commencing the execution phase (Turner and Cochrane, 1993). In such cases management expects design, plan, allocate, and execute stages to take place alternately on a rolling basis, with achievement of one milestone triggering detailed design, plan, allocate, and execute stages of the next part of the project deliverable. In this scenario, previous *go* decisions in the design, plan, and allocate stages are made on the understanding that subsequent control evaluation steps will send the process through further design, plan, and allocate stages as necessary when the appropriate milestone has been achieved. In effect, the design, plan, allocate, and execute stages are managed as a sequence of miniprojects.

Prototyping is a special case of this scenario and a natural approach where the intention is to mass-produce a product, but the product involves novel designs or new technology. For the production project, the PLC conceive and design stages are managed as a prototype project (with its own PLC). On completion of the prototype, the production PLC proceeds from the plan stage through to the support stage in Table 2.1.

The value of a detailed stage–step structure

The value of a *basic* PLC structure at the level of detail used in Table 2.1 might be questioned on three grounds:

1. these steps and stages will be difficult to distinguish cleanly in practice;
2. in practice some of these steps may not be necessary;
3. this level of detail adds complexity, when what is required to be useful in practice is simplification.

For example, it might be argued that some of the later evaluation steps may be regarded as non-existent in practice because the decision to proceed is not usually an issue beyond a certain point. However, we would argue that it is worth identifying such steps beforehand, given their potential significance in managing sources of process uncertainty.

Many of the really serious sources of project uncertainty are late realizations of unmanaged uncertainty from earlier project stages. The detailed stage and step structure of Table 2.1 and the associated Figure 2.1 help to make this clear. In many projects there is a failure to give sufficient attention to *go/no-go/maybe* decisions. Such decisions should involve careful evaluation of uncertainty, both to appreciate the sources of uncertainty inherent in a *go* decision and the rewards forgone in a *no-go* decision. Equally important is the need to recognize when a *go/no-go* or *maybe* choice should be on the agenda. Many projects appear to involve just one *go/no-go* decision—at the end of the conceive stage. Yet the large number of projects that run into major problems of cost escalation, time overruns, and quality compromises suggests that explicit *go/no-go/maybe* decision points in later stages would often have been worthwhile.

A further reason for the detailed step structure is to highlight the process of objectives formation and its significance for project risk management. As noted in

Chapter 1, risk is measured in terms of uncertainty about the attainment of project objectives. In the PLC, objectives and performance criteria are often initially vague for good reasons, but they must be progressively clarified and refined during the conceive, design, plan, and allocate stages. This process needs to be recognized and the implications understood. A situation where the objectives of a project change imprecisely during the project without proper recognition of the new situation implied is particularly risky. From a risk management viewpoint, any changes in objectives and performance criteria at any stage of the PLC need to be carefully evaluated for risk implications.

Beyond a single-project perspective

As well as recognizing the detailed internal structure of individual project life cycles, it is also important to recognize the role of a project as part of a larger, corporate picture. Projects are invariably embedded in a wider context, which involves other projects. Three basic context structures are the chain configuration, the parallel configuration, and the project hierarchy. Figure 2.2 illustrates these configurations.

In the chain configuration a sequence of component projects follow one another over time to complete an overarching, primary project. In the parallel configuration a number of component projects run in parallel, perhaps with interdependencies, to complete an overarching, primary project. In either case the 'primary project' may be thought of by senior management, in terms that go beyond that associated with individual component projects, as a strategy or long-term programme, using 'programme' in the 'portfolio of projects' sense, with links between the component projects defined by shared objectives, resources, or other issues. The discipline and techniques of project management may be considered of limited use in managing strategy or programmes in this sense, leading to a separation of strategy ('primary project' or programme) management and project management of the component projects. This separation may be formalized by organizational structures and may increase the chances of risk management of component projects being treated separately from consideration of strategic risk.

An obvious example is a contracting organization where the ongoing business involves tendering for individual contracts. Each contract won is treated as a project, and these contracts form a mixture of the chain and parallel configurations. Interdependencies exist between contracts to the extent that they utilize common corporate knowledge, skills, and other resources. An important task for senior management is to manage the (often implicit) 'primary project'—the organization's short- and long-term strategy. Unless this is managed explicitly at 'the top', strategy is likely to emerge *ad hoc* and 'bottom-up' in an unintended rather than deliberate manner (Mintzberg, 1978).

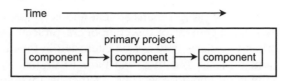

(a) Chain configuration: primary project as a chain of component projects.
Stages in a primary project may be managed as a chain of component projects.

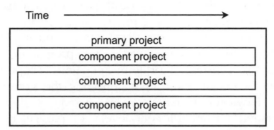

(b) Parallel configuration: primary project as a set of parallel component projects.
Aspects of a project may be managed as a set of parallel projects.

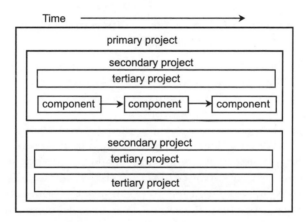

(c) Project hierarchy: primary project as a three-level hierarchy of component projects.

Figure 2.2—Configuration of project systems

In a project hierarchy the 'primary project' is broken down by management into a hierarchy of component projects. The project hierarchy shown in Figure 2.2 is a simple example with embedded parallel and chain configurations. Much more complex configurations involving a combination of these three configuration types exist in most organizations.

Large engineering or construction projects are invariably managed as project hierarchies. As noted earlier, large projects may be managed as a set of component projects running in parallel, with each parallel component comprising a hierarchy of component projects. Management of the 'primary project' can be tackled as a complex version of project management and is typically managed at a more senior level than management of the component projects. As a practical matter, managers of primary projects may not be interested in the 'nuts and bolts' of individual component projects, but they will have to understand them well enough to make sure the component projects fit together as a whole. To achieve this they need to pay special attention to how the six Ws of each of the various component projects fit together, with obvious implications for managing risk.

More generally, a project hierarchy can be thought of as a hierarchy of an organization's long-, medium-, and short-term planning activity. In a top-down approach, long-term strategy leads to the development and implementation of medium-term projects. These may be achieved by a programme of short-term projects or may otherwise constrain short-term operations. Scope for managing sources of uncertainty exists at each level, reflecting the corresponding key issues at each level. However, management at each level also needs to be aware of potential impacts from adjacent levels. In particular, managers of medium-term projects need to take into account potential impacts on their projects from both short-term and long-term issues.

Example 2.1   Planning projects at different levels in an electric utility

An electric utility, providing electricity to a set of private and corporate consumers, might start with a corporate level assessment of annual profit P_t, equal to annual revenue R_t, less annual costs C_t, for $t = 1, 2, \ldots, n$, up to the chosen long-term planning horizon.

Revenue might be a key source of uncertainty, worthy of major risk management effort. Forecast demand might be important here, but existing competing utilities, possible new competitors, market regulators, and other political players may be important parties to consider.

Cost might also be important. At the corporate level, cost may be driven by long-term strategic planning decisions: what mix of sources of power should be aimed for 25 years hence, what proportion of nuclear, gas-fired, coal-fired units should be planned for, and so on. Through-life costs will be important, including fuel costs, the effects of environmental legislation or technology development, and liability for pollution or accidents.

At an operational level, management is concerned with the day-to-day utilization of existing units. At an intermediate level, an important management concern is the timing of decisions to start building new power-generating units. Such decisions may be coupled to both short-term, operational issues and longer-term strategic issues. Sudden failure of an existing unit may trigger a need to bring plans forward. Political events may alter the need for a planned unit significantly, perhaps even eliminate the need for a unit, possibly doing so when construction of the unit is already under way.

> The project manager for the construction of such a unit clearly needs to manage the project in a way that deals effectively with the sources of uncertainty he or she is responsible for and ensure that the sources of uncertainty other members of the organization are responsible for are managed in a supportive manner.

Motivation to undertake risk analysis in a top-down strategic manner needs to come from the organization's board level managers. This involves issues beyond the scope of this book, but discussed elsewhere (Chapman and Ward, 2002, chap. 11, develops Example 2.1). However, even if a project manager's organization chooses to ignore such issues completely, a competent project risk manager should not do so. At the very least, it is important to identify the complete set of corporate risks that impact on the project manager's project and may require responses from the project manager or other parties.

For some purposes and from some perspectives, it can be important to distinguish project management and programme management, to see whether uncertainty is an issue or not. For example, see CCTA (1995a, b, and 1999). We will not develop this distinction for risk management purposes in either/or terms, but treat programmes as the strategic end of a strategy–tactic or programme–project dimension that characterizes projects in an important way for RMP purposes—a driver that should shape the nature of the RMP used, directly comparable in this sense with the stage in the PLC.

Conclusion

To be fully effective, risk management needs to address the whole PLC rather than selected stages, guiding and informing each and every stage of the PLC. The scope and depth of analysis should increase as the project progresses toward the execute stage. Prior to each stage a preliminary risk analysis should guide the first step, but as more details and options are considered in subsequent steps, further risk analysis should be performed with increasing detail and precision to continuously guide and inform the project management process. Risk management should be an integral part of project management at each stage of the PLC, designed to accommodate the focus of each stage in an integrated, holistic manner.

Taking a wider perspective, any designated project is but a particular reference point in a larger system, affected by the wider system, and with potential to affect the wider system in turn. A key management issue, with risk management implications, is the degree of interdependency between (component) projects. The desirability of an approach to risk management that addresses the overall system increases dramatically as the interdependency between projects increases.

3 Motives for formal risk management processes

The Light of Lights looks always on the motive, not the deed, The Shadow of Shadows on the deed alone.—William Butler Yeats

Introduction

Chapter 1 argued for an uncertainty management perspective in project risk management concerned with understanding where and why uncertainty is important and where it is not. Proactive management of this uncertainty leads to benefits beyond improved control and neutralization of threats. It can facilitate enhanced project performance by influencing and guiding a project's objectives, parties, design, and plans.

For effective and efficient risk management to produce these benefits requires formal approach, in much the same way as effective and efficient project management requires formal processes. The nature of an appropriate formal risk management process (RMP) is the subject of later chapters. This chapter considers some key motives for adopting a formal RMP, related to documentation, quantification of uncertainty, and consideration of risk efficient options. These motives are important because they underpin all the potential benefits achievable from an RMP, and they need to be viewed as potential objectives when choosing or shaping an effective RMP for any given context.

Documentation

Documentation is a key feature of all formal processes. This documentation is a key process output, but it also facilitates the operation of the process, and it provides a means of assessing the performance of the process. All project managers are aware of the importance of documentation for effective project management. Formal RMPs require appropriate documentation for all these basic and common reasons, but it is especially important because of the need to deal with uncertainty in terms of both variability and ambiguity. This can include information in a wide variety of forms: describing designs, activities, sources of uncertainty, responses, decisions taken, identified trigger points, and so on. Such documentation might be regarded as a by-product of project risk management, rather than a central concern, but it serves a number of useful purposes that may be worth pursuing in their own right:

1. *Clearer thinking.* A focus on documentation can clarify the initial thinking process. If people have to set down their thinking in writing, this forces clarification of what is involved.
2. *Clearer communications.* Documentation can provide an unambiguous vehicle for communication at any given point in time. If people explain what they mean in terms of designs and activities, sources of uncertainty and responses, and in writing in detail, the scope for misunderstanding is significantly reduced. This can be particularly important in communications between different organizational units or in client–contractor situations. In such settings a number of questions concerning the risk management effort need to be addressed. For example: who is responsible for which activities?, who bears the financial consequences of which sources?, and who will respond to realization of shared sources? Clear documentation can also be an essential part of making all threats and opportunities and all key assumptions clearly visible to all interested parties. A key role for any formal analysis process is the collective use of team input to a joint decision, drawing on a range of expertise as appropriate. Communication is a vital aspect of this process.
3. *Familiarization.* Documentation can provide a record to assist new project team members to 'get up to speed' quickly. Staff turnover on a project can be a significant source of risk, which documentation helps to mitigate. Risk management documentation is a very valuable training tool specific to the project to which new staff are attached.
4. *A record of decisions.* Documentation can provide a record that explains the rationale for key decisions. In some industries (and for some careers), this may become a very important document if a decision goes badly wrong due to bad luck, as illustrated by Example 3.1 (see p. 37).
5. *A knowledge base.* Documentation can provide a record that captures corporate knowledge in a manner useful for subsequent similar project teams. If the kernel of the thinking behind one project is available in a readily accessible form for those doing the next project, the value of this information can be very great. For contracting organizations this information can amount to a competitive advantage over rival firms. Such information can also be the basis of ongoing training as well as an individual learning tool, and a basis for fundamental research.
6. *A framework for data acquisition.* When organizations first introduce a formal RMP, appropriate data are usually difficult to come by. However, the use of a formal RMP clarifies the nature of appropriate data and generally leads to the systematic collection and appreciation of such data, as part of the documentation process. The importance of this development is difficult to understand for organizations that have not been through the process of introducing a formal

RMP, but it is recognized as a major benefit by those who have introduced such processes. It is important to ask whether this issue is relevant upfront, because it means the current lack of data that could be collected in the future does not distort the development of an approach that best serves long-term needs.

If only the first of these six purposes is of interest, limited documentation may be appropriate. However, the other purposes deserve careful prior attention, even if the design of the documentation has a fairly free format. The key underlying purpose of documentation is to integrate the expertise of teams of people so they can make effective, collective decisions based on clearly articulated premises.

Qualitative or quantitative analysis?

Some RMPs focus on qualitative analysis, some on quantitative analysis, and some use both. We argue for both, with use varying at different stages in the Project Life Cycle (PLC) and at different points in the RMP. What is important for present purposes is understanding that an effective RMP will necessarily be a largely qualitative identifying-and-structuring process early on and a more quantitative choosing-and-evaluating process later on. The effectiveness and efficiency of quantitative analysis is driven to an important extent by the quality of the qualitative analysis and the joint interpretation of both. Many of the key motives for formal risk analysis may seem to be driven directly by quantitative risk analysis, but the underlying role of the qualitative analysis this depends on should never be forgotten, and some of the key corporate learning motives are met by the qualitative aspects of the process.

Targets, expectations, and commitments

An important reason for quantifying uncertainty at some stage is that doing so helps to force all members of an organization's management to appreciate the significance of differences between 'targets' that people can aspire to, 'expected values' used to provide an unbiased predictor of outcomes, and 'commitments' that provide some level of contingency allowance. Targets, expected values, and commitments need to be distinguished in terms of cost, time, and all other relevant measures of performance.

Commitments usually involve 'asymmetric penalties' if they are not met or exceeded, with respect to costs, durations, and other performance measures (e.g., the implications of being over cost are not the same as being under cost). This in turn helps to force management to clarify the distinction between 'provisions' (e.g., additional cost to be expected) and 'contingency

allowances' (e.g., additional cost allowance to provide an acceptably low probability of failing to meet commitments). This clarification produces further insight
when ownership of provisions and contingencies is addressed. All these issues
were a central concern when BP International introduced RMPs in the 1970s, and
they should be a central concern for most organizations. However, many organizations with a long history of RMPs still do not understand these issues.

In cost terms, expected values are our best estimate of what costs should be
realized on average. Setting aside a contingency fund to meet costs that may
arise in excess of the expected cost, and making a 'commitment' to deliver within
the expected cost plus the contingency, involves a probability of being able to
meet the commitment that an organization may wish to standardize to clarify
what 'commitments' mean. The contingency allowance provides an uplift from
the expected value, which is not required on average if it is properly determined.
Determining this level of commitment ought to involve an assessment of perceived threats and the extent to which these may be covered by a contingency
fund, together with an assessment of the opportunities and the implications of
both over- and underachievement in relation to the commitment. High penalties
associated with being over cost relative to the penalties associated with being
under cost can justify setting commitment levels that have a higher probability of
being met than the 50–60% chance an expected value might provide. Setting
commitment levels that have an 80 or 90% chance of not being exceeded is
common.

In cost terms, targets are set at a level below expected cost, with provisions
accounting for the difference. Targets need to reflect the opportunity aspect of
uncertainty and the need for goals that stretch people. Targets are sometimes
referred to as 'stretch targets' to reflect this and might be set at a level that has
less than a 20% chance of being achieved. Targets need to be realistic to be
credible, but they also need to be lean. If targets that are optimistic are not aimed
for, expected costs will not be achieved on average and contingency funds will
be used more often than anticipated. If expected costs together with contingency
funds are treated as targets, following a version of Parkinson's law, work will
expand to fill the time available for its completion, leaving insufficient margin
when anything goes wrong. Sometimes differences between targets, expectations, and commitments are kept confidential, or left implicit. We argue that
they need to be explicit, and a clear rationale for the difference needs to be
understood by all, leading to an effective process of managing the evolution from
targets to realized values. Ownership of provisions and contingencies is a central
issue when making this work and is a critical aspect of uncertainty and risk
allocation between parties.

Organizations that do not quantify uncertainty have no real basis for distinguishing targets, expected values, and commitments. As a consequence, single-
value performance levels are employed to serve all three purposes, often with
disastrous results, not to mention costly and unnecessary dysfunctional organizational behaviour: 'the cost estimate', 'the completion date', or 'the promised

performance' become less and less plausible, there is a crisis of confidence when the goal posts are moved, and then the process starts all over again. Senior project managers involved when RMPs were introduced by BP in the 1970s stated that the avoidance of this cycle was the key benefit of RMPs for them. In organizations with a long history of RMPs which still do not deliver this insight some senior managers see its absence as their central problem. The ability to manage the gaps between targets, expected values, and contingency levels, and the ability to set these values appropriately in the first place, is a central concern of risk management. The recommended basis for managing the relationship between targets, expected values, and commitments is developed briefly at various points in later chapters, and in more detail in Chapman and Ward (2002).

Risk efficiency

A central reason for employing formal risk management is the pursuit of 'risk efficiency'. Arguably the most difficult motive to understand, it is certainly the most important. It is the central reason why risk management should not be seen as an 'add-on', an overhead, with limited focus on questions like 'is this project worth investing in?' It is the central reason why risk management should be seen as an integrated 'add-in', an improvement to the basic project planning process that is always worthwhile. BP understood this and acted on it in the 1970s, and it was a published aspect of their process at an early date (Chapman, 1979). However, many organizations with long-standing RMPs still do not understand it. Example 3.1 illustrates what is involved.

Example 3.1   Identifying a risk efficient alternative

A major North Sea offshore oil project was about to seek board approval and release of funds to begin construction. Risk analysis was undertaken to give the board confidence in the plan and its associated cost. One activity involved a hook-up, connecting a pipeline to a platform. It had a target date in August. A 1.6-m barge was specified—equipment that could work in waves up to a nominal 1.6 m height. Risk analysis demonstrated that August was an appropriate target date and a 1.6-m barge was appropriate in August. However, risk analysis also demonstrated that, because this hook-up was late in the overall project sequence and there was considerable scope for delays to earlier activities, there was a significant chance that this hook-up would have to be attempted in November or December. Using a 1.6-m barge at this time of year would be time-consuming and might mean delays until the following spring, with severe opportunity cost implications. A revised analysis was undertaken assuming a 3-m wave height capability barge, costing more than twice as much per day. This more capable barge avoided the risk of going into the next season, significantly reducing risk in terms of the threat of a significant cost overrun. It also significantly reduced the expected cost. This significant improvement with respect to both expected cost and risk in terms of the threat of a major overrun provided a significant improvement in risk efficiency. The base plan was changed, and it was recognized at board level that this one change paid for the risk analysis study many times over. An expected return on RMPs in the 100 to 1,000% range motivated the company to immediately adopt the current RMP worldwide. In the event, hook-up was actually completed in October in good weather conditions.

The risk efficiency concept was originally developed for managing portfolios of investment opportunities afforded by the financial securities markets and is fundamental to understanding how financial markets work. Markowitz (1959) was awarded the Nobel Prize for Economics for his contribution to this 'portfolio analysis' perspective, and the associated mean variance approach to portfolio risk management is now basic undergraduate university material in courses on economics, finance, and accountancy. In its basic form risk efficiency involves one attribute (profit, or return) and a two-criteria view of a portfolio of risky investment opportunities. One criterion is the 'expected value', an unbiased estimate of the performance outcome that can be expected, and the best measure of what should happen on average. The other criterion is 'risk', defined as 'downside variability of the level of performance achievable relative to expected outcome', traditionally measured by the variance or downside semivariance of the distribution of possible levels of performance (Markowitz, 1959). The mean variance approach to investment selection involves selecting alternative portfolios of investments on the basis of their expected performance and their risk as measured by variance in anticipated performance. The mean variance decision rule says that if a portfolio B has both a preferable expected value for performance and lower variance than another portfolio A, then B should be preferred to A, and B is said to be 'risk efficient' with respect to A.

There are problems with the use of variance or semivariance as a measure of risk associated with an investment. However, assuming measurement of risk is appropriate, these problems can be avoided by the use of cumulative probability distribution curve comparisons to make choices between portfolios. The same is true of other management strategy choices couched in portfolio analysis terms.

Project management plans can be viewed in a portfolio analysis framework. Project management plans involve allocating money and other resources to a portfolio of contracts, purchases, tasks, and other components, and we want to achieve risk efficiency. We usually start with cost risk rather than addressing profit risk directly, and we need to think in terms of time and quality (perform-

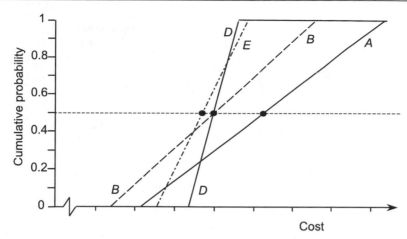

Figure 3.1—Example cumulative probability distribution portrayals

ance other than that measured by cost and time) risk as well, on our way to profit risk, which means our portfolio problem involves multiple attributes. However, we have a portfolio risk management problem to confront if overall risk is the concern.

Figure 3.1 portrays a choice between a project plan B and a project plan A comparable with the portfolio choice described above, with A and B described in terms of cumulative probability cost distributions. In practice both distributions would be asymmetric S-shaped curves, but Figure 3.1 assumes linear cumulative probability distributions (associated with uniform probability density functions) to simplify comparisons for initial illustrative purposes. One virtue of this initial simplicity is that the mean, median, and mode of each distribution all coincide at the midpoint of the range, indicated by dots on the cumulative probability curves for A and B in Figure 3.1. Plan B clearly has a lower expected cost than plan A and less risk by any measure concerned with downside variability. The gap between the curves for plans A and B is a direct measure of their relative risk efficiency, the shape of the gap providing information about the nature of the difference. For example, parallel curves would indicate that the difference between distributions is purely a difference in expected values, while a flatter curve indicates more variability.

In a project context, risk efficiency has to be addressed in terms of cost, time, and all other relevant measures of performance. However, assume for the moment that achieved performance can be measured solely in terms of cost out-turn and that achieved success can be measured solely in terms of realized cost relative to some approved cost commitment. In a project context, risk can then be defined in terms of the size of possible cost overruns and their likelihood. More formally, when assessing a particular project plan in relation to alternative plans, we can consider the expected cost of the project (what

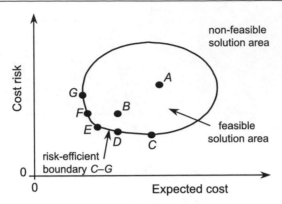

Figure 3.2—Risk efficient options

should happen on average) as one basic measure of performance and associated risk defined by the potential for costs greater than expected cost as a second basic measure of performance.

In this context some project plans will involve less expected cost and less cost risk than others—they will be better in both respects and are referred to as 'risk efficient', like B relative to A in Figure 3.1. The most risk efficient plan for any given level of expected cost will involve the minimum feasible level of risk. The most risk efficient plan for any given level of cost risk will involve the minimum feasible level of expected cost. Given a set of risk efficient plans, expected cost can only be reduced by increasing the cost risk and cost risk can only be reduced by increasing the expected cost. This concept is most easily pictured using a graph like Figure 3.2. Consider a set of feasible project plans, portrayed in relation to expected cost and cost risk as indicated in Figure 3.2. The feasible set has an upper and lower bound for both expected cost and cost risk because there are limits to how good or bad plans can be in both these dimensions. The boundary of the feasible set of plans need not be a smooth and continuous curve as shown in Figure 3.2, but it is convenient to assume this for illustrative purposes.

The 'risk efficient boundary' portrayed by the curve $C–D–E–F–G$ is that set of feasible, risk efficient project plans that provides a minimum level of cost risk for any given level of expected cost, or the minimum level of expected cost for any given level of cost risk.

Any points inside the boundary, like A and B, represent risk inefficient plans. B is more risk efficient than A, but B can be improved on with respect to both expected cost and cost risk (e.g., moving to E).

Figure 3.1 illustrates the implications of points A and B in relation to D and E in Figure 3.2. D has the same level of expected cost as B, but a lot less risk. E has a little more risk than D, indicated by the area between the curves above the

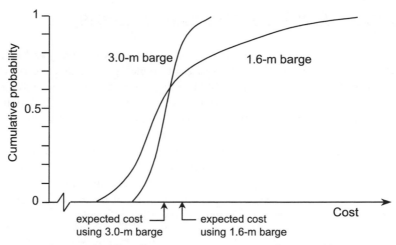

Figure 3.3—Illustrative asymmetric S curves for Example 3.1

crossing point, but less expected cost. *D* and *E* are both risk efficient choices. *A* and *B* are both risk inefficient choices in overall terms, relative to the risk efficient boundary. The simple linear form of the cumulative probability distributions used to illustrate the Figure 3.1 format make it relatively easy to learn to read such curves. It is then a relatively simple matter to graduate to interpretation of differences between the asymmetric, S-shaped distributions that arise in practice.

Figure 3.3 illustrates the nature of the probability distributions used to make decisions in practice, associated with the decision discussed in Example 3.1. The 1.6-m choice will be cheaper most of the time, indicated by the probability level where the curves cross. However, the 3.0-m barge distribution curve is much steeper, because the outcome is less uncertain. The 1.6-m barge distribution has a much longer tail to the right, because of the low probability but high cost of a lost season. It is the long tail to the right that drags the expected cost of the 1.6-m barge option to the right of the expected cost for the 3.0-m barge option.

In practice it is important to limit the number of cumulative probability distributions portrayed on one diagram, to make interpreting them as simple as possible, even when a large number of sequential decisions is necessary. This issue is discussed in detail in Chapman and Ward (2002, chap. 10).

Example 3.1 illustrates three separate roles for risk management in relation to risk efficiency:

1. diagnose desirable changes in plans;
2. demonstrate the need for such changes;
3. facilitate, demonstrate, and encourage 'enlightened caution'.

Diagnose desirable changes in plans

Sometimes risk analysis can diagnose difficulties and opportunities, and identify a need for changes in project base plans or contingency plans that were previously obscure and not recognized. Risk analysts should be motivated to search for such changes, their RMPs should facilitate the search, and they should enlist the support of the project team as a whole to join the search. In this context risk management can be usefully portrayed as a treasure hunt—the 'treasure' is increases in risk efficiency through changes in plans. Put another way, risk management is a search for opportunities and ways to manage them, as well as threats. This positive perspective is extremely important for staff motivation and morale, as well as for the direct pay-off in terms of more efficient plans and designs and a more effective approach to achieving efficiency.

Demonstrate the need for such changes

Sometimes risk analysis is not necessary to identify a need for changes in plans in the sense that exploring the intuitions of project team members will reveal an understanding of the need for such changes. However, whether or not recognition by specific project team members is the result of risk management, risk management can allow the demonstration of the need for that change to others, like the board in Example 3.1. Demonstration of this need is a separate and very important aspect of making the changes. For a variety of reasons, if it is not possible to demonstrate clearly the need for changes, such changes may not be made, even if most of those involved acknowledge the need to make the changes. One basic reason is determined resistance to changes by those with vested interests. Another is inertia. Yet another is a business culture that discourages the 'enlightenment' essential to achieve risk efficiency.

Facilitate, demonstrate, and encourage enlightened caution

'Enlightened caution' is a willingness to commit resources that may not be needed, because in expected value terms (on average) it will be cost-effective to commit them.

Had problems in the earlier part of the project of Example 3.1 caused the hook-up to take place in November or December, with seasonably bad weather, the change to a 3-m barge would have been clearly justified. The enlightened caution associated with the changes would have been verified empirically. The hook-up taking place in October in good weather demonstrated enlightened caution, which was not verified empirically. This was a very important demonstration, because if enlightened caution is part of a corporate culture, money will be spent which 20 : 20 hindsight will suggest would have been saved whenever we are lucky, and it is important to appreciate that this money was not wasted.

If no formal RMP had been followed in relation to the Example 3.1 decision to use a 3-m barge—the decision being made on intuitive grounds by the project manager—the project manager's career might have looked much less promising when it became clear he could have got away with a 1.6-m barge. That is, the risk analysis made it clear that the project manager had done well to achieve hook-up by October and that he had been lucky with the weather. Without a formal risk analysis, his good luck might have been confused with bad management regarding this decision, overlooking completely his good management of the project (getting to the hook-up by October), and blighting his career. A worldly-wise project manager would explicitly recognize this possibility and might opt for the 1.6-m barge in the absence of formal risk analysis, deliberately making a bad management decision because good luck would subsequently be confused with good management, and bad luck would subsequently just be interpreted as plain bad luck. If an organization cannot distinguish between good luck and good management, bad luck and bad management, individuals will manage risk accordingly. Without risk analysis to demonstrate support for their decisions, astute managers who are naturally and reasonably cautious with respect to their own careers will see risk efficient decisions comparable with choosing the 3-m barge in Example 3.1 as unwise, potentially dangerous to their careers, seeming to demonstrate a 'wimpish' uncalled for caution whenever they actually manage the preceding work effectively. Very astute managers will avoid even looking for opportunities to increase risk efficiency in this way, to avoid the moral hazard of the obvious conflict of interests. More generally, if good luck and good management cannot be distinguished, such opportunities will not be looked for and for the most part they will be passed over if they are stumbled on.

Risk management can facilitate and demonstrate enlightened caution in particular instances and by doing so encourage a more general culture change associated with circumstances that are not worth formal analysis as used in relation to Example 3.1.

If everyone involved understands the lesson of examples like Example 3.1, the culture can change as a consequence of everyone looking for and making changes that increase risk efficiency through enlightened caution. This means that sometimes most people will spend money on 'insurance' that is not needed. However, any organization that never spends money on 'insurance' that is sometimes not needed is habitually 'underinsured'. Enlightened caution needs to be facilitated and demonstrated to overcome this widespread cultural phenomenon; the demonstration of instances when enlightened caution was not empirically verified is of particular importance.

Risk efficiency in terms of expected cost and cost risk has direct analogies in terms of duration, quality, and all other relevant performance criteria that need joint management, as addressed later and further explained in Chapman and Ward (2002). Further, risk efficiency in this multiple attribute sense links project risk management to project value management, project quality management, and so on—project management *in toto*. The objective is jointly optimizing the design associated with a project, the duration of the project, its resource usage, its cost, and the quality of what is delivered, in terms of expected performance and associated risk, with appropriate trade-offs. All six *W*s are involved and their relationships. Much of the uncertainty and associated risk to be managed is ambiguity about how best to do this. What might go wrong (or better than expected) with a particular way of approaching the project is part of what project risk management has to address, but it is a small part of a much bigger picture if the scope for opportunity management in the context of uncertainty that includes ambiguity is fully realized. Project risk management is about doing the right things in every sense, as well as doing them the right way—effectiveness as well as efficiency in general terms. Risk efficiency in a multiple attribute sense embraces all of this in a holistic and integrated manner.

Trade-offs between risk and expected performance

Closely linked with the concept of risk efficiency is the possibility of making trade-offs between alternative risk efficient project plans.

Return for the moment to the assumption that expected cost and associated cost risk are adequate measures of performance. For most-risk efficient plans, the level of cost risk can be decreased given an increase in expected cost, and the level of expected cost can be decreased given an increase in cost risk. In relation to Figure 3.1, point *G* represents the minimum expected cost project plan, with a high level of cost risk despite its risk efficiency. Point *C* represents the minimum cost risk project plan, with a high level of expected cost despite its risk efficiency. If an organization can afford to take the risk, *G* is the preferred solution. If the risk associated with *G* is too great, it must be reduced by moving toward *C*. In general, successive movements will prove less and less cost-effective, larger increases in expected cost being required to achieve the same reduction in absolute or relative risk. In practice, an intermediate point like *E* usually needs to be sought, providing a cost-effective balance between risk and expected cost, the exact point depending on the organization's ability to take risk.

The scale of the project relative to the organization in question is a key issue in terms of the relevance of plans *D*, *E*, *F*, or *G*. If the project is one of hundreds, none of which could threaten the organization, plan *G* may be a sensible choice. If the organization is a one-project organization and failure of the project means failure of the organization, a more prudent stance may seem to be appropriate, closer to *C* than *G*.

Traditional portfolio theory discussions of alternative choices on the risk efficient boundary (e.g., Markowitz, 1959) usually treat these decisions as a simple matter of preference: how much risk does the decision maker want to take? The Synergistic Contingency Planning and Review Technique (SCERT) (Chapman, 1979) followed this lead, using the term 'risk balance' to discuss the balance between expected cost and cost risk. Later work with IBM UK made it clear that in the context of an ongoing portfolio of projects, choosing between D, E, F, and G is better viewed as a matter of corporate level risk efficiency, as distinct from the project level of risk efficiency involved in defining these plans. That is, corporate risk efficiency means never reducing risk for a project by increasing expected cost when the risk involved does not threaten the organization as a whole more than a proportionate increase in the expected cost of all projects. In these terms an aggressive approach to risk taking at a project level is part of a risk efficient approach to corporate level risk management. IBM UK developed project risk management in the early 1990s to facilitate taking more risk, not less, to exploit this perception of corporate risk management, and both authors of this book were involved in a linked culture change programme. Chapman and Ward (2002) develop this extended risk efficiency notion in more detail, in the context of both projects and security portfolios. It can be viewed as a matter of project versus corporate risk efficiency, or as a matter of dynamic versus static risk efficiency, or as both. It implies decisions about 'risk balance' which involve a higher level form of risk efficient choice, not a simple preference statement.

If an organization can afford to minimize expected project cost and not worry about cost risk at the individual project level, this has the very great merit of simplicity. This in turn implies it is very worthwhile defining a level of potential cost overrun below which the organization can accept cost risk, above which cost risk needs to be considered in terms of risk efficient trade-offs at a corporate level. Similar arguments apply to risk in terms of other measures of performance.

Risk analysis can serve three separate roles in relation to trade-offs between risk and expected performance: two almost (but not quite) directly analogous to those associated with risk efficiency and the third somewhat different (but complementary):

1. diagnose possibly desirable changes in plans;
2. demonstrate the implications of such changes in plans;
3. facilitate, demonstrate, and encourage 'enlightened gambles'.

Diagnose possibly desirable changes in plans

The treasure hunt for difficulties and opportunities associated with current plans and associated changes in plans to improve risk efficiency may identify desirable moves around the risk efficient boundary. Consider a fabricated alternative to Example 3.1 to illustrate this issue.

Example 3.2   Taking an enlightened gamble

Assume that Example 3.1 involved different perceived uncertainty. Assume risk analysis suggested that the 3-m barge would effectively avoid the risk of major delays (a lost season) costing £100 to £200 million, but increase expected cost by £15 million. Assume that after due consideration the board decided to specify the 1.6-m barge, taking an enlightened gamble. Assume that, in the event, hook-up activity was reached in October, but the weather proved unseasonably bad and hook-up completion was delayed until the following spring.

The outcome of Example 3.2 might make some boards wish they had not been told about the gamble. However, we argue that whatever the decision and whatever the outcome, boards should be pleased such decisions are brought to their attention. Further, we argue that decisions involving trade-offs at lower levels also benefit from formal diagnosis in a similar manner. The rationale may become clearer as we consider the two further roles of risk analysis in relation to trade-offs between risk and expected performance.

Demonstrate the implications of changes in plans

It might be obvious to all involved that a change in approach, like using a 3-m barge instead of a 1.6-m barge as in Example 3.2, would increase expected cost but reduce risk. Identification of the trade-off situation involved might not be an issue.

Demonstration of the implications as just discussed is still extremely valuable and a separate and very important part of the process of ensuring appropriate trade-offs between risk and expected performance are made. Indeed, arguably the importance of demonstration increases when a trade-off is involved, relative to a case like the basic Example 3.1, because the judgement is a much finer one.

Facilitate, demonstrate, and encourage enlightened gambles

The quantification of uncertainty in Example 3.2 might lead many people to the conclusion that a 3-m barge was clearly worthwhile. Had risk analysis not been carried out but figures of this order of magnitude been generally anticipated, caution might seem even more obviously desirable. However, while promoting enlightened caution, formal risk analysis can and should also encourage 'enlightened gambles', defined as risk efficient gambles involving significant risk that is considered bearable.

For oil majors involved in £1,000 million projects in the 1970s and 1980s, potential losses much greater than £100–200 million were part of the territory. To enable them to live with these risks, joint ventures were common. Over 10 such projects, taking the risk described in Example 3.2, equate to an expected cost saving of £15 million times 10, or £150 million. Oil companies could not afford to pass up expected cost savings on this level in order to reduce risks that did not need to be reduced. Enlightened gambles were a key part of the culture. Organizations that do not take enlightened gambles reduce their average profitability and may guarantee eventually going out of business. The authors have experience of programmes specifically designed to demonstrate the need for such enlightened gambles in organizations that spend too much on avoiding gambles—the equivalent of persistent overinsurance. Formal risk management can facilitate, demonstrate, and encourage enlightened gambles as a basis for engineering associated organization culture changes.

In the context of Example 3.2, if the gamble had paid off, the virtue of the enlightened gamble would have been verified empirically. However, the occasional, visible, high-level failure of such gambles is extremely important, because it demonstrates that good managers who take risk efficient gambles are sometimes unlucky. If no quantified risk analysis had been undertaken to demonstrate the expected cost saving associated with the Example 3.2 enlightened gamble, this message would have been lost, whatever the outcome. In the absence of a demonstrated expected cost benefit and an organizational culture that promotes enlightened gambles, astute managers do not take such gambles and very astute managers don't even look for them.

Risk management can facilitate a search for opportunities to take enlightened gambles, demonstrate that such gambles are worth taking, and encourage a culture change where this mode of thinking and behaviour becomes the norm even when formal risk analysis is not involved. Enlightened caution means that sometimes money will be spent on proactive risk management that in the event proves unnecessary. Enlightened gambles mean that sometimes money will not be spent on proactive risk management that in the event proves unlucky. The general cultural issue is concerned with distinguishing between good luck and good management, bad luck and bad management, in order to persuade people to take the right risks and avoid the wrong ones, in risk efficiency and risk/ expected performance trade-off terms.

Particularly at middle and lower levels of management involving decisions that risk analysis may not reach directly, changing the culture to promote enlightened gambles can have a significant impact on organizational performance. 'Unenlightened gambles' (gambles that are not risk efficient, or risk efficient but inappropriate) are an obvious concern of risk analysis—to be rooted out and avoided. 'Unenlightened caution' (risk reduction measures that are not risk efficient, or risk efficient but not necessary) is arguably an even more important target for risk analysis and associated culture change. Risk management as opportunity management is particularly concerned with enlightened gambles and the need to distinguish between bad management and bad luck.

Expected value and associated risk trade-offs in terms of cost, duration, quality, and other measures of performance need joint management. Trade-off considerations may be quite different for issues like safety or quality when corporate image is involved. For example, an aggressive approach to taking cost risk might be coupled to a very cautious approach to safety risk, for a range of very sensible reasons. Chapman and Ward (2002) provide a much deeper development of risk efficiency and associated trade-offs than is appropriate here. It is difficult to overstate the central importance of the risk efficiency concept for *all* risk and uncertainty management, and it is worth the reader spending some time ensuring that this and the previous section are understood as clearly as possible before proceeding.

Defining 'risk' and 'opportunity'

Recognition and exploitation of risk efficiency requires an appropriate definition of 'risk'. Unfortunately, many standard definitions of risk are unhelpful in this respect. Definitions of risk as *causes of an effect* on project performance do not facilitate a focus on the risk efficiency concept. The common definition of risk as *probability multiplied by impact* precludes consideration of risk efficiency altogether, because it means risk and expected value are formally defined as equivalent.

Using the risk efficiency concept requires a definition of 'risk' that accommodates the portfolio analysis definition used earlier in this chapter: 'downside variability of the level of performance achieved relative to expected outcome'. Given our recommended use of diagrams like Figure 3.3 and our short-form definition in Chapter 1, a more operational definition of 'risk' is:

> *the implications of uncertainty about the level of performance achievable, portrayed by adverse variability relative to expected outcomes, assessed for each performance attribute using comparative cumulative probability distributions when measurement is appropriate.*

This provides an operational definition of risk that is new in the form quoted above, but well established in the sense that organizations like BP and IBM have been using it successfully for years. It is substantially different from those adopted by the PMI and APM cited in Chapter 1, and many other definitions. A debate about which is most appropriate would be useful in our view.

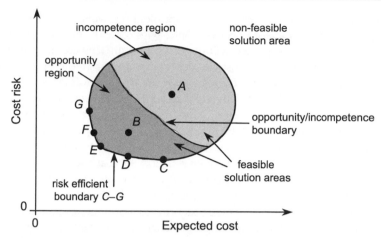

Figure 3.4—An illustrative opportunity/incompetence boundary

Relative to the APM and PMI approach to the definition of risk, the key to the difference is treating opportunities and threats—or events, conditions, and circumstances—as sources of uncertainty that cause risk, rather than as risk in themselves. A holistic and integrated approach to risk management requires this perspective, and risk management without it is severely crippled, be it project risk management, safety management, or any other form of risk and uncertainty management.

'Risk' as defined here has a downside variability focus, but opportunities as well as threats are seen as part of the uncertainty that needs to be managed source by source to the extent that decomposition of sources of uncertainty is useful. To maintain an opportunity management perspective it is useful to revisit Figure 3.2 in the augmented form of Figure 3.4.

The basic idea is to move away from relatively inefficient plans like *A* in Figure 3.4 toward more risk efficient points like *B* and hopefully to points like *E*. If achieved, such moves should be interpreted as captured opportunities, comparable with that identified in Example 3.1, with the RMP facilitating the hunt and the capture. Examples 1.1 and 1.2 also illustrate this kind of opportunity hunt and capture. Approaches to the project involving plans with a cost and cost risk profile like point *A* will be in an 'incompetence region' if it is reasonably obvious that they involve significant risk inefficiency in overall project management terms. The 'opportunity region' represents potentially feasible improvements in plans that are not obvious. They require an effective RMP to identify them. The location of the opportunity/incompetence boundary and the extent of the opportunity region will always be subjective and debatable. But its existence can be conceptually useful. It helps to maintain a focus on upbeat opportunity management when the RMP is effective. And it puts into perspective an RMP that is crippled by a failure to address risk efficiency in terms of a holistic and integrated approach to project management *in toto*.

We can never be sure our plans are risk efficient. However, we need to search systematically for risk efficient improvements, with a clear understanding of what we are looking for; otherwise, we will never find them. This implies that the form of risk management selected must be geared to a search for opportunities to improve risk efficiency—to do things better in the risk efficiency sense. If a project's plans are already very effective and efficient in general terms, usually what is involved is identifying where extra money or other resources expended upfront will reduce later uncertainty, risk, and overall expected cost, but more fundamental lateral thinking may be key. Example 1.2, turning a threat into an opportunity by managing potential delays in a way that improved the project's cash flow, is a good example. If a project's plans are not risk efficient, any lack of effectiveness and efficiency in general terms will reveal itself as risk ineffi-ciency. Diagnosis of potential changes to base or contingency plans to improve risk efficiency is the central purpose of effective project risk management. Con-sideration of risk efficient choices in Example 3.1 motivated BP to adopt formal risk management on a worldwide basis for all significant or sensitive projects as indicated earlier. Improvements in risk efficiency are what they were looking for.

In terms of the old adage 'an optimist always sees a glass as half-full while a pessimist sees it as half-empty', the opportunity/incompetence boundary is a half-way mark. Most people and most organizations tend to be optimists about their abilities. Most organizations will wish to place their adopted plans in the opportunity region, or even assume their plans are in the risk efficient set. However, an assertion that adopted plans are (relatively) risk efficient is not good enough. Such an assertion needs to be tested. It can be tested by the organization itself, in terms of externally assisted assessment of the quality of the design and selection processes used, which depends on the quality of the concepts they rest on, the culture of the organization they operate in, and the quality of the people. Or it may be tested by the stock market, relevant govern-ment watchdogs, or other interested parties. Sooner or later it will be tested by one or the other, and an ineffective or complacent internal test will lead to a negative external test. This 'test' in one form or another is as inevitable as death and taxes. This is a 'stick' incentive to understand and pursue risk efficiency, but the 'carrot' incentive of improved project performance will be more profitable and more fun.

Creative thinking

The culture changes associated with facilitation, demonstration, and encourage-ment of enlightened caution and enlightened gambles discussed earlier are extremely important in their own right. They are also extremely important drivers of second-order effects that result from taking a more positive attitude to uncertainty and the elimination of associated risk inefficiency. If uncertainty is seen as a 'bad thing', a source of fear to be avoided, people develop blinkers as a natural defence mechanism. If uncertainty is seen as a 'good thing', a source of opportunity and satisfaction to be seized, people take off their blinkers. They start to look at all the angles, and their expectations and aspirations rise. This can go well beyond enlightened caution and enlightened gambles, to include entirely new ways of seeing an organization's purpose, as Example 3.3 illustrates.

Example 3.3   A change of purpose for new production equipment

The established manufacturer of a branded household product suddenly found its market growing rapidly, severely taxing its outdated production process. With outside help, new production equipment had been designed that would improve both the consistency of the product and productivity. Although the equipment was new to this application, it was based on known technologies from other fields and promised twice the output per square foot of plant and per employee, with an investment per unit of capacity comparable with the old equipment. The new process appeared to more than meet cost requirements and the production manager planned to replace the old production equipment with the new as quickly as possible.

At a senior management meeting concern was raised that the production manager had no contingency plan in the event that the new production process experienced unexpected start-up problems. This prompted a discussion of the critical role of additional capacity in exploiting the substantial growth in demand. Further investigation indicated that the cost of creating and maintaining excess capacity was minimal compared with the high margin obtainable on the product. Moreover, if the firm was unable to meet all of the demand for its products, the penalty would not only be a loss in market share but a waste of advertising dollars equivalent to a capital investment required for 30% idle capacity. The senior management team concluded that in the short term the new production equipment should be acquired to provide additional production capacity, rather than as a replacement for the existing equipment.

Adapted from Wheelwright (1978)

When people take their blinkers off and start searching for opportunities (risk inefficiencies) they generally enjoy themselves. Lateral thinking becomes the order of the day and people start to think of risk management as 'fun'. It is fun because it is tackled in advance, in a calm and creative way, while there is time to work around the obvious and important problems. Reactive crisis management is not eliminated but is reduced to a tolerable level. For years we have suggested to seminar audiences that *good* formal risk analysis processes are not inhibiting, that they are not about 'doom and gloom', but they are about creative thinking, seizing opportunities, and having fun. The acid test of a good risk management process is 'do the people involved have a smile on their face?'

While it may not seem so at first sight, this is a *very* serious point. The biggest source of risk and risk inefficiency for most projects and organizations is a failure to attract and keep the best people. If a manager wants to attract and keep the best people, and get the most out of them, morale is a key issue. Good morale cannot be bought, it has to be developed. Good risk management processes can help to build good morale in a number of ways. Encouraging creative and lateral thinking is one way. Other ways include the order-of-magnitude increases in communication between all project staff that tend to flow from the process, breaking down 'them and us', enlarging co-operation across group and company boundaries, and so on. These benefits should not simply be allowed to happen, they should be encouraged by designing them into the process.

Constructive insubordination

A common experience for risk analysts is being expected to answer what they soon perceive to be 'the wrong question'. It is important for analysts, and for those who ask them questions, to understand that this does not necessarily imply an error of judgment on the questioner's part—it may be the natural consequences of a need for focus prior to the insights provided by analysis. It may be useful for analysts to assume that this is the case and indulge in 'constructive insubordination', attempting to answer 'the right question', after some time spent attempting to formulate 'the right question'.

When first questioned, analysts often respond with a provisional answer to what is perceived as 'the wrong question'. This too may be the natural consequence of a need for focus, or part of the process of negotiating 'the right question', which may be usefully understood as 'constructive insubordination', not an error of judgement on the analyst's part.

Encouraging a dialogue—an interactive process that both facilitates and promotes constructive insubordination—can be an important part of the overall culture change process. It is vital to teams working across different management levels. Example 3.4 illustrates what may be involved.

Example 3.4   Risks associated with an offshore gravity platform

An offshore project on the east coast of Canada being planned in the early 1980s involved two possible technologies.

One technology involved a gravity platform, a larger-scale version of an approach used by the Norwegians for North Sea projects. A large concrete doughnut is cast in a deepwater harbour, sunk, and another section cast on top. This process is repeated until a large concrete 'pipe' about 100 m across and 200 m long is formed. This 'pipe' is then floated and towed to the site. After sinking it at the desired location, it is half-filled with iron ore to make it heavy enough to withstand the impact of icebergs. The other half is used to store oil when production begins.

The other technology involved a submarine well head connection via a flexible hose to 'ship-shapes' (effectively tankers that produce the oil), moving off-station if icebergs become a threat.

Political pressures were an important part of the decision process. Gravity platforms would have to be constructed in an east coast Canadian harbour, an area of high unemployment. Ship-shapes could come from anywhere. A number of other factors also favoured the gravity platform approach.

Initially it was assumed that the gravity structure was the preferred approach, and the focus of a risk assessment Chapman was asked to undertake was on the cost of a gravity platform. However, the initial analysis concentrated on the technology choice question, in terms of uncertainty associated with recoverable oil in the reservoir, the price of oil when it is produced, and the capital costs and operating costs for both technologies. A key issue was the high capital cost and low operating cost structure of the gravity platform approach versus the low capital cost and high operating cost structure of the ship-shape approach. This analysis demonstrated that as things then stood a gravity platform approach involved unacceptable risk. A low oil volume/low oil price/high platform capital cost scenario involved betting the company and losing. A ship-shape approach did not pose this threat, because of its low capital cost.

The company's management were not pleased by this result, addressing a question they had not asked, but they accepted its validity and managed the risks it identified.

Subsequent to this analysis, further exploratory wells confirmed the anticipated volume of oil, and the risk associated with the gravity approach was managed in other ways, to make this technology (design) choice effective and efficient.

An important motive for RMPs can be the much more effective working relationships that result from the encouragement of big picture perspectives, the discouragement of tunnel vision, and the encouragement of productive questioning of sacred cows. This does not imply an absence of discipline or a tolerance of unconstructive insubordination. The goal is a process that is creative and supportive, built on mutual confidence and trust, give, and take. It deliberately avoids the assumption that more senior management 'know better' than their juniors and seeks to liberate creativity of all levels of management responsibility. Even hard-nosed military commanders in the heat of real battle understand the value of constructive insubordination, the origin of the term, and the obvious illustration of a context in which unconstructive insubordination would not be tolerated.

Conclusion

Successful risk management is not just about reducing threats to project perform-ance. A key motive is the identification of opportunities to change base plans and develop contingency plans in the context of a search for risk efficiency, taking an aggressive approach to the level of risk that is appropriate, with a view to long-term corporate performance maximization. Risk measurement can be a vital tool in this process, especially if the full potential value of cultural changes is to be realized and dysfunctional organizational behaviour associated with confusing targets, expectations and commitments, provisions and contin-gency sources is to be avoided. But qualitative analysis and its documentation can also help to capture corporate knowledge in an effective fashion, for use in both current and future projects. And explicit corporate culture management can pay major dividends.

4   An overview of generic risk management processes

Some people regard discipline as a chore. For me it is a kind of order that sets me free to fly.—Julie Andrews

Introduction

The idea of a formal risk management process (RMP) is central to this book. Formality is desirable because it provides structure and discipline, which facilitates efficient and effective risk management. A key message of this book is that this structure is not a source of restriction, but a source of liberation.

Formality is not about the pursuit of a closely defined, inflexible procedure; it is about providing a framework that guides and encourages the development of best practice. Formality in RMPs is partly about making sure the right questions get asked and answered and partly about making sure everyone who needs to know understands the answers. Helping people to develop the right answers is a third aspect, which lies between these two aspects, but while it can be a focus of attention for risk analysts, it may be of less concern to others. Giving people the comfort that all the key questions have been asked and addressed is the basic rationale of a formal RMP. *How* they are addressed is orders of magnitude less important.

This chapter outlines a particular generic RMP framework for projects, referred to as the SHAMPU (Shape, Harness, And Manage Project Uncertainty) process. To some readers the acronym SHAMPU may suggest yet another brand label in a marketplace already awash with similar products under different labels. No irony was intended when choosing this acronym, and the authors share a widely felt dislike of all acronyms, especially new ones. Our concern is the content of the RMPs people use, not what they call them. SHAMPU is a convenient label for a coherent set of operational process concepts, not a new product.

If an organization or an individual is starting from scratch, the SHAMPU process is a good place to start. However, for organizations or individuals with some experience of risk management, it may be important to accommodate preferences and pressures for alternative processes. For example, some readers may prefer an alternative RMP because they are familiar with it, some readers may see advantages in following an RMP promoted by a professional organization they belong to, and some readers may be required to employ a particular RMP framework. Nevertheless, whatever their circumstances, *all* readers need a basic understanding of the concepts and issues encompassed by the SHAMPU process framework if they are to develop and improve their risk management practice.

After a brief introduction to key features of the SHAMPU framework, this chapter considers some alternative RMP frameworks and compares them with the SHAMPU framework. In part this serves to clarify the pedigree and the rationale of the SHAMPU process, in part to clarify key differences and in part to help readers understand process design choices.

To simplify the acquisition of a working understanding of the key issues for all readers, a historical perspective is adopted in most of this chapter. This shows how the SHAMPU framework has emerged from a synthesis of earlier RMPs. It also sheds some light on the evolution of key ideas that are central to all effective RMPs. This historical perspective also includes particular consideration of three established RMP frameworks: those outlined in the *PRAM Guide* (Simon et al., 1997), the *PMBOK Guide* (PMI, 2000), and the *RAMP Guide* (Simon, 1998; see also Lewin, 2002). SHAMPU is recommended as an operational generic framework for direct use, or for synthesis with other RMP frameworks, as the best means of addressing the concepts and issues discussed in this book. Other RMP frameworks vary in their attention to these concepts and issues, and some important differences are subtle.

Ultimately, all organizations that intend to make extensive use of risk management need to develop a formal RMP framework that is tailored to the specific kinds of project and context that organization faces. Comparing SHAMPU and some alternatives should provide readers with an initial idea of some of the design choice issues.

The SHAMPU framework

The SHAMPU framework involves nine phases, with purposes and tasks as outlined in Table 4.1. For comparison and exposition purposes, two simplified (macrophase) frameworks are defined in Table 4.2.

The simplest (three phase) framework in Table 4.2 provides a top-down overview of the process that the SHAMPU acronym is based on. The starting point is *shape* the project strategy, which involves shaping project uncertainty at a strategic level to make the chosen approach to project uncertainty both effective and efficient in a risk efficient sense. This is followed by *harness* the plans (defined in terms of all six Ws), which involves harnessing the uncertainty shaped at a strategic level by developing risk efficient plans at a tactical level. These tactical level plans are necessary for implementation. *Manage* implementation, managing this harnessed uncertainty, is the third key ingredient. In very simple terms *shape*, *harness* and *manage* project uncertainty is what the SHAMPU process is about. 'Shape' is used in the effective strategic crafting sense adopted by Miller and

Table 4.1—A nine phase portrayal of the SHAMPU process outlining purposes and tasks

phases	*purposes and tasks in outline*
define the project	Consolidate relevant existing information about the project at a strategic level in a holistic and integrated structure suitable for risk management. Fill in any gaps uncovered in the consolidation process, and resolve any inconsistencies.
focus the process	Scope and provide a strategic plan for the RMP. Plan the RMP at an operational level.
identify the issues	Identify sources of uncertainty at a strategic level in terms of opportunities and threats. Identify what might be done about it, in terms of proactive and reactive responses. Identify secondary sources of uncertainty associated with responses.
structure the issues	Complete the structuring of earlier phases. Test simplifying assumptions. Provide more complex or alternative structures when appropriate.
clarify **ownership**	Allocate *both* financial *and* managerial responsibility for issues (separately if appropriate).
estimate variability	Size the uncertainty that is usefully quantified on a first pass. On later passes, refine earlier estimates of uncertainty where this is effective and efficient.
evaluate implications	Assess statistical dependence (dependence not modelled in a causal structure). Synthesize the results of the estimate phase using dependence assumptions that are fit for the purpose. Interpret the results in the context of *all* earlier phases. Make decisions about proactive and reactive responses, and about refining and redefining earlier analysis, managing the iterative nature of the process as a key aspect of these tasks.
harness the plans	Obtain approval for strategic plans shaped by earlier phases. Prepare detailed action plans. These are base plans (incorporating preventative responses) and contingency plans (incorporating reactive responses with trigger points) ready for implementation within the action horizons defined by appropriate lead times. Commit to project plans that are fit for implementation.
manage implementation	Manage the planned work. Develop action plans for implementation on a rolling basis. Monitor and control (make decisions to refine or redefine project plans as required). Deal with crises (unanticipated issues of significance) and be prepared to cope appropriately with disasters (crises that are not controlled).

Table 4.2—Alignment of simplified (macrophase) portrayals of the SHAMPU process

the basic nine phase SHAMPU process	*middle level (five phase) portrayal*	*simplest (three phase) portrayal*
define the project **focus** the process	clarify the **basis of analysis**	**shape** the project strategy
identify the issues **structure** the issues clarify **ownership**	execute the **qualitative analysis**	
estimate variability **evaluate** implications	execute the **quantitative analysis**	
harness the plans	**harness** the plans	**harness** the plans
manage implementation	**manage** implementation	**manage** implementation

Lessard (2000), except that we explicitly associate 'shape' with seeking risk efficiency in the extended corporate/dynamic sense discussed in Chapter 3. 'Harness' is a word chosen to emphasize the need to transform project strategy into operational plans at a different level of detail for implementation purposes. The *harness* phase is a clarification of the PRAM (Project Risk Analysis and Management) *planning* phase (Simon et al., 1997), and clarification is facilitated by another label.

The middle level (five phase) framework in Table 4.2 provides more detail for '*shape* the project strategy'. The *basis of analysis* must be clarified, executing *qualitative analysis* provides the necessary holistic structure, and *quantitative analysis* serves essential roles within this holistic structure.

Identifying the phases of the SHAMPU process in Table 4.1 and Table 4.2 terms provides only a partial description of the SHAMPU process. A key aspect not captured in these tables is the iterative nature of the process. Iterations involve revisiting or looping back to earlier phases to develop, refine, or reconsider aspects of the analysis undertaken to date.

The way iterations between phases are managed has a major impact on the effectiveness and efficiency of the project's strategy and on the effectiveness and efficiency of the SHAMPU process itself. In *project* strategy terms, effectiveness and efficiency involve explicit attention to *risk efficient* choices as discussed in Chapter 3. In risk management *process* terms, effectiveness and efficiency involves a related *simplicity efficiency* concept. Simplicity efficiency is about achieving the maximum amount of insight for any given level of effort by choosing an approach to each successive pass through the SHAMPU phases in a way that copes efficiently and effectively with uncertainty (Chapman and Ward, 2002). The concept of simplicity efficiency is developed and illustrated via examples in Chapters 5–15.

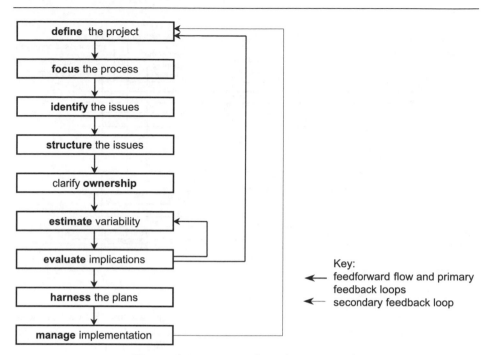

Figure 4.1—SHAMPU flow chart portrayal

If a single pass (linear) approach to all SHAMPU phases is attempted, it will be highly inefficient and seriously ineffective. Time will be wasted on issues that turn out to be unimportant, and not enough time will be spent on the important issues not anticipated when the SHAMPU process was started. Figures 4.1 and 4.2 portray possible iterative loops between phases as the SHAMPU process progresses. Figure 4.1 portrays the two key iterative loops to be managed formally, but selective informal looping back to other phases will also be used.

The *basis of analysis* in the SHAMPU process has two key elements: a *define* phase and a *focus* phase. '*Define* the project' involves consolidating relevant existing information about the project at a strategic level in a holistic and integrated form suitable for analysis, filling in any gaps uncovered in the consolidation process, and resolving any inconsistencies. '*Focus* the process' involves scoping the analysis to be performed, providing a strategic plan for the RMP, and planning the RMP at an operational level. As indicated in Figure 4.2, the *define* and *focus* phases can proceed in parallel at the outset for a brief period of intense activity, providing a basis for following phases that is fit for the purpose at this stage in the process. *Focus* activity is ongoing for the rest of a first pass through the SHAMPU process, but *define* activity is intermittent.

Qualitative analysis in the SHAMPU process has three key elements: the *identify*, *structure*, and *ownership* phases. *Identify* the issues involves identifying sources of uncertainty at a strategic level in terms of opportunities and threats,

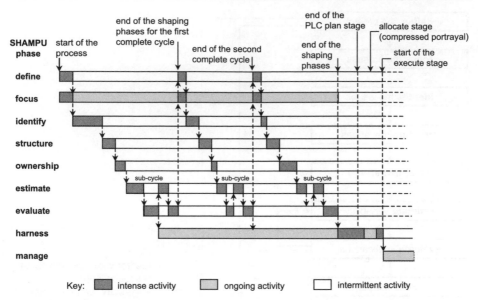

Figure 4.2—An example SHAMPU process over time. The figure assumes SHAMPU process initiation is toward the end of the plan stage of the project life cycle (PLC) and the timescale is days, weeks, or months, depending on the nature of the project

identifying what might be done about it in terms of reactive and proactive responses, and identifying secondary sources of uncertainty associated with responses. *Sources* is a convenient short form for 'sources of uncertainty' that *may* matter. A source of uncertainty will matter if it needs to be understood in order to:

- estimate expected values, targets, or commitments, because it is a *source of confusion* or a *source of bias*;
- reduce *sources of risk inefficiency*;
- evaluate *sources of risk* in a project or corporate sense;
- resolve ambiguity that is a *source of concern* for any other reasonable reason.

Issues is a convenient term for one or more 'sources' and associated 'responses'. 'Responses' are things we can do about sources in the conventional proactive or reactive response sense.

The *structure* phase involves completing the structuring of earlier phases, testing key simplifying assumptions, and providing more complex structures or alternative structures as appropriate. The clarify *ownership* phase involves allocating *both* financial *and* managerial responsibility for issues (separately if appropriate). In all three of these *qualitative analysis* phases it is important to operate at a level of detail and clarity that is fit for the purpose in each iteration.

As indicated in Figure 4.2, a first pass through each of these phases in turn can proceed at an initial intense level of activity following a first pass through the *define* and *focus* phases.

Quantitative analysis in the SHAMPU process has two key elements: the *estimate* and *evaluate* phases. As indicated in Figure 4.2, the two *quantitative analysis* phases sequentially follow the initial treatment of the first five SHAMPU phases. The *estimate* phase involves two components: on a first pass, sizing uncertainty that is usefully quantified; and on later passes, refining estimates of uncertainty where earlier analysis suggests this would be both effective and efficient. The *evaluate* phase involves assessing statistical dependence (dependence not modelled in a causal structure) and using this assessment to synthesize the results of the *estimate* phase, interpreting the results in the context of *all* earlier SHAMPU phases, making decisions about proactive and reactive responses, and making decisions about refining and redefining earlier analysis. Managing the iterative nature of the SHAMPU process is a key aspect of these tasks.

As indicated in Figure 4.2, an iterative loop back to the *estimate* phase might be expected in order to refine estimates for issues that matter. Further, this might be followed by an iterative loop back to the *define* phase to refine or redefine the *basis of analysis* and the *qualitative analysis* for sources of uncertainty revealed to be important, initiating a second complete pass through the *shape* phases. This might be followed by further iterative loops of this kind. In practice, '*shape* the project strategy' has to be pursued in a highly iterative fashion, the illustrative looping structure of Figure 4.2 oversimplifying what can be expected.

The *harness* phase provides a bridge between the *shape* and *manage* phases, and, as Figure 4.1 shows, this is outside the looping structure of the *shape* phases. The *harness* phase has two aspects that should follow sequentially without iterations if the *shape* phases have been effective: obtaining approval for the project strategy that emerges from the earlier phases and preparing detailed action plans that are then approved. The action plans consist of project base plans (incorporating proactive responses) and contingency plans (incorporating reactive responses with trigger points) ready for implementation within action horizons defined by appropriate lead times. Commitment to plans that are fit for implementation may involve commitment to designs, contracts, partnerships, and other arrangements associated with all six Ws in a holistic and integrated project plan.

The particular portrayal of a SHAMPU process in Figure 4.2 assumes that the *shape* phases take place toward the end of the plan stage of the project life cycle (PLC), the allocate stage of the PLC begins after the strategic part of the *harness* phase, and the execute stage of the PLC coincides with the start of the *manage* phase. Part II will make these assumptions in order to elaborate what is involved in each of the SHAMPU phases, and Part III will consider the implications of alternative assumptions. It is not feasible to discuss *any* RMP at a detailed level without making assumptions (implicitly if not explicitly) about key drivers that should shape the RMP in their equivalent of the *focus* phase, and the point of application of the RMP in the PLC is particularly crucial. Other key drivers of this kind include where the organization is on its risk management learning curve, whether it is in a project owner or contractor position, and the strategic/tactical level of the project in a programme/project hierarchy sense.

The *manage* implementation phase of the SHAMPU process has four key aspects: managing the planned work; developing action plans for implementation on a rolling basis; monitoring and controlling (making decisions to refine or redefine project strategy as required); dealing with crises (unanticipated issues) and being prepared to cope appropriately with disasters (crises that are not controlled). As Figure 4.1 indicates, iterative looping back to the *define* phase from the *manage* phase should be a planned part of the process, but at a much lower level of intensity than the loops within the *shape* phases, because loops back from the *manage* phase are comparatively expensive.

A historical perspective, the late 1950s to the early 1990s

The SHAMPU process framework and much of its content is not new. The SHAMPU label is new, but the SHAMPU process has emerged from the synthesis of earlier project RMPs and models. These processes and models have themselves evolved over a considerable period of time, as the range of issues addressed was extended. The nature of these developments may be of interest in their own right, but they are outlined here to provide a rationale for the SHAMPU structure and to indicate the content and importance of each phase.

PERT (Program Evaluation and Review Technique) as originally developed in the late 1950s for the Polaris Missile Project (Moder and Philips, 1970) is usefully thought of as the first formal project-planning technique to address project risk and uncertainty in an activity-based planning framework. The PERT 'technique' involves a *model* that consists of an activity network with activity duration probability distributions assumed to be defined by an approximation of the Beta distribution. Using this model in its original 1950s' form, the expected duration of the project is defined by an expected critical path identified using a standard CPA (Critical Path Analysis) algorithm with expected durations for each activity. Project duration is assumed to exhibit a Normal probability distribution with an associated variance defined by summing the variances of activities on the expected critical path. The PERT 'technique' also involves a *process* (or method) involving the following steps: decompose the project into activities, define precedence relationships, diagram the activities, estimate activity duration probability distributions, and so on. The PERT *process* and associated CPA processes (sometimes referred to as CPM for Critical Path Method) use the *model* in a highly iterative fashion, to develop an initial plan, test for and resolve timetable restrictions, optimize project duration approximately, test for and resolve resource restrictions, and optimize overall project resource use approximately (Chapman et al., 1987, chap. 29). The PERT and CPA/CPM processes may have been *designed* in part, drawing on the Operations Research/Operational Research (OR), industrial engineering, or systems process traditions of the consultants who designed the models, but in part these processes also *evolved* through use, as captured best practice.

By the 1960s most PERT software used Monte Carlo simulation to avoid assuming that only one path may be critical and that the project duration probability distribution must be Normal. Such software also allowed activity duration probability distributions that need not be Beta approximations (Moder and Philips, 1970). Modified in this way PERT is still used by many organizations, but it is a very primitive approach to project planning unless more sophisticated models are employed as and when appropriate. PERT and associated processes, including CPA/CPM processes, are embedded in SHAMPU, as part of its heritage and as a special case form of the process and models. The same applies to a series of generalizations considered next.

By the early 1960s, many authors were arguing for the use of decision branches embedded in both deterministic CPA models and probabilistic PERT models. Decision branches in deterministic CPA models reflect alternative ways of approaching activities and activity sets even if duration variability is not an issue. They are about optimizing technical, resource, and duration choices. These approaches adopted a 'decision CPM' label (e.g., Chapman and El Hoyo, 1972). Decision branches in a probabilistic PERT context usually focussed on contingency responses to delays (Moder and Philips, 1970). These approaches adopted a 'generalized PERT' label. The pursuit of risk efficiency as discussed in Chapter 3 requires both of these perspectives.

By the late 1960s, some authors were arguing for probabilistic models involving decision trees embedded in Markov processes. GERT (Graphical Evaluation and Review Technique) is one label used to describe this type of model (Moder and Philips, 1970). GERT allows activities to be addressed time period by time period, greatly enhancing our ability to understand both simple and complex repetitive processes, to accommodate contingency responses that do not wait until an activity has been completed, and to deal with time dependencies like weather windows. Early major users in the USA included the space industry. The Shell Corporation made extensive early use of these models for North Sea oil projects. Chapman applied them to a proposed major Canadian oil pipeline project, looking at trade-offs between time, cost, and demand for scarce resources, in 1975.

Starting in 1975, Chapman and BP International developed probabilistic models for planning and costing offshore North Sea projects, which embedded the fault tree and event tree concepts used for safety analysis (NUREG, 1975) in GERT models. SCERT (Synergistic Contingency Planning and Review Technique) is one label used to describe this model in the PERT and GERT tradition

(Chapman, 1979). The SCERT approach provided a detailed understanding of where uncertainty and associated risk was coming from. It allowed modelled responses to be specific to a particular source of uncertainty or general in the sense of dealing with the residual effect of combinations of uncertainty sources after specific responses.

To make effective use of the SCERT models in conjunction with a family of simpler PERT, generalized PERT, decision CPM, GERT, and SCERT derivatives, Chapman and BP International developed an associated SCERT process (Chapman, 1979), a *designed* process that was tested and *evolved* by developing corporate best practice within BP and a range of other organizations in the UK, USA, and Canada over the following decade (Chapman, 1992b). Key insights from the design and testing of this process included:

- a recognition of the important role of structured documentation;
- the need for a formal process that integrates qualitative 'issue-structuring' methodologies (e.g., Rosenhead, 1989) and quantitative modelling methodologies;
- the need for a clear understanding of which sources of uncertainty are best modelled quantitatively and which are best treated as assumed conditions;
- the great value of a formal process in terms of capturing and integrating the knowledge of different people who have different perspectives 'to bring to the party';
- the great value of a process that indirectly integrates issues that are too complex to model directly, like the 'decision CPM' search for optimal activity definitions with respect to time, cost, and quality in the context of a search for risk efficiency as discussed in Chapter 3;
- the great value of a process that pursues other objectives as discussed in Chapter 3.

The SCERT process had four phases: *scope, structure, parameter*, and *manipulation*. Each contributed directly to the shape of the SHAMPU process. The SCERT *scope* phase corresponds to the activity-based planning aspects of the SHAMPU *define* and *identify* phases. In the context of a SCERT focus on sources of uncertainty associated with activity-based planning, the SCERT *structure, parameter*, and *manipulation* phases correspond closely to the SHAMPU *structure, estimate*, and *evaluate* phases, respectively.

During the 1980s and early 1990s, Chapman and Cooper applied variants of the BP models and processes, and some new models and processes, to a range of different contexts and decision types with a range of clients in the UK, Canada and the USA, mostly associated with the generic label 'risk engineering' (Chapman and Cooper, 1983a; Cooper and Chapman, 1987; Chapman, 1990). The basis of the approach was designing specific RMPs or methods tailored to the context, based on generic decision support process ideas developed in both 'hard' and 'soft' OR and related systems areas as well as experience with earlier specific RMPs (Chapman, 1992b). The more specific the process design the more process efficiency could be improved, by exploiting the context characteristics. But the loss of generality carried costs in terms of reduced effectiveness if inappropriate assumptions about the context were made. Managing these trade-offs was a key process design issue. Designed decision support processes were sometimes used for important single decisions, sometimes embedded in organizational decision processes, both providing tests that fed back into subsequent process design work.

During the late 1980s and early 1990s, Ward and Chapman began to focus on a wider set of issues associated with competitive bidding (Ward and Chapman, 1988), general decision support process issues (Ward, 1989), contract design (Curtis et al., 1991; Ward et al., 1991; Ward and Chapman, 1995a), process enhancement (Ward and Chapman, 1991, 1995b), process establishment within the organization, the nature of drivers that shape processes (Chapman and Ward, 1997), linked capital investment decision choice issues (Chapman and Howden, 1997), and linked strategic management issues (Chapman, 1992a).

All the citations in the last two paragraphs and many of the earlier citations in this chapter are selections from the authors' publications to give the flavour of what lies behind this book. There is of course a substantial literature by others, some of which helped to shape our thinking, and some of which develops quite different perspectives. Major influences are cited when appropriate throughout this book, but a more detailed bibliography is provided by Williams (1995) and in Chapman and Ward (2002).

Post-1997 processes: the *Project Risk Analysis and Management (PRAM) Guide*

In the mid-1990s the APM (Association for Project Management) started to develop the *Project Risk Analysis and Management (PRAM) Guide* (Simon et al., 1997). PRAM is a core contributor to the heritage of the SHAMPU process. The PRAM process description was drafted by Chapman, as chap. 3 of the *PRAM Guide*. It was a distillation of the experience of a large number of UK organizations that had used RMPs successfully for a number of years, as understood by a working party of more than 20 people drawn from an APM Specific Interest Group on Project Risk Management of more than 100 who reviewed working party drafts and provided feedback. The draft PRAM process was based on a synthesis of designed and evolved processes using a nine-phase structure similar to Table 4.1. The SHAMPU *harness* phase was called the *planning* phase, and this and several other phases were interpreted less precisely, but there were no other significant differences in terms of phase structure.

The PRAM process used nine phases from an early stage in its development, rather than the four of the SCERT process (Chapman, 1979), or the various three to six phase structures used by other SIG members, because of the need to seek a 'common basis'. There was a clear need to make sure everyone involved could map their process onto the agreed PRAM process, to ensure collective ownership, if possible. This required more divisions than might otherwise seem sensible and suggested phase divisions as defined by Table 4.1. It was clear that if people could not see how the process they used currently mapped onto what was proposed, they were not going to buy into it. Nine phases as defined by Table 4.1 was the simplest structure that came close to achieving this 'common basis' criterion. *Any* process defined via synthesis involving a group of people and organizations faces a range of similar issues, and how these issues are managed is important.

The key reason Chapman was soon convinced that this nine-phase structure was appropriate in operational terms was the separability (but not the independence) of the phases in terms of different purposes, deliverables, and tasks. This suggested each phase could be thought of as a project in its own right, and all nine-phases could be regarded as a programme (portfolio of nine projects). This in turn suggested that everything we know about good programme and project management could be applied to managing the RMP. As for any programme or project, alternative structures are feasible, but this nine phase structure seemed robust and effective at a generic level at the time, and experience since confirms this. Much of the structure was tested operationally prior to the PRAM synthesis, in a SCERT context and in the context of other RMPs that contributed to its form.

Between agreeing the nine-phase structure portrayed by Table 4.1 and the publication of the *PRAM Guide*, editing to link chaps 2 and 3 of the *PRAM Guide* resulted in recasting the nine phases as six phases with four subphases, as indicated in Table 4.3. A new *assessment* phase was defined, incorporating *structure, ownership, estimate* and *evaluate* as subphases. This phase/subphase distinction is not an issue of importance, and the alignment between the PRAM and SHAMPU processes is clear. Indeed, Table 4.3 is a useful illustration of differences between process descriptions that should matter very little in practice. However, the merit of an *assessment* phase that aggregates the *structure, ownership, estimate* and *evaluate* phases as subphases is debatable. It is usefully interpreted as an illustration of the pressure within the PRAM working party to 'keep it simple' in terms of well-loved familiar structures. Such pressure is understandable, but when it is useful to simplify the recommended nine phase structure of Table 4.1, our preference is for the structures of Table 4.2 for a number of reasons that should become clear by the end of this book.

Some process insights

To the authors of this book, chapter 3 of the *PRAM Guide* provided four very important insights relating to *process*, in addition to useful advice on a range of other topics in other chapters.

Table 4.3—Aligning SHAMPU with PRAM

the nine phase portrayal of the SHAMPU process of Table 4.1	*PRAM phases and subphases from the PRAM Guide (Simon et al., 1997)*
define the project **focus** the process **identify** the issues	**define project** **focus PRAM** **identification**
structure the issues clarify **ownership** **estimate** sources of variability **evaluate** overall implications	**assessment—structure** **—ownership** **—estimate** **—evaluate**
harness the plans **manage** implementation	**planning** **management**

First, 'planning *the project*' in risk management terms and 'planning *the planning of the project*' in risk management terms are well worth separation, in the *define* and *focus* phases respectively, to clarify the *basis of analysis*. A separate *focus* phase formally acknowledges that there is no one best way to undertake an RMP for all projects. Deciding how to proceed in a given context is a particularly difficult process to conceptualize and make operational; so, recognizing the need for this phase is crucial. To some extent the *focus* phase is home territory for skilled consultants, in intuitive if not formal terms, but it is virgin territory for planners or estimators who do not have a sophisticated understanding of RMPs or other decision support processes. If no explicit focus phase is involved in an RMP, the process is seriously defective in ways naive users may not even recognize, using 'naive' in Hillson's (1997) risk maturity sense (discussed later in Part III). PRAM working party discussions about the relative value of different approaches in different contexts, looking for a systematic explanation of different practices, served as a trigger for the insight that a *focus* phase is essential.

Second, both the *define* and *focus* phases have to be part of an ongoing iterative framework, not part of a one-shot 'start-up' or 'initiation' phase. The importance of an iterative approach was recognized early in the development of PERT and CPA/CPM, although this insight has been lost along the way by some. It is particularly important with respect to initial assumptions including framing assumptions.

Third, ownership of risk is so important that it deserves separable attention in its own phase (or subphase), as a part of an ongoing iterative process. Isolating it from the iterative loops in a one-shot 'start-up' or 'initiation' phase is not appropriate, and it is usefully conceived as a final part of *qualitative analysis* in SHAMPU terms. PRAM was the first RMP to have a separate explicit *ownership* phase.

Fourth, the PRAM *planning* and *management* phases as defined by Table 4.3—the basis of the SHAMPU *harness* and *manage* phases—are important parts of the RMP. SCERT did not include these aspects of the RMP. Other RMPs did so in part in various ways. In particular, phases with these labels were part of the MoD (1991) RMP, and there was a rapid and clear agreement to include them in the PRAM process, acknowledging this heritage. However, there were competing views as to what these labels should imply, and what they involved was not agreed as clearly as might have been the case.

In summary, from our perspective the four SCERT phases (Chapman, 1979) formed the starting point for the SHAMPU/PRAM *define, identify, structure, estimate*, and *evaluate* phases, augmented by ideas from other processes, most of which have *define, identify, estimate*, and *evaluate* equivalents. The SHAMPU/PRAM *harness (planning)* and *manage* phases were borrowed from the MoD (1991) RMP in a form modified by ideas stimulated by the PRAM working party. The SHAMPU/PRAM *focus* and *ownership* phases were entirely new concepts as separate formal phases, triggered by PRAM working party discussions. The iterative nature of the process as a whole, including the *basis of analysis* phases, was endorsed by the PRAM working party as a very important feature of the process.

Some important differences between the PRAM and SHAMPU frameworks

The first edition of this book (Chapman and Ward, 1997) was profoundly influenced by drafting chapter 3 of the *PRAM Guide*. It used the nine phase PRAM structure directly, employing the same dependent chapter structure used in this edition. It was published prior to the *PRAM Guide*, and it did not allude to the Table 4.3 differences or any other differences, presenting itself as a direct elaboration of a PRAM process. However, this elaboration was based on a SCERT and 'risk engineering' perspective, and revisiting the *PRAM Guide* to revise Chapman and Ward (1997) has crystallized differences that need clarification here.

The first difference concerns the central importance of risk efficiency as developed in the SCERT process (Chapman, 1979). The *PRAM Guide* does not mention risk efficiency, because Chapman was unable to convince the PRAM working party that this is a central issue. In the SCERT process the pursuit of risk efficiency and associated risk balance issues (risk efficiency at a corporate level) are explicit steps in the equivalent of the *evaluate* phase, and this aspect of SCERT is reflected in Chapters 3 and 11 of this book. This different view of what risk management is about at a fundamental level has important implications, which are explored later.

A second difference is Ward's development of the six *W*s framework, as outlined in Chapter 1, which is central to our thinking. This framework is not mentioned in the *PRAM Guide*, because it was not fully developed at the time chap. 3 of the *PRAM Guide* was developed. An operational *define* phase that is holistic and integrated requires a six *W*s structure equivalent. In addition, Ward's development of the PLC structure (Ward and Chapman, 1995b), as outlined in Chapter 2, is central to our thinking, but its use in the *PRAM Guide* is limited to describing risk management in the plan stage of the PLC. The role of the PLC as a driver of the focus phase was clear at the time chap. 3 of the *PRAM Guide* was developed, but its use as a basis for the *define* phase was not developed at that time. Like the six *W*s, it is crucial to a holistic and integrated *define* phase. A holistic *define* phase needs to consider the cash flow and associated multiple criteria models that integrate the six *W*s and the PLC. This issue was not addressed by the PRAM working party.

A third difference relates to the *harness* phase. As described in this book, the harness phase is broadly equivalent to the *planning* phase of the PRAM framework. However, the *PRAM Guide*'s section 2.6 description of the *planning* phase embraces aspects of risk response development (seeking risk efficiency in our terms) that we associate with the *shape* phases, and it omits the initiation of detailed planning for implementation within an action horizon determined by lead times that we believe should be deferred until looping back to earlier phases is largely over. Figure 4.1 shows two important loops back from the *evaluate* phase, but no loops back from the *harness* phase. The *harness* phase is about using the results of previous analysis to gain approval for a project strategy shaped by the earlier iterative process and then preparing a detailed project base plan and contingency plans for implementation. This process is outside the earlier iterative looping structure of Figure 4.1. Figure 4.1 is as used in the first edition of this book and submitted for PRAM in terms of this looping iteration structure, but the *PRAM Guide* version of Figure 4.1 was altered to show feedback from the *planning* phase. Moving tasks from one phase to another may not be particularly important and reordering tasks in the context of an iterative process may have little effect in practice, but the additional content of the *harness* phase as we define it is important. Also important is the removal of feedback from the *harness* phase to the *define* phase, as this allows the *shape* phases to work at a relatively high 'strategic' level. This has important ramifications (developed in Chapter 12), as well as implications for Chapters 5 to 11. In brief, the development of responses in order to achieve risk efficiency and balance has to start at a strategic level, then progress to a tactical level, with a simple, possibly deterministic, approach to the most detailed plans required for implementation.

A fourth difference is that the *PRAM Guide* does not adequately reflect the recent shift in emphasis from project *risk* in the downside risk sense to project *uncertainty*, involving upside and downside issues. Jordanger (1998) reported Stat Oil's use of the term *uncertainty management* at the beginning of the period when this shift in perception occurred, and Stat Oil deserves considerable credit for initiating this shift in emphasis, which is central to Chapman and Ward (2002).

It has been picked up by many other authors (e.g., Hillson, 2002b). However, full consideration of the implications of uncertainty management demands a risk efficiency perspective and a related simplicity efficiency approach to analysis, which Hillson does not adopt.

If the reader wishes to embed the SHAMPU phase structure of Table 4.1 and the ideas developed in the rest of this book in a process defined by the *PRAM Guide*, three things need attention:

1. Expand the *define* phase scope to embrace the six *W*s and the PLC, integrating cash flow and multiple criteria models. Make associated adjustments to all following phases.
2. Adopt the risk efficiency concept and the associated primary definition of risk (as outlined in Chapter 3) and use these changes to fully embrace the management of good luck as well as bad luck. Embed the wider scope this gives risk management in all the phases, driven by a search for risk efficiency and simplicity efficiency in an evaluate *phase* that is served by all preceding phases.
3. Associate this use of the *evaluate* phase and all preceding phases with the *PRAM Guide*'s chapter 2 concept of planning risk responses, distinguish this from the *PRAM Guide*'s chapter 3 concept of the *planning* phase, and revise the *manage* phase to reflect the rolling nature of detailed action plans developed in Chapter 13 of this book.

Post-1997 processes: *PMBOK Guide*

The large membership, global reach, and accreditation programme of the Project Management Institute makes its *Project Management Book Of Knowledge* (*PMBOK Guide*: PMI, 2000, chap. 11) an important RMP description to relate to that adopted here. Table 4.4 is a useful starting point for comparison, recognizing that this alignment is very approximate. The only compatible boundaries between phases are indicated by the two solid lines dividing the first two and the last two SHAMPU phases from the rest.

A number of key differences are worth clarification in terms of a general understanding for all readers and are especially important for those working with an RMP defined by the *PMBOK Guide*. First, at a background level, in the *PMBOK Guide* framework:

- *an inputs, techniques & tools*, and *outputs* structure for each phase replaces the *purposes, deliverables (outputs)*, and *tasks* structure of PRAM and this book;
- risk efficiency is not addressed;
- an iterative approach to the overall process is not explicitly advocated,

Table 4.4—Approximate alignment of SHAMPU and the *PMBOK Guide*

the nine phases of Table 4.1	PMBOK Guide phases (major processes)
define the project **focus** the process	**Risk Management Planning**
identify the issues **structure** the issues clarify **ownership**	**Risk Identification**
estimate variability	**Qualitative Risk Analysis** **Quantitative Risk Analysis**
evaluate implications	**Risk Response Planning**
harness the plans **manage** implementation	**Risk Monitoring and Control**

although within phases like the *Risk Identification* phase iteration is recommended;

- because an iterative approach across phases is not considered explicitly, the relationships between phases do not reflect significant interdependencies or overlaps;
- upside risk is not emphasized, although it is recognized as important.

A second key difference is the absence of a *harness* phase in the Table 4.1 sense in the *PMBOK Guide* framework. Planning in the *PMBOK Guide*'s *Risk Response Planning* phase sense is part of the *shape* phases. It is not concerned with augmenting strategic plans with tactical plans ready for implementation within an action horizon, which can be taken to imply no distinction between tactical and strategic level planning. This distinction is important, even for very small projects, like weekend do-it-yourself ventures, a lesson most of us learn the hard way.

A third key difference is the relatively late location of the *Risk Response Planning* phase in the *PMBOK Guide*'s process description. Where the tasks associated with this PMBOK phase are placed would not matter a great deal in the context of an iterative approach, but in the context of what is presented as a one-shot linear process, it is particularly ineffective to leave this risk response planning so late. The concerns addressed by the *PMBOK Guide*'s *Risk Response Planning* phase receive their first attention in the context of the SHAMPU process in the *identify* phase, with important follow-on aspects embedded in all the other SHAMPU phases within the *shape* phases set. The *PMBOK Guide*'s description of *Risk Identification* notes that an iterative approach to this phase is important and that 'simple and effective responses can be developed and even implemented as soon as the risk is identified', but there is no significant sense of an overall iterative process that uses early passes to filter out which risks need careful consideration in terms of responses and which do not.

A fourth key difference is that the *PMBOK Guide*'s *Qualitative Risk Analysis* is not interpreted in the SHAMPU (Table 4.2) *qualitative analysis* sense, but in terms of the use of Probability Impact Matrices (PIMs), as a first-pass version of an *estimate* and *evaluate* phase in the Table 4.1 sense. The *PRAM Guide* was neutral about the use of PIMs (the working party agreed to differ), but in this book we argue strongly that the use of PIMs ought to be killed off. The *PMBOK Guide*'s *Quantitative Risk Analysis* phase is not interpreted in the SHAMPU (Table 4.2) *quantitative analysis* sense, but in terms of a selective one-shot numerical follow-up to the use of PIMs. The use of PIMs, the timing of *Risk Response Planning*, and the lack of emphasis on process iterations might be coupled to the definition of risk adopted (which is comparable with the PRAM definition, as noted in Chapter 1) and the absence of a concern for risk efficiency—they are certainly interdependent *PMBOK Guide* framing assumptions.

A fifth key difference is that there is no explicit *define* and *focus* phase distinction in the *PMBOK Guide*'s *Risk Management Planning* phase, nor are there explicit *structure* or *ownership* phase components.

Seven issues need to be addressed to embed a SHAMPU approach in the *PMBOK Guide* framework:

1. Reinterpret the PMBOK process as highly iterative overall, as part of a simplicity efficiency perspective on effective and efficient process design.
2. Adopt the risk efficiency concept and the associated primary definition of risk as outlined in Chapter 3, embrace upside as well as downside risk and uncertainty in general, and embed the wider scope this gives risk management in all the phases.
3. Insert the *define* and *focus* phase concepts in the *Risk Management Planning* phase.
4. Insert the *identify*, *structure*, and *ownership* phase concepts in the *Risk Identification* phase, including associated aspects of *Risk Response Planning*.
5. Omit the *Qualitative Risk Analysis* phase.
6. Relocate most of the residual *Risk Response Planning* plus all of the SHAMPU *evaluate* phase concepts in the *Quantitative Risk Analysis* phase.
7. Insert the SHAMPU *harness* phase in front of the *Risk Management and Control* phase. Merge this with some residual aspects of the *Risk Response Planning* phase, which are best seen as outside the iterative loops of the *shape* phases, because they are about converting approved project strategy, post-risk analysis, into detailed action plans for implementation. Supplement the *Risk Monitoring and Control* phase accordingly, in line with the SHAMPU *manage* phase as developed in Chapter 13.

Post-1997 processes: the *RAMP Guides*

Risk Analysis and Management of Projects (*RAMP Guide*) was first published in 1998 (Simon, 1998), with a revised edition (Lewin, 2002) edited by the chairman of the working party responsible for both editions. This guide is a joint publication of the Faculty and Institute of Actuaries and the Institution of Civil Engineers, with a working party for both editions drawing on members of these institutions.

The RAMP perspective was defined to a significant extent by Chris Lewin, as chair of the working party and an enthusiastic contributor, and by Mike Nichols, who set out the process structure and much of its content. Contributions to the process content were made by Luke Watts (initially as part of an MSc in Risk Management at the University of Southampton) and by Chapman, both of whom brought aspects of a PRAM approach to the flavour of the process content. Other members of the working party also made significant contributions to process content. Like the *PRAM Guide*, the *RAMP Guide* offers advice that goes beyond process issues which is well worth reading.

One key characteristic of the RAMP process structure is a strategic view of projects within a financial modelling perspective. It operates at a more strategic level than PRAM and PMBOK, with a stronger focus on financial issues. SHAMPU involves both revisions and clarifications with respect to the first edition of this book (Chapman and Ward, 1997) which were stimulated in part by this RAMP perspective, especially in the *define*, *evaluate*, and *harness* phases.

A second key characteristic of the RAMP process structure is a multiple-level approach that combines both the eight stage PLC and the nine phase PRAM structure in four 'activities': A = process launch; B = risk review; C = risk management; and D = process close-down. These 'activities' are each decomposed into from two to seven components—A_i ($i = 1$ and 2), B_i ($i = 1, \ldots, 7$), and so on—that can be aligned in approximate terms with phases of the SHAMPU structure. These second-level components are further decomposed into third-level steps—A_j ($j = 1, \ldots, 7$), and so on—with flow charts provided in appendix 10, roughly comparable with the flow charts provided for each of Chapters 5 to 13 in this book. Given the iterative approach to RAMP and the comparable content, exact alignment of phases should not be a significant issue in practice, although detailed mapping of one onto the other is difficult and detailed comparisons are not appropriate here.

A particularly interesting difference between RAMP and both PRAM and SHAMPU is the way the latter use the *focus* phase to drive changes in the shape of the Table 4.1 process, including changes that are functions of the PLC, while the RAMP process effects a blending of the Table 4.1 process structure and a version of the Table 2.1 PLC structure. This blending offers a simplification some will find very attractive, while others may prefer decomposition for some purposes.

If the reader wishes to embed the SHAMPU phase structure of Table 4.1 and the ideas developed in the rest of this book in a process defined by RAMP, three things need to be remembered:

1. The search for risk efficiency in RAMP could be more explicit. The concept of risk efficiency is not addressed explicitly, but it is implicit in the definition of risk adopted (Lewin 2002, p. 62) and in the step structure. Managing upside risk and uncertainty more generally also needs more emphasis.
2. The RAMP process embraces the PLC of the project and the PLC of the risk management process in a joint manner, but it may be useful to decompose them in the way this book and the *PRAM Guide* do, conceptually if not operationally.
3. The *focus* phase could be more explicit. Drivers of the *focus* phase other than the PLC should not be forgotten, and simplicity efficiency considerations could be explicitly developed.

Other process frameworks

PRAM, PMBOK, and RAMP are a useful representative sample of alternative RMP frameworks that the reader may wish to relate to the SHAMPU process elaborated in the rest of this book. Any other process framework of interest could be characterized in relation to these three to gain some insights about the relationships. Although some alternatives may require a quite new approach to comparison, the basic issues will be similar. Examples that may be of interest of which we are aware include: Construction Industry Research and Information Association (CIRIA) (Godfrey, 1996), CAN/CSA-Q850-97 (1997), ICAEW (1999), AS/NZS 4360 (1999), BS6079-3 (2000), AIRMIC, ALARM and IRM (2002), and Office of Government Commerce (OGC, 2002). No doubt we have missed some, and others will be forthcoming. Williams (1995) provides a useful review of earlier research, Williams (2003) some more recent views.

RMPs developed and promoted by professional organizations, like PRAM, RAMP and PMBOK, have an important role to play in the development of best practice, for a number of reasons. For example, they can bring together experts with different experience, synthesize that experience in a unique way, and tailor completely general 'best practice' approaches to particular types of context, which facilitates constructive detail. However, they have limitations imposed by the need for group consensus. Like all views, different RMPs need to be subjected to constructive critique from alternative perspectives, and our collective best interests are served if these RMPs support each other and move toward common basic concepts. The comparisons provided by this chapter were much more difficult to analyse than the authors anticipated, and they will surprise some readers by their complexity. This difficulty and complexity arises because of differences in quite basic framing assumptions, like what we mean by risk and uncertainty, and whether or not risk efficiency is seen as relevant.

The RAMP working party has now established a separate, associated working party involving representatives from those responsible for the *PRAM*, *PMBOK*, *CIRIA*, and *OGC Guides*. A more coherent view of best practice is the clear aim of all those involved, and the importance of this is obvious. However, convergence of RMP guides should not be anticipated as imminent. Hook (2003) begins with the following quote:

> *The Heffalump is a rather large and very important animal. He has been hunted by many individuals using various ingenious trapping devices, but no one so far has succeeded in capturing him. All who claim to have caught sight of him report that he is enormous, but they disagree on his particularities.*

Hook then explains that this quote from A. A. Milne's *Winnie the Pooh* describes a character in the world of Pooh, but it has been used by entrepreneurial theorists to describe the differing and complex theories of the entrepreneur. There is a touch of the Heffalump about the best possible generic RMP.

Some common failures in processes

A series of recent confidential reports by the authors on RMP audits suggests that there are a number of common shortcomings in most operational RMPs, even in those RMPs employed by organizations with considerable experience of risk management. Chapman and Ward (2002, chap. 5) illustrate some of these shortcomings in terms of a well-disguised 'tale', but principal shortcomings include:

1. A *define* phase that is too detailed in terms of activities and fails to address the other five Ws, the PLC, and the linking financial cash flow model in a balanced manner.
2. A *focus* phase that is not really visible and is unclear about the motives for the RMP in relation to the various interested parties, or the links between motives for analysis and the models selected.
3. An *identify* phase that fails to provide a useful structure for sources of uncertainty, associated risk, and responses.
4. Absence of a *structure* phase, with little evidence of robustness testing or effective structuring decisions, including the lack of a significant search for common responses and a failure to identify significant linkages and interdependences between issues.

5. Lack of an explicit *ownership* phase, with a marked failure to comprehend the implications of contractual arrangements for motivating parties to manage uncertainty, including inappropriate use of simple contracts.
6. An *estimate* phase that is costly but not cost-effective, resulting in biased estimates that are usually highly conditional on scope and other assumptions that are lost sight of.
7. An *evaluate* phase that combines different sources of uncertainty without capturing crucial dependence or without providing the insight to clarify how revisiting to earlier analysis can clarify uncertainty where appropriate, develop effective responses where appropriate, facilitate crucial choices to achieve risk efficiency and balance, or demonstrate the robustness of those choices when necessary.
8. Absence of a *harness* phase, to manage the transition from an iterative *shaping* process to the detailed planning necessary for managing implementation of the project plan.

This book is about how to address these shortcomings in terms of established ideas that have been tested successfully in a range of applications. The use of the SHAMPU acronym and some associated modifications are new to this edition, and significant changes have been made to the first edition of this book to clarify issues, but most of the SHAMPU ideas have a long-established track record, albeit 'wearing different hats' in some cases.

Part II
Elaborating the generic process framework

Part II elaborates the nine phase generic process framework outlined in Chapter 4: one chapter for each phase in Chapters 5 to 13. As indicated in Part I, a number of drivers should shape any formal risk management process (RMP). It follows that any detailed RMP description must assume a position in relation to each of these drivers. Part II assumes:

1. *Project life cycle (PLC) position.* The end of the plan stage of the PLC has almost been reached and the project is well defined at a strategic level (that definition needs to be tested by the RMP).
2. *Project uncertainty level.* The project is large enough, complex enough, and novel enough to warrant a thorough RMP. No significant short cuts need consideration.
3. *Learning curve position of the organization responsible for the RMP.* The organization undertaking the RMP is early on its RMP learning curve, so short cuts that might be feasible for a more experienced organization are best avoided for the time being, a full analysis serving as a corporate learning process as well as addressing the project of direct interest.
4. *Learning curve position with respect to the project.* No earlier applications of a formal RMP are available to draw on, so in RMP terms there is no history or heritage to deal with.
5. *Client/contractor perspective.* The RMP will be done by the client (project owner) or on behalf of client, so it is the client's interests that are being considered.
6. *Decisions of interest.* These include developing and approving the shape of the project at a strategic level, with a focus on activity-based plans.

Part III will relax these assumptions and consider additional issues that this raises in designing and operating efficient and effective RMPs.

Part II
Elaborating the genetic process framework

5   Define the project

If you are sure you understand everything that is going on, you are hopelessly confused.—Walter F. Mondale

Introduction

As indicated in Chapter 4, the first phase of the SHAMPU (Shape, Harness, And Manage Project Uncertainty) process is the define phase. The define phase is concerned with clarifying the project definition for risk management purposes. It provides a basic foundation for everything that follows. If this phase is flawed, everything that follows will be flawed. This chapter explores in more detail what is involved.

The purpose of the define phase is to consolidate the project effort to date at a strategic level in order to define the project in a form suitable for the rest of the project risk management process and resolve any problems this raises. Two somewhat different but closely linked tasks are involved:

1. *consolidate* relevant existing information about the project and its management in a suitable form;
2. *elaborate and resolve*, to fill in any gaps uncovered in the consolidation process and resolve any inconsistencies, by stimulating the project team to develop and integrate their plans and management processes in an appropriate form.

These two tasks are 'specific tasks' in the sense that they are unique to the define phase. In addition to these specific tasks, four 'common tasks' are involved, 'common' in the sense that all SHAMPU phases require comparable tasks:

1. *document*—record in text and tables with diagrams as appropriate;
2. *verify*—ensure that all providers of information agree as far as possible, important differences in opinion are highlighted if they cannot be resolved, and all relevant providers are referred to;
3. *assess*—evaluate the analysis to date in context, to make sure it is 'fit for the purpose' given the current status of the risk management process;
4. *report*—release verified documents, presenting findings if appropriate.

Comments on these common tasks are provided in Chapters 5 to 13 when appropriate, but, with the exception of specific versions of the common *assess*

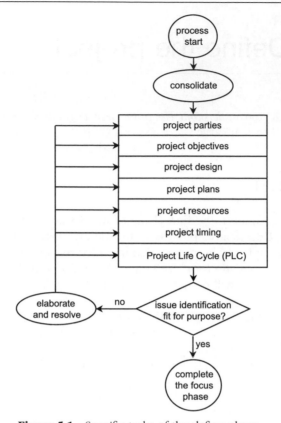

Figure 5.1—Specific tasks of the define phase

task, they are not included in the summary flow chart depictions of each phase provided in Chapters 5 to 13, like Figure 5.1.

The target deliverable for the define phase is a clear, unambiguous, shared understanding of the project and its management processes at a strategic level suitable for the risk management process to work on.

To explain how the specific tasks of 'consolidate' and 'elaborate and resolve' relate to the purpose and deliverable, it is convenient to adopt a structure based on the six *W*s introduced in Chapter 1, plus the project life cycle (PLC) structure introduced in Chapter 2. This involves addressing each of the six *W*s as one of six steps within the define phase, followed by a seventh step considering the PLC, as shown in Figure 5.1. Figure 5.1 is an idealization that helps to capture and illustrate the spirit of the process in simple terms.

Figure 5.1 portrays starting the define phase in a *consolidate* mode. The definition (verbal and graphic descriptions) of each of the six *W*s and the PLC is addressed in turn and the overall results assessed. If the overall project definition is fit for the purpose, the process proceeds to the next phase of the

SHAMPU process: the focus phase. If not, loops back to individual *W*s or the PLC are initiated as appropriate, in an *elaborate and resolve* mode to fill in the gaps and resolve inconsistencies. In practice it may be more effective to aim for separate *consolidate/elaborate and resolve* loops for each of the seven steps, as well as the overarching loop structure of Figure 5.1. Our intent is to make Figure 5.1 complex enough to say something interesting and useful, but simple enough to say it clearly and concisely, as a basis for discussion of an effective definition process that may involve greater complexity, or simplification, depending on the context. When attempting to implement this process, the distinction between the steps may seem artificial, with fuzzy overlaps being a routine fact of life. However, the purpose of a detailed specification of the define phase with separate steps is to provide focus and keep the implementation in practice as simple as possible. Even at this level of detail the method described here is not a 'cookbook' recipe, to be followed blindly. It is more a description of culinary techniques, to be used to create specific recipes. Figure 5.1 is not a restrictive definition of the ideal process, it is a caricature.

Project parties, the *who*

The identity, nature, and relationships between the key players in a project, the *who*, is clearly a general project management issue. It is inseparable from the management of project uncertainty. It is the starting point in Figure 1.1, usefully revisited at this point.

In any organizational setting, even small projects invariably involve two or more parties working together. Parties may be individuals, units of an organization, or organizations as a whole. The relationships between the various parties may be complex, often involving a hierarchy of contractual arrangements. Such relationships bring fundamental complications that have a profound influence on project uncertainty and project risk. As indicated in Figure 1.1, later players and other interested parties may require attention as the project evolves. Indeed, project initiators may cease to dominate. The other interested parties in Figure 1.1 reflect the potentially important roles of regulators and others who are not direct players, but may require careful attention, because they are important sources of uncertainty. It is important to ensure a *broad* view of the *who*, to include all relevant interested parties, and a *rich* view, to distinguish individual players or groups within single organizations who may have significantly different agendas. For example, in marketing terms distinguishing between the purchaser and ultimate user of a product can be very important. A memorable illustration concerns the launch (some time ago) of a new carbon paper for copy typing that did not make black smudges on secretaries' fingers and clothes. Initial marketing effort was targeted at corporate supply departments. It failed. A revised approach aimed at secretaries was an overwhelming success.

For definition purposes, it may suffice to draw up a simple list of the project parties, supplemented by a paragraph or two about their nature and a paragraph or two about each key relationships. This information may be readily available. However, fundamental information is often not available in a concise, documented form because it is presumed to be too basic to bother to record.

Two sets of parties are worth distinguishing: 'agents of the client' and 'other stakeholders'. The latter set includes parent organizations, partners, regulatory bodies, competitors, and customers. Clients may have little choice about their involvement in the project and have limited ability to control their objectives and actions, but their ability to influence the project and its performance may be substantial. Agents of the client are often assumed to be controllable by the client, but this set of parties may include subcontractors not directly under the control of the client. Their potential for liquidation is an obvious concern. Their ownership may be an issue, as illustrated by Example 5.1. The value of documenting the identity, nature, and affiliations of all parties to a project is further illustrated by Example 5.2.

Example 5.1   A subcontractor owned by the client

Government managers of a weapon system contract believed that no risk was involved because they had a very tight specification with onerous performance penalties. When the prime contractor reported a major shortfall on performance, it was assumed that the contractual provisions could be used. It was discovered, too late, that the prime contractor could pass the liability to a subcontractor and the subcontractor was owned by the government.

Example 5.2   Recognizing conflict of interests among multiple owners

A government-established organization was partly owned by its major customers. Defining the project *who* was a particularly useful starting point because the risk arising from the built-in conflict of interest inherent in the ownership/customer structure was identified formally for the organization's board of directors by a third party. Steps were taken to resolve the position, and the subsequent risk management process clearly allocated significant particular risks to specific customers/shareholders.

It is important to understand that 'the home team' is worthy of careful inspection as well as 'the opposition'. For example, two nations that are partners in a new weapon system development project may seem to want the same thing, but one may be desperate for completion by the agreed date and the other may prefer significant delay. Those party to the negotiation of the agreements between the two countries may understand this very clearly, but those implementing the contract may not, with obvious implications. A few pages of background to the agreement making such issues clear to everyone involved can be very valuable. Complex relationships may benefit from formal exploration using the identification methodologies discussed in Chapter 7.

An essential deliverable of the define phase is a comprehensive list of all the players who may prove central to the project. The purpose is to provide sufficient detail for following steps and sufficient summary information to trigger later recognition of sources of uncertainty that can be generated by all parties to the project.

Project objectives, the *why*

A key aspect of project risk analysis is appraising the implications of project objectives and related performance criteria: the project *why*. It follows that any changes in objectives and performance criteria at any stage of the PLC need to be carefully evaluated for uncertainty implications. Lack of clarity about objectives makes this more important, not less important.

A clear idea of prevailing project objectives is important for the project itself. It is also important in planning for risk analysis because the structure and form of project objectives ought to drive the structure and form of the risk analysis. This process assessment needs to consider the nature of the objectives, their relative importance, how they might be measured, and the extent to which trade-offs can be made between them. For example, project managers must generally consider the relative priorities to be placed on cost, time, and quality, recognizing that trade-offs are possible between these basic performance criteria. If this is not done, different parts of the project team will make internally inconsistent decisions and the project organization as a whole will show confusion and lack of focus.

It is important to be clear about the full range of relevant performance criteria that may relate to a corporate perspective. For example, corporate concerns about strengthened market position, a more favourable position with regulating authorities, or a 'greener' public image may be important. In the context of an oil major, strengthened market position is a subset of the issues ultimately driving profit, a more favourable position with regulatory authorities is a subset of the considerations driving market position, and a 'greener' public image is a subset of the considerations driving the position with regulatory authorities. Each successive member of this quartet (profit–market position–regulatory position–perceived 'greenness') is more difficult to describe in formal terms. Other performance criteria may not have a simple hierarchical structure like this, and relatively difficult criteria to describe and manage like perceived 'greenness' may be extremely important. More than one major engineering project has failed as a direct result of a failure to manage these issues, which can be a much more important driver of profit (through revenue, project capital cost, and operating costs) than the direct technical choices that tend to receive the attention of technically driven project teams.

It may be appropriate to consider the relative importance of criteria in the context of the project as a whole, although different parts of a project may involve different priorities. In both cases it may be useful to consider these priorities and consequent sources of uncertainty in an analytical structure that records different objectives and related activities explicitly. For example, in projects with a high science content, clarification, detailing, and hierarchical structuring of project objectives to correspond with activity structures can be extremely useful. The basis of the rationale is that planned activities are only one way of achieving objectives and may currently seem the best way of executing the project. However, serious threats to completion of those activities may be best responded to by doing something quite different or simply abandoning the associated objective. If the relationship between activities and objectives is made explicit at the outset, the subsequent risk management process becomes much more efficient and effective.

In a risk management context, if quantification of uncertainty is involved, the need to be clear about priorities is intensified, because the risk management process must exploit these priorities and the structure of the uncertainty involved. Quantification can serve to force organizations to clarify priorities. An important motive for quantification can be forcing this clarification.

Often it is feasible and sufficient to select one primary performance criterion and convert other performance criteria into primary criterion equivalents. Other performance criteria may also be treated as constraints, and the effect of varying these constraints on performance in terms of the primary criterion may be investigated. This point is illustrated in Example 5.3.

Example 5.3 Initial priorities reconsidered after analysis

The structure of the initial risk analysis of a civil engineering construction project assumed that the primary criterion was cost. Delay was treated as a secondary performance criterion and converted into cost equivalents by assessing (in probability distribution terms) a cost per unit time for delay during construction. Quality (performance in relation to the design specification) was treated as a constraint. When the analysis was complete, in terms of a representation that users believed broadly reflected the reality of the situation, trade-offs began. In particular, the project as planned at that stage was deemed too expensive and re-engineering was applied to reduce the cost. It was not just a question of reducing quality or increasing duration; the project objectives were revisited, and a significant change in approach adopted.

Initial risk analysis often adopts time (duration delay) as the primary performance criterion in the first instance. Cost is defined later as a function of time and of the variability of other costs that are not time-dependent. This is particularly true of North Sea projects and is implicit in associated risk management methods (e.g., see Chapman, 1979). Other ways of relating cost and time, or other possibilities for treating quality, may be preferable in other cases. For example, safety-critical software for a weapon platform or a nuclear power station may require a very different approach. Functionality may be the primary criterion, followed by cost, with time dependent on functionality and cost risk choices. These issues are not relevant just because project risk management is a concern; they are central to project management in general.

A further consideration is how project objectives should be measured. If time uncertainty is the key concern, choosing a suitable metric is relatively straightforward, but some important issues need considering. For example, time to milestone payments may be the key concern for a contractor, and time until a system achieves a satisfactory level of performance may be the key concern for a client. Earlier sensitizing to the *who* is important if this kind of distinction is going to get recognized. Delay may have very different cost implications for different parties, so which party is considered is crucial. Defining payments in terms of milestones to ensure contractor performance may be the client's ultimate concern, to ensure a compatible sense of urgency applies to all parties.

For cost uncertainty these issues become more complex. For example, is life cycle cost the issue or just capital cost? Both can involve a common starting point, but the overall approaches are very different.

In respect of uncertainty related to 'quality', these issues become still more complex. For example, the trade-off between complete and partial degradation of a system may raise very complex issues that affect basic system design. If risk analysis is insensitive to key issues it may prove a costly waste of time, so these issues need upfront treatment.

In some cases it may be useful to define a metric for performance criteria measurement that links time, cost, and quality in a more direct manner. For example, computer software projects have a long-standing love–hate relationship with 'the mythical man-month' (Brooks, 1975). 'Standard-months' can be used as a basis for estimating work content, cost, and time, with associated performance risk analysis and efficiency risk analysis working on a standard-month basis.

Project design, the *what*

Review of project design, the *what*, is an important part of the consolidation, elaboration, and resolving inconsistencies process that is often ignored, at considerable cost.

A highly valued feature of successful project risk management reports is often a carefully crafted strategic-level summary of project design issues: the project *what*. Usually the material is selected from design reports prepared by the project team as part of the normal project planning process. In such cases the added value of the risk analysis reports is simply pulling it together in an integrated form accessible to all project staff. Sometimes this integration process reveals missing detail, occasionally it reveals major flaws. In effect, it is an independent review by a risk analyst who is by vocation someone prepared to ask lots of dumb questions, in order to write his or her simplified view of what the design is all about, with a strong drive for internal consistency and clear definitions of relationships. Sometimes the apparently dumb questions have no effective answers, revealing cracks that need serious attention.

Linking design issues or components to objectives or benefits of the project in a more formal and structured way would seem to be a key area for method development. Science-based projects, like research or research and development projects, lend themselves to formalization of these links. Another good example is the development of 'benefit management' processes for information technology projects. The benefit structure used to justify a project is formally mapped onto the system design, and the tasks required to achieve the product of the project, and the sources of uncertainty associated with the tasks and design, are linked back to the benefits. Benefits have to be measurable to be managed in this way, but they can be quality measures, addressed by a balanced scorecard (Kaplan and Norton, 1996). Whether or not this is done, an early review of the project *what* is vital, and the positioning suggested in this section has worked well in practice in many successful studies.

Project plans, the *whichway* (or how)

The need for a simple strategic-level project activity structure for risk management purposes is now widely understood, although not universally practised. The advice 'target about 20 activities, with an upper limit of about 50' (Chapman, 1979) has proven appropriate for a wide range of project types involving major investments, as has the advice to scale this down in a non-linear manner for smaller investments. One activity may be appropriate for very small projects, but four or five is more common.

Example 5.4   Activities for a North Sea oil platform

Offshore North Sea projects in the late 1970s could involve total expenditures of the order of £1,000 million. Even in the context of projects of this size, aiming for 20 activities in a strategic-level activity structure was deemed appropriate, with 50 activities perceived as the upper limit for effective risk analysis. Example activities were: design the platform, fabricate the platform, design the modules (which sit on the platform), fabricate the modules, install the platform, install the modules, design the pipeline, procure the pipe, coat the pipe, lay the pipe, hook-up (connect the pipe to the platform), and so on.

In Example 5.4 each of the project activities is clearly a project in its own right. Separating components of a project into activities at this level allows for the separation of sources of risk that are largely different and unrelated, the responsibility of different people, amenable to different types of responses or solutions, and other rules of thumb of this nature. There is no point attempting detailed risk management at a tactical level within these activities until risk associated with the relationships between these activities is managed at a strategic level. For example, in the context of Example 5.4, purchase of the pipe, delivery of the pipe, coating the pipe, and laying the pipe, might be treated as separate activities, but it would be important to consider how pipe-laying operations vary in different seasons of the year and how this could affect interactions between these activities, prior to addressing how best to manage the details of pipe purchase, delivery, or coating. If the detailed questions are addressed at the outset, we tend to 'lose sight of the wood for the trees'.

It is vital not to assume that risks associated with different activities are independent or unconnected. A useful rule of thumb is 'don't separate activities that involve complex interactions' when defining an initial activity structure for risk management purposes. Another basic rule of thumb is 'keep things as simple as possible'. Only break down an activity into more detailed activities if it seems it will be useful to do so. For overall risk management purposes, fabrication of the modules to be installed on an offshore platform (providing power, accommodation, and so on) might be treated as one activity and their installation might be treated as another activity, without attempting to deal with the complex interactions within and between these activities. When planning implementation, later in the process, more detailed definition of the exact nature of interconnections is clearly critical. But keeping it simple is the priority in the definition phase.

The discipline required to 'keep it simple' is not always easy, and the issues associated with where to decide to draw the line dividing (defining) activities are complex. Associated expertise is a craft rather than a science to a significant extent, requiring practice and, inevitably, some mistakes.

Project resources, the *wherewithal*

A review of resource requirements implied by the project activity plans must be part of the *consolidate/elaborate and resolve* tasks because an obvious source of risk is key resources not being available when needed. If a risk management process has not been in place from the outset of the project, the identification of resource requirements is usually part of a process to provide base cost estimates. This process can be somewhat separate from the design and activity-planning processes, which may proceed in parallel to some extent.

In large engineering or construction projects, usually the group doing the base cost estimation is not the same as the group doing the activity planning, and the designers are a third group. Often they have very different backgrounds. Sometimes these functional and cultural differences are exacerbated by departmental or contractual structures. Risk analysts often feel like they have been parachuted into the middle of a 'three-ring circus', with quite separate unco-ordinated acts in the three rings. They may be viewed by the three acts as a new clown, but they have to operate to some extent as a ringmaster, without offending the ringmaster.

The relationships between professions needs to be tackled directly to avoid associated sources of uncertainty being realized; otherwise, they may have to be addressed on a contingency response basis that may prove extremely costly. This point raises the issue of the order for the *whichway* and *wherewithal* steps. For convenience it is usually safe to assume the order used here, but the project design process may suggest considering *wherewithal* first, then *whichway*.

Project timing, the *when*

In the authors' experience, it is very important to construct a simple activity-on-node precedence diagram to portray clearly the assumed precedence relationships between the activities selected for the *whichway* portrayal of the project. It is also important to construct a separate but directly related Gantt chart to portray the implied timing. Modern linked bar chart software makes it tempting to combine these two traditional graphs in a single graph, but clarity and generality is lost if this is done.

At a very detailed planning level, it may seem that precedence relationships are always strict and simple, and defined by the task nature of the activities (e.g., the water must be boiled before we make the tea). At the strategic-planning level—the level most appropriate for initial risk management—precedence relationships tend to be fuzzy and complex, and defined by design and resource issues as well as the task nature of activities.

The strategic-level views of activity precedences and timing used for project risk management should capture very important alternative approaches to the project that detailed portrayals obscure. Consider Examples 5.5 and 5.6.

> **Example 5.5   Trade-offs between onshore and offshore fabrication**
>
> Planning the fabrication of modules for offshore platforms (for accommo-
> dation, control functions, etc.) in a conventional, critical path network
> manner—focusing on the project *whichway*—naturally assumes modules
> are completed before taking them out to install on the platform. In practice
> it is much more expensive to complete fabrication offshore, but it may be
> cheaper to do so than missing a weather window. Hence, the planning
> process ought to reflect the trade-off between the cost of onshore/offshore
> fabrication and the expected cost of missing a weather window.

> **Example 5.6   Trade-offs in resource utilization for a mining project**
>
> Two sequential activities associated with preparing to sink a deep-mining
> shaft project were assumed to be on a subcritical path. When it became
> apparent that they might be critical, the possibility that they might take
> place in parallel was raised. It transpired they had been put in series
> because it was assumed that the same resources would be used. This
> was cost-effective if this path was subcritical, but not if it was critical.

Being aware of the trade-offs described in these two examples was essential for
good project management, whether or not formal project risk management was
an issue. These examples also illustrate an interdependency between the project
whichway, wherewithal, and *when* that needs explicit attention. The questions of
whichway, wherewithal, and *when* are not really separable in many situations.
However, it is useful to distinguish them for consolidation purposes, because
they are often treated separately in project planning.

The project life cycle (PLC)

A brief, documented outline of the earlier, current, and future stages of the PLC is
a useful seventh step in the define phase. Like the six *W*s, a summary description
of the PLC stages provides a basis for the SHAMPU identify phase. For example,
identification of sources of uncertainty associated with the deliver stage or the
support stage of the PLC needs to be based on a clear, documented understanding of what these stages involve.

Clarity about the PLC can also assist with the SHAMPU focus phase, in terms
of clarification of the objectives for current risk management in relation to later
risk management.

The ongoing nature of the define phase

The define phase deliverable is a clear, unambiguous, shared understanding of all relevant key aspects of the project, appropriately documented, verified, assessed as 'fit for the purpose', and reported. The written form of this deliverable may be a single document or parts of several documents. Whatever its form, a comprehensive and complete define phase should clarify all relevant key parts of the project that the risk management process addresses, in a manner accessible to all relevant client staff. A single document achieving these ends is often held to be a key benefit of a formal risk management process, especially by senior managers.

Part of the purpose of this documentation is the provision of a 'reference plan' for the project that may be modified and augmented as a result of the subsequent risk analysis. Usually ensuring an appropriate reference plan is available is not just a question of capturing in simplified form an existing common perception of the six Ws and the PLC; in practice, this step is a risk analysis of the project-planning process itself that requires responses to errors of omission and commission in the project management process. Responses may involve project management as distinct from project risk management, involving people and organizations not necessarily part of the risk management process.

Even if project risk management is first implemented when the project is well developed, the define phase as just outlined may reveal gaps in the reference plan that need to be filled and inconsistencies that need to be resolved. In theory, such gaps and inconsistencies should not exist, but in practice they are inevitable. Because some aspects of the project may not be clearly defined when the define phase begins and they may take some time to be defined, important and central aspects of the define phase may be ongoing. Figure 4.2 portrays the way the effort associated with the define phase might be timed in a typical SHAMPU process. The initial concern should be to make as much progress as possible with the define phase before moving on to the other phases. In general, the greater the level of unfinished business from the define phase the lower the efficiency and effectiveness of the following phases.

6   Focus the process

If the only tool in your toolbox is a hammer, every problem looks like a nail.— Anon.

Introduction

The opportunities for risk management in projects are considerable, pervasive, and diverse. Any systematic efforts at project risk management must be carefully designed and managed if cost-effective use of risk management resources is to be achieved.The generic SHAMPU (Shape, Harness, And Manage Project Uncertainty) process provides a framework for risk management, but the precise scope and detail of analysis in each phase will depend on the context. There is no single 'best approach' for all circumstances.

For expository convenience, Part II considers a situation where risk analysis is to be undertaken on a 'green field site' in the sense that an approach has not been prespecified. In these circumstances the focus phase involves two specific tasks:

1. *Scope the process*—this task addresses issues such as: who is doing the analysis for whom?; why is a formal risk management process (RMP) being undertaken (what benefits must be achieved)?; and what is the scope of the relevant uncertainty? It culminates in a 'strategic' plan for the RMP. This provides a framework for more detailed planning of the RMP. It also ensures that management is aware of any limitations of the proposed analysis that may warrant further attention outside the project RMP of immediate concern.
2. *Plan the process*—this task addresses issues such as the appropriate structure and level of detail in the analysis using what models and methods (techniques), what software, what other resources over what time frame, and so on and culminates in a 'tactical' plan for the RMP, to make the process operational.

The deliverables provided by the focus phase may be a single document or parts of several documents. Whatever their form, a comprehensive and complete focus phase should clarify all the key aspects of the chosen approach as a project in its own right and in a manner accessible to all relevant client staff. The target deliverable is a clear, unambiguous, shared understanding of the proposed approach.

Viewing the application of an RMP as a project in its own right involves basic concerns associated with the six *W*s, and the life cycle of the RMP:

1. *who* wants risk analysis to support a formal RMP, and *who* is to undertake the analysis? (identify the parties to the process);
2. *why* is the analysis being undertaken? (clarify the process objectives);
3. *what* issues should the analysis consider? (structure the sources of uncertainty via a top-down issue appreciation);
4. *whichway* should the analysis be carried out? (select a process approach);
5. *wherewithal* needed? (determine the resources required);
6. *when* should the analysis take place? (determine the process timing);
7. how might this analysis relate to later analysis in the life cycle of the RMP? (assess the process strategy and plan).

As with the define phase in Chapter 5, it is useful to address these questions in terms of a series of steps, as shown in Figure 6.1. This portrays starting the focus phase in *scope the process* mode, addressing each of the first three *W*s in turn, plus the process strategy. If the process strategy is assessed as fit for the purpose, *plan the process* mode can begin. If not, earlier steps are revisited as appropriate. In *plan the process* mode a detailed operational plan is developed, working within the strategy and revisiting earlier steps if necessary. Both specific *assess* tasks can fail to reach an acceptable position, potentially stopping the project or the RMP. In practice it may be more effective to aim for separate development loops for each of the seven basic steps, with parallel, converging, strategic- and tactical-planning processes once the shape of the strategic plan is in place. Figure 6.1 is not a restrictive prescription of the focus phase, but an idealization to capture the considerations involved.

Clarify the parties to the process

The first step in the focus phase is concerned with clarifying who is undertaking risk analysis for whom and how the reporting process will be managed. Major doubts about who is undertaking risk analysis for whom may invalidate all following steps in the focus phase, so this is a good reason for putting this step first. The key players should be:

1. senior managers, to empower the process, to ensure the risk analysis effort reflects the needs and concerns of senior managers, and to ensure it contains the relevant judgements and expertise of senior managers;
2. all other relevant managers, to ensure that it services the whole project management process;
3. all relevant technical experts, to ensure it captures all relevant expertise for communication to all relevant users of that expertise in an appropriate manner;
4. a risk analyst or risk analysis team, to provide facilitation/elicitation skills,

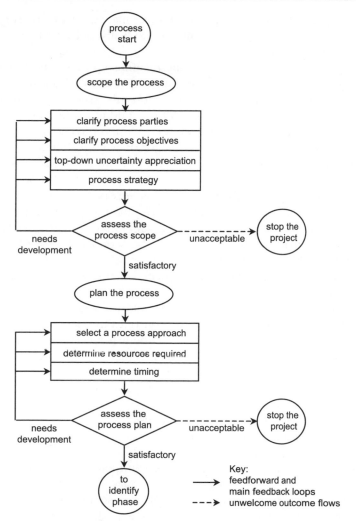

Figure 6.1—Specific tasks of the focus phase

modelling and method design skills, computation skills, teaching skills that get the relevant messages to all other members of the organization, and the management skills needed to allow the risk analysis function to develop and evolve in a way that suits the organization.

Some organizations refer to risk analysts in the above sense as risk *managers*. This can imply a confusion of roles. Risk and associated uncertainty are pervasive aspects of a project, which can be delegated in terms of analysis but not in terms of management. Proper integration of project risk management and project management generally requires that the project manager takes personal responsibility for all uncertainty management not explicitly delegated to managers of components of the project.

In the context of any given project, the relationship between the risk analysis team and other players needs early and clear definition. When the risk analysis team is part of the project-owning organization this issue may seem straightforward, but very important issues still need to be addressed in an explicit manner. For example, does the risk analysis team report to the project manager and act as a support function for the project manager, or does the risk analysis team report to the board and act as an auditor of the project team on behalf of the board? In the authors' view the risk analysis team should, if possible, be seen by the project team as a support function providing feedback of immediate practical value to the project team. If this is not the case, the co-operation necessary to do the job may not be forthcoming and the RMP may flounder. However, it is equally important that the risk analysis team be seen by the board as unbiased, with a demonstrable record for 'telling it as it is', as providers of an 'honest broker' external review as part of the process. If this is not the case, the RMP may sink without trace.

In relation to all key players the RMP should be seen as immediately useful and valuable, in the sense that it more than justifies the demands made on them. If it threatens any of the players, there must be a balance of power in favour of meeting that threat rather than avoiding it. Often the project planning team provide a high-risk environment for risk management because, for example, project management is ineffective, or project team members:

- are not familiar with effective project RMPs;
- are familiar with inappropriate RMPs;
- come from very difficult cultures;
- come from competing organizations or departments.

If the quality of project management or staff is a serious issue, this can be the biggest source of uncertainty for the RMP as a project, as well as an obvious threat to the project itself. If this is the case, it deserves careful management, for obvious reasons.

To clarify the importance of the reporting process, consider a simple practical issue. If the project risk analyst reports to the project manager, using information obtained from a set of groups within the project team, it is very important to keep the whole team onside. This means each group must be aware of the implications of their assessments before these go beyond the group, and they must have time to change their minds, perhaps several times, until they are confident about exposing their assessments to the rest of the project team. Some project teams may be fairly uninhibited about this, but others may be extremely sensitive, with consequential major impacts on risk management plans. A project team made up of contractors who have scope for competition as well as collaboration can be a source of this problem and a source of risk inefficiency of sufficient importance to warrant a project team design that avoids it.

A common question at risk management seminars is 'can I as a client ask my prime contractor to do a risk analysis for me?' The answer is yes, but while such an analysis may be a useful starting point for the client, it is only that. The problem here is that, to the extent that the client and contractor have different objectives and information, their perceptions of project risks will be different. In particular, what the client sees as threats or problems, the contractor may see as opportunities. The contractor may be unwilling to reveal such opportunities to the client if doing so is likely to lead to a reduction in those opportunities. This issue is considered in more detail in Chapter 16.

Addressing the *who* question associated with the RMP can also help to clarify who is working for whom in the project team as a whole. To take this a bit further, the RMP *who* can be defined in a broad sense to include the whole project team, as part of the integration of project management and project risk management. If the risk analyst, or the project manager or some other member of the project team, does not take it on him or herself to clarify process party issues in this broad sense, they will be mismanaged or unmanaged. In addition, this broadened RMP *who* can be usefully compared with the project *who* discussed in Chapter 5, to check for consistency and clarity.

Clarify the process objectives

Explicit consideration of why risk analysis is to be carried out helps to clarify further the scope of the RMP. In particular, an awareness of the purpose and scope of the proposed risk analysis can help determine the desirability or necessity for quantification. Consider two contrasting examples.

> **Example 6.1 Quantitative analysis defines a realistic budget**
>
> An engineering construction project was approaching the point of a board level *go/no-go* decision. It was the first project the organization had subjected to a formal risk analysis process. If a *go* decision was taken, the project could be executed within a few years, with no major anticipated changes in management. The project management team wanted board approval for a budget they could live with and control within the organization in an effective manner, but they recognized that if they asked for funds they did not need, they would increase substantially the risk of a *no-go* decision. This was a very unwelcome possibility. These concerns made

a quantitative risk analysis essential, in order to distinguish clearly between targets, expectations, and commitments.

Example 6.2 Forecasting completion times of aircraft helps manage deliveries

A commercial aircraft manufacturer managed production as a 'programme' of projects, with each aircraft treated as a project. Each aircraft was costed on a materials and labour basis, using standard-hours for all tasks. Production was planned using standard CPA (Critical Path Analysis) deterministic planning tools. The basics of most aircraft conformed to a standard production model, but each aircraft involved significant variations according to the instrumentation and finishing requirements of the airline or other customers ordering the aircraft. Two sources of uncertainty plagued the manager in charge of each aircraft's production: materials might not arrive when they were required; and staff might not be available when they were required, because another aircraft manager might 'steal' them by pleading higher priority or because of illness and staff turnover.

If materials did not arrive on time they were 'chased' and work rescheduled to use materials and staff that were available.

Airlines wanted to know how long it would take to deliver an aircraft when ordering it. Keeping delivery promises was an important marketing strategic weapon. Forecasting delivery dates to the day over the last 30 days was also a contractual matter, with a cost of about £10,000 per day early or late, because of the airline's need to put new aircraft into their service schedules.

Consistent failure to deliver on time with substantial variations in performance suggested the need for a formal risk management system.

Discussions with those involved in managing the system suggested that replacing the CPA-based planning system with one capturing the uncertainty involved would hinder rather than help the shop floor managers. No changes to the existing system were recommended at this level.

To deal with the forecasting problem, a system was suggested that went back to the basic standard-hours calculations used for costing, measuring the efficiency associated with converting standard-hours into completed work as a function of aircraft percentage completion, and using this model plus forecast staff availability to forecast completion.

The efficiency associated with converting standard-hours into work achieved could be shown to fall off in a predictable way as aircraft neared completion, because work was increasingly difficult to do out of order due to missing components and less flexibility was available when rescheduling to cope with shortages of components or key labour.

> This modelling also provided a 'what-if' capability for addressing higher-level programme management questions, such as: would it be better to let one aircraft that is in trouble carry on as planned, rather than borrow staff from two others that are currently ahead of schedule, but could be induced to fail if we 'steal from Peter to pay Paul'?; or would it be a good idea to recruit 10% more staff than we think we need over the next six months?; or how much is it costing us to have materials arrive late and what is the most cost-effective way to reduce these costs?

These examples illustrate the value of being clear about the purpose of any risk analysis before it is attempted. A basic axiom of those who build successful models for decision support purposes is 'there is no one best model for all purposes'. The same can be said for the processes built around such models. A corollary is that there is no best way to pursue all risk analyses—much of the need to vary the approach taken hinges on why it is being undertaken. A requirement for effectiveness and efficiency demands that we design or select our models and processes according to our purposes. If more than one purpose is being pursued, we may need more than one model and process, running in a separate but linked manner.

Top-down uncertainty appreciation

To design an effective RMP for a particular application, experience suggests that a limited top-down strategic view of project uncertainty is a sensible starting place. Sources of uncertainty internal to the project and corporate sources of uncertainty can be related and sized to provide an overview that is useful in its own right, as well as providing a basis for further more detailed analysis. Simple forms of quantitative approaches are needed, as illustrated later in Example 11.3. Such approaches must recognize that some sources of uncertainty are best left as conditions (assumptions), but semiquantitative risk-ranking approaches like that proposed by Baccarini and Archer (2001) are to be avoided, for reasons comparable with our case against 'qualitative' approaches to estimation and evaluation in Chapters 10 and 15. Uncertainty associated with the obvious lack of a structured bottom-up analysis basis means the tendency to optimism and under-estimation of uncertainty discussed in Chapter 10 needs to be neutralized as far as possible, overstating uncertainty when in doubt.

This kind of initial top-down uncertainty appreciation may reveal levels and forms of uncertainty some people do not want to address. However, from a risk management perspective, it really is a waste of everybody's time to do otherwise. If bearing this kind of bad news involves 'constructive insubordination' that is likely to be so unwelcome that it may cut short the project risk analyst's career in this organization, he or she may wish to keep this part of the analysis to themselves for the time being; but, helping to keep bodies buried for any length of time is inappropriate.

Example 6.3 illustrates that an important reason for undertaking a top-down view of uncertainty is to determine where the limits of the project manager's responsibilities for managing project-related uncertainty lie. The rest of Part II assumes a simple division of 'external' and 'internal' sources of uncertainty between board level and project management for most illustrative purposes, but a more complex, hierarchical division of risks can be helpful, for reasons considered in Chapter 9.

Example 6.3   Corporate risks set project risk management in context

When Chapman started work on one organization's risk management processes his remit did not include an assessment of strategic risks, but an early priority was to persuade the directors that such an analysis would be a good idea. Several preliminary analyses were undertaken to indicate what would be involved. The highly political nature of the project made the issues identified extremely sensitive. A full analysis was not undertaken by Chapman, but he was encouraged to provide the directors with a suitable framework and to clarify key sources of corporate uncertainty as he saw them. This process helped to shape corporate policy on major strategic issues, was used as the basis for a report to the board, and added substantial value to the overall risk management process.

Apart from its direct value as a strategic analysis for the directors, the strategic overview set the project risk management process in context. It was recognized in a formal corporate sense that a range of major design changes might take place for political reasons or for reasons related to customer plans. However, those responsible for the design underlying the project were explicitly relieved of responsibility for worrying about such changes, responsibility being formally placed with the board.

Process strategy and the project life cycle (PLC)

RMP objectives associated with immediate concerns and concerns later in the RMP need joint consideration to design effective and efficient RMPs. For example, if quantification of uncertainty is not an immediate priority, but will be essential shortly, the case for immediate, very simple quantification is greatly strengthened. There is no need for a detailed, formal RMP plan in project life cycle (PLC) terms, but an outline of current and future issues agreed by all the relevant players can pay sizeable dividends.

Assess the process scope

The first four steps of the focus phase provide a 'strategic' framework that serves to guide detailed planning of the RMP, completing the *scope the process* specific task. *Assess the process scope* is the next specific task, providing a convenient place to pause and consider project uncertainty as it is perceived at this point.

Stopping the project may be a possibility if the previous steps raise serious questions about the project's viability. However, answering such questions usually becomes central to the objectives of the RMP, requiring further development of the RMP strategy and operational plans. At its simplest, these assessments may identify a single potential 'show-stopper', and the *scope* and *plan the process* tasks may then address how best to assess the extent to which this show-stopper can be revised, removed, resolved, or dissolved. This specific *assess* task as a whole may reduce to deciding whether it is worth undertaking an RMP or whether it is better to bring the whole project to a stop without further work.

When a project is in doubt, a different kind of RMP is required to one based on the assumption the project will proceed. What is particularly critical is an understanding, on the part of the whole project team, that the whole purpose of project planning changes if the viability of a project is seriously called into question. If a project that was assumed to be 'a goer' suddenly looks like 'a maybe', project planning and risk management need to address the question 'is the project worth doing?', considering how to do the project only in so far as it is necessary to do so to address this question to avoid excessive delay. Developing details of how to undertake the project will be a complete waste of time should the project be stopped, and resources should be allocated with this potential nugatory expenditure effect clearly in mind.

In principle, this issue should be addressed via an appropriate RMP much earlier in the PLC than the end of the plan stage, as discussed in Chapter 14. Otherwise, obtaining unbiased estimates of performance from the project team may be difficult, particularly if the project team are threatened by the possibility of the project stopping and if cancellation threatens their livelihood.

Select a process approach

As shown in Figure 6.1, the first *plan the process* specific task involves considering how the risk analysis effort is to be carried out, addressing the process approach or *whichway* question.

It is very important to understand that there is no one best approach for all project risk management purposes. We would not expect to use the same approach for the construction of all buildings, or the development of all weapon systems, or the implementation of all information systems. Even within these industry sectors, we must expect to create plans in a manner tailored to the needs of the specific project. The same applies to planning the project risk management effort.

Planning for a RMP begins with selecting an appropriate model or set of models. A 'model' in this context is the deliberate simplification of reality we use as a basis for analysis. Most models of interest have a mathematical form, but of particular concern is their associated graphical form, which can clarify our understanding of their implications.

Even in an organization with a well-established formal RMP, decisions need to be made consciously and regularly about which models to use in individual applications. If these decisions are not made consciously, then decisions are being made by default, which may prove very costly. On some occasions the models used may be too simple, obscuring important issues that should be addressed. On other occasions the models may be too complex, involving effort that is not cost-effective. Using an inappropriate model to analyse uncertainty and related issues is a risk management planning error directly comparable with undertaking a construction project with an inappropriate plan.

Failing to consider this issue is rather like operating a car hire firm that always offers a Rolls Royce, or a Mini, regardless of the potential customer's wallet or needs. It is difficult to overemphasize this point because the systematic, generic nature of some RMP frameworks can easily seduce those who ought to know better into the adoption of a single modelling approach for all purposes in all projects. 'If the only tool in your toolbox is a hammer, every problem looks like a nail,' is a situation to be avoided.

It is also worth noting that the selection of suitable models for risk management purposes can influence other project planning models in important ways, and these issues need joint consideration. For example, in terms of project *whichway* activity based models, modelling could take progressively more sophisticated approaches, from simple PERT (Program Evaluation and Review Technique) models, generalized PERT models that embed decision trees, GERT (Graphical Evaluation and Review Technique) models that further embed Markov processes, through to SCERT (Synergistic Contingency Planning and Review Technique) models that embed fault tree or event tree representations of sources of risk, as discussed in Chapter 4. Choosing an appropriate level of model sophistication can be left to later in the RMP if a nested set of compatible models of the SCERT variety is employed. However, specific simplifications in the focus phase that preclude more sophisticated models later can have serious ongoing consequences. Comparable arguments apply to models used to consider the other five project *W*s in conjunction with activity-based models.

Determine the resources required

Just as resources for the project require explicit consideration, so too do resources for effective risk analysis: the RMP *wherewithal* question. In a given project context, there may be specific constraints on cost and time. Resource questions are likely to revolve around the availability and quality of human resources, including the availability of key project personnel and the availability of information-processing facilities.

Computing power is no longer a significant constraint for most project planning, with or without consideration of uncertainty. Even very small projects can afford access to powerful personal computers. However, software can be a significant constraint, even for very large projects. It is important to select software that is efficient and effective for an appropriate model and method. It is also important to prevent preselected software from unduly shaping the form of the analysis.

Our current preference is a flexible, unstructured software system to get started, @Risk being a typical industry standard example. It is effective in expert hands because it is flexible, but it is not very efficient because this flexibility requires expert users. When the type of models used and the associated methods or processes have become reasonably well defined, more specific and more efficient software may deserve attention, involving at the very least 'macros' or subroutines constructed from a basic software system.

In the early stages of an RMP the risk analysis team may be seen as the project-planning player doing most of the risk management running. However, it is vital that all the other players (as listed earlier) see themselves as part of the team and push the development of the RMP as a vehicle serving their needs. This implies commitment and a willingness to spend time providing input to the risk analysis and exploring the implications of its output.

In any given project, key people's time may become extremely precious. In the terms economists would use, the marginal cost of an extra hour (or the last hour) spent on RMPs by *all* the staff involved (not just specialist RMP staff) ought to be assessed in terms of the value of the best alternative use these hours might be put to. At a critical point in the development of a project, the time of the staff involved will be very valuable, perhaps two, three, or even ten times their gross salary cost; effective use of their time is a key concern. The effects of this are easily observable in terms of the project team that is 'too busy fighting alligators to think about how to drain the swamp they are in.' An effective RMP should avoid this kind of panic, but crisis management is not going to be eliminated entirely if the project plan is risk efficient and high short-term opportunity costs for the time required for RMPs is going to remain an issue. In the longer term we need to anticipate the opportunity costs associated with all staff involved in an RMP and resource the RMP accordingly. In a given context, the resources available for risk management are key considerations in the focus phase.

Determine the process timing

If a client of the authors' asks 'how long will it take to assess my project's risk?', the quite truthful response 'how long is a piece of string?' will not do. A more useful response is 'how long have we got?' (the process *when*), in conjunction with 'how much effort can be made available?' (the process *wherewithal*), 'who wants it?' (the process *who*), and 'what do you want it for?' (the process *why*). The answer to this latter question often drives the processes *what* and *whichway*. It is important to understand the interdependence of these considerations. Six months or more may be an appropriate duration for an initial, detailed project risk analysis of a major project, but six hours can be put to very effective use if the question of the time available is addressed effectively in relation to the other process *W*s. Even a few minutes may prove useful for small projects, or specific decisions, as Example 6.4 illustrates.

Example 6.4 Allocating time to steps in a bidding process

A formal bidding process used by a contractor experienced in risk management involves the following steps:

1 decide how to do the project;
2 assess the expected cost;
3 assess the chance of winning given a bid equal to expected cost and two or three higher or lower bids;
4 construct a table that shows the expected profit and associated probability of winning for the different levels of bid;
5 consider the most appropriate bid price in relation to trade-offs between maximization of expected profit and other criteria;
6 record the chosen bid and estimate of the associated probability of winning, and feed the analysis of this information back into step 3 the next time a bid is developed.

In the absence of a formal process, most people instinctively spend most of their time on steps 1 and 2, but only by articulating the above steps, and spending much more time on each reveals the true relative importance of steps 3, 4, 5, and 6.

Experience with this process suggests that if only 10 minutes are available to prepare a bid, rather than concentrate on steps 1 and 2 a more effective allocation of time would be: 2 minutes each on steps 1–3, 1 minute on step 4, and most of the remaining 3 minutes on step 5.

Example 12.1 employs this process, and a more sophisticated version of this process is developed in Chapman and Ward (2002, chap. 3).

Fitting an RMP to available time and other resources is central to the issue of short cuts (addressed in Chapter 15). For present purposes, we assume any necessary time is available.

If the process timing is not predetermined by the need to make decisions by particular dates, a Gantt chart like that of Figure 4.2 can be used to plan the first pass of the iterative process and an allowance made for further passes, as discussed in Chapter 4. The time required for the first and later passes can reflect what has to be done and the resources available to do it. In this case the process *when* flows from the first five *W*s in the ideal project-planning manner. If *when* is constrained, the earlier *W*s will have to be constrained to make the process feasible, as discussed earlier.

Assess the process plan

Assess the process plan is the final specific task within the focus phase. This provides a convenient place to pause and consider the risks associated with the execution of the risk analysis. The results of the common tasks *document, verify, assess,* and *report* with respect to each previous step need to be consolidated at this point.

A key reason for identifying this specific task is to provide a *go/no-go/maybe* decision point in the planning of the RMP. One possibility is to move directly on to the identify phase of the RMP. Another possibility is the need to carry out another pass through the plan the process part of the focus phase, taking in selected steps as appropriate. Stopping the RMP is a third possibility. There are inappropriate reasons for stopping the RMP at this point, such as more uncertainty revealed than the client wishes to see. There are also good reasons, such as nothing can be done about the key sources of uncertainty for the time being, because they are beyond the control of the organization, and putting the whole process on hold is a sensible strategy. Note that 'stop' need not imply 'abandon'.

The ongoing nature of the focus phase

A first pass through the focus phase of the SHAMPU process may be largely concurrent with the define phase, as indicated in Figure 4.2. Updating risk management plans is necessarily ongoing, with further passes initiated by a perceived need to revise the approach to analysis, reflecting RMP success or failure. As a particular RMP becomes fairly stable (e.g., in terms of routine updates), the *scope the process* task becomes less relevant and more detail is required with respect to *plan the process* issues.

7 Identify the issues

Zaphod ... put on the sunglasses ... They were a double pair of Joo Janta 200 Super Chromatic Peril Sensitive Sunglasses, which had been specially designed to help people develop a relaxed attitude to danger. At the first hint of trouble they turn totally black and thus prevent you from seeing anything that might harm you.—D. Adams, *The Restaurant at the End of the Universe*

Introduction

Most project risk management process (RMP) descriptions emphasize a need to identify 'risks' early in the process, typically restricting this to risk events and sometimes to just threats. As discussed in Part I, effective risk management needs to address uncertainty in a broad sense, with early consideration of all sources of uncertainty and associated responses. As indicated in Chapter 4, the SHAMPU (Shape, Harness, And Manage Project Uncertainty) identify phase involves identifying 'sources' *and* associated possible responses *and* secondary sources arising from these responses. For convenience, we use the word 'issues' to refer to individual sources, their associated responses, and secondary sources. It is these 'issues' rather than 'risks' that need identification and subsequent management. Identifying issues involves two specific tasks:

1. *search*—for sources and responses, employing a range of techniques;
2. *classify*—to provide a suitable structure for defining sources and responses, aggregating or disaggregating particular issues as appropriate.

The key deliverable is a clear, common understanding of the sources of uncertainty facing the project and what can be done about them. Opportunities need to be identified and managed with the same resolve as threats, as part of the same process. Sometimes opportunities and threats are closely coupled, but this need not be the case. Often an RMP is particularly successful because the process of generating and reviewing responses to threats leads to the identification of important opportunities, with implications well beyond the uncertainty that led to their identification.

The identify phase can be treated as an iterative five step process, as shown in Figure 7.1, with each step involving both search and classify tasks. The first step involves a simple first cut at the identification of sources associated with the key performance criterion. Step 2 explicitly expands this focus in three important

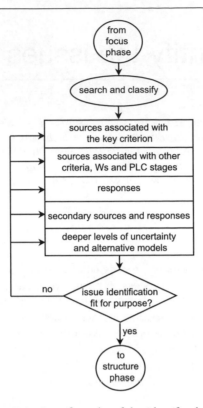

Figure 7.1—Specific tasks of the identify phase

dimensions. Step 3 considers associated responses. Step 4 considers associated secondary sources and responses. Step 5 elaborates on the very basic search process used to kick off the first five steps. A specific *assess* task then initiates loops back to earlier steps if necessary. As with Figures 5.1 and 6.1, the Figure 7.1 portrayal of the identify phase is deliberately simplified to illustrate the spirit of what is involved. In practice, things may not happen according to this model, but the model is a useful target that can help to maintain focus and order.

The identify phase involves the identification of at least one assumed response for each identified source. A generic 'do nothing' response is one option, but this will not be appropriate in some cases. A preliminary list of obvious response options indicating preferences associated with all sources is a recommended output on a first pass. Detailed lists of response options may be deferred until later passes for those sources that prove significant, but early identification of response options can form the basis of a concerted opportunity identification process that goes beyond simple threat management. Risk efficiency is about generating options that may lead to better plans, responses to sources providing the starting point from an RMP perspective.

In terms of documentation, the identify phase involves the production of a list or register of sources. However, it is important to co-ordinate SHAMPU 'source list' equivalents with associated 'upstream' lists generated in the define phase and 'downstream' lists involving responses and secondary issues. Generalizing the SCERT (Synergistic Contingency Planning and Review Technique) approach developed for BP and later 'risk engineering' versions for other contexts involves a numbering system of the form u, v, w, x for response x specific to source w arising in the context of activity v where u is defined as follows:

$$u = 1 \text{ is concerned with parties} \quad (who)$$

2	motives	(why)
3	design	(what)
4	activities	(whichway)
5	resources	(wherewithal)
6	timing	(when)
7	PLC	(project life cycle)

When relevant, secondary sources and responses involve extending this numbering system to the form u, v, w, x, y, z, for secondary response z to secondary source y. A key increase in process efficiency and effectiveness is provided by the use of simple 'labels' ('handles') for each u, v, w, x, y, and z element, and enough associated text ('descriptions') to clarify what is involved. Being able to access this information flexibly can be very useful (e.g., producing a list of issues a particular individual or team is responsible for). The common *verify*, *assess*, and *report tasks* are dependent on an effective approach to this *document* task. Example 7.1 illustrates the two specific tasks of searching and classifying involved in all the identify phase steps. The *search* task was concerned with the identification of issues like pipe 'buckles'. The *classify* task was concerned with recognizing the significant difference between 'wet buckles' and 'dry buckles' for risk management purpose.

Example 7.1 Identifying and classifying 'buckle' issues in pipe laying

Laying offshore pipelines in the North Sea in the mid-1970s was deemed a particularly risky activity, so examination of sources received considerable attention. About 40 sources were identified, including the lay barge arriving late, the lay barge not operating as quickly as planned given good weather, encountering bad weather, pipe 'buckles', and so on.

The large number of sources involved made it particularly obvious that rules of thumb needed to be developed to help decide how many separate sources should be identified, and how some different sources might be grouped under a common heading or label and treated collectively. This process issue is usefully illustrated in relation to pipe 'buckles', which could take two basic forms: a 'dry buckle' or a 'wet buckle'.

A dry buckle involves a kink in the pipe and/or the loss of some of the concrete coating. If a dry buckle occurs, the pipeline can be pulled back on board the lay barge, the buckled section cut off, and pipe-laying can then continue. Very little pipe or time are lost.

A wet buckle involves a fracture in the pipe that allows water to rush in. The pipe quickly becomes too heavy for the barge to hold, ripping itself off the barge unless it is released quickly. It then sinks to the ocean floor and continues to fill with water and debris.

It was very important to distinguish between wet and dry buckles. Dry buckles were a minor problem, conveniently put together with other 'productivity variations' to cover a range of problems not worth separate analysis, although identification in terms of a comprehensive list of examples was useful. Wet buckles were a major problem, worth designating as a separate source (called 'buckles' without the need to use the word 'wet' every time they were referred to).

All sources need to be classified as 'wet buckle equivalents' or 'dry buckle equivalents', initiators of major issues to be treated separately or minor issues to be treated collectively.

Technical sources of the kind illustrated by Example 7.1 are useful for illustrative purposes throughout this book, because they are unambiguous. Market-related sources and institutional sources may be just as important in practice (Miller and Lessard, 2001), and some technical sources may be much more difficult to deal with (Klein and Cork, 1998), but the same principles apply.

Some descriptions of identify phase tasks concentrate initially on assessing the effects of sources without reference to associated responses, leaving consideration of responses until later and then only consider alternatives in relation to major issues. We recommend an early, proactive approach to responses as indicated above. The essence of the matter is:

1. do not waste time considering alternative responses if the first one thought of is both effective and efficient;
2. do not overlook key responses;
3. do not overlook the apparently minor problem that has no effective fix once it occurs;
4. identify opportunities that may have implications beyond the issues that triggered their consideration;
5. explore deeper levels of uncertainty where this is particularly important.

Sources associated with the key performance criterion

The simplest way to begin the identify phase is to adopt a simple ponder approach to the identification of what might be termed *key criterion, level one, primary* issues (more conveniently referred to as KLP issues). *Key criterion* issues are sources and associated responses that impact directly on the most important or central project performance criterion. *Level one* issues are sources of uncertainty and responses that can be linked directly to an uncertain effect on a performance criterion of interest, without reference to an uncertainty structure involving multiple levels of disaggregated or contributory sources. *Primary* issues are issues associated with base plans or designs or other base assumption aspects of the project, as distinct from secondary issues associated with sources arising from primary responses. The following example clarifies what is meant by KLP issues.

Example 7.2 Identifying key criterion, level one, and primary issues (KLP issues)

Offshore oil and gas projects in the early 1970s experienced widespread planning and costing failure, in that many projects came in late and over cost.

The key criterion was time. Most cost uncertainty was driven by time uncertainty (delay), and trade-offs between time and cost or performance were not a significant issue. Time uncertainty was directly linked to the execution of project activities, the *whichway* in terms of the six *W*s, at the *execute* stage of the PLC (project life cycle).

Part of the reason for the planning and costing failure was the absence of a formal process for considering sources of uncertainty. However, most of the people involved could provide a list of primary sources that could directly impact on project duration without much hesitation given a carefully executed define phase in terms of the project's activity structure. When a formal RMP (risk management process) was introduced, identification of a list of primary sources in level-one terms was reasonably straightforward.

Examples of such sources were provided in Example 7.1: the lay barge arriving late, the lay barge not operating as quickly as planned given good weather, encountering bad weather, pipe buckles, and so on.

Sources associated with other performance criteria

As noted in Chapter 1, there are a number of problems associated with defining uncertainty and risk in relation to performance that can be viewed as opportunities. One problem (or opportunity) is the multidimensional nature of project performance. In some circumstances a case can be made for keeping the measurement of performance and success very simple, but such conditions are comparatively rare. More commonly, project objectives might be viewed in terms of cost, time, or quality. Cost might be addressed in terms of capital cost or 'whole life' cost and quality might be divided into technical specification, functionality, and appearance, each of which may be 'at risk' to different degrees. Often performance is perceived primarily in terms of dimensions that can be measured, such as time and cost or particular aspects of quality. The implication is that variations are possible and measurable, and hence uncertainty exists in respect of these performance criteria. Other criteria that are not readily quantified may be treated as inviolate constraints for project management purposes. This may lead to neglect of uncertainty in these dimensions, even though they represent important performance criteria. These problems (opportunities) need to be addressed in this step.

Even if one criterion clearly dominates, such as time in a North Sea offshore project context, other criteria will be important. Uncertainty not identified in the frameworks used for the key criteria will need explicit attention. Consider an example, building on Example 7.2.

> ### Example 7.3   Building cost uncertainty on a time uncertainty framework
>
> When North Sea offshore project teams were satisfied that time uncertainty had been properly assessed, aspects of cost uncertainty not addressed as part of the process of responding to time uncertainty were assessed. For example, the uncertain duration of pipe-laying activity was multiplied by the uncertain cost of lay barge per unit time needed to compute lay barge cost.

In this case it is relatively simple to build cost uncertainty on a time uncertainty framework. When a clear structure linking criteria exists, it is worth exploiting. When it does not, more complex approaches may be required, and this complexity requires great care. For example, many weapon system and information system RMPs identify sources in terms of time, cost, and performance impacts simultaneously, using matrix formats. This may seem sensible for a first-pass approach to the identify phase. However, it poses two somewhat different potential problems. First, it does not facilitate a clear, sequential focus on performance criteria, which helps to avoid omissions. Second, it leaves structural and trade-off issues to be addressed later as they must be for quantification, and this can mitigate against appropriate quantification. By impeding quantification, it impairs the iterative process that is central to a complete RMP.

Much more detailed analysis of objectives, including their decomposition in a structure directly related to project activities or design components, may be useful in some cases. For example, in a high-technology product development project, if a set of components is assessed as very risky, it may be possible to design out the uncertainty by changing the basic nature of the design, perhaps as part of a formal value management process (Green, 1994). This will require a clear understanding of the functional role of the components in the overall design. It involves an interaction between the project *why* and *what*. The groundwork for identification of such issues should have been provided back in the define phase.

It is important to address these difficulties explicitly as part of the focus phase or the closely linked structure phase. Guidance on how to manage such difficulties is beyond the scope of this book, but a starting point for those interested is provided by Chapman et al. (1985a), Klein (1993), and Chapman and Ward (2002).

Even if only one project party is of concern, it is very important to define objectives in writing and their relative priorities. Often different parts of the same organization have different objectives. At the very least, agreed priorities in terms of time, cost, and performance are essential. If differences are very important, treating the different parts of the organization as separate partners may be appropriate. This takes us into different criteria related to different parties and uncertainty associated with other *W*s.

Sources associated with other *W*s

It is convenient to start with a focus on the KLP issues, then generalize to consider other criteria from the perspective of the key player (assumed to be the client here), then move on to other *W*s. For present purposes assume that time is the key criterion, with cost driven by time as in Examples 7.2 and 7.3, and we now want to move on.

Project risk management, which is largely focused on time uncertainty (a project *why*), is naturally addressed in terms of project activities (the project *whichway*), but the other project *W*s are usually important and associated uncertainty will usually need explicit attention. As a consequence, this step is concerned with considering the other four *W*s: *who*, *what*, *when*, and *wherewithal*, using as a basis the documentation of all six *W*s from the define phase and other interactions of all six *W*s as a complete set.

Considering the complete set of *W*s can reveal some key sources, associated responses, and in some cases secondary sources, with important interactions that require management. Below we consider each of these four *W*s in turn, not to generate an exhaustive, generic list of possible sources, which would be impracticable and inappropriate, but to illustrate the range of areas that could be considered.

Sources associated with other parties, the *who*

Chapter 5 indicated the importance of documenting clear descriptions of all the interested parties during the define phase. The concern here is an effective issue identification process using this earlier identification of the relevant parties. Examples 5.1 and 5.2 illustrate what is involved to some extent, but consider another example.

Example 7.4   The need to keep partners informed of possible changes

Joint venture partners are important to address explicitly, in terms of the interests and roles of all the partners. Many offshore oil projects involve a lead partner who takes operational responsibility and other partners who help to fund the project and share the product. A significant change in plans will require approval by all the partners. If they are not all kept informed of the possible need to make such changes, managing the decision to change the plan can be a question of crisis management rather than risk management, adding to the cost of the incidents necessitating the change or eliminating the possibility of responding to an opportunity.

Multination military joint ventures, such as the development of new weapon systems or their platforms (aircraft, ships, etc.), make the *who* dimension very rich indeed, due, for example, to different technical requirements, different needs in terms of timing, and different contracting systems between the partners and their contractors. It clearly complicates the *why*, in the sense that each party's objectives need attention.

Regulators, planning authorities, and others providing approvals may also prove to be key players. For example, combined cycle gas turbine power stations involve warm water discharges into rivers and vapour plumes that are regulated, in addition to the planning permission issues associated with such plant. Nuclear power stations involve obviously increased levels of regulation, including safety standards that may be changing during construction, necessitating redesigns with delays that yield still more regulation-induced design changes in a vicious circle, which can prove extremely expensive. Channel tunnel rolling stock development and production encountered this kind of difficulty. To manage this kind of source it is important to understand what is driving changes in the regulatory environment and to endeavour to meet the regulations that will be relevant at the appropriate time in the future, rather than those currently in force.

Competitors for limited resources (*wherewithal*) can also prove a profitable area of study. For example, oil majors have attempted to avoid bidding up the price for key scarce resources by timing their projects (moving the *when*) to avoid excessive competition. If only a half a dozen players are involved, individual study and perhaps direct collaboration may be feasible. More generally, it may be appropriate to look at the markets for specific resources as a whole. Successful commercial property developers are aware of the need to time new building construction, hopefully while the market for resources and cash are depressed, just before the market for office space takes off. Many failed developers are also well aware of the importance of these considerations too late.

Much of the uncertainty inherent in project management arises from agents appointed by the client, such as contractors and subcontractors. The client may not be able to rely on an agent performing as the client wishes for reasons related to the nature of the work and the agent's motivation, ability, and understanding of the work. In theory, it should be possible for the client to maximize the chances of satisfactory performance from the agent by careful selection of a suitable agent, careful monitoring of the agent's activities, and ensuring that the agent is appropriately motivated. Unfortunately, lack of knowledge on the part of the client and the presence of uncertainty can make these things difficult to achieve.

The so-called 'principal–agent' relationship, whether between parties in the same organization, or between a client and contractor, is prone to three fundamental problems: *adverse selection*; *moral hazard*; and *risk allocation* (Eisenhardt, 1989).

Adverse selection refers to misrepresentation of ability by the agent and the principal's difficulty in selecting an agent with appropriate skills. The agent may claim to have certain skills or abilities when hired, but the principal cannot completely verify these skills or abilities either at the time of hiring or while the agent is working. A 'selection' problem can also arise where a contractor misrepresents the work that will be done or the likely final price. Once a contractor has been hired, it may be difficult for the client to ensure that costs are contained and work promised is what is actually delivered.

Moral hazard refers to an agent's failure to put forth the contracted effort. This can be of greatest concern to the principal when it is particularly difficult or expensive for the principal to verify that an agent is behaving appropriately, as when task specifications are inadequate or the principal lacks knowledge of the delegated tasks.

Risk allocation concerns the manner in which responsibility for project-related issues (sources and responses) is allocated between principal and agent. Risk allocation is very important because it can strongly influence the motivation of principal and agent and the extent to which uncertainty is assessed and managed. In so far as principal and agent perceive risks differently and have different abilities and motivations to manage uncertainty, then their approach to risk management will be different. In particular, either party is likely to try to manage uncertainty primarily for his or her own benefit, perhaps to the disadvantage of the other party. This issue is explored in more detail in Chapter 16.

The uncertainties arising from problems of adverse selection, moral hazard, and risk allocation are more likely to arise where principal and agent are separate organizations, as in most client–contractor relationships. Where principal and agent belong to the same organization it might be expected that such problems would be less likely to arise, to the extent that the parties can share information, responsibilities, and objectives more readily. Unfortunately, this is not always the case. Chapman and Ward (2002, chap. 6) explores 'internal contracts' to address such issues.

Sources associated with project design, the *what*

Many of the important sources associated with a project relate to the specific physical nature of the project and its design, to the *what* of the project. The relationship may be direct and obvious or indirect and easily overlooked. For example, many risk management methods for high technology products (such as advanced weapon systems) suggest an explicit focus on technical issues arising from design because using a design based on the latest technology may involve sources associated with technical failures or reliability problems. Using a design based on established technology may avoid certain technical sources but involve other sources associated with more aggressive competitors who are willing and able to manage the uncertainty involved in new technology. That is, avoiding a technical source may involve generating a competitor-based source, but where the choice of technology is implicit, competitor-based sources may not be seen as a related issue.

Design changes are often a major threat. However, freezing the design is often not a viable option. Hospitals, military equipment, computer software, and comparatively simple consumer products may require design updates during development and production to remain viable. Anticipating these changes in needs may be the key to successful design, as well as the key to a successful project more generally. Attention to procedures for 'change control' (design changes) should be recognized as central to any project involving a design that is neither simple nor stable.

Effective anticipation of design changes is part of the RMP. Links to other *W*s may be quite simple but very important, requiring an understanding of the *what*, with the *whichway* and *why* assumed to have been covered earlier, and the *wherewithal* and *when* yet to be considered. For example, property developers will be sensitive to issues like how many car-parking places a planning department may require for a new building now, and whether or not this is likely to increase by next year. A design that fails to reflect this sort of change can seriously threaten a project. At the very least it requires a clear understanding of the technologies involved and the interface between technological choices and related issues. For example, the development of computer-controlled fly-by-wire technology revolutionized aircraft design because inherently unstable designs that previously would not have been able to fly became feasible, but a whole new set of sources were generated that were not all anticipated at the outset.

It is important to appreciate that *what* is the recipient of effects from other *W*s as well as a primary source, and these effects can generate substantial second-order effects. For example, if some combination of problems from a variety of sources threatens the viability of the target project completion time or date, or its cost, the response may be a change in design. This may have the desired effect or it may make the situation worse. This impact is well understood in theory in terms of the standard time–cost–quality triangle (Barnes, 1988), but it is often overlooked in practice. Part of the role of documenting the six *W*s in the define phase, and review of this documentation in the identify phase, is explicit identification of these issues.

Sources associated with project resources, the *wherewithal*

The importance of risk management involving resources, the *wherewithal* of the project, is obvious. Lack of the right resources in the right place at the right time is a source of serious risk inefficiency. Making sure this does not happen is central to project management. Example 5.6 is a relatively low-key illustration of resource-related sources. In the following example, the availability of one resource was a major issue.

> **Example 7.5   Factors influencing the supply of welders**
>
> A very early study by Chapman was totally driven by the impact of a scarce resource: welders needed for the fabrication of a proposed, large-diameter, gas pipeline to bring Arctic gas to US markets. The availability of welders was central to the project because political pressures were forcing a short project duration (a *when* issue) that required a significant proportion (of the order of 10%) of the suitably skilled welders available in Canada. Other factors influencing the availability of welders also needed to be understood, such as immigration rules that would make importing labour difficult or impossible and a recognition that Arctic construction of this kind often leads to a pattern of employment that involves long hours (and weeks)

> for an extended period when cash is accumulated by the workforce, followed by a spell on a sunny island until the cash runs out, the duration of both periods depending on the welders' circumstances and whims.

Potential shortage of various resources is not the only resource-related source of uncertainty. In the context of computer software projects, there is a widely held view that adding more staff to a software project that is running very late is rather like attempting to drown a fire by pouring on petrol. Usually economic usage of resources suggests self-imposed constraints even if there are no externally imposed constraints. For example, employing 300 people one week, 100 the next, and 200 the next, is generally very uneconomic compared with 200 throughout. If all the resources required are readily available in the required quantities at the required times with no difficulties associated with quality or performance, and no costs associated with highly variable resource usage patterns, the *wherewithal* issue is not worth pursuing. At the very least it is worth confirming that this is the case, in writing if appropriate.

It may be convenient to identify and describe resource requirements (*wherewithal*) within the activity (*whichway*) structure, but resources shared with other projects mitigate against this, making separate *wherewithal* documentation useful. If a project is subject to political pressure to employ local labour or other resources it makes obvious sense to identify this type of consideration in relation to those resources that are relevant, which has implications for how the resource units are defined. As in the case of activities, the basic rule of thumb is disaggregate resource types only when it looks useful to do so.

Sources associated with project timing, the *when*

Like design (*what*), timing (*when*) can be an important primary source of uncertainty over and above the timing implications of delay considered earlier and a recipient of impacts from other *W*s, which can generate important second-order effects. Formal documentation of the *W*s is concerned with making sure these issues do not fall down cracks and get lost from sight until they generate a crisis. Example 5.6 illustrates a timing/resource link, in terms of overstated time uncertainty if common resource usage is overlooked.

Even if no first- or second-order implications are involved, project duration is an economic choice that needs explicit attention. For example, the study concerned with welders described in Example 7.5 addressed the question of an optimal target project duration explicitly, in response to the political pressure for a shorter duration. But even if no one outside the project team asks questions about project duration, the issue of trade-offs between time (indirect cost) and direct cost is important. At this stage in the process the question needs to be raised in broad terms. For example, if the proposed project duration is five years, the question is why not four, or six? If the answer is not clear, further attention to the issue will be required and the need to give it attention should be flagged. From the outset it is important to be clear what level of overhead costs per unit time will be incurred in relation to any project extensions.

A simple first cut at identifying primary sources might involve a simple list of all the sources associated with each *W* and brief notes on relevant issues in relation to each source, merging steps 1 and 2 of Figure 7.1. At any stage in the process the use of a simple label (or 'handle') for each source can be very helpful for discussion purposes, while back-up descriptions for each source document what is involved. However, no matter how clear the output looks, *if all key sources for all six Ws* have not been properly understood and that understanding documented and shared by the project team, issue identification cannot be effective. For example, failure to consider market and political sources associated with *why* or *what* can render detailed planning and risk analysis of *whichway* and *when* somewhat superfluous. Additionally, market and political sources may be driven by technical choices.

A complementary second-cut (or alternative first-cut) approach is to look for uncertainty associated with the elements of a hierarchical framework based on one or more of the six *W*s, starting with the obvious framework for the key criteria, as suggested by the separate steps 1 and 2 of Figure 7.1. Thus a starting point might be a work breakdown structure based on a decomposition of the *whichway*, a product breakdown structure based on a decomposition of the *what*, or an objectives breakdown structure based on a decomposition of the *why*. Whichever hierarchical basis is chosen, the other five *W*s provide a prompt list for identifying sources at each level in the adopted hierarchy.

Whatever the exact nature of the first-pass approach, it is important to see Figure 7.1 as a portrayal of tasks to be achieved to a 'fit for the purpose' level for each pass, with an emphasis on early aspects of step 2 on the early passes, moving the emphasis toward later aspects on later passes.

Sources in other stages of the project life cycle (PLC)

A project risk management focus on time uncertainty associated with *whichway* uncertainty is almost a basic instinct if the RMP is initiated at the end of the plan stage as assumed here. Step 1 and the part of step 2 of the identify phase addressed in the previous sections of this chapter were concerned with ensuring that other criteria and other *W*s did not get ignored. An obvious further elaboration is a review of uncertainty associated with other stages in the PLC. Chapter 14 will address the process implications of being at other stages, but a useful step at this point in the RMP is making sure sources of uncertainty that may not materialize until later in the PLC and sources that may have been overlooked in earlier stages are addressed now.

Table 7.1—Typical uncertainty management issues in each stage of the
project life cycle (PLC)

stage	uncertainty management issues
conceive the product	level of definition definition of appropriate performance objectives managing stakeholder expectations
design the product strategically	novelty of design and technology determining 'fixed' points in the design control of changes
plan the execution strategically	identifying and allowing for regulatory constraints concurrency of activities required capturing dependency relationships errors and omissions
allocate resources tactically	adequate accuracy of resource estimates estimating resources required defining responsibilities (number and scope of contracts) defining contractual terms and conditions selection of capable participants (tendering procedures and bid selection)
execute production	exercising adequate co-ordination and control determining the level and scope of control systems ensuring effective communication between participants provision of appropriate organizational arrangements ensuring effective leadership ensuring continuity in personnel and responsibilities responding effectively to sources that are realized
deliver the product	adequate testing adequate training managing stakeholder expectations obtaining licences to operate
review the process	capturing corporate knowledge learning key lessons understanding what success means
support the product	provision of appropriate organization arrangements identifying extent of liabilities managing stakeholder expectations

As noted in Chapter 2, many important sources are associated with the fundamental management processes that make up the PLC. A fair number of sources are implicitly acknowledged in lists of project management 'key success factors'. Potential sources typically identified in this way are listed in Table 7.1 against the appropriate PLC stages identified in Chapter 2.

The identification of these sources of uncertainty in the project management literature is based on substantial project management experience, but it is somewhat haphazard. Different writers identify different success factors or problem areas, describe them in more or less detail, or identify as single-problem areas what may in practice be a whole series of separate issues. Another difficulty is that sources of uncertainty are identified as adverse effects rather than in terms of underlying causes or uncertainties. For example, potential problems in the execute stage of a project can often be related to weaknesses in particular earlier stages of the project: 'failure of prototype to pass performance trials' may be a consequence of faulty workmanship, unreasonable performance requirements, a choice of new technology, or novel design features.

Conceive the product

Stakeholder expectations associated with a conceive stage that is not subjected to formal risk management until the end of the plan stage can be a major issue, as can performance objectives in terms of relative priorities. This is never an acceptable reason for avoiding these issues, but it can make managing an RMP a very high-risk operation.

Designing and planning

A common source of project risk inefficiency is a failure to carry out steps in the design and plan stages thoroughly enough. Thus a project proceeds through to execution with insufficient well-defined specifications for production. During execution this gives rise to difficulties necessitating additional design development and production planning, and consequently adverse effects on the performance criteria of cost, time, and quality. Related risk inefficiency associated with 'premature definition' is also difficult to avoid entirely, except on very routine, repeated projects, and the problem is most acute in novel, one-off projects involving new technology. The basis of both problems is that it is extremely difficult to specify in advance how every part of the execution and termination phase will take place; neither is it cost-effective to seek to do so. In any case, some uncertainty about operating conditions and related factors outside the control of project management will always remain. Inevitably, judgements have to be made about the degree of detail and accuracy practicable in the design and plan stages. However, these judgements should be supported and informed by appropriate risk analysis that is undertaken no later than the end of the plan stage.

Allocation

The allocate stage is a significant task involving decisions about project organization, identification of appropriate agents, and allocation of tasks between them. As noted on p. 113, the introduction of an agent is prone to the three problems of adverse selection, moral hazard, and risk allocation. In particular, this stage of a project can introduce several sources of uncertainty with significant risk inefficiency implications:

1. participants have different priorities and risk/uncertainty perceptions;
2. unclear specification of responsibilities (including those relating to the management of uncertainty and risk);
3. communications between different departments or organizations;
4. co-ordination and control tasks.

Even if client and agents all work for the same organization, the problems presented by these uncertainties can be substantial. When agents are different organizations, these problems can be particularly challenging.

In a client–contractor situation, the client exerts influence over the contractor primarily via conditions laid down in a contract between the two parties. The contract sets out what is to be produced, what the client will pay, how the client can assess and monitor what the contractor has done, and how things should proceed in the case of various contingent events. In theory, the contract seeks to reduce uncertainty about each party's responsibilities. In practice, substantial uncertainties can remain associated with items such as the following:

1. inadequate or ambiguous definition of terms (specifications; responsibilities of parties to co-operate, advise, co-ordinate, supervise);
2. inappropriate definition of terms (performance specifications; variations; extensions);
3. variations (powers to order; express and implied terms; pricing and payment mechanisms);
4. payment and claims arrangements (timing and conditions for payment);
5. defects liability (who has to be satisfied; who could be responsible; extent of liability).

Effective risk management toward the end of the plan stage should look forward and anticipate these issues, putting effective responses in place.

Execution

During the execute stage, the essential process issue is the adequacy of co-ordination and control procedures. Thus co-ordination and control ought to include risk management practices as 'good project management practices' that amount to:

1. milestone management;
2. adequate monitoring of activities likely to go wrong;
3. ensuring realistic, honest reporting of progress;
4. reporting problems and revised assessments of future issues.

A common source of risk inefficiency in the execution phase is the introduction of design changes. Such design changes can lead to disruption of schedules and resourcing, and affect cost, time, and quality measures of performance directly. A potentially serious concern is that changes are introduced without a full appreciation of the knock-on consequences. Apart from direct consequences, indirect consequences can occur. For example, changes may induce an extension of schedules, allowing contractors to escape the adverse consequences of delays in works unaffected by the change. Changes may have wider technical implications than first thought, leading to subsequent disputes between client and contractor about liability for costs and consequential delays (Cooper, 1980; Williams et al., 1995a, b). Standard project management practice should establish product change control procedures that set up criteria for allowable changes and provide for adequate co-ordination, communication, and documentation of changes. However, adjustments to production plans, costs, and payments to affected contractors ought to be based on an assessment of how project risks are affected by the changes and the extent to which revised risk management plans are needed.

In a repetitive, operational context, human failings can be a significant source of risk inefficiency. Studies of accidents and disasters often identify 'human error' and 'management error' as major contributory causes (Kletz, 1985; Engineering Council, 1993, app. 3). Such risk inefficiency may be evident in a project setting. Although the novelty of a project can discourage complacency and carelessness to some degree, the project context is often characterized by sufficient novelty, complexity, work pressure, and uncertainty as to increase greatly the likely significance of human failure or error.

In any organizational context, a number of factors influence the performance of an individual participant, as shown in the left-hand column of Table 7.2. Failure in individual performance, whether amounting to inadequate or incorrect performance, may be related to one or more of these factors in a wide variety of ways, as shown in the right-hand column of Table 7.2.

In a project context, sources of risk inefficiency of the kind listed in Table 7.2 could feature in any stage of the PLC. However, seeking to identify such sources associated with individuals at every PLC stage may represent an excessive level of analysis. More usefully the factors in Table 7.2 might be applied to particular groups of individuals or to individual participating organizations. In the latter case it is easy to see how the sources of risk inefficiency of Table 7.2 might be associated with individual departments or whole organizations acting, for example, in the capacity of contractors or subcontractors.

Table 7.2—Possible causes of inadequate or incorrect performance by individuals

factors	*sources of risk inefficiency*
task perception	following instructions that are incorrect failure to realize responsibility personal interpretation of a task required mistaken priorities, such as taking short cuts through safety rules to save time
capability and experience	lack of appropriate training or skills to perform a task failure to follow instructions lack of appreciation of consequences of actions inappropriate choice of procedure to achieve desired outcome jumping to conclusions about the nature of a situation

work environment	information overload makes it difficult to identify important
	    pieces of information and easier to ignore or delay scrutiny
	task overload impairs ability to monitor developments and
	    formulate reactive or proactive responses
	difficult working environment
	inadequate work environment, equipment, or procedures
	    increase the chance of mistakes

mistake	random slips failure to detect very unusual situations or rare events incorrect assessment of a situation
motivation	lack of incentive for high level of performance lack of concentration on a task personal objectives
actions of others	failure to communicate information frustration of actions incorrect or faulty components supplied insufficient quality of contribution

Deliver and support

Looking forward to the deliver and support stages, and developing appropriate responses for key sources while still in the plan stage, can reduce or eliminate potential later problems at relatively low cost. The key here is identifying which issues need this attention in the plan stage and which do not.

Responses

As shown in Figure 7.1, the next step in the identify phase is concerned with responses. This step involves searching for and classifying primary responses for each primary source identified earlier, in the process *documenting*, *verifying*, *assessing*, and *reporting* what is involved.

Often the identification of a possible response to a particular source is a simple task. Once a source has been identified it is frequently obvious how one could respond. However, the most easily identified possible response may not be the most effective or the most risk efficient response; other responses may be worth identifying and considering. Where an issue is particularly significant, a systematic examination of a range of possible responses, perhaps with a view to applying several responses in parallel, may be worthwhile. There are nine types of response that can be considered, as shown in Table 7.3.

A key response option is to *modify objectives*, as noted earlier. For example, as a proactive response, the time allowed to complete a decommissioning task may be extended before a contract for the work is let because an assessment of the base plan shows that the initial target would be virtually impossible to meet. As a reactive response, certain performance targets may be relaxed during the execution and termination phases of the PLC, if difficulties in meeting original targets become insuperable or the value of achieving the original targets is reassessed. Setting different levels of cost, time, or quality objectives can have varying effects on the achievement of other objectives. These effects depend on a variety of situational factors, not least of which are the nature of the project and the behaviour of the contractors and professionals employed. For example, good-quality building work is fostered by allowing contractors time to analyse and properly price what is required, and to conduct the work without excessive

Table 7.3—Generic response types

types of response	method of handling uncertainty
modify objectives	reduce or raise performance targets, changing trade-offs between multiple objectives
avoid	plan to avoid specified sources of uncertainty
influence probability	change the probability of potential outcomes
modify consequences	modify the consequences if an event occurs
develop contingency plans	set aside resources to provide a reactive ability to cope
keep options open	delay choices and commitment, choose versatile options
monitor	collect and update data about probabilities of occurrence, anticipated effects, and additional sources of uncertainty
accept	accept uncertainty, but do nothing about it
remain unaware	ignore uncertainty and take no action to identify (or manage) it

haste and paring of costs. In setting goals for attainment on each project objective, trade-offs must be made between levels of attainment on each objective.
Unfortunately, deciding trade-offs is often complicated by uncertainty about the
nature of the interdependencies between the different performance objectives.
Thus, a decrease in the time available to complete a project can cause an
increase in total project cost, but it may cause a decrease. Similarly, improvements in quality can mean an increase or a decrease in project time associated
with an increase or a decrease in project cost.

In the face of these difficulties, a pragmatic approach is common. Trade-offs
may be expressed simply in terms of one objective having clear priority over
another. Alternatively, project objectives are often expressed in terms of satisfying
target levels of achievement that are assumed to be mutually compatible. This
typically results in a series of *ad hoc* trade-offs being made through the life of the
project. For example, in a construction project, the client's representative on the
building site might accept work of lower performance than specified in the
contract where specifications appear excessively tight, in exchange for work of
higher performance in other areas, to secure an overall balance in the terms of
exchange.

A second response—*avoid*—is often a feasible and desirable response to
uncertainty. However, risk management strategies formulated as avoidance
options in practice may operate only as influence or modify options. This may
still be useful, but the residual uncertainty should be recognized. In a multiparty
context, transferring uncertainty to another party may be perceived by the transferring party to be an obvious and natural way of avoiding one or more sources
of uncertainty. However, uncertainty may not be eliminated for the transferor
unless the party receiving the uncertainty adopts appropriate risk management
strategies, and the consequences may include secondary sources that fall on the
transferor. This is a particularly significant issue in contractual relationships, often
with profound implications for risk management and project performance. This
issue is examined in more detail in Chapters 9 and 16.

A third response option is *influence probability*. This is a very common type
of response that typically has the intention of reducing the probability of adverse
events occurring. Viewing risk management as opportunity management involves
increasing the probability of desirable events occurring. In terms of sources of
uncertainty more generally, this response involves changing the probability of the
various potential outcomes.

A fourth response option is *modify consequences*. This involves modifying the
potential consequences of a source on project performance. It certainly includes
reducing adverse impacts (e.g., reducing delays likely to be caused should a
particular event occur). However, modification may also involve modifying
potential consequences by changing their nature, perhaps by transforming an
impact on one performance criterion into an impact on another criterion. For
example, if an event occurs that will delay the project, it may be possible to
counter this by paying for overtime work or other additional resources.

A fifth type of response option is to *develop contingency plans*. This involves consciously accepting uncertainty but setting aside resources to provide a reactive capability to cope with adverse impacts if they eventuate. Thus the project manager may set aside a contingency reserve of physical resources, finance, or time in case of need. Risk analysis may be useful to determine the appropriate level of contingency provision.

A sixth type of response—*keep options open*—involves deliberate delaying decsions, limiting early commitment, or actively searching out versatile project strategies that will perform acceptably under a variety of possible future conditions.

Monitor, a seventh type of response, implies a willingness to undertake more active risk management at some point, but the criteria for active management intervention may not be clearly articulated. Delaying risk management is always an option. Uncertainty may decrease (or increase), associated risk may change, and the need for real-time problem solving may increase or decrease. Adopting this response ought to involve conscious assessment of the likely costs and benefits of delaying more active responses.

Accept, with recognition of the risk exposure, but with no further action to manage or monitor associated uncertainty, is an eighth type of response.

In an important practical sense the final response option is to *remain unaware* that uncertainty exists. This is a sensible option in cases where threats and opportunities can be dealt with effectively and efficiently as and when they arise. It has obvious dangers in other cases. Remaining unaware is the default option if none of the other options in Table 7.3 are pursued.

The scope for complex source–response management is clearly considerable. Example 7.6 provides an extension to Example 7.1 to clarify part of what is involved. Example 7.7 illustrates some further issues, complementing Example 7.6.

Example 7.6   Responses to the wet buckle source in pipe laying

Consider the potential occurrence of a pipe wet buckle as described in Example 7.1.

One kind of response is purely reactive, after the fact, using readily available resources: the buckled pipeline can be repaired. This involves sending down divers to cut off the damaged sections and put a cap containing valves on the pipe. A 'pig', a torpedo-like metal cylinder, is then sent through the pipe under air pressure from the other end to 'dewater' the pipeline. The pipeline can then be picked up and pipe laying recommenced.

A second kind of response is proactive and preventive action upfront that reduces the chance of the source being realized: a more capable lay barge could reduce the probability of a buckle occurring (capability for this purpose being maximum wave height conditions for safe working). This response is also a proactive, mitigating response, because buckle repair can be completed more quickly in the face of bad weather with a more capable barge.

A third kind of response is also after the fact, but requires essential prior actions: the buckled pipeline can be abandoned and a new pipeline started. If the buckle occurs before very much pipe has been laid and sufficient additional spare pipe has been ordered in advance, this is a risk efficient solution because of the time saved. This kind of response is an example of a proactive/reactive combination.

Some responses have important implications for other responses, other sources, or the base plan, all of which need to be identified. For example, a more capable barge reduces the chances of a buckle and allows faster repair of buckles as noted. It also allows faster pipe laying, especially in the face of bad weather, with an impact on base plan performance.

Simply accepting the possibility of a buckle, in the sense of living with it with no direct risk management responses, was not an option. However, oil majors operating in the North Sea in the 1980s often transferred some of the risk associated with buckles to their contractors, via fixed price contracts for a complete pipeline. This did not transfer all the uncertainty, as contractors could not bear the consequential costs or lost revenues associated with delaying the start of oil or gas production. Insurance for such risks was taken into account, but generally considered inappropriate.

Designing out the possibility of a buckle, by using flexible pipe and reel barges, was not to our knowledge explicitly identified as a response to buckles in the early days of North Sea pipe laying, but it was considered later. Designing out important sources of risk inefficiency is an important response.

Example 7.7   Managing weather risk on a sailing holiday

Spending August sailing a small yacht from Southampton to Falmouth in Cornwall and back, along the south coast of England, is Chapman's idea of a summer holiday project. Bad weather is the central source of uncertainty. It can be designed out only by staying at home. Monitoring, keeping options open, and modifying objectives when appropriate, are the basic response strategies.

The trip each way is planned to take a week to ten days, with four or five stops on the way, sailing in daylight. The most desirable stops are anchorages in sheltered bays, which are usable only in certain wind conditions. A buoy in a quiet river is the next preference and a marina a poor third, unless water or fuel are required. Stopovers are for walks, pub meals, and visits to historic houses, gardens, and other places of interest. Staying in port is also a response to a poor weather forecast. Avoiding planning long passages without alternative ports if the weather is bad, or potentially bad, is an important variant of this response to the monitoring process. If the forecast is bad for a week, going anyway becomes almost inevitable as priorities change. Further responses once under way include shortening sail (reefing or, in extremes, changing to a storm jib and/or trisail), putting on lifelines, and securing the main hatch. The basic objective is enjoyment while on passage, but extensive delays can make getting there more of a priority, and the ultimate priority is the safety of the boat and crew. Sometimes carrying on to the planned destination has to be replaced by heading for the nearest port in a storm, and in extremes that option may have to be abandoned in favour of making sea room.

Many new strategic information system projects for competitive advantage share most of these characteristics, as do a wide range of other projects, even if having fun is not the basic intent and ending up dead in the water is not a potential outcome in a literal sense.

Most experienced sailors and most experienced managers in other contexts, where the basis of risk management is monitoring, keeping options open, and modifying objectives when appropriate, can recount tales of when it all went wrong, with disastrous or near-disastrous consequences. Yachting magazines carry regular features in this vein, which make educational as well as interesting reading. Corporate disaster stories also receive such attention (e.g., Lam, 1999). Common features are a series of largely unpredicted events whose significance was not recognized, coming together at a time when options were reduced for predictable reasons, and there was a failure to take radical action based on a change of objectives early enough.

In a risk management process centred around monitoring, keeping options open, and modifying objectives when appropriate, a further characteristic of actual or near disasters is a presumed set of primary responses that don't work. For example, on a sailing trip the radio needed for a Mayday may not work because the mast carrying the aerial has fallen down and the emergency aerial, perhaps tested when new, has been stored for many years in a way that has led to its failure.

In a first pass at least one response should be identified for each primary source, if only because the consequences of a source cannot be considered without some assumed response. This initial response may be simply 'accept the uncertainty', but such a response may not be feasible and a more active response may need to be identified. For example, in Example 7.6 there is a range of things that can be done, but just accepting the exposure to possible buckles is not one of them. On a first iteration, one response per issue may be enough, especially for those issues that are clearly unlikely to prove significant. Later iterations can add additional responses for issues of importance. Very important issues may warrant careful consideration of possible options under each type of response in Table 7.3.

Sometimes it is particularly important to stress, and extensively develop, the primary response part of the identify phase as early as possible in the very first pass. One reason is to address low project team morale. Looking for problems can be very depressing when a project that is your sole source of income is already looking decidedly risky. Encouraging the project team to look for responses to each problem before going on to the next can be a vital aspect of success.

Another reason to stress early primary response development arises where a project is based on a design that is so tentative that a major source is best dealt with by redesign.

A third reason arises where a project's objectives are receptive to the response: 'if at first it doesn't look like you will succeed, redefine success.' Software projects with a shopping list of deliverables ranging from 'must have' to 'nice to have' are obvious examples, but not so obvious possibilities may be worth consideration in these terms.

In general it is useful to see this early response development as part of the process of searching for risk efficiency that needs to go beyond simple threat management.

Whether or not early primary response development is stressed for the kinds of reasons just cited, it is very important to see responses in terms of all six Ws as part of a process concerned with maximizing flexibility and enabling appropriate monitoring.

Secondary sources and responses

The fourth step associated with the identify phase involves identifying secondary sources and responses as appropriate, and documenting what is involved. The extent to which it is worth identifying and documenting secondary, tertiary, and further potential levels of sources and responses is very much a matter of judgement, necessarily dependent on a variety of issues. Once again, the key lies in keeping the analysis as simple as possible without overlooking any important issues. An extension of Example 7.6 illustrates this point.

Example 7.8   Secondary sources and responses when repairing a pipe buckle

If repair becomes the primary response to a pipe buckle, an important secondary source involves the pig running over a boulder or other debris in the pipe and becoming stuck.

A secondary response is to send down divers, cut off the pipe behind the pig, put a cap on the shortened pipeline, and try again. This response involves the loss of pipe and time. Another secondary response is to increase the air pressure, hoping to pop the pig through, with the tertiary source that the pipeline may fail to withstand the additional pressure some considerable distance from the stuck pig, resulting in the loss of even more pipe and even more delay.

It was very important to identify these secondary and tertiary source–response chains, for several reasons.

First, it clearly makes sense to assess, well in advance, how far the air pressure should be turned up in the event of a stuck pig. This is not a decision that should be left to a lay barge operator in the midst of a crisis. The decision requires the expertise of pipeline designers and pipeline manufacturers who will understand the safety margins in their design and production and are best placed to judge the probability of damage and the extent of that damage as the pressure increases. It also requires the expertise of those members of the project team who understand the cost implications of delay to the pipe laying, including opportunity costs.

Second, once it is clear that 'repair' involves considerable scope for loss of pipe and that additional pipe will have to be ordered if a repair strategy is adopted, 'abandon and start again' begins to look a much more attractive option and fast supply of extra pipe becomes a key issue.

Ultimately such considerations helped to motivate fundamental changes in design, including the use of more flexible pipe laid from reel barges, greatly speeding up the whole process of pipe laying.

A key issue illustrated by this example is the insight provided by the identification process. Insight and understanding are what motivate and drive the process.

Many analysts prefer to look at source–response–secondary issue chains within each activity on a chain basis. However, there is some merit in taking the steps, in order, for the project as a whole.

Approaches to identification

Identification of sources and responses can be an individual activity or involve other people in a variety of ways, including: interviewing individuals, interviewing groups, or various group processes such as brainstorming and decision conferencing. A key concern is to stimulate imaginative thinking and draw on the experiences of different individuals.

An obvious, simple approach is what might be called 'pondering', involving a single person with a 'clean sheet of paper and a pencil' (or the computer-based equivalent) to identify sources or responses. This is the most basic approach possible. It may serve as a default option if other approaches are not feasible or suitable. While simple and potentially limited, pondering should not be dismissed or usurped too readily as a starting point. Most experienced risk analysts start with it intuitively.

A straightforward ponder approach to the identify phase in a first pass can be useful: to guide a second pass back through the focus phase and to provide a basis for further passes through the identify phase. We rely on it explicitly as part of the ongoing focus phase of the SHAMPU process and the subsequent structure phase. Its explicit use before involving other people or undertaking a systematic review of available documentation can be very effective for a number of reasons. For example, it can help to kick off an interview process by providing examples of the level of issue aggregation/disaggregation of interest and stimulating other thoughts. The effectiveness of pondering can be enhanced by simple techniques such as prompt lists or identification frameworks. For example, an analyst could consider in turn each of the detailed activities making up each of the project activities consolidated for risk management purposes and ask the question 'what are the uncertainties associated with this component activity?'

Alternatively, techniques that are more resource-intensive could be applied from the outset, or applied to selected areas where earlier passes suggest the additional resource commitment would be worthwhile. Choosing between alternative identification techniques is a question of trading off different levels of analysis costs against effectiveness, a judgment that has to be made in relation to the importance of the uncertainty at all levels. It may require very different approaches in different areas. The most effective approach usually involves successive passes through the whole process. Early passes are used to distinguish between those areas that warrant the most effective process available and those that do not, and later passes return to apply more effort where this appears to be warranted.

Harnessing creativity and experience

The use of formal procedures to systematically capture personal experience can be very effective in identifying issues and possible responses. However, it is important that the experiences of a wide range of personnel are sought, particularly early on in the identify phase, to ensure a comprehensive set of issues are identified. Individual project managers may not have sufficient breadth of experience to provide this comprehensive view. Pooling of experience needs to include not only project managers, but specialists concerned with all aspects of projects, including, for example, designers, user representatives, engineers, lawyers, financial personnel, and managers responsible for administration, sales, personnel, logistics, and so on. Even with input provided from a variety of sources, the quality of what is obtained depends heavily on the ability of individuals to recall events accurately, without selectivity. Some issues may not be identified, because they were effectively managed in the past and are not so readily brought to mind.

An obvious limitation of identification based on experience is that such experience may not be entirely applicable to future projects. In particular, it may be of limited value in respect of changing project environments and novel aspects of future projects. 'The real sources of risk are the one's you can't identify' is a common view, recognizing that the 'unknown' can have a far greater effect on projects than all of the anticipated sources of uncertainty. For example, Hall (1975) cites examples of firms that were taken by surprise by substantial environmental changes: a mining company's assets seized by a foreign government and the rapid rise in oil prices in the early 1970s. These are perhaps examples of issues a project manager should be able to regard as 'external' to the project (as discussed in Chapter 6) and indicate a failure to identify and manage 'external' issues rather than a failure to identify and manage 'internal' issues. Although we may wish to place responsibility for 'external' issues higher in the organizational hierarchy than the project manager, the identify phase still needs to identify both 'external' and 'internal' issues.

'Thinking the unthinkable' calls for creativity and imagination. One of the best-known techniques for fostering creativity is brainstorming, which is used to improve problem analysis by providing more possible solutions and unusual approaches to a problem. The process typically involves a group of six to twelve individuals with a variety of backgrounds in order to facilitate the analysis of a problem from different points of view. In a typical brainstorming session the emphasis is on generating a large number of ideas. In problem-solving situations it is hoped that this will increase the chances of obtaining an excellent idea. In the initial ideas generation session, wild ideas are encouraged on the basis that ideas are easier to modify than to originate, and participants are encouraged to utilize the ideas of others to develop additional ideas. Throughout this process judgement of ideas is withheld. Ideas generated are criticized and evaluated in a later stage. Large problems may need to be made more manageable by breaking them into smaller parts, and samples should be available if products are being discussed (Whiting, 1958). There are important pitfalls to overcome (Furnham, 2000), but brainstorming is a valuable and widely used approach.

A less well-known but potentially significant technique is synectics, developed by Gordon (1956, 1968). A synectics team consists of a carefully selected group of individuals best equipped, intellectually and psychologically, to deal with problems unique to their organization. After selection, members are assigned to the synectics team on a full-time basis to solve problems for the entire organization (Crosby, 1968). The synectics process involves two steps. The first step is 'making the strange familiar'. This requires that a problem and its implications be understood. The second step is 'making the familiar strange'. This involves distorting, inverting, and transposing the problem in an attempt to view the problem from an unfamiliar perspective.

In the context of issue identification, creativity techniques such as brainstorming and synectics may be too creative. So many potential issues may be identified that the project team becomes overwhelmed with the number of issues to consider. Nevertheless, certain features of these approaches are attractive for issue identification purposes, including: the involvement of individuals with a variety of backgrounds, withholding judgement about identified issues, utilizing the thoughts of others, and attempting to view situations from an unfamiliar perspective.

More recently a number of 'decision-conferencing' techniques have been developed (e.g., see Finlay and Marples, 1991; Marples and Riddle, 1992; Dennison and Morgan, 1994). Decision-conferencing techniques are designed to improve the efficiency and effectiveness of group processes involving the exploration of problems and decision-making situations. Typically decision-conferencing techniques involve a facilitator and real-time computer support operated by one or more analysts. The facilitator manages the group's deliberations, guiding discussion in appropriate directions as necessary. Computer support may be used to help the group develop an understanding of the different aspects of the problem being addressed and to document the proceedings. For example, Williams et al. (1995a) describe the development of a cognitive map during a decision-conferencing process that was used to elicit an enhanced, shared understanding among the project management team of the reasons for project cost overruns.

Checklists and prompt lists

It is important in the search for issues and possible responses not to unduly constrain the process if available experience and expertise is to be fully exploited. We explicitly advise against the use of highly structured techniques, such as questionnaires that can straitjacket respondents, and strongly caution against over-reliance on checklists to drive the identification of sources and responses. Given the popular appeal of checklists, this advice warrants some explanation.

A simple, 'checklist' approach to source identification is often taken on the grounds that a 'quick and dirty' approach can yield substantial benefits despite its conceptual shortcomings. The checklist approach typically takes a view of project uncertainty that is very simple. The approach is illustrated in Table 7.4, which shows a typical list of broad headings under which individual, more specific sources might be identified. Sources are presumed to be independent and are presented in a standard list. This list may be very extensive and cover a variety of categories. It may be extended as risk management experience accumulates over time.

Checklist approaches can be very effective in focusing attention on managing sources of uncertainty, provided they are supported by appropriate administra-

Table 7.4—The checklist approach

source of uncertainty	impact	likelihood	exposure
definition of project			
concept and design			
financing arrangements			
logistics			
local conditions			
resource estimates			
industrial relations			
communications			
project organization			

tive procedures. For example, a corporate risk manager or risk analysis team may operate an internal audit function using the checklist as a basis for interrogating project managers at key stages in the life cycle of projects. More-detailed documentation related to individual sources and progress in managing them may accompany the checklist, as considered necessary.

Selection of the sources to be included on a checklist is usually based on experience. An initial list may be drawn up by a small group of experienced project managers, with a view to augmenting the list in the light of new experiences. Even without the help of creativity techniques, some checklists, developed and added to over several years, can become very intimidating, particularly to new members of project teams. Worse still, the length of some checklists may actively discourage further selective analysis of key sources.

There is no doubt that the checklist approach is a convenient and relatively simple way of focusing attention on project risk management. However, the checklist approach has a number of potentially serious shortcomings, as follows:

1. important interdependencies between sources are not readily highlighted;
2. a list, particularly a long one, provides limited guidance on the relative importance of individual sources;
3. individual entries may encompass a number of important, separate sources implicitly;
4. sources not on the list are likely to be ignored;
5. the list of sources may be more appropriate for some projects than others;
6. individual sources may be described in insufficient detail to avoid ambiguity and varying interpretations;

7. a checklist presents an overly simplistic view of the potential effects of individual sources;
8. a checklist does not encourage the development of a more sophisticated
attitude to assessing and quantifying uncertainty.

The main problem is that a checklist does not offer a sufficiently structured
examination of sources from which to discover key sources in a cost-effective
manner. In our view, if any kind of 'checklist' is used it should be referred to as a
'prompt list' and used in that spirit as a catalyst and stimulant, not as a definitive
statement of possibilities.

Uncertainty at deeper levels and alternative models

As noted in Chapter 6, an important aspect of the SHAMPU focus phase is a top-
down appreciation of uncertainty, to determine where the limits of the project
manager's responsibilities for managing project-related uncertainty lie and to size
the big uncertainty areas, as a basis for RMP design. This involves identifying
which sources are 'internal' to the project and therefore the responsibility of the
project manager, and which are 'external' and therefore the responsibility of
higher-level management. It also involves a first-pass, top-down view of internal
project uncertainty, quantifying this in terms of cost, revenue, and duration as
appropriate.

It is important to appreciate the three separate roles this kind of top-down
perspective can provide. It provides a background initial view of uncertainty
from a senior management perspective. It provides a basis for designing a
bottom-up, detailed RMP process. And it provides a consistency check against
a bottom-up analysis. Top-down and bottom-up analyses should confirm each
other and adjustment to one or both pursued until they do.

In order to allocate analysis effort efficiently and effectively, the bottom-up
RMP proper as described in Chapters 5 to 13 needs to start at a reasonably
simple level on the first pass and facilitate deeper (lower-level) subsequent analysis on later passes, wherever this is most effective (i.e., the level of 'the bottom'
needs to be moved down selectively as successive iterations unfold). Further, it is
important to appreciate that the PERT*/Generalized PERT/GERT*/SCERT model
set that underlies the structure of this analysis in a *whichway* dimension, and
comparable structures for other Ws, may be complemented or replaced in some
areas by alternative frameworks that better capture the structure of issues. As we

*PERT = Program Evaluation and Review Technique; GERT = Graphical Evaluation and
Review Technique

go deeper, dependencies become more and more important and a switch to other *W*s can require major model structure changes. For example, the use of a systems dynamics model structure to capture positive and negative feedback loops can prove useful in some circumstances (Williams et al., 1995a, b).

Even if the structure remains the same, further decomposition of categories of uncertainty can be undertaken in subsequent iterations through the steps in Figure 7.1. One key consideration is ensuring that deeper levels of uncertainty are identified whenever appropriate, as distinct from more detail at the same level. Another key issue is understanding the issues identified well enough to identify responses in an effective manner. Consider an example, described in more detail elsewhere (Chapman, 1988), which illustrates one way of considering uncertainty at different levels.

Example 7.9   Exploring the threat to submarine pipelines from 'ice scour'

A Beaufort Sea oil project involved oil production on artificial islands. The oil would be sent through pipes to the shore in a sea area known for very deep ice scours in the ocean bed. These deep scours would threaten a pipeline even if it were buried 3 or 4 m beneath the sea bed, many times deeper than conventional pipe burying. The key criterion, level-one, primary source of uncertainty Chapman was asked to address (by the project manager) was 'ice scour damage' to the pipeline. He addressed this question in terms of a second level of uncertainty involving two components to the question 'what was the chance of ice scour damage?':

- What was the chance ice would strike the pipeline?
- What was the chance that an ice strike would seriously damage the pipeline?

Chapman was also asked to take the second of these questions to deeper levels by the company ice scour experts, addressing the questions:

- What was the uncertainty in their data, with a view to assessing what type of additional data would be most useful (e.g., more seasons or a wider area within a season)?
- What was the uncertainty in the statistical model used to estimate the likelihood of scours at different depths?

Further deeper levels could be associated with the alternative mechanisms associated with generating scour (ice heave during freezing versus grounded ice during thaws), and so on.

Issue identification fit for the purpose?

Figure 7.1 shows the identify phase terminating once the identification of issues is 'fit for the purpose'. It can be very difficult to decide when this point has been reached. On the first pass it should be anticipated that there will be a return to the identify phase from later phases in the RMP as insights and issues from analysis emerge. On a first pass it is appropriate to aim for a higher-level overview than is likely to be necessary in later passes, to avoid detailed analysis, which would later prove wasted. This principle should be followed on subsequent passes too, but there is always a risk that further iterations do not happen. Further, inefficiencies associated with too many iterations to get to a given level of analysis in a given area may add to the cost of analysis significantly, depending on how iterations are managed. This reinforces the case for making the identify phase as complete as possible before proceeding to the next phase. If sources, and responses, and associated secondary issues (response chains) are not properly understood, any subsequent risk management can be a complete waste of resources. That said, time management pressures and the availability of key people may require getting on with some of the next phase while the identify phase is still in progress. Delays associated with an incomplete define phase can aggravate this difficulty. Regarding an RMP as a project in its own right, this is 'fast-tracking' in a fairly extreme form, rather like starting to put up a building before the foundations are fully in place. Any attempt to 'fast-track' the RMP needs to be managed with great care.

8 Structure the issues

... for want of a nail the shoe was lost; for want of a shoe the horse was lost; and for want of a horse the rider was lost.—Benjamin Franklin (1758)

Introduction

All the earlier phases in the SHAMPU (Shape, Harness, and Manage Project Uncertainty) process necessarily involve some structuring of identified issues. The structure phase is concerned with reviewing and extending this earlier structuring. The objective is to improve understanding of the relative importance of different sources given identified responses, to explore the interactions between issues, and to test the assumptions implicit or explicit in all earlier steps. This can lead to refinement of existing responses and prompt the development of new, more effective responses. It can also lead to new models or analyses.

In general, we want the structure used to be as simple as possible, but not misleadingly so. The structure phase involves testing the simplifying assumptions and developing a more complex structure when necessary. Failure to do so can render project risk management dangerously misleading. For example, assuming a large number of sources are independent will allow their individual effects to tend to cancel out with respect to the overall effect, on a 'swings-and-roundabouts' basis. If, in practice, they are positively correlated (things tend to go well or badly at the same time), this cancelling effect will be significantly reduced, and such circumstances need to be appreciated. Failure to structure can also lead to lost opportunities. For example, some responses to particular sources operate in practice as general responses in that they can deal with whole sets of sources, possibly all sources up to that point in a project, including sources that have not been identified. It is important to recognize the opportunities provided by such general responses.

Structuring involves four specific tasks:

1. *Develop orderings*—this involves developing an ordering of sources and associated responses for several purposes, including priorities for project and process planning, and for expository (presentation) purposes. In addition, this task involves developing a priority ordering of responses that takes effects into account, including secondary issues.
2. *Explore interactions*—this involves reviewing and exploring possible interdependencies or links between project activities, other *W*s, sources, and

responses, and seeking to understand the reasons for these interdependencies.

3. *Refine classifications*—this involves the review and development (where appropriate) of existing issue classifications, in the sense that a 'new' response may be defined because the understanding associated with an 'old' response may be refined and in the sense that a new classification structure may be introduced (e.g., distinguishing between specific and general responses).

4. *Other selective restructuring*—insights derived from the above may lead to revisions to precedence relationships for activities assumed in the define phase and comparable relationship adjustments in terms of the other *W*s.

Most risk management process (RMP) frameworks do not promote an explicit, separate, stand-alone structure phase. Some traditional modelling approaches, such as basic PERT (Program Evaluation and Review Technique), may seem to not need a separate structure phase because the approach used inherently assumes a particular, simple, standardized structure. However, even in this case testing the way the standard structure is implemented can be useful. A conventional management science approach to the use of any model-based approach requires such a step, usually referred to in terms like 'test the model'. A variety of techniques have been developed by a number of individuals and organizations that are directly relevant to structuring in a SHAMPU context. This chapter attempts to integrate these considerations in a five-step process, as shown in Figure 8.1. Each of these steps may involve all four of the above specific tasks, as well as the four tasks of document, verify, assess, and report that are common to all SHAMPU phases. Figure 8.1 portrays the process in a simplified form, consistent with Figures 5.1, 6.1, and 7.1.

This five-step process is more detailed than any other implicit or explicit project risk management structuring process we are aware of, and we hope it offers some useful new insights. The approach to the first four steps is comparable with the 'ponder' approach associated with a first pass through the identify phase, prior to considering alternative approaches. It is the sort of approach a single analyst could take, and should use, as a check on any specific diagramming techniques adopted in the fifth step.

Ponder the activities and associated issues

Chapter 5 indicated the need for a summary-level project activity structure represented by an activity-on-node (precedence) diagram and a Gantt chart. Part of the purpose of 'ponder the activities and associated issues' is to ensure that no important sources of precedence flexibility have been overlooked and that the constraints on precedence flexibility are clearly defined where they are important. A simple, direct approach to this task is to question each and every

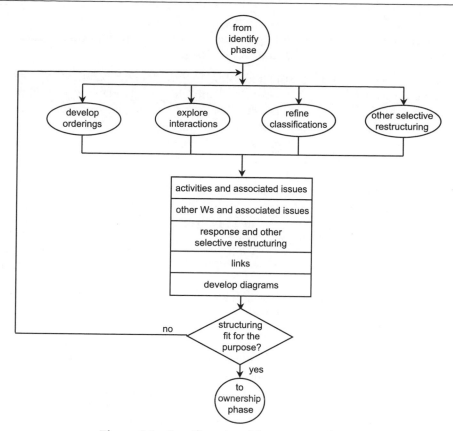

Figure 8.1—Specific tasks of the structure phase

precedence assumption, to make sure that no potentially significant assumptions of convenience are treated as inflexible imperatives. Example 5.6 illustrates the potential value in considering this explicitly: a precedence sequence was assumed so that the same resources could be used, but the rationale for the precedence relationship was not documented.

Part of the rationale for the top-down uncertainty appreciation of Chapter 6 is to clarify the difference between internal risks owned by the project and external risks owned by the corporate management team or some other party. This, together with subsequent source–response analysis, has to be used to clarify which aspects of the project are relevant for risk management purposes. Important judgements about discarding or acquiring aspects of project responsibility may be necessary somewhere in the overall process. This step is concerned with ensuring that they are not overlooked. Important links may drive these decisions, as illustrated by the following example.

Example 8.1   A close linkage between regulation, technical, and construction issues

The engineering and construction of a major pipeline planned to take Arctic oil to markets in the USA was clearly the project manager's responsibility, but he preferred to assume that associated regulation issues were 'external' (corporate) issues. However, preliminary risk analysis of the permissions process, using lawyers experienced in such processes, indicated that regulatory uncertainty was a major source of project uncertainty, and management of this uncertainty could not be effective if it was treated separately from the management of technical and construction issues. Consequently, the project was redefined to recognize the need for this integrated treatment, and the regulatory risk lawyers became key players in the project risk management team.

When clarifying project boundaries, it is often useful to recognize pervasive activities, sometimes associated with pervasive sources of uncertainty. For an environmentally sensitive project, 'maintain public confidence' may be such an activity, linked to one or more specific permission process activities, but also linked to other specific corporate activities within and beyond the project. It may be very important to recognize such pervasive activities formally, in order to ensure basic things get done to avoid the obvious associated threats.

A further aspect of this step is making sure all activity definitions correspond to a common date for the 'snapshot' that the RMP will provide. This is a change control aspect of the RMP (as distinct from the project). However, addressing change control for the RMP may serve as a reminder to ensure all necessary project change control processes are in place, as part of the risk assessment of the project management process. This illustrates the cross-checking that an RMP can stimulate. Having captured one new important idea or link, the instinctive question that should be asked is 'does this apply anywhere else?'

A goal of this step is a documented structure for the activities that reflect interactions with all other aspects of the analysis and portray the project *which-way* in terms that are both effective and efficient. Some of the interactions will be clarified later in the structure phase, as part of the iterative nature of this phase, but drawing together all the interactions and their effects that were identified earlier in the SHAMPU is a sensible part of this first step.

In the define phase, a key skill is the ability to choose an activity structure that is effective, but simple. This skill is tested in the structure phase. A similar issue arises when identifying source and response categories. For example, if two important sources both warrant the same response it may be sensible to aggregate them, while if different responses are involved separation is important. One way to address this is to formally identify some sources as 'collectable', to indicate they need to be collected together into a pool of the 'productivity variations' variety, leaving a relatively small residual of sources treated separately. Anticipation of appropriate choices in the identify phase is a key skill, illustrated by the wet buckle and dry buckle distinctions in Example 7.1.

The basic rules of thumb for collective/separate treatment at this stage in the process on a first pass are:

1. put all significant sources into the separate category if their responses are unique, but consider treating significant sources that have a common response as a single source;
2. put all small-effect sources with similar or common responses into the collectable category;
3. consider all intermediate cases on their individual merits, in terms of the value of insights expected from separate treatment versus the cost/effort/time required.

Statistical dependence is one of the issues that can make judgements related to the third category complex. Any difficult decisions are best deferred until quantification takes place, on a later pass.

There is a natural tendency simply to omit recording some sources altogether in the identify phase because they are immediately considered to be of a minor nature. The merit in not doing so, leaving such judgements until now, is to ensure that:

1. there is a complete audit trail, to protect organizations and careers should such sources prove important and questions are asked about their identification;
2. apparently minor issues that do not have an effective response are less likely to be overlooked;
3. prior to any estimation effort, sources are given an effective and efficient estimation structure, with separate treatment of sources that merit such treatment and collective treatment of those that do not;
4. the nature of the sources treated collectively is clarified, with a rich range of examples, which makes underestimation of the effect of such sources less likely.

Ponder the other *W*s and associated issues

Analogous issues may need to be dealt with for other project *W*s besides the *whichway*, and some basic structural linkages between the *W*s usually require attention. Consider some illustrations.

A Gantt chart, defined by the precedence relationships between activities and base estimates for activity durations, provides a base estimate of the overall project *when*. It may be useful to ensure that formal links between Gantt charts and activity-on-node network diagrams are in place in terms of a joint computer-based model at this stage. This allows rapid assessment of the effect of a change in the *whichway* on the *when*, and vice versa.

Project resource usage can be linked to Gantt charts via standard resource-planning models. If resource usage is a potential area of restriction, it may be worth using these models to explore just how much flexibility is available. In the limit, some projects are resource-driven and should be managed in a manner that reflects this.

Project direct and indirect costs can be linked to Gantt charts via resource usage and cost, or directly via time–cost functions. These can be used to explore the flexibility associated with the project *when*, in overall project terms, and in relation to specific activities. The possible use of such models was alluded to in Chapter 7. At this stage ensuring such a model is not required if it is not already in place becomes an issue.

It may be useful to recognize formal links between project *whichway/when/ wherewithal* issues and the project *what*. For example, in a generalized PERT (Program Evaluation and Review Technique) model framework decision trees can be used to embed design change decisions into a base plan network, using what are called 'decision nodes' as well as precedence nodes. For example, if a test on a high-risk component is successful the project proceeds using it, but if the test fails an alternative approach is adopted.

Develop responses and other selective restructuring

Responses require development in the structure phase for much the same reasons as the project's six *W*s and associated sources do. Two aspects of this development are worth highlighting:

1. distinguishing between specific and general responses;
2. ordering specific and general responses.

Distinguish between specific and general responses

Some responses are specific to particular sources. For example, in relation to a pipeline buckle, as discussed earlier in Example 7.6, 'repair' or 'abandon and start again' are feasible specific responses. Other responses may be identified in the context of a particular source, but serve as general responses in the sense that they offer a solution to a wide range of sources. This aspect of this step involves a careful and systematic search for all general responses. As a simple, practical matter, all project managers should try to make sure they have at least one general response available to deal with combinations of sources, including sources they may not have been able to identify. Consider a further extension of Example 7.6.

> ### Example 8.2   Use of a second lay barge as a general response
>
> It was recognized that the delay associated with a pipe buckle could be recovered by using a second lay barge working from the other end, with a submarine connection to join the two parts of the pipeline, provided an option on a second barge was in place. This response would also recover time lost due to bad weather, equipment failures, a delayed start to pipe laying, and a wide range of other difficulties, including some that may not have been identified in the first place.
>
> Planning to lay pipe from both ends using two barges was not a cost-effective base plan, nor was it a cost-effective response to buckles in isolation. However, being able to use a second barge in this way as a contingency plan provided a very powerful way to buy back lost time resulting from earlier delays, triggered by a wide range of identified sources, and was a source of comfort in relation to unidentified sources. This made the purchase of an option on the use of a second barge in case of need a particularly important issue. If this powerful general response was not available when needed because the importance of the option was not recognized earlier, a major failure of the proactive RMP would have occurred.

Example 1.2, concerned with the implications of a take-or-pay gas contract for a gas turbine electricity-generating project, provides a further illustration of the important role of this step in the process. Using standard British Gas supplies for testing purposes was a viable response to possible delay caused by a wide range of factors, including those not identified. The key here lies in being aware of any particularly useful general responses and ensuring that they can be implemented if necessary, if it is risk efficient to do so.

General responses can be viewed as a source of flexibility, and building in flexibility is a key generic response to risk, which deserves attention from several perspectives.

Order specific and general responses

It is useful to identify a preliminary ordering of responses in a preferred sequence in terms of which response is the most effective first choice, if that fails what is the next best choice, and so on. Ordering of responses may be useful for each set of specific responses associated with particular sources and for each set of general responses associated with particular activities. While comparable with the ordering of activities in precedence terms to some extent, ordering of responses is a rather different process, with no prior formal analysis to provide its basis. In early iterations the judgements may be purely intuitive. Later on in the process analysis can be used to test these intuitions.

Examine links

Examination of links involves a systematic search for dependencies between sources, responses, and the six *W*s of the project.One aspect of link identification involves reassessing all specific and pervasive sources in the light of preferred responses and secondary issues. The basic approach is to ask, for each source, the question: '*Could this source initiate problems in any directly or indirectly related response, base activity, or other project W?* Another aspect of link identification is to ask, for all identified responses that are reasonably likely to be implemented, the question: '*if this response is implemented will it affect other activities, responses, or sources?*' One product of this search will be the identification of responses that are mutually exclusive or incompatible, or that affect other activities in an adverse manner. Alternatively, economies of scale or synergies between possible responses may be identified that offer opportunities for further improvements in project performance.

Ensuring any pervasive sources have been identified as pervasive is an essential starting point, comparable with, and linked to, the search for pervasive activities and general responses. Pervasive sources may be sources that operate as underlying causal factors for several different 'level-one' sources or sources that impact on a number of different activities or responses.

Example 8.3   Weather as a pervasive source

When considering pipe laying in the North Sea in the mid-1970s, weather was a major source of uncertainty in terms of its direct impact on the ability to operate equipment. A 3-m laying barge was a barge deemed capable of working in wave conditions up to a nominal 3 m maximum, so weather in terms of wave height was a direct source of uncertainty in relation to pipe-laying performance.

In addition to this direct effect, bad weather greatly increased the chance of a buckle, and the probability of a buckle increased significantly as the amount of work in the 'shoulder season' (early spring or late autumn) increased because of the weather implications. It was important to recognize and model this effect.

Often dependence between different sources can be identified in causal terms. Sometimes the relationship is not clearly definable in these terms and may be best described in terms of statistical dependence (see Chapter 11). For example, preliminary 'macro'-level assessments of the relationship between capital cost items and direct cost rates associated with North Sea projects suggested an average of about 70 to 80% dependence (equivalent to a coefficient of correlation of 0.7 to 0.8 approximately—dependence measures and approaches to dependence are discussed in Chapter 11). This level of dependence was driven by the prevailing level of construction activity and other specific market pressures as well as more general economic conditions. Attempts to describe this dependence in causal terms were not fruitful, in the sense that too many different factors were clearly driving a similar joint movement to make individual identification and modelling of the factors worthwhile. However, it became clear that it was essential to model this statistical dependence to avoid bias, which otherwise made cost risk estimates misleading to a dangerous degree.

Statistical or causal dependencies can also be generated by responses. For example, in a construction project based on the use of two cranes, if one crane should fail and the response is to press on using only one crane, a significant increase in use may be required from the surviving crane, possibly increasing its failure probability. In the limit, such dependencies can cause a cascade or domino effect. Reliability engineers are familiar with the need to understand and model such effects, but many project managers are not.

It may be important to address dependence very carefully. Failure to do so, as in using a basic PERT model and assuming independence that does not exist, can be dangerously misleading as well as a complete waste of time. For example, in the context of a basic PERT network, with activity A followed by activity B, the durations of activities A and B may be positively dependent. If A takes longer than expected, B may also take longer than expected. This can arise because the sources for A and B are common or related. Causal relationships underlying this dependence might include:

1. the same contractor is employed for both activities, who if incompetent (or particularly good) on activity A will be the same for activity B;
2. the same equipment is used for both;
3. the same labour force is used for both;
4. the same optimistic (or pessimistic) estimator provided estimates for both activity duration distributions.

An important form of dependency is knock-on or 'ripple' effects. In the simple example above, when things go wrong in activity A the cost of A goes up and the delays impact on B. The cost of B then increases as a consequence of contingency responses to stay on target. As a consequence of contingency responses, which induce negative time dependence, the positive statistical dependence between the durations of A and B tends to disappear from view.

However, the negative dependence introduced into the activity duration relationships by contingency planning induces strong, positive dependence between associated costs. If *A* costs more than expected, *B* tends to cost very much more than expected, because of the need to keep the project on target, quite apart from other market-driven sources of dependence. Put another way, cost and duration modelling of uncertainty that does not explicitly consider contingency planning tends to estimate time uncertainty erroneously (usually optimistically) and fails to structure or explain it and tends grossly to underestimate direct cost uncertainty. Considering the impact of contingency planning will clarify apparent time uncertainty and increase apparent direct cost uncertainty.

Common causes of knock-on effects are design changes and delays, which not only have a direct impact but also cause ripple effects termed 'delay and disruption'. Often direct consequences can be assessed fairly readily in terms such as the number of man-hours required to make a change in design drawings and the man-hours needed to implement the immediate change in the project works. Ripple effects are more difficult to assess and may involve 'snowballing' effects such as altered work sequences, conflicting facility and manpower requirements, skill dilution, undetected work errors, and so on.

Example 8.4 Widening fire doors causes substantial delays

In 1991 apparently small changes in the design of fire doors on Channel Tunnel rolling stock was expected to lead to a delay of up to six months in providing a full service for car and coach passengers, substantially reducing expected revenue for Eurotunnel, operators of the tunnel. The problem was caused by the insistence of British and French authorities that the width of the fire doors separating the double-deck car shuttles should be widened from 28 to 32 inches (Taylor, 1991).

Example 8.5 A delay-and-disruption claim

Cooper (1980) has described how a computer simulation based on influence diagrams was used to resolve a $500 million shipbuilder claim against the US Navy. By using the simulation to diagnose the causes of cost and schedule overruns on two multibillion dollar shipbuilding programmes, Ingalls Shipbuilding (a division of Litton Industries Inc.) quantified the costs of disruption stemming from US Navy-responsible delays and design changes. In the settlement reached in June 1978, Ingalls received a net increase in income from the US Navy of $447 million. It was the first time the US Navy had given such a substantial consideration to a delay-and-disruption-claim.

The need to appreciate fully the implications of knock-on effects in a project is clear, especially for activities late in an overall project sequence that may be considerably delayed, with possible contractual implications of great importance. As Example 8.5 illustrates, this process of appreciation can be greatly facilitated by appropriate diagramming of activity–source–response structures and their interdependencies.

Develop diagrams

The use of a range of diagrams is advantageous throughout the structure phase to document and help develop insights in the structuring process. Precedence networks and Gantt charts are key documents because they capture key aspects of the project base plan. However, other diagrams are important in terms of capturing a range of wider considerations. For example, if a formal model is used to link Gantt charts to resource usage and associated resource constraints, these issues will require appropriate diagrams. If direct/indirect cost models are used, other standard diagrams will be required. Of particular concern here is diagrams that summarize our understanding of source–response structures, and links between activities, sources, and responses.

Ensuring that the earlier steps in the structure phase result in a set of diagrams that summarize the classification, ordering issues, and then linking them is extremely important. Complexity is inherent in most projects, but it must be made manageable to deal with it effectively. A summary diagram structure, which all those who need to be involved can discuss as a basis for shared understanding, is very important. Organizations that have used such diagrams often stop doing so because they are difficult to construct, but start using them again because they realize these diagrams are difficult to produce precisely because they force a proper disciplined understanding, which is otherwise not achieved. One such diagram is the source–response diagram of Figure 8.2, which was initially developed for offshore oil projects and subsequently adopted by a range of organizations.

In principle, a numbering system of the kind described early in Chapter 7 (u, v, w, x, y, z designations) could be used to drive a computer-generated version of Figure 8.2. However, manual approaches, with computer graphics when appropriate, have been employed to date.

Example 8.6 Source–response diagrams for an offshore platform jacket

Figure 8.2 provides an illustration of source–response diagrams in the context of the fabrication of an offshore project jacket (the structure that

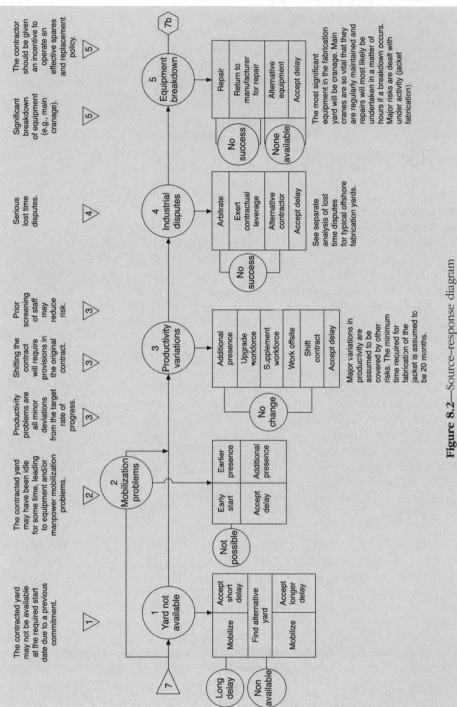

Figure 8.2—Source-response diagram

From Chapman et al. (1987), reproduced by permission of John Wiley & Sons

sits in the water to hold production and accommodation facilities)—this is the first section of a diagram that continues in the same vein for several pages. The '7' in the large triangle indicates this is the start of the diagram for activity 7 (jacket fabrication). The '7b' label at the end of the diagram's horizontal centre line indicates a continuation to a further page (diagram section), which will start with '7b' on the left-hand side.

Primary sources are represented by circles along the diagram's horizontal centre line and linked parallel lines. The first source (labelled 1) in a time-of-realization sense is 'yard not available', because another jacket is still under construction in the contracted yard (a dry dock construction area like a big shipyard), and our jacket has to await its completion. A close second in this time-of-realization sense (labelled 2) is 'mobilization problems': we can get access to the yard, but it has not been used for some time, so it will take time to get up to speed.

These two sources are mutually exclusive: we can have one or the other, but not both—this is why they appear in parallel. All the other sources are in series, indicating they can all occur, without implying additive or multi-plicative effects at this stage. Their sequence is nominal. Dependence relationships could be indicated on the diagram and lead to ordering sources, but independence is assumed with respect to those sources shown.

Links in this diagram are limited to links from earlier activities discussed in notes along the top of the diagram. Links could appear as arrows between sources and responses, with links out to other diagrams if appro-priate. Identification of all these links, dependence, and ordering issues is part of the structure phase steps identified earlier.

Responses are represented by boxes, ordered to reflect the preferred implementation sequence. Secondary sources are represented by circles at the side of the primary responses. For example, if the yard is not available, the preferred response is to 'mobilize' (get ready to start work, making temporary use of another site) and 'accept a short delay'. The secondary source here is a 'longer delay', which would lead to the second-ary response 'find an alternative yard'. The secondary source here is 'none available', at which point 'mobilize' and 'accept a longer delay' are the only remaining option.

These responses and secondary sources illustrate further the complexity of the generic types of response we may have to consider to capture the most effective response to uncertainty. They also make it clear why a diagram to capture the structure provided earlier is a very good test of understanding, which may lead to redefinitions in earlier steps.

The final source on the last page of the source–response diagram for each activity is a collector/dummy risk that represents residual uncertainty after specific responses. The ordered boxes that appear below this residual

uncertainty collector are the general responses. The importance of the
structuring process as a whole is highlighted by the need for this feature.
It also indicates that the residual uncertainty of real interest is the combined
effect of all individual sources (net of specific responses) less the effect of
general responses. This serves to emphasize further the importance of
structure.

Implicit in the identify phase is a very complex decision tree that will remain an
implicit, ill-understood 'bushy mess' unless the structure phase is pursued until
source–response diagrams like that of Figure 8.2 can be drawn. Completion of
such diagrams by risk analysts, and subsequent verification by all relevant
players on the project team, is a watershed in the overall RMP.

Fault trees and event trees

Two common approaches used in a system failure analysis context that underlie
the Figure 8.2 approach are fault tree analysis and event tree analysis. It can be
useful to adopt these approaches in their basic or standard forms as a preliminary
or an alternative to the use of source–response diagram formats like Figure 8.2. A
good classic reference is NUREG (1975).

Event tree analysis involves identifying a sequence of events that could follow
from the occurrence of particular source–response configurations and then representing the possible scenarios in a tree diagram where each branch represents an
alternative possibility.

In fault tree analysis the process is reversed, working backward from a particular event known as the top event, in an attempt to identify all possible
sequences of events giving rise to the top event.

Ishikawa or fish bone diagrams (Ishikawa, 1986) adopt a similar approach,
showing necessary inputs to a particular final position.

Influence diagrams

In event tree and fault tree analysis there is still the problem of ensuring
completeness in the set of possible failure modes included. A more versatile
representation of causes and effects can be achieved with influence diagrams,
as used in 'systems dynamics' (Forrester, 1958, 1961; Richardson and Pugh, 1981;
Senge, 1990) and 'cognitive mapping' (Eden, 1988). One advantage of influence
diagrams over tree diagrams is that much more complex interactions can be
shown, including feedback and feedforward loop effects.

Example 8.7   Cognitive mapping shows the knock-on effects of design changes

Williams et al. (1995a, b) describe the study of a large design-and-manufacturing engineering project, undertaken as part of a delay-and-disruption litigation. Design changes and delays in design approval would have caused delay to the project. In order to fulfil tight time constraints, management had to increase parallel development in the network logic, reducing delay but setting up feedback loops that markedly increased the total project spend. Cognitive mapping using specialist computer software called 'Graphics Cope' was used to elicit the relationships. The cognitive map contained some 760 concepts and 900 links. Over 90 positive feedback loops were identified, illustrating the complex dynamics of the real situation. Figure 8.3 summarizes some of the key feedback loops.

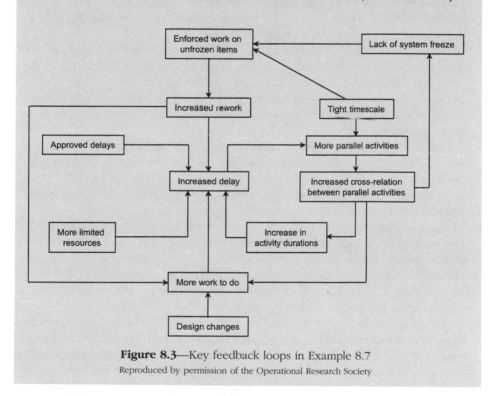

Figure 8.3—Key feedback loops in Example 8.7
Reproduced by permission of the Operational Research Society

The situation in Example 8.7 is similar to that described in Example 8.5. It is unfortunate that the very considerable benefits of constructing cognitive maps to explore source–response dependencies were sought *after* these projects got into serious difficulties, rather than *before*.

Influence diagrams such as Figure 8.3 are essentially a qualitative tool, although they can provide a starting point for quantitative, systems dynamics models (Rodrigues and Williams, 1998; Eden et al., 2000; Howick, 2003). They do not indicate the magnitudes or the timing of influence relationships that would be quantified in systems dynamics model simulations. Thus a link between two factors X and Y does not indicate the strength of the link: whether it is continuous or intermittent, or whether the impact on the influenced factors is immediate or delayed. Nevertheless, an influence diagram can be a useful aid to understanding a complex situation, particularly if effectively interpreted. It explores positive and negative feedback loops in a way Figure 8.2 does not accommodate directly, providing a very useful complementary or alternative technique. Diffenbach (1982) suggests a number of guidelines for interpreting influence diagrams:

1. *Isolated factors.* A factor not linked to any other factor suggests either that the isolated factor is not relevant to the depicted situation or that not all important links and factors have been identified.
2. *Influencing-only factors.* A factor that influences other factors but is not itself subject to influence from other factors prompts questions about overlooked links and factors that might influence this factor.
3. *Influenced-only factors.* A factor that does not influence any other factors prompts questions about overlooked links and factors by which this factor might influence.
4. *Secondary and higher-order consequences.* Chains of influence suggest possible secondary and higher-order consequences of a change in a given factor in the chain.
5. *Indirect influences of A on B.* Chains can reveal potentially significant indirect influences of one factor on another.
6. *Multiple influences of A on B.* One factor may influence another in more than one way. These multiple influences could be direct (by link) or indirect (by chain) and of the same or opposite sign.
7. *Self-regulated loops.* A chain with an odd number of negative links that cycles back to meet itself is a self-regulating, negative loop. Successive cycles of influences result in counteracting pressures.
8. *Vicious circles.* A chain with zero or an even number of negative links that cycles back to meet itself is a self-reinforcing, positive loop. Since it is unlikely that vicious circles will operate endlessly, unresisted by countervailing forces, one should look for one or more negative loops that are interrelated with the positive loop by means of a common factor.

The process of construction and interpretation of influence diagrams goes beyond identification of direct source–response and cause–effect relationships. It also assists in identifying potentially important links, such as the nature of source–response chains associated with vicious circles, or particular sources that influence many other sources either directly or indirectly. Increased understanding of cause–effect relationships can also prompt the formulation of additional responses.

More general soft systems models

The use of influence diagrams can be viewed as a special (reasonably 'hard') version of a range of 'soft' approaches usually referred to as soft systems, soft operational research, or other labels that span the two, like problem structuring methods (Rosenhead, 1989; Checkland and Scholes, 1990). All these ideas are directly relevant to the structure phase.

Structure fit for the purpose?

As with other phases of the SHAMPU process, the structure phase is itself an iterative process. In particular, we cannot assess the importance of some sources until we have identified responses and considered possible interactions between sources and responses. However, some prior assessment of the importance of identified sources is necessary to guide the initial structuring, to avoid too many or too few source and response categories.

The structure phase clearly links to all previous phases, because it is a form of robustness analysis associated with earlier phases, as well as ordering issues for subsequent phases. In particular, changes to the structure phase outputs may be triggered by later changes to identified sources and responses. Figure 4.1 limits the feedback loops assumed to two from the evaluate phase and one from the manage phase, but the impact of the obvious linkages here in terms of selectively revising earlier structuring is important. However, the structure phase should always be as complete as possible given the progress made in the identify phase before moving on to the ownership phase.

Conclusion

The structure phase as described here is a very important part of the SHAMPU process. It is about transforming the information generated earlier into a qualitative model of project uncertainty, ideally summarized in diagrams, with underlying computer-based models to handle changes where appropriate and feasible. The richer the information generated in the identify phase the greater the need for care in the structure phase to provide a sound basis for inferences to follow.

In the authors' experience some key points to bear in mind in the structure phase are:

1. independence, or lack of it, is one of the most important assumptions made in any modelling of uncertainty;
2. in a cost dimension high levels of dependence are endemic, and in an activity dimension important instances of dependence are endemic;
3. making inappropriate assumptions about dependence or avoiding quantification because of dependence are potentially dangerous cop-outs that may negate the whole process—it is the difficult bits that can be particularly important;
4. the most effective way to understand uncertainty dependence is to model it in causal terms;
5. 'statistical' dependence is best thought of as a causal dependence of several kinds that cannot be sorted out or that it is not cost-effective to sort out at this stage;
6. ensuring a simple but effective structure for sources and responses as well as activities is greatly facilitated by diagrams like Figure 8.2;
7. being prepared to experiment with different forms of diagram, like Figure 8.3, can greatly enhance the RMP as a whole.

9 Clarify ownership

It is an equal failing to trust everybody and to trust nobody.—18th century English proverb

Introduction

In principle, making sure that every source of uncertainty and all associated responses have a manager *and* an owner in financial terms (possibly different parties) is recognized as basic good practice. In practice, this worthy ambition is not often achieved. One obvious reason for this is a failure to identify issues early in the Project Life Cycle (PLC) that later prove to be a serious source of difficulties or a serious lost opportunity. Another is a failure to identify relationships between issues that prove to be important. These are fundamental failures in other phases of the Risk Management Process (RMP), not failures of the ownership phase *per se*. However, even if issues are duly identified and links between them appreciated, effective management of these issues requires appropriate and effective allocation of issues to those parties involved in a project. This is the focus of the ownership phase in the SHAMPU (Shape, Harness, and Manage Project Uncertainty) process.

Failures of risk management associated with the allocation of ownership of issues tend to arise because this activity is not recognized explicitly, or not given sufficient attention. Issue allocation always occurs in any situation where more than one party is responsible for the execution of a project. Just as roles and responsibilities are allocated to parties concerned, so too are uncertainty management issues associated with the enterprise. However, allocation of issues, and consequently risk, can take place by default and need not be explicit, intentional, or clearly articulated. The consequences of an allocation, particularly a default allocation, may not be fully appreciated, and the manner in which allocated issues are to be managed may be unclear, if they are managed at all.

This chapter attempts to provide a framework for efficient and effective issue allocation processes, in terms of an explicit ownership phase in the SHAMPU process. Locating the ownership phase after the structure phase of the SHAMPU process is appropriate because it is in some respects a particular kind of structuring. Locating the ownership phase before the estimate phase of the SHAMPU process is appropriate because some ownership issues need attention before starting the estimate phase, although some ownership phase tasks can be completed quite late in the SHAMPU process.

The ownership phase has three purposes:

1. to distinguish the sources and associated responses that the project client (owner or employer) is prepared to own and manage from those the client wants other parties (such as contractors) to own or manage;
2. to allocate responsibility for managing uncertainty owned by the client to named individuals;
3. to approve, if appropriate, ownership/management allocations controlled by other parties.

The first of these three purposes should be achieved before moving on to a first attempt at the estimate and evaluate phases of the SHAMPU process. Some organizations will consider this first purpose as a part of project strategy that the SHAMPU define phase should identify. Deferring achievement of the other purposes until later is usually appropriate, with the amount of effort expended on ownership issues increasing in subsequent passes through the SHAMPU process as indicated by Figure 4.2.

Ownership issues often have such great importance that it is very useful to treat this phase as a project in its own right, with attention given to the associated six Ws in the same way as the earlier focus phase. Indeed, ownership issues are so important and complex that they are considered in more detail in Chapter 16.

The deliverables provided by the ownership phase are clear allocations of ownership and management responsibility, efficiently and effectively defined, and legally enforceable as far as practicable. The tasks required to provide this deliverable may be very simple or extremely complex, depending on contract strategy. For expository purposes we assume no fixed corporate contracting policy. In these circumstances the ownership phase involves two specific tasks, which are the focus of two modes of analysis:

1. *Scope the contracting strategy*—this mode concentrates on issues such as what are the objectives of the contracting strategy (the *why*), which parties are being considered (the *who*), and what aspects of uncertainty and associated risk require allocation (the *what*). This mode culminates in a strategy for issue allocation.
2. *Plan/Replan the contracts*—this mode builds on the definition of the *what*, considers the details of the approach (the *whichway*), the instruments (the *wherewithal*), and the timing (the *when*). This mode transforms issue ownership strategy into operational form.

Figure 9.1 elaborates the structure of the ownership phase. It portrays starting the ownership phase in *scope the contracting strategy* mode. Each of the first three Ws is addressed in turn in the first three steps, followed by a switch to *plan/replan the contracts* mode for the last three Ws. A specific *assess* task initiates possible loops back to the first three steps, until the strategy is 'fit for the

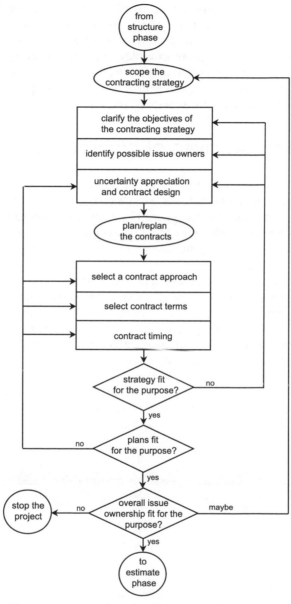

Figure 9.1—Specific tasks of the ownership phase

purpose'. This task is not shown immediately after the first three steps because of the difficulty in separating uncertainty appreciation and contract design issues at the levels of contracting strategy and contracting plan. A second specific *assess* task initiates loops back to the last four steps, until the contract plan is 'fit for the purpose'. A final specific *assess* task considers the more fundamental overall issue ownership, with stopping the project as an option.

Figure 9.1 is an idealization to capture and illustrate the spirit of the process, recognizing that in practice more complex processes may be effective. As in previous phases, recurring, common *document, verify, assess*, and *report* tasks are not shown, to keep the diagram simple, but they play an important contracting role, and it is important to remember the Part II perspective.

Clarify the objectives of contracting strategy

From a client's point of view, the fundamental reason for being concerned about who owns what sources is that this will influence how uncertainty is managed and whether it is managed in the client's best interest. This suggests that a client needs to consider explicitly who the uncertainty owners could be and make conscious decisions about how uncertainty and associated issues should be allocated to various parties.

A fundamental point is that the different parties involved in a project frequently have different perceptions of project uncertainty and associated issues, and have different abilities and motivations to manage these issues. As a consequence, they may wish to adopt different strategies for managing project uncertainty. One reason for this is that different parties typically have different knowledge and perceptions of the nature of sources. Another reason is that project parties are likely to have different objectives or at least different priorities and perceptions of performance objectives. Example 9.1 illustrates one common context in which these considerations are important. Chapter 16 discusses these problems and their management in more detail.

Example 9.1   Risk analysis in a competitive bidding context

Consider the nature of risk analysis carried out in three closely related but quite different contexts:

- risk analysis by the client prior to putting a contract out to competitive tender;
- risk analysis by a bidding contractor prior to submitting a tender;
- post-tender risk analysis by the winning contractor.

In each case the scope of the risk analysis undertaken will be influenced by the predominant concerns of the party undertaking the risk analysis and the information about uncertainty available.

Analysis by the client—Uncertainty is evaluated and the project design is developed to manage uncertainty in the client's best interests. Tender documentation and the contract may be drafted to allocate uncertainty to the contractor. However, even with the help of advisers, the client may not be in a position to assess many of the sources of uncertainty associated with the project. Such sources may be better assessed by potential contractors. Some of the key sources will be associated with contractor selection and contract terms.

Analysis by a bidding contractor—Risk analysis by each bidding contractor could be based on the client's risk analysis if it is provided in the tender documentation. The greater the detail provided by the client in relation to uncertainty that is to be borne in whole or in part by the contractor the less the contractor has to price for risk related to the contractor's uncertainty about what the project involves. Risk analysis here needs to evaluate not only the uncertainty about the tasks required to perform the work specified in the tender documents but also assess bids that give an appropriate balance between the risk of not getting the contract and the risk associated with profits and losses if the contract is obtained. Some of the key sources of uncertainty will be associated with client selection (addressing questions like 'is the client's business secure?') and contract terms.

Analysis by the winning contractor—Risk analysis by the winning contractor should be undertaken to reduce uncertainty and risk associated with the contractor's profits, to pursue risk efficiency and check the risk/expected profit balance. If the client has already undertaken such an analysis and provided it to all bidding contractors, the winning contractor can use it as a starting point. If the contractor has to start from scratch, two drawbacks are involved:

- The scope for modifications to the project specification and base plan will be less than would be the case during the client's risk analysis. This implies a less efficient project specification and base plan.
- The level of detail adopted by the contractor will be determined by the benefit to the contractor of more or less detail. Sources that involve costs that can be recovered from the client, and contingency plans associated with the contractor's possible bankruptcy, will not be relevant. This implies less efficient project specification, base, and contingency plans.

It may be that these two effects discourage contractors from undertaking risk analysis. They certainly strengthen the case for a client's risk analysis prior to the development of tender documentation. If the client chooses the wrong contractor, if the contractor chooses the wrong client, or if either agrees to inappropriate contract terms, both may have serious problems on their hands that require crisis management more than risk management.

As a first step in the ownership phase of the SHAMPU process, *clarify the objectives of the contracting strategy* is not usually about project-specific issues. The key principles are generic ones, and they are usually equally applicable to all projects undertaken by the organization. Nevertheless it is useful to distinguish this step to ensure that these principles are duly acknowledged by the appropriate personnel.

Identify possible issue owners

The second step in *scope the contracting strategy* involves identifying parties who could be expected to own some sources of project-related uncertainty and associated responses. An obvious starting point is the list of key players identified in the SHAMPU define phase. As noted in Chapter 5, this list includes agents of the client such as contractors and subcontractors, 'other stakeholders' such as parent organizations, regulatory bodies, competitors, and customers. Clearly not all of these parties are relevant for issue ownership purposes, although potential owners need not be confined to the client and agents of the client. Other potential issue owners might have been implicitly identified in the consideration of responses in a first cut of the SHAMPU identify phase. These might include particular groups and individuals within the client, contractor, and subcontractor organizations, or third parties (such as insurers).

Within the client's organization, it is clearly important to distinguish between 'the project' and 'the board'. Further subdivisions within the project are often important, in terms of project financing and the associated ownership of issues. For example, if the project is an Information Systems (IS) project undertaken by an external third party and managed by an internal IS group, for an internal client, issues associated with the external third party, the internal client, the IS group, and the board may need to be identified and managed separately.

In a given project, different divisions of labour and organizational arrangements may be possible, and the choice between these may be usefully driven by risk management considerations as well as the physical nature of the project works. For example, a large construction project that Chapman was associated with involved an RMP that included examining all the major components of the project in relation to their key sources and responses with a view to minimizing the number of issues that would require managing across contractor boundaries. The number of contractors and the division of work between them were designed to minimize problems with risk management during construction.

Example 9.2 illustrates the potential complexity of issue ownership when considering various forms of management contracting systems for construction projects. Because the parties in each system and the contractual arrangements between them are different, each system gives rise to somewhat different sources of uncertainty and allocations of issues, and each system varies in its ability to manage project risk efficiency and risk. Choice between the different systems is not clear-cut and depends on a variety of factors, including the nature of the project and performance criteria, the skills of the management contractor, and the role the client is willing to take during project execution. A detailed discussion of these issues is given in Curtis et al. (1991).

Example 9.2   Risk allocation in management contracting systems of procurement

Management contracting systems involve the employment by the client of an external management organization to co-ordinate the design and construction phases of the project and to control the construction work. The concept underlying management contracting systems is that the Management Contractor (MC) joins the client's team of professional advisers and devotes efforts unequivocally to pursuing the client's objectives. The MC is able to do this by being employed on a fee basis so that there is no clash of interest on the MC's part between looking after the client and protecting the MC's own earnings. The MC normally accepts no liability for the site works other than any detriment to the client that is attributable to the MC's negligence.

The MC is normally brought in at an early stage in the preconstruction period in order to contribute management and construction expertise to the design, and prepare a construction schedule linking works packages with design decisions. Competitive tenders are sought by the MC from construction contractors for specific packages of construction work. As the construction work is let in a succession of packages, each one can reflect the particular conditions and sources of uncertainty applicable to that part of the work. In this way the issues can be looked at separately and decisions made on the extent to which issues need to be incorporated in a work package contract.

Four types of management contracting system can be distinguished in the construction industry:

- construction management;
- management contracting;
- design and manage;
- design, manage, and construct.

The basic form of management contracting involves the MC directly employing works contractors to undertake all construction packages. The MC does none of the construction work, but exercises co-ordination, time, cost, and quality control over the work package contractors and provides facilities for their common use. The permanent works are constructed under a series of construction contracts placed by the MC after approval by the client.

A variation of this system that is more frequently used in North America is termed 'construction management'. It involves the MC performing the same co-ordination and control functions, but contracts for construction are formed between the client and the work package contractors. This arrangement gives the client more direct contractual involvement with the construction work, but can reduce the managerial impact of the MC.

Recognition of the importance of managing design has led to the emergence of a third variation, the 'design-and-manage' system. This system gives the management organization a specific responsibility to oversee the design work on behalf of the client. This responsibility is normally exercised in a purely professional manner and gives the management organization a seniority among the designers that ostensibly enables it to impose a stronger discipline.

The fourth kind of management contracting system, 'design, manage, and construct', places a degree of responsibility on the MC for the performance of the construction operations. It moves the MC away from the purely professional role that restricts the MC's liability to negligence in performing contractual duties. The additional liability can occur in two ways. First, the MC is allowed to take on some elements of the construction work using the MC's own workforce. Second, the MC is expected to accept some responsibility for achieving cost and time targets, and for meeting quality specifications.

Uncertainty appreciation and contract design

As noted in Chapter 6, an important part of scoping the RMP for a project is deciding what issues are 'internal' to the project and therefore the project manager's responsibility to manage, and which are 'external' to the project and therefore issues that the project manager is not expected to manage.

Usually ownership of an issue implies responsibility for the management of that issue as well as responsibility for bearing its consequences. However, it is often important to distinguish between responsibility for managing an issue and responsibility for bearing the consequences of the issue. In particular it may be desirable to allocate these responsibilities to different parties, recognizing that the party best able to manage an issue may not be the party best able to bear the consequences of that issue. Thus, while one party, perhaps a contractor, may be best placed to manage a source, it may not be appropriate or desirable for that party to bear all the associated financial consequences. The following example illustrates the nature of this question, which is explored in more detail in Chapter 16.

> ## Example 9.3 Ability to manage an issue and ability to bear the consequences
>
> An example of a source of uncertainty that raised this responsibility question occurred in the context of a late 1970s' analysis of a North Sea oil pipeline that had to cross three other existing pipelines. Given the way lay barges were positioned, with lots of anchors in front under considerable tension, the chance of damaging one (or more) of the existing pipelines was seen as significant. The consequences of one of the existing pipelines being fractured were very significant. Apart from the environmental impact and clean-up costs, and compensation required by the other pipeline owners, pipe-laying equipment would have to be diverted from the task in hand to sort out the damaged pipeline, which would involve the loss of a weather window and cost a season.
>
> This source of uncertainty provides a good example of a low to medium-probability issue with large impact that does not average out with other issues. Such issues either happen or they do not, with a major impact either way relative to the expected outcome. For example, assume a £200 million impact in this case with a 0.10 probability, resulting in an expected cost of £200 million × 0.10 = £20 million. If this issue had been quantified and rolled into the analysis used by the corporate board to set the budget for the project, the implicit effect would have been to give the project manager financial ownership of this issue with a budget of £20 million. If the issue was subsequently realized, this budget would not have sufficed and the project manager would have had to go back to the board for more money. If the issue was not subsequently realized, the project would have had £20 million to spend on other things that the board would not have appreciated. Whatever the outcome, it would not be appropriate for the project to bear the financial consequences of this kind of issue. Responsibility for this issue in financial terms had to be retained by the board, along with a portfolio of other similar issues associated with other projects.
>
> It was clearly important for the project team to accept responsibility for physically managing this issue, including developing procedures and plans to avoid the issue being realized and developing contingency plans should it happen. It might have been worth indicating to those responsible for avoiding the issue what sort of unpleasant futures might be forthcoming if the issue was realized. But there was no point in making the project financially responsible for it with an extra £20 million in the budget.

In addition to distinguishing between project management and board-level financial responsibilities, some organizations are moving toward distinguishing between issues owned financially by the project manager, issues owned by those at the sharp end of specific aspects of the project, and issues owned by a number of intermediate management levels, in the context of control budgets that recognize the target, expected value, and commitment distinctions discussed in Chapter 3. Control budgets and associated issue allocations in a hierarchical structure represent an interlocking set of organizational agreements, all of which can be viewed as 'contracts' for present purposes. External contracts and sub-contracts with other organizations extend this structure. It is important to define, and in some instances to design, this structure. Chapman and Ward (2002, chap. 6) consider these concerns in terms of internal and external contracts designed to manage good luck as well as bad luck, generalizing aspects of Goldratt's (1997) 'critical chain' perspective. This kind of analysis suggests that *uncertainty appreciation and contract design* should be a step that is an integral part of both contracting strategy and contract planning that is more detailed.

Select a contract approach

The *plan/replan the contracts* specific task involves considering how the con-tracting strategy is to be implemented, in terms of formal and informal contracts, first addressing the *select a contract approach* or *whichway* question to expand on the closely related *what* or *contract design question*.

The contract approach adopted is highly dependent on the parties involved in working on the project and the way in which project tasks have been divided and distributed between these parties. For example, the novelty and technical nature of a construction project may warrant the employment by the client of an architect, engineer, quantity surveyor, prime contractor, and a variety of subcontractors. The presence of these parties may imply clear allocation of particular issues to particular parties. A very different and perhaps simpler allocation strategy is implied for a client who opts for a 'turnkey' contract to procure a building, where the client has only to deal with a single prime contractor.

As noted in Chapter 7, in a client–contractor situation the client exerts influ-ence over the contractor primarily via conditions laid down in a contract between the two parties. The contract sets out what is to be produced, what the client will pay, how the client can assess and monitor what the contractor has done, and how things should proceed in the case of various contingent events. The contract may identify and allocate sources and responses explicitly, but very often par-ticular issues are not identified explicitly and allocation of issues is implicit in the nature and size of contract payment terms. In these cases, the consequences of such allocation may not be fully appreciated. In particular, the manner in which issues are to be managed may be unclear.

From a risk management perspective, it is very important to identify sources of uncertainty that are:

1. controllable by the contractor;
2. controllable by the client;
3. not controllable by either party.

Different payment arrangements should be adopted for each of these categories, implying different levels of issue sharing for each category, so that appropriate allocation and positive management of uncertainty in each category is encouraged where possible.

The acquisition of information about sources plays a key role in the ability of contractual parties to allocate and manage associated uncertainty. Given the potential conflict of contractual party objectives, a central question is the extent to which contractual parties can obtain mutual benefit by sharing issue-related information. A related question is how this information can be used to allocate issues on a rational basis and in a mutually beneficial way. Chapter 16 discusses this issue in more detail.

Select contract terms

The *whichway* and *wherewithal* in an ownership phase context can be associated with contract details, including budgets, fees, and penalties—the operational details that make internal or external contracts work.

This is one reason for the development of a wide range of 'standard' forms of contract that serve as familiar 'models' for the contracting process. For example, the Institute of Civil Engineers'' (ICE, 1995) *New Engineering Contract* (NEC) has been designed so that its implementation should contribute to rather than detract from the effectiveness of management of the project works. This is based on the proposition that foresighted, co-operative management of the interactions between the parties can shrink the risk (and risk inefficiency) inherent in construction work. The NEC main options offer six different basic allocations of issues between the 'employer' (client) and contractor, and whatever variations in strategy between different contracts within a project are adopted the majority of the procedures will be common to all contracts.

Internal contracting, and associated incentive and target-setting mechanisms, have not received the same attention, but the problems can be equally complex and equally important. Intelligent choices that reflect the circumstances can be crucial to effective and efficient allocation and subsequent management of issues. Chapman and Ward (2002, chap. 6) consider this question in some detail.

Determine the timing of issue transfer

'When should transfer of responsibility take place?' is an important basic question among a number of associated questions that need early consideration. Where project issues are ongoing, answering this question can substantially alter the allocation of issues between parties. Obvious examples include the length of warranties, or the determination of 'vesting' or handover dates. Such issues cannot be addressed in detail until earlier steps in the ownership phase have been addressed comprehensively. However, failure to consider them early enough in the RMP can lead to project delays and contract arrangements that are not risk efficient.

A further important (but often neglected) aspect of ownership assessment timing is the time allowed for tenders and contract negotiations. In particular, bidding contractors ought to be given sufficient time to price for the uncertainty they will be expected to carry. This issue is discussed in more detail in Chapter 16.

Overall issue ownership fit for the purpose?

Separate *assess* tasks for the contracting strategy and the contracting plan as shown in Figure 9.1 need no further comment, but the final *assess* task does. It provides a convenient place to pause and consider the issues associated with the contracting strategy as a whole as well as individual planned contracts developed to this point. The possibility of multiple contracts with many parties makes this overall integrative assessment crucial. For example, if the constraints imposed by other parties collectively put the project at risk in unacceptable ways, it may be worth explicitly addressing the possibility of stopping at this stage, or going back to rescope the strategy.

The ongoing nature of the ownership phase

This has been a short chapter, because the concerns addressed are not usually treated as a part of the mainstream process of project risk management and we do not want to unduly interrupt the flow of the other chapters. However, the issues involved are of fundamental importance and should be addressed in any RMP.

A first pass through the ownership phase should focus on contracting strategy because initial concern in the next phase of the SHAMPU process, the estimate phase, may be restricted to issues the client proposes to own, as identified in the ownership phase. Subsequent passes through the ownership phase can then focus on contract planning at a more detailed level, followed by estimating contractor costs and verifying contractor cost estimates. This will require estimation of the implications of all associated sources and associated responses, possibly using a somewhat different approach and different people than those involved in estimating client-owned issues. Part of the rationale for being clear about who owns issues before estimation is to verify the feasibility of assumed responses and their effects. For example, client-initiated redesign is a response that may invalidate all allocations of risk to a contractor, with knock-on cost implications that are orders of magnitude greater than the cost of the redesign itself.

10 Estimate variability

But to us, probability is the very guide of life.—Bishop Joseph Butler (1756)

Introduction

This chapter, and the next, may seem too technical to be of interest to senior managers. In our view this is not the case. Probability as it is addressed here is not high science, it is common sense captured in a manner that provides structure to guide decision making. The principles discussed, and their implications, need to be understood by everyone involved in Risk Management Processes (RMPs).

The estimate phase of the SHAMPU (Shape, Harness, and Manage Project Uncertainty) process is usefully associated with two main purposes that are related but important to distinguish:

1. on the first pass, size uncertainty;
2. on later passes, refine estimates of uncertainty where this is effective and efficient.

A single-pass approach to the shaping phases (Table 4.2) is neither effective nor efficient. We want to minimize the time spent on relatively minor sources with simple response options, so as to spend more time on major issues involving complex response options. To do this, a first pass with a focus on sizing uncertainty can be used. Looping back from the evaluate phase to the estimate phase can refine estimates of uncertainty that are identified as important. Further loops from the evaluate phase to the define phase can provide more attention to detail and some revisions in relation to all the previous phases in those areas where unresolved issues suggest it is worth applying more effort in this way. Figure 4.2 shows one loop (subcycle) within each of the three complete loops back to the define phase as an illustration of the kind of pattern we might expect.

The deliverables provided by the estimate phase are numeric estimates of uncertainty associated with issues identified earlier in terms of cost, duration, or other project performance criteria. Some approaches to project risk management suggest numeric probability distributions from the outset. Others suggest a non-numeric approach initially, using likelihood and criteria ranges associated with scenario labels such as 'high', 'medium', and 'low', commonly referred to as a 'qualitative assessment', with numeric measures later if appropriate. However, qualitative statements of beliefs about uncertainty in this sense are of limited use and are open to different interpretations by different people. This book suggests avoiding this approach for reasons touched on in this chapter, further developed in Chapter 15. Indeed, we suggest reserving the term *qualitative analysis* to its interpretation in Table 4.2: the identify, structure, and ownership phases of the SHAMPU process.

Example 10.1   Ambiguity in qualitative labels

As part of a seminar on decision analysis conducted for a private company, the seminar leader included a demonstration called the 'verbal uncertainty exercise'. This exercise was designed to show that different individuals assign very different probabilities to the same qualitative expressions. In the exercise the seminar participants were individually asked to assign probabilities to common expressions, such as 'very likely to occur', 'almost certain to occur', etc. The seminar leader had just completed the demonstration and was about to move on to another topic when the president of the company said, 'Don't remove that slide yet.' He turned to one of his vice presidents and, in essence, said the following: 'You mean to tell me that last week when you said the Baker account was almost certain, you only meant a 60 to 80% chance? I thought you meant 99%! If I'd known it was so low, I would have done things a lot differently' (from Merkhofer, 1987).

Some people argue that quantitative analysis is a waste of time if it has to be based on subjective estimates of probabilities. There are obvious concerns about the validity of subjective estimates. These concerns are reinforced by the recognition that no probability assessment (except 1 or 0) can be proven to be wrong. However, given that individuals are guided by their perceptions of uncertainty whether or not quantification is attempted, it makes sense to articulate these perceptions so that uncertainty can be dealt with as effectively as possible. In addition to the general benefits of quantifying uncertainty set out earlier in Chapter 3, quantifying subjective beliefs encourages more precise definition of issues, motivates clearer communication about uncertainty, and clarifies what is and what is not important.

Desirable as quantification is, concerns about the basis for subjective estimates of probability and their validity are reasonable concerns. Any method used to elicit probability estimates from individuals needs to address these concerns.

Sometimes good data are available to provide 'objective' probability estimates. One of the benefits of breaking out various sources of uncertainty is the ability to use such data.

> **Example 10.2   Weather data as a basis for estimating available operating days**
>
> Equipment laying pipe in the North Sea is designated by maximum wave height capability: 1.6 m, 3 m, and so on. Even in the early days of North Sea offshore projects, weather data spanning 15 or so years was available that indicated the number of days in each month that waves were above various nominal heights according to sea area (e.g., see Mould, 1993). This provided a very good basis for estimating how many days a lay barge might operate or not due to weather. Direct use of these data in a semi-Markov process context allows very complex weather window effects to be modelled directly, enhancing understanding with good hard data (Cooper and Chapman, 1987).

It is worth recognizing that even the above example introduces a subjective element into the assessment process. In practice, a lay barge operator does not stop immediately when waves go above the equipment's nominal wave height and start again as soon as the waves drop below the nominal wave height. For important practical reasons, judgements are made about carrying on for short spells of bad weather, stopping early for anticipated prolonged bad spells, and starting later after prolonged bad spells, because starting and stopping pipe laying may involve picking up or putting down a pipeline, operations that are prone to 'buckles' (see Examples 7.6, 7.8, and 8.2).

There is always a gap between the circumstances assumed for data analysis purposes and the actual circumstances. Decisions about whether or not to ignore such gaps are always required, the basis of any associated adjustments is inherently subjective, and the validity of any unadjusted estimates is an equally subjective judgement. In this sense there is no such thing as a truly objective probability estimate for practical situations. Even the card or dice player has to make important assumptions about bias and cheating. All practical estimates are conditional on assumptions that are subjectively assumed to hold, and we need to recognize that such assumptions never hold exactly. The issue is the extent to which these assumptions fail to hold. In this sense, all practical 'objective' estimates are conditional, and any 'objective' conditional estimate is necessarily 'subjective' in the unconditional form required for practical analysis.

Often there are aspects of a project where uncertainty is very important, but appropriate data are not available. Even where past experience is relevant, the required data may not have been collected, may not exist in sufficient quantity or detail, or may not have been recorded accurately or consistently. In such situations, quantification may have to rely heavily on subjective estimates of probability distributions.

Assessment of some sources may be best handled by identifying them as conditions, with associated assumptions, that deliberately avoid estimation in the usual sense. Earlier chapters have emphasized the importance of this part of the process. On occasion, estimation in the usual numeric (or 'qualitative' scenario) terms may be a waste of time and best eliminated (e.g., if on a first pass the concern is identifying and then managing any 'show-stoppers', estimation reduces to looking for show-stoppers).

The key deliverable of the estimate phase is the provision of a basis for understanding which sources and associated responses are important. Three specific tasks are required to provide this deliverable, as follows:

1. *Select an appropriate issue*—As the basis of a process of successive estimation for a set of issues, select an appropriate place to start and each successive issue in terms of initial estimates and refinement of those estimates.
2. *Size the uncertainty*—Provide a simple numeric, subjective probability estimate, based on the current perceptions of the individual or group with the most appropriate knowledge, to 'size' the uncertainty associated with the issue.
3. *Refine earlier estimates*—If the implications of the uncertainty warrant it, refine the initial sizing estimate. This may be undertaken in conjunction with refining the response-related decision analysis or the earlier definition of the source and its context.

These last two specific tasks are so different that they divide the estimate phase into two quite different subphases (versions), *scope estimates* and *refine estimates*, illustrated by Figures 10.1a and b.

The first pass through the process as a whole will normally use the *scope estimates* subphase, as will the first pass through an extensively revised structure. Figure 10.1a portrays starting the scope estimates subphase in *select an appropriate issue* mode. Making sure that the first issue selected is the most appropriate place to start is worth specific attention, as part of the process of determining an effective sequence. Assessing each successive issue in terms of the question 'is it useful to quantify this issue?' follows.

Estimating then moves into *size the uncertainty* mode. The objective is an unbiased 'sizing' of the uncertainty, with an explicit numeric interpretation that is understood to be crude by all concerned. Nine steps are involved in the recommended approach, as indicated in Figure 10.1a, referred to here as the *simple scenario* approach. Chapter 15 develops a particular simplification of this simple scenario approach, the *minimalist* approach to estimation and associated evaluation, which we recommend strongly. The minimalist approach is a special case of the more general simple scenario approach developed in this chapter.

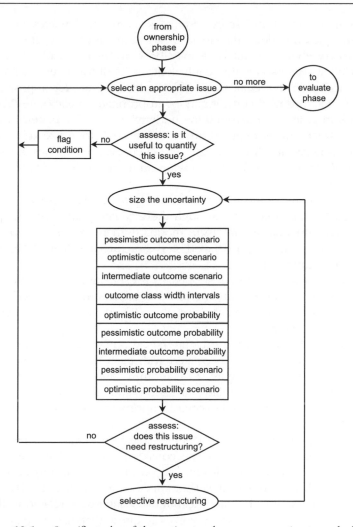

Figure 10.1a—Specific tasks of the estimate phase: scope estimates subphase

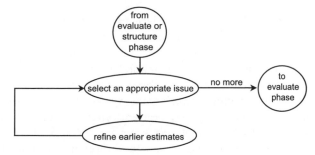

Figure 10.1b—Specific tasks of the estimate phase: refine estimates subphase

The final aspect of the scope estimates subphase involves an *assess* task asking the question 'does this issue need restructuring?' If the issue is too small to worry about separately, it may be convenient to add it to a pool of 'productivity variations' or the equivalent, a pool of issues with identified examples that can be dealt with effectively without decomposition. If the uncertainty is surprisingly large, it may be appropriate to elaborate the definition of the issue in order to understand the underlying structure better. In either case selective restructuring is required and looping back to resize (or confirm) the uncertainty is necessary. If neither of these circumstances applies, a loop back to *select an appropriate issue* follows, moving on to the evaluate phase if no further issues need scoping.

Figure 10.1b portrays the *refine estimates subphase*. This follows on from, and is motivated by, an earlier pass through the evaluate phase. This subphase also starts in *select an appropriate issue* mode. It then moves into *refine earlier estimates* mode. Portraying a detailed step structure like that of Figure 10.1a is not useful in Figure 10.1b.

The ultimate objective of both subphases is estimation of all sources involving a level of precision and estimation effort that reflects the value of that precision and the cost of the effort, recognizing that different issues are likely to merit different levels of attention.

This chapter adopts a section structure based on Figure 10.1. The following six sections outline the processes associated with each of the tasks associated with the operational stages of Figure 10.1 in turn. Subsequent sections consider specific techniques for probability elicitation and detailed practical issues, to support and develop the simple scenario approach, and explain the nature of some alternatives.

For *generality* this chapter considers the basis of the simple scenario approach in terms of threats and opportunities, considers sources that may or may not have an effect, and accommodates all criteria of interest in terms of 'outcomes'. For *simplicity* all the numerical illustrations in this chapter are based on one example, which assumes that the uncertainty of interest is related to time (duration) uncertainty and the source involves a threat that has a chance of being realized (or not). Chapter 15 illustrates what is involved in terms of more general numerical examples.

Issues may involve potential variability in terms of whether or not associated events occur, and implications if they occur. This potential variability may be inherent in nature, in the sense that severe storms may or may not occur, and if they do their impact may be variable. However, a holistic view of uncertainty must embrace ambiguity as well as variability inherent in nature. Portraying ambiguity as variability can be very useful, and on a first pass analysis ambiguity may be the dominant source of variability. Such ambiguity is associated with lack of clarity because of lack of data, lack of detail, lack of structure to consider the issues, assumptions employed, and sources of bias.

Select an appropriate issue

Starting the estimate phase by selecting the issue that earlier phases suggest is the most important is a simple and effective rule of thumb. This rule of thumb generalizes to successive selections based on an overall ordering of the issues for treatment in terms of a perceived order of importance, usually within activities or other subdivisions of the project, which in turn may be selected because of the relative importance of issues as currently perceived. No matter how crude the basis of this judgement, it is preferable to using an alphabetic ordering or some other totally arbitrary ordering.

Any estimation process involves 'getting up to speed', even if everyone involved is experienced in this kind of analysis. If inexperienced people are involved, going down a learning curve is part of the process. It makes sense to spend extra time as part of this process on the most important issues. It also makes sense to grip people's interest and involvement by starting with particularly important issues. When in doubt, err on the side of issues that have aspects that intrigue or touch on common experience, provided this is a cost-effective use of training time.

Having identified a suitable candidate in these terms, a key question follows: 'is this a useful issue to quantify?'

Assess the usefulness of quantification

In some projects it may be useful to quantify no issues at all. There are two reasons for this:

1. the client is not prepared to accept any significant sources, so all significant sources need to be transferred to other parties or avoided in some other manner, and there are no significant opportunity management issues usefully addressed in quantitative terms, so quantitative risk analysis is not required;
2. one or more 'show-stoppers' have been identified earlier, and managing the show-stoppers is the most effective next move.

Assuming these general reasons do not apply, a range of other specific reasons for non-quantification might apply, such as significant changes in the project environment.

Example 10.3 No need to quantify show-stoppers

A multinational weapon platform project was approaching an early feasibility assessment. It was the first project those responsible had subjected to a formal risk analysis process. Most other risk analyses undertaken elsewhere in the organization were quantitative. However, while quantitative risk analysis was an objective, it was not a commitment. When qualitative risk analysis clearly defined a small set of show-stoppers, risk management focused on managing away the show-stoppers. There was no need at this stage for quantitative analysis, because it would not have served any useful purpose.

Example 10.4   No value in quantifying the probability of changes of direction

The North Sea, offshore, pipe-laying project examples cited earlier involved a number of issues that were usefully quantified in most cases: buckles, weather, equipment failures, and so on. Of the 40 or so pipe-laying issues typically identified, about 30 were not quantified, but flagged as important 'conditions', assumptions that the analysis depended on.

As an example of an issue not usefully quantified, one project involved a source identified as 'the management may change its mind where the pipeline is to go' (because the company was drilling for oil on an adjacent site and a strike would probably lead to replanning a 'collector network'). It was important to keep the plan as flexible as possible to respond effectively to a possible change in route. However, the board owned this issue, not the project, and there was clearly no point going to the board with an estimate that says 'we think there is an $x\%$ chance you will change your mind about what you want and, if you do, it will cost y and take z days longer'.

It is important to stress that the identification of conditions of the kind illustrated by the above example can be *much more important* than the identification of sources that are subsequently quantified. Such conditions may be the key to effective contract design, claims for 'extras', and risk avoidance or reduction management, which is central to the overall risk management process. As well as quantified issues, flagged conditions are an important output of the estimate phase.

Sizing the uncertainty

The next task, *size the uncertainty*, involves making 'sizing' estimates of potential implications for project performance by roughly assessing the range of possible outcomes and associated probabilities. Example 10.5 on p. 180 illustrates what is involved, but first consider the description of each step summarized in Figure 10.1a.

1 Pessimistic outcome scenario

The first step in this task is to estimate the range of possible outcomes commencing with a pessimistic outcome scenario if the issue in question is realized. This estimate should be a 'nominal' pessimistic outcome in the sense that it has:

1. a rounded value that makes it easy to work with and indicates clearly its approximate nature;
2. a perceived chance of being exceeded of the order of 10% for a threat and 90% for an opportunity, given the issue is realized.

2 Optimistic outcome scenario

The next step in this task is to estimate a complementary optimistic outcome scenario. This estimate should be nominal in a similar sense, in that it has:

1. a rounded value on the same scale as the pessimistic outcome scenario that makes it easy to work with and indicates clearly its approximate nature;
2. a perceived chance of being exceeded of the order of 90% for a threat and 10% for an opportunity, given the issue is realized.

3 Intermediate outcome scenarios

The third step in this task is to designate one or two intermediate outcome scenarios. Usually it is convenient to choose these intermediate scenarios such that the distances between each pair of adjacent scenario values are equal.

4 Outcome class width intervals

The fourth step in this task is to define class width intervals centred on each of the outcome scenario values. Usually it is convenient to make these class width intervals equal to the distance between scenario values.

Rationale for steps 1 to 4

The rationale for this procedure in terms of beginning with the extremes (initially, the pessimistic extreme) is to mitigate against 'anchoring' effects, which are discussed later, and ensure residual bias is conservative (safe), while 'keeping it simple'. With a bit of practice, optimistic and pessimistic outcome scenarios can be selected on a common scale with one or two intermediate points on the same common scale quickly and easily. The simplicity of the scenario set is more important than whether the probabilities associated with values exceeding or being less than the extreme scenarios are closely in line with the guidelines. The priority is 'keep it simple'.

The next part of the simple scenario process is concerned with assessing the probabilities associated with each of the designated intervals, *working to one significant figure*. For *size the uncertainty* purposes it is convenient to assume that all values in a particular interval are equally likely.

5   Optimistic outcome probability

Step 5 involves assessing the probability of an outcome in the interval centred on the optimistic outcome scenario value. In the context of a threat, given the nominal 10 percentile interpretation of the optimistic outcome scenario, a probability of 0.2 is a reasonable estimate for this interval. In the context of an opportunity, a nominal 90 percentile interpretation also suggests a probability of 0.2 for this interval. An estimate of 0.3 may be preferred, and 0.1 is a possibility. However, usually these are the only viable choices, a simplicity driven by the optimistic outcome scenario definition. Even modest experience makes selecting the most appropriate value in the context of this first-pass process fairly quick and efficient.

6   Pessimistic outcome probability

Step 6 involves assessing the probability of an outcome in the interval centred on the pessimistic outcome scenario value. Given an estimated 0.2 probability for the interval centred on the optimistic outcome scenario value and the complementary nominal 90 or 10 percentile interpretation of the pessimistic outcome scenario, 0.3 is a reasonable expectation, rounding up to reflect the usual asymmetry of both threat and opportunity distributions. In general there is more scope for things to go badly than there is for things to go well relative to expectations. An estimate of 0.2 may be preferred, and 0.4 is a possibility, but 0.1 would be a cause for query. As in the context of the optimistic outcome probability, the process is efficient and quick for participants of even modest experience, with simplicity driven by the scenario interpretations.

7   Intermediate outcome probabilities

Step 7 involves assessing the probability of outcomes in the central intervals. If a single intermediate outcome scenario is involved, the associated probability is simply a residual. Two intermediate scenarios require a split, rounding to the nearest 0.1. Again, simplicity is the key. A little practice should make the process easy, fast, and efficient.

8 Pessimistic probability scenario

Step 8 involves assessing the chance that the issue will occur at all, again to one significant figure (to the nearest 0.1, 0.01, 0.001, etc.), in terms of a pessimistic probability scenario. Like the pessimistic outcome scenario, it should be nominal in the sense that it has:

1. a rounded value that makes it convenient to work with and indicates clearly its approximate nature;
2. a perceived chance of being exceeded of the order of 10% for a threat and 90% for an opportunity.

9 Optimistic probability scenario

Step 9 involves the complementary optimistic probability scenario, nominal in the sense that it has:

1. a rounded value on the same scale as the pessimistic probability scenario;
2. a perceived chance of being exceeded of the order of 90% for a threat and 10% for an opportunity.

Rationale for steps 5 to 9

The rationale for the sequence of steps 5 and 6 is to encourage an assessment that spreads the distribution. Reversing the order will tend to yield a narrower distribution: 0.2 followed by 0.1, instead of 0.2 followed by 0.3. The rationale for steps 8 and 9 coming last is clarifying the overall nature of the outcome probability distribution given the issue occurs, prior to estimating the probability that the issue will occur. If the issue involves uncertain outcomes but the source always occurs, both the optimistic and the pessimistic probability scenario will have values of 1 by definition. In the general case the probability that the issue will occur will be uncertain. The rationale for the ordering of steps 8 and 9 is dealing with anchoring effects (explored later). The rationale for intermediate outcome scenarios but no intermediate probability scenarios is a balance between generality and simplicity, assuming that impact uncertainty is greater than probability of occurrence uncertainty, an issue explored further in Chapter 15.

An illustration

The following simple example illustrates the procedure.

Example 10.5   The simple scenario approach

Suppose an issue is the occurrence of an event that could give rise to delay in a project with a pessimistic outcome scenario of 12 months and an optimistic outcome scenario of 8 months. A single value of 10 months is the obvious intermediate outcome scenario choice. If the optimistic and pessimistic outcome scenarios were 11 and 14 months, respectively, it would be more convenient to use the two intermediate outcome scenarios: 12 and 13.

If 8, 10, and 12 months are the outcome scenarios used, the intervals centred on these points are each of 2 months' width: 7 to 9, 9 to 11, and 11 to 13.

Assuming all values in a given interval are equally likely, suppose probabilities of 0.2 and 0.3 are assigned, respectively, to the intervals 7 to 9 and 11 to 13. The interval 9 to 11 is assigned the residual 0.5 probability.

Figures 10.2a and 10.2b show the resulting probability density function and the associated, piece-wise, linear cumulative probability distribution. The 0.2 probability associated with the interval centred on 8 months is uniformly distributed over the range 7 to 9 in Figure 10.2a, causing the cumulative probability to rise from 0 to 0.2 over the interval 7 to 9 in Figure 10.2b. The two other classes involve similar relationships.

Assume the pessimistic probability scenario is 0.3 and the optimistic probability scenario is 0.1, with a uniform probability density over the whole range: this implies an expected value of 0.2 for the probability that the event occurs.

Figures 10.2c and 10.2d show the resulting probability density function and the associated linear cumulative probability distribution. The single-interval approach makes Figures 10.2c and 10.2d special cases of the multiple-interval approach of Figures 10.2a and 10.2b. The probability value 0.2 is the class mark (centre point in the interval), expected value, and median value.

If the event occurs, the expected delay is given by $8 \times 0.2 + 10 \times 0.5 + 12 \times 0.3 = 10.2$ days and the expected impact is 10.2 times the probability the event occurs: $10.2 \times 0.2 = 2.04$ days, about 2 days.

In practice the uncertainty associated with the probability of the event may be greater than the uncertainty associated with the outcome, in which case more than one interval to capture probability uncertainty may be appropriate, with or

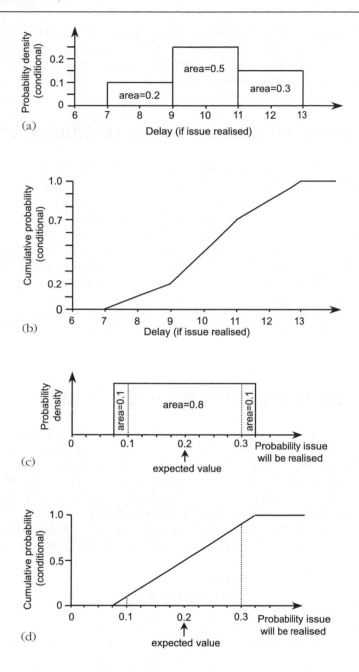

Figure 10.2—(a) Conditional, rectangular density function for *outcome*;
(b) Conditional, piece-wise, linear cumulative function for *outcome*;
(c) Rectangular density function for *probability*;
(d) Linear cumulative function for *probability*.

without dropping a multiple-interval approach to outcome uncertainty. More-sophisticated conversion processes embedded in suitable computer software could dispense with the use of a common class interval, while keeping the basic simplicity of a simple scenario approach.

Assess the need for selective restructuring

Sizing the uncertainty associated with a given source may be usefully followed by an immediate assessment of whether the revealed uncertainty warrants more detail or simplification. If the simple scenario estimate indicates that the issue involves a very modest effect, restructuring in terms of putting this issue into a 'productivity variations' pot of issues that are not worth separate quantitative treatment may be an obvious useful short cut. If the simple scenario approach indicates that the issue involves a major effect, it may be worth immediately decomposing (restructuring) the issue into components that clarify its nature and facilitate more accurate estimation. In both these cases Figure 10.1a indicates a selective restructuring that may be limited to a revised issue structure, but may involve more fundamental changes—in effect looping back to the define phase in selective terms.

Select an appropriate estimate to refine

A first pass through the shaping phases will be primarily concerned with using the scope estimates subphase to identify which issues warrant further attention in the evaluate phase, to help allocate estimating time effectively and efficiently. How this is done will be addressed in the next chapter. This section assumes that it has been done and some issues worthy of further attention in terms of refinement (as distinct from restructuring) have been identified.

The purpose of the refine estimates subphase is to refine initial scoping estimates in a credible and useful manner. Concerns in this subphase include:

1. what level of detail to aspire to;
2. what approach to use to obtain more detailed estimates;
3. the reliability of estimates;
4. how best to manage the elicitation of probabilities;
5. the relationship between objective data and subjective probabilities.

These concerns are discussed in the remainder of this chapter.

For reasons similar to those discussed in relation to the scope estimates subphase, it makes sense to start this subphase with one of the most significant sources. For present purposes suppose the issue in question is the uncertain

Table 10.1—Conditional tabular format for interpreting Example 10.5

delay if the delaying event occurs (months)	probability (given the delaying event occurs)	contribution to expected value (delay × probability)
8	0.2	$8 \times 0.2 = 1.6$
10	0.5	$10 \times 0.5 = 5.0$
12	0.3	$12 \times 0.3 = 3.6$
expected delay given delaying event occurs (via column sum)		10.2

Table 10.2—Unconditional tabular format for interpreting Example 10.5

delay (months)	probability	contribution to expected value
0	$1 - 0.2 = 0.80$	$0 \times 0.80 = 0$
8	$0.2 \times 0.2 = 0.04$	$8 \times 0.04 = 0.32$
10	$0.2 \times 0.5 = 0.10$	$10 \times 0.10 = 1.00$
12	$0.2 \times 0.3 = 0.06$	$12 \times 0.06 = 0.72$
expected delay (unconditional, via column sum)		2.04

effect of a delaying event that may or may not occur, associated with Example 10.5 (as characterized by Figure 10.2 and Tables 10.1 and 10.2).

Table 10.1 provides a probability distribution for the possible delay conditional on the delaying event occurring. Table 10.2 provides an unconditional probability distribution for possible delay by building in a 0.2 probability of the delay event occurring (and therefore a 0.8 probability of no delay at all), and provides an unconditional form and an unconditional expected outcome. It also clarifies the discrete nature of the zero impact case if continuous distributions are used for the unconditional equivalents of Figures 10.2a and 10.2b. The simple rectangular histogram format of Figure 10.2a and the associated piecewise linear format of Figure 10.2b mean that expectations for the continuous variable forms are the same as expectations for the discrete variable form of Tables 10.1 or 10.2.

Even if an issue is of only moderate importance, presenting results to the project team may raise unnecessary questions if the portrayal is too crude, particularly if members of the project team are inexperienced in the use of the simple scenario approach. All issues modelled separately may require more probability distribution detail as a cosmetic issue. Further precision and accuracy may be required because an issue is recognized as important. Still more precision and accuracy may be required because demonstrating the validity of decisions dependent on the issue is important. The task here is assessing how much precision and accuracy is appropriate with respect to this pass through the estimate phase for each issue being addressed.

Provide more probability distribution detail

A reasonable concern about estimates like those of Tables 10.1 and 10.2 and Figure 10.2 is their clearly nominal nature. People may be uncomfortable making significant decisions based on estimates that are so overtly crude.

Second and third cuts to develop an estimate

More detail can be associated with Table 10.1 outcomes using 'second- and third-cut' refinement of 'first-cut' estimates without significantly altering the intended message, as illustrated in Table 10.3.

The second-cut probabilities of Table 10.3 are typical of the effect of still working to one significant figure, but pushing an estimator to provide more detail in the distribution tails. The probability associated with the central value of 10 months drops from 0.5 to 0.3 to provide the probability to fill out the tails. It might be argued that if the second cut is unbiased, the first cut should have had a 0.3 probability associated with 10 months. However, this implies probability values for 8, 10, and 12 months of 0.3, 0.3, and 0.4, which sends a different message. Further, we will argue later that most probability elicitation techniques are biased in terms of yielding too small a spread. The design of the process described here is explicitly concerned with pushing out the spread of distributions, to deliberately work against known bias.

The third-cut probabilities of Table 10.3 are typical of the effect of pushing an estimator to provide still more detail in the tails, using a 20-division probability scale instead of 10, working to the nearest 0.05. A further slight decline in the central value probability is motivated by the need for more probability to fill out the tails.

Table 10.3—Second-cut and third-cut examples

delay (months)	probability of each delay, given a delay occurs		
	first cut	second cut	third cut
4			0.05
6		0.1	0.10
8	0.2	0.2	0.15
10	0.5	0.3	0.25
12	0.3	0.2	0.20
14		0.1	0.15
16		0.1	0.10
conditional expected delay	10.20	10.60	10.60
expected delay	2.04	2.12	2.12

It is worth noting that the expected values for each successive cut do not differ significantly. If expected value were the key issue, the second cut would provide all the precision needed and the first cut would suffice for many purposes. The difference in expected values between cuts is a function of the skew or asymmetry of the distribution, which is modest in this case. Extreme skew would make more intervals more desirable.

It is worth noting that the variance (spread) increases as more detail is provided. This is a deliberate aspect of the process design, as noted earlier. It is also worth noting that the third cut provides all the precision needed for most purposes in terms of variance.

Further, it is worth noting that any probability distribution shape can be captured to whatever level of precision is required by using more intervals: the simple scenario approach involves no restrictive assumptions at all and facilitates a trade-off between precision and effort that is clear and transparent.

A range of well-known, alternative approaches to providing more detailed estimates are available, which may or may not help in a given situation. Some of these approaches are considered below.

Provide a probability distribution function

Some people believe specific probability distribution functions provide more reliable estimates than the simple scenario approach described above. However, while specific probability distribution functions can provide more precision, this additional precision is often spurious. Specific probability distributions often provide less accurate estimates, because the assumptions are not appropriate and distort the issues modelled. The exceptions to this rule arise when the assumptions inherent in some distribution functions clearly hold and a limited data set can be used to estimate distribution parameters effectively. In such cases it may be appropriate to replace a specification like that of Table 10.1 with a distribution function specification. However, it is counterproductive and dangerous to do so if the nature of these assumptions are not clearly understood and are not clearly applicable. For example, Normal (Gaussian) distributions should not be used if the 'Central Limit Theorem' is not clearly understood and applicable (e.g., for a discussion of what is involved, see Gordon and Pressman, 1978). Table 10.4 indicates the distributions that are often assumed and their associated assumptions.

Instead of estimating parameters for an appropriate theoretical distribution, an alternative approach is to fit a theoretical distribution to a limited number of elicited probability estimates. This can serve to reduce the number of probabilities that have to be elicited to produce a complete probability distribution.

This approach is facilitated by the use of computer software packages such as MAINOPT or @Risk. MAINOPT is a tool that models 'bathtub' curves for reliability analysis. The generic bathtub-shaped curve shows the probability of failure of

Table 10.4—Applicability of theoretical probability distributions

distribution	applicability
poisson $P(n) = \lambda^n e^{-\lambda}/n!$ mean $= \lambda$ variance $= \lambda$	distribution of the number of independent rare events n that occur infrequently in space, time, volume, or other dimensions. Specify λ, the average number of rare events in one unit of the dimension (e.g., the average number of accidents in a given unit of time)
exponential $f(x) = \begin{cases} e^{-x/k}/k, \ k > 0, 0 \leq x \leq \infty \\ 0 \quad \text{elsewhere} \end{cases}$ mean $= k$ variance $= k^2$	useful for modelling time to failure of a component where the length of time a component has already operated does not affect its chance of operating for an additional period. Specify k, the average time to failure, or $1/k$ the probability of failure per unit time
uniform $f(x) = \begin{cases} 1/(U - L), \ L \leq x \leq U \\ 0 \quad \text{elsewhere} \end{cases}$ mean $= (U + L)/2$ variance $= (U - L)^2/12$	where any value in the specified range $[U, L]$ is equally likely. Specify U and L
standard Normal $f(x) = \exp(-x^2/2)/\sqrt{2\pi}$ mean $= 0$ variance $= 1$	appropriate for the distribution of the mean value of the sum of a large number of independent random variables (or a small number of Normally distributed variables). Let $Y_1, Y_2, \ldots, Y_n$ be independent and identically distributed random variables with mean μ and variance $\sigma^2 < \infty$. Define $x_n = \sqrt{n}(\bar{Y} - \mu)\sigma$ where $\bar{Y} = \sum_{i=1}^{n} Y_i$. Then the distribution function of x_n converges to the standard Normal distribution function as $n \to \infty$. Requires μ and σ^2 to be estimated
standard normal $f(x) = \exp(-x^2/2)\sqrt{2\pi}$ mean $= 0$ variance $= 1$	if y represents the number of 'successes' in n independent trials of an event for which p is the probability of 'success' in a single trial, then the variable $x = (y - np)/\sqrt{np(1 - p)}$ has a distribution that approaches the standard Normal distributions as the number of trials becomes increasingly large. The approximation is fairly good as long as $np > 5$ when $p \leq 0.5$ and $n(1 - p) > 5$ when $p > 0.5$. Requires specification of p and n

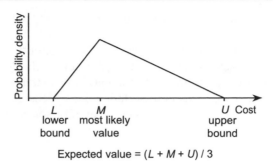

Expected value = $(L + M + U) / 3$

Figure 10.3—The triangular distribution

a component at a particular time, given survival to that point in time. The analyst specifies parameters that specify the timing of the 'burn-in', 'steady-state' and 'wear-out' periods, together with failures rates for each period. The software then produces appropriate bathtub and failure density curves. Woodhouse (1993) gives a large number of examples in the context of maintenance and reliability of industrial equipment.

A popular choice for many situations is the triangular distribution. This distribution is simple to specify, covers a finite range with values in the middle of the range more likely than values of the extremes, and can also show a degree of skewness if appropriate. As shown in Figure 10.3, this distribution can be specified completely by just three values: the most likely value, an upper bound or maximum value, and the lower bound or minimum value.

Alternatively, assessors can provide 'optimistic' and 'pessimistic' estimates in place of maximum and minimum possible values, where there is an x% chance of exceeding the optimistic value and a $(100 - x)$% chance of exceeding the pessimistic value. A suitable value for x to reflect the given situation is usually 10, 5, or 1%.

In certain contexts, estimation of a triangular distribution may be further simplified by assuming a particular degree of skewness. For example, in the case of activity durations in a project-planning network Williams (1992) and Golenko-Ginzburg (1988) have suggested that durations tend to have a $1:2$ skew, with the most likely value being one-third along the range (i.e., $2(M - L) = (U - M)$ in Figure 10.3).

The triangular distribution is often thought to be a convenient choice of distribution for cost and duration of many activities where the underlying processes are obscure or complex. Alternative theoretical distributions such as the Beta, Gamma, and Berny (Berny, 1989) distributions can be used to model more rounded, skewed distributions, but analytical forms lack the simplicity and transparency of the triangular distribution (Williams, 1992). In the absence of any theoretical reasons for preferring them and given limited precision in estimates of distribution parameters, it is doubtful whether use of Beta, Gamma, or Berny distributions have much to offer over the use of the simple trianglular distribution.

In our view, for reasons indicated earlier, it is doubtful that triangular distributions offer any advantages over the use of the approach illustrated in Example 10.5. They may cause significant underestimation of extreme values. The use of an absolute maximum value also raises difficulties (discussed in the next subsection) about whether or not the absolute value is solicited directly from the estimator.

Fractile methods

A common approach to eliciting subjective probabilities of continuous variables is the 'fractile' method. This involves an expert's judgement being elicited to provide a cumulative probability distribution via selected fractile values. The basic procedure as described by Raiffa (1968) is:

1. Identify the highest (x_{100}) and lowest (x_0) possible values the variable can take. There is no chance of values less than x_0 and there is a 100% chance that the variable will be less than x_{100}.
2. Identify the median value (x_{50}). It is equally likely that the actual value will be above or below this figure (i.e., 50% chance of being below x_{50} and a 50% chance of being above x_{50}.
3. Subdivide the range x_{50} to x_{100} into two equally likely parts. Call the dividing point x_{75} to denote that there is a 75% chance that the true value will be below x_{75} and a 25% chance that it will be in the range x_{75} to x_{100}.
4. Repeat the procedure in step 3 for values below x_{50} to identify x_{25}.
5. Subdivide each of the four intervals obtained from step 3 and step 4, depending on the need to shape the cumulative probability distribution.
6. Plot the graph of cumulative percentage probability (0, 25, 50, 75, 100) against associated values (x_0, x_{25}, x_{50}, x_{75}, x_{100}). Draw a smooth curve or series of straight lines through the plot points to obtain the cumulative probability curve.

A variation of Raiffa's procedure is to trisect the range into three equally likely ranges, rather than bisect it as in step 2 above. The idea of this variation is to overcome any tendency for the assessing expert to bias estimates toward the middle of the identified range.

In our view this approach is fundamentally flawed in the context of most practical applications by the dependence on identification of x_{100} in the first step. Most durations and associated risks are unbounded on the high side (there is a finite probability that the activity may never finish), because the project may be cancelled, for example. This means any finite maximum is a conditional estimate, and it is not clear what the conditions are. Further, it is very difficult in practice to visualize absolute maximums. For these reasons most serious users of PERT (Program Evaluation and Review Technique) models redefined the original PERT minimum and maximum estimates as 10 and 90 percentile values 30 years ago (e.g., as discussed by Moder and Philips, 1970). The alternative provided by Tables 10.1 and 10.3 avoids these difficulties. However, variants of Raiffa's approach that avoid the x_0 and x_{100} issue may be useful, including direct, interactive plotting of cumulative probability curves.

Relative likelihood methods

A common approach to eliciting subjective probabilities of discrete possible values like Table 10.3 is the method of relative likelihoods (Moore and Thomas, 1976). The procedure to be followed by the assessing expert, as Moore and Thomas describe it, is as follows:

1. Identify the most likely value of the variable (x_m) and assign it a probability rating of 60 units.
2. Identify a value below x_m that is half as likely to occur as x_m. Assign this a probability rating of 30 units.
3. Identify a value above x_m that is half as likely to occur as x_m. Assign this a probability rating of 30 units.
4. Identify values above and below x_m that are one-quarter as likely as x_m. Assign each of these values a probability rating of 15 units.
5. Identify minimum and maximum possible values for the variable.
6. On a graph, plot the probability ratings against associated variable values and draw a smooth curve through the various points.
7. Read off the probability ratings for each intermediate discrete value. Sum all the probability ratings for each value and call this R. Divide each individual probability rating by R to obtain the assessed probability of each discrete value.

The above procedure may be modified by identifying variable values that are, for example, one-third or one-fifth as likely to occur as the most likely value x_m.

In our view the Table 10.3 development of the simple scenario approach is simpler, but some of the ideas associated with this Moore and Thomas procedure can be incorporated if desired.

Reliability of subjective estimates of uncertainty

Techniques used to encode subjective probabilities ought to ensure that estimates express the estimator's true beliefs, conform to the axioms of probability theory, and are valid. Testing the validity of estimates is extremely difficult, since it involves empirical observation over a large number of similar cases. However, it is possible to avoid a range of common problems if these problems are understood.

An important consideration is ensuring honesty in estimates and that explicit or implicit rewards do not motivate estimators to be dishonest or biased in their estimates. For example, a concern to avoid looking inept might cause estimates to be unrealistically optimistic.

Even if honest estimating is assumed, estimates may still be unreliable. In particular, overwhelming evidence from research using fractiles to assess uncertain quantities is that people's probability distributions tend to be too tight (Lichtenstein et al., 1982, p. 330). For example, in a variety of experiments Alpert and Raiffa (1982) found that when individuals were asked to specify 98% confidence bounds on given uncertain variables, rather than 2% of true values falling outside the 98% confidence bounds, 20–50% did so. In other words, people tend to underestimate the range of possible values an uncertain variable can take. The simple scenario approach associated with Tables 10.1 and 10.3, deliberately pushing out the tails, helps to overcome this tendency.

Slovic et al. (1982) suggest that 'although the psychological basis for unwarranted certainty is complex, a key element seems to be people's lack of awareness that their knowledge is based on assumptions that are often quite tenuous.' Significantly, even experts may be as prone to overconfidence as lay people when forced to rely on judgement.

The ability of both the layperson and experts to estimate uncertainty has been examined extensively in the psychology literature (e.g., Kahneman et al., 1982). It is argued that, as a result of limited information-processing abilities, people adopt simplifying rules or heuristics when estimating uncertainty. These heuristics can lead to large and systematic errors in estimates.

Adjustment and anchoring

Failure to specify adequately the extent of uncertainty about a quantity may be due to a process of estimating uncertainty by making adjustments to an initial point estimate. The initial value may be suggested by the formation of a problem or by a partial computation. Unfortunately, subsequent estimates may be unduly influenced by the initial value, so that they are typically insufficiently different from the initial value. Moreover, for a single problem different starting points may lead to different final estimates that are biased toward the starting values. This effect is known as 'anchoring' (Tversky and Kahneman, 1974).

Consider an estimator who is asked to estimate the probability distribution for a particular cost element. To select a highest possible cost H it is natural to begin by thinking of one's best estimate of the cost and to adjust this value upward, and to select the lowest possible cost L by adjusting the best estimate of cost downward. If these adjustments are insufficient, then the range of possible costs will be too narrow and the assessed probability distribution too tight.

Anchoring bias can also lead to biases in the evaluation of compound events. The probability of conjunctive 'and' events tends to be overestimated while the probability of disjunctive 'or' events tends to be underestimated. Conjunctive events typically occur in a project where success depends on a chain of activities being successfully completed. The probability of individual activities being completed on time may be quite high, but the overall probability of completion on time may be low, especially if the number of events is large. Estimates of the probability of completing the whole project on time are likely to be over-optimistic if based on adjustments to the probability of completing one activity on time. Of course, in this setting unbiased estimation of completion time for identified activities can be achieved with appropriate project-planning software, but the anchoring may be an implicit cause of overestimation when a number of conjuncture events or activities are not explicitly treated separately.

The rationale for the simple scenario process in terms of the sequencing of defining pessimistic and optimistic extremes is minimization of this anchoring effect and ensuring the direction of any bias is conservative (safe).

The availability heuristic

The availability heuristic involves judging an event as likely or frequent if instances of it are easy to imagine or recall. This is often appropriate in so far as frequently occurring events are generally easier to imagine or recall than unusual events. However, events may be easily imagined or recalled simply because they have been recently brought to the attention of an individual. Thus a recent incident, recent discussion of a low-probability hazard, or recent media coverage, may all increase memorability and imaginability of similar events and hence perceptions of their perceived likelihood. Conversely, events that an individual has rarely experienced or heard about, or has difficulty imagining, will be perceived as having a low probability of occurrence irrespective of their actual likelihood of occurring. Obviously experience is a key determinant of perceived risk. If experience is biased, then perceptions are likely to be inaccurate.

In some situations, failure to appreciate the limits of presented data may lead to biased probability estimates. For example, Fischoff et al. (1978) studied whether people are sensitive to the completeness of fault trees. They used a fault tree indicating the ways in which a car might fail to start. Groups of subjects were asked to estimate the proportion of failures that might be due to each of seven categories of factors including an 'all other problems' category. When three sections of the diagram were omitted, effectively incorporating removed categories into the 'all other problems' category, subjects overestimated the probability of the remaining categories and substantially underestimated the 'all other problems' category. In effect, what was out of sight was out of mind. Professional mechanics did not do appreciably better on the test than laypeople.

Such findings suggest that fault trees and other representations of sources of uncertainty can strongly influence judgements about probabilities of particular sources occurring. Tables 10.1, 10.2, and 10.3 can be interpreted as a way of exploring the importance of these kinds of issues.

Presentational effects

The foregoing discussion highlights that the way in which issues are expressed or presented can have a significant impact on perceptions of uncertainty. This suggests that those responsible for presenting information about uncertainty have considerable opportunity to manipulate perceptions. Moreover, to the extent that these effects are not appreciated, people may be inadvertently manipulating their own perceptions by casual decisions about how to organize information (Slovic et al., 1982). An extreme but common situation is where presentation of 'best estimates' may inspire undue confidence about the level of uncertainty. The approach recommended here is designed to manipulate perceptions in a way that helps to neutralize known bias.

Managing the subjective probability elicitation process

It should be evident from the foregoing section that any process for eliciting probability assessments from individuals needs to be carefully managed if it is to be seen as effective and as reliable as circumstances permit.

Spetzler and Stael von Holstein (1975) offer the following general principles to avoid later problems in the elicitation process:

1. Be prepared to justify to the expert (assessor) why a parameter or variable is important to the project.
2. Variables should be structured to show clearly any conditionalities. If the expert thinks of a variable as being conditional on other variables, it is important to incorporate these conditions into the analysis to minimize mental acrobatics. For example, sales of a new product might be expected to vary according to whether a main competitor launches a similar product or not. Eliciting estimates of future possible sales might be facilitated by making two separate assessments: one where the competitor launches a product and one where it does not. A separate assessment of the likelihood of the competitor launching a rival product would then need to be made.
3. Variables to be assessed should be clearly defined to minimize ambiguity. A good test of this is to ask whether a clairvoyant could reveal the value of the variable by specifying a single number without requesting clarification.

4. The variable should be described on a scale that is meaningful to the expert providing the assessment. The expert should be used to thinking in terms of the scale used, so in general the expert assessor should be allowed to choose the scale. After encoding, the scale can be converted as necessary to fit the analysis required.

Let us develop point 2 in a slightly different manner. If a number of potential conditions are identified, but separate conditional assessments are too complex because of the number of variables or the partial dependency structure, the simple scenario approach can be developed along the lines of the more sophisticated approaches to scenario building used in 'futures analysis' or 'technological forecasting' (Chapman et al., 1987, chap. 33). That is, estimation of the optimistic and pessimistic scenarios can be associated with consistent scenarios linked to sets of high or low values of all the conditional variables identified. This approach will further help to overcome the tendency to make estimated distributions too tight. For example, instead of asking someone how long it takes them to make a journey that involves a taxi in an unconditional manner, starting with the pessimistic value suggest it could be rush hour (so taxis are hard to find and slow), raining (so taxis are even harder to find), and the trip is very urgent and important (so Sod's Law applies).

Example 10.6 Probability elicitation for nuclear power plant accidents

An instructive case study that illustrates many of the issues involved in probability elicitation is described by Keeney and van Winterfeldt (1991). The purpose of this study, funded by the US Nuclear Regulatory Commission, was to estimate the uncertainties and consequences of severe core damage accidents in five selected nuclear power plants. A draft report published in 1987 for comment was criticized because it:

1 relied too heavily on scientists of the national laboratories;
2 did not systematically select or adequately document the selection of issues for assessing expert judgements;
3 did not train the experts in the assessments of probabilities;
4 did not allow the experts adequate time for assimilating necessary information prior to assessment;
5 did not use state-of-the-art assessment methods;
6 inadequately documented the process and results of the expert assessments.

Following criticisms, project management took major steps to improve substantially the process of eliciting and using expert judgements. Subsequently probabilistic judgements were elicited for about 50 events and quantities from some 40 experts. Approximately 1,000 probability distributions were elicited and, counting decomposed judgements, several thousand probability judgements were elicited. Given the significance of this study it was particularly important to eliminate discrepancies in assessments due to incomplete information, use of inappropriate assumptions, or different meanings attached to words.

Nevertheless, uncertainties were very large, often covering several orders of magnitude in the case of frequencies and 50 to 80% of the physically feasible range in the case of some uncertain quantities.

Various protocols for elicitation of probabilities from experts have been described in the literature (Morgan and Herion, 1990, chap. 7). The most influential has probably been that developed in the Department of Engineering–Economic Systems at Stanford University and at the Stanford Research Institute (SRI) during the 1960s and 1970s. A useful summary of the SRI protocol is provided by Spetzler and Stael von Holstein (1975), and Merkhofer (1987). A similar but more recent protocol is suggested by Keeney and van Winterfeldt (1991), drawing on their experience of the study in Example 10.6 and other projects. Their procedure involves several stages as follows:

1. identification and selection of issues;
2. identification and selection of assessing experts;
3. discussion and refinement of issues;
4. assessors trained for elicitation;
5. elicitation interviews;
6. analysis, aggregation, and resolution of disagreements between assessors.

For completeness each stage is described briefly below, but it will be noted that stages 1–3 relate to the SHAMPU define, focus, identify, and structure phases examined in previous chapters. Stage 3 raises the question of restructuring via disaggregation of variables, which is shown as an *assess* task in Figure 10.1a.

1 Identification and selection of issues

This stage involves identifying questions about models, assumptions, criteria, events, and quantities that could benefit from formal elicitation of expert judgements and selecting those for which a formal process is worthwhile.

Keeney and van Winterfeldt (1991) argue for the development of a comprehensive list of issues in this stage, with selection of those considered most important only after there is reasonable assurance that the list of issues is complete. Selection should be driven by potential impact on performance criteria, but is likely to be influenced by resource constraints that limit the amount of detailed estimation that is practicable. This stage encapsulates the spirit of the focus, identify, and structure phases discussed in earlier chapters.

2   Identification and selection of experts

A quality elicitation process should include specialists who are recognized experts with the knowledge and flexibility of thought to be able to translate their knowledge and models into judgements relevant to the issue.

Analysts are needed to facilitate the elicitation. Their task is to assist the specialist to formulate the issues, decompose them, to articulate the specialist judgements, check the consistency of judgements, and help document the specialist's reasoning. Generalists with a broad knowledge of many or all project issues may be needed in complex projects where specialists' knowledge is limited to parts of the project.

3   Discussion and refinement of issues

Following issue and expert selection, a first meeting of experts and analysts should be organized to clearly define and structure the variables to be encoded. At the start of this first meeting, the analyst is likely to have only a rough idea of what needs to be encoded. The purpose of the meeting is to enlist the expert's help in refining the definition and structure of variables to be encoded. The aim is to produce unambiguous definitions of the events and uncertain quantities that are to be elicited. For uncertain quantities the meaning, dimension, and unit of measurement need to be clearly defined. All conditioning events also need to be clearly defined.

At this stage it is usually necessary and desirable to explore the usefulness of disaggregating variables into more elemental variables. Previous chapters have discussed the importance of breaking down or disaggregating sources and associated responses into appropriate levels of detail. A central concern is to ensure that sources are identified in sufficient detail to understand the nature of significant project risks and to facilitate the formulation of effective risk management strategies. From a probability elicitation perspective, disaggregation is driven by a need to assess the uncertainty of an event or quantity derived from a combination of underlying, contributory factors.

Disaggregation can be used to combat motivational bias by producing a level of detail that disguises the connection between the assessor's judgements and personal interests. Disaggregation can also help to reduce cognitive bias (Armstrong et al., 1975). For example, if each event in a sequence of statistically independent events has to occur for successful completion of the sequence, assessors are prone to overestimate the probability of successful completion if required to assess it directly. In such circumstances it can be more appropriate to disaggregate the sequence into its component variables, assess the probability of completing each individual event, and then computing the probability of successful completion of the whole sequence.

Often more informed assessments of an uncertain variable can be obtained by disaggregating the variable into component variables, making judgements about the probabilities of the component variables, and then combining the results mathematically. In discussions between analyst and assessor a key concern is to decide on an appropriate disaggregation of variables. This will be influenced by the knowledge base and assumptions adopted by the assessor.

Cooper and Chapman (1987, chap. 11) give examples of disaggregation in which more detailed representation of a problem can be much easier to use for estimating purposes than an aggregated representation. These examples include the use of simple Markov processes to model progress over time when weather effects involve seasonal cycles. Disaggregation also facilitates explicit modelling of complex decision rules or conditional probabilities and can lead to a much better understanding of the likely behaviour of a system.

4   Training for elicitation

In this stage the analyst leads the training of specialist and generalist assessors to familiarize them with concepts and techniques used in elicitation, to give them practice with assessments, to inform them about potential biases in judgement, and to motivate them for the elicitation process.

Motivating assessors for the elicitation process involves establishing a rapport between assessor and analyst, and a diplomatic search for possible incentives in which the assessor may have to prove an assessment that does not reflect the assessor's true beliefs.

Training involves explaining the nature of heuristics and cognitive biases in the assessment of uncertainty and giving assessors an opportunity to discuss the subject in greater depth if they wish. Training may also involve some warm-up trial exercises based around such commonplace variables as the journey time to work. This familiarization process can help assessors to become more involved in the encoding process and help them understand why the encoding process is structured as it is. It can also encourage assessors to take the encoding process more seriously if the analysts are seen to be approaching the process in a careful and professional manner (Morgan and Herion, 1990).

In the study outlined in Example 10.6, Keeney and van Winterfeldt (1991) found that the elicitation process worked largely due to the commitment of project staff to the expert elicitation process and to the fact that the experts were persuaded that elicitation of their judgements was potentially useful and worthy of serious effort. Also they considered that training of experts in probability elicitation was crucial because it reassured the experts that the elicitation process was rigorous and showed them how biases could unknowingly enter into judgements.

5   Elicitation

In this stage, structured interviews take place between the analyst and the specialist/generalist assessors. This involves the analyst reviewing definitions of events or uncertain quantities to be elicited, discussing the specialist's approach to the issue including approaches to a decomposition into component issues, eliciting probabilities, and checking judgements for consistency.

Conscious bias may be present for a variety of reasons, such as the following:

1. An assessor may want to influence a decision by playing down the possibility of cost escalation or by presenting an optimistic view of possible future revenues.
2. People who think they are likely to be assessed on a given performance measure are unlikely to provide an unbiased assessment of uncertainty about the performance measure. Estimates of the time or the budget needed to complete a task are likely to be overestimated to provide a degree of slack.
3. A person may understate uncertainty about a variable lest they appear incompetent.
4. For political reasons a person may be unwilling to specify uncertainty that undermines the views or position of other parties.

Where such biases are suspected, it may be possible to influence the incentive structure faced by the assessor and to modify the variable structure to obscure or weaken the incentive for bias. It can also be important to stress that the encoding exercise is not a method for testing performance or measuring expertise.

Spetzler and Stael von Holstein (1975) distinguish three aspects of the elicitation process: conditioning, encoding, and verification. Conditioning involves trying to head off biases during the encoding process by conditioning assessors to think fundamentally about their judgements. The analyst should ask the assessor to explain the bases for any judgements and what information is being taken into account. This can help to identify possible anchoring or availability biases. Spetzler and Stael von Holstein (1975) suggest that the analyst can use the availability heuristic to correct any central bias in estimates by asking the assessor to compose scenarios that would produce extreme outcomes. Careful questioning may be desirable to draw out significant assumptions on which an assessment is based. This may lead to changes in the structure and decomposition of variables to be assessed.

Encoding involves the use of techniques such as those described earlier, beginning with easy questions followed by harder judgements. Spetzler and Stael von Holstein (1975) provide some useful advice for the encoding analyst:

1. Begin by asking the assessor to identify extreme values for an uncertain variable. Then ask the assessor to identify scenarios that might lead to

outcomes outside these extremes and to estimate the probability of outcomes outside the designated extremes. This uses the availability heuristic to encourage assignment of higher-probability extreme outcomes to counteract central bias that may otherwise occur.

2. When asking for probabilities associated with particular values in the identi- fied range, avoid choosing the first value in a way that may seem significant to the assessor, lest subsequent assessments are anchored on their value. In particular, do not begin by asking the assessor to identify the most likely value and the associated probability.

3. Plot each response as a point on a cumulative probability distribution and number them sequentially. During the plotting process the assessor should not be shown the developing distribution in case the assessor tries to make subsequent responses consistent with previously plotted points.

The final part of the elicitation stage involves checking the consistency of the assessor's judgements and checking that the assessor is comfortable with the final distribution. Keeney and van Winterfeldt (1991) suggest that one of the most important consistency checks is to derive the density function from the cumula- tive probability distribution. This is most conveniently carried out with online computer support. With irregular distributions, the cumulative distribution can hide multimodal phenomena or skewness of the density function. Another im- portant consistency check is to show the assessor the effect of assessments from decomposed variables on aggregation. If the assessor is surprised by the result, the reasons for this should be investigated, rechecking decomposed assessments as necessary.

6   Analysis, aggregation, and resolution of disagreements

Following an elicitation session the analyst needs to provide feedback to the assessor about the combined judgements, if this was not possible during the elicitation session. This may lead to the assessor making changes to judgements made in the elicitation session.

Where elicitation of a variable involves more than one assessor, it is necessary to aggregate these judgements. This may involve group meetings to explore the basis for consensus judgements or resolve disagreements. Keeney and van Win- terfeldt (1991) found that whether or not substantial disagreements existed among expert assessors, there was almost always agreement among them that averaging of probability distributions (which preserved the range of uncertain- ties) was an appropriate procedure to provide information for a base case analysis.

It should be clear from the foregoing discussion that probability encoding is a non-trivial process that needs to be taken seriously for credible results. To be effective the encoding process needs to be carefully planned and structured and adequate time devoted to it. The complete process should be documented as well as the elicitation results and associated reasoning. For subsequent use, documentation should be presented in a hierarchical level of detail to facilitate reports and justification of results in appropriate levels of detail for different potential users. In all of these respects the encoding process is no different from other aspects of the risk analysis and management process.

Merging subjective estimates and objective data

Subjective probability estimates often have a basis in terms of objective data. The use of such data was touched on in the introduction to this chapter (e.g., fitting specific probability distribution curves to data).

On occasion there is a need to make important subjective adjustments to data-based estimates to reflect issues known to be important, even if they are not immediately quantifiable in objective terms.

> **Example 10.7   Subjective updating of objective estimates**
>
> When Chapman was first involved in assessing the probability of a buckle when laying offshore pipelines in the North Sea in the mid-1970s, data were gathered. The number of buckles to date was divided by the number of kilometres of pipe laid to date in order to estimate the prob-ability of a buckle. When the result was discussed with experienced engineers, they suggested dividing it by two, because operators had become more experienced and equipment had improved. In the absence of time for revised time series analysis (to quantify the trend), this was done on the grounds that dividing by 2 was a better estimate than not dividing by anything.

When Chapman worked for IBM in Toronto in the 1960s, advice provided by a 'wise old-timer' on the estimation of software costs was 'work out the best estimate you can, then multiply it by 3.' A more recently suggested version of this approach is 'multiply by pi', on the grounds that 'it has a more scientific ring about it, it is bigger, and it is closer to reality on average.' Such advice may seem silly, but it is not. Formal risk management processes are driven at least in part by a wish to do away with informal, subjective, hidden uplifts. However, the operative words are informal and hidden. Visible, subjective uplifts are dispensed with only by the very brave, who can be made to look very foolish as a consequence. Chapter 15 develops this issue further, in terms of a 'cube factor'.

Dealing with contradictory data or a complete absence of data

As argued earlier, subjective estimates for the scope estimates subphase are useful even if no data exist, to identify which aspects of a situation are worth further study.

Where no data exist, or the data are contradictory, it can be useful to employ sensitivity analysis directly. For example, a reliability study (Chapman et al., 1984) involving Liquefied Natural Gas (LNG) plant failures used increases and decreases in failure probabilities by an order of magnitude to test probability assumptions for sensitivity. Where it didn't matter, no further work was undertaken with respect to probabilities. Where it did, extensive literature searches and personal interviews were used. It transpired that LNG plant failure probabilities were too sensitive to allow operators to provide data or estimates directly, but they were prepared to look at the Chapman et al. estimates and either nod or shake their heads.

In some situations, where experience and data are extremely limited, individual assessors may feel unable or unwilling to provide estimates of probabilities. In such situations, providing the assessor with anonymity, persuasion, or simple persistence may be sufficient to obtain the desired co-operation (Morgan and Herion, 1990, chap. 7). However, even where assessors cannot be persuaded to provide probability distributions, they may still provide useful information about the behaviour of the variables in question.

Nevertheless, there can be occasions where the level of understanding is sufficiently low that efforts to generate subjective probability distributions are not justified by the level of insight that the results are likely to provide. In deciding whether a probability encoding exercise is warranted, the analyst needs to make a judgement about how much additional insight is likely to be provided by the exercise. Sometimes a parametric analysis or simple order-of-magnitude analysis may provide as much or more insight as a more complex analysis based on probability distributions elicited from experts and with considerably less effort. In the following example, probability estimates were unavailable, but it was still possible to reach an informed decision with suitable analysis.

Example 10.8   Deciding whether or not to protect a pipeline from sabotage

During a study of the reliability of a water supply pipeline Chapman was asked by a client to advise on the risk of sabotage. The pipeline had suffered one unsuccessful sabotage attack, so the risk was a real one; but, with experience limited to just one unsuccessful attack there was clearly no objective basis for assessing the subsequent chance of a successful attack. Any decision by the client to spend money to protect the pipeline or not to bother needed justification, particularly if no money was spent and there was later a successful attack. In this latter scenario, the senior executives of the client organization could find themselves in court, defending themselves against a charge of 'professional negligence'.

The approach taken was to turn the issue around, avoiding the question 'what is the chance of a successful sabotage attack?', and asking instead 'what does the chance of a successful sabotage attack have to be in order to make it worthwhile spending money on protection?' To address this latter question, the most likely point of attack was identified, the most effective response to this attack was identified, and the response and consequences of a successful attack were costed. The resulting analysis suggested that one successful attack every two years would be necessary to justify the expenditure. Although knowledge was limited it was considered that successful attacks could not be this frequent. Therefore, the case for not spending the money was clear and could be defended.

Had a successful attack every 200 years justified the expenditure, a clear decision to spend it might have been the result.

A middle-ground result is not a waste of time. It indicates there is no clear case one way or another based on the assumptions used. If loss of life is an issue, a neutral analysis result allows such considerations to be taken into account without ignoring more easily quantified costs.

The key issue this example highlights is *the purpose of analysis is insight, not numbers*. At the end of the day we usually do not need defendable probabilities: we need defendable decisions. The difference can be very important.

Example 10.8 illustrates a number of issues in relation to two earlier examples in this chapter:

1. Data availability is highly variable, ranging from large sets of directly relevant data to no relevant data.
2. Analysis of *any* available and relevant data is a good starting point.
3. To capture the difference between the observed past and the anticipated future, subjective adjustment of estimates based on data is usually essential.
4. Even when good data are available, the assumptions used to formulate probability distributions that describe the future are necessarily subjective. Thus it is useful to think of all probability distributions as subjective: some based on realistic data and assumptions, others more dependent on judgements made in a direct manner.
5. The role of probabilities is to help us make decisions that are consistent with the beliefs of those with relevant expertise and knowledge, integrating the collective wisdom of all those who can usefully contribute. The validity of the

probabilities themselves is not really relevant unless misconceptions lead to ill-advised decisions. Understanding why some decision choices are better than others is what the process is about.

6. The validity of probability distributions in terms of our ability to verify or prove them may be an issue of importance in terms of legal or political processes. In such cases it is usually easier to demonstrate the validity of recommended strategies.

Conclusion

This chapter suggests a particular estimation process, based on the simple scenario approach, that can be developed in various ways. In its simplest *size the uncertainty* form, it provides a simple alternative to high, medium, and low scenarios defined in purely qualitative terms, explicitly linking a comparable scenario approach to full quantitative analysis via a simple quantitative interpretation of the scenarios.

Chapter 15 develops further key ideas underlying this chapter. In particular, the minimalist approach special case of the simple scenario approach provides a useful short cut, which also clarifies why a high, medium, and low qualitative approach is ineffective and inefficient. A key feature of the minimalist approach is using what we know about anchoring and other sources of bias to design them out in so far as this is feasible (e.g., choosing the most effective sequence of steps).

There is a large amount of literature on probability elicitation, for good reason. Much of it complements the approach suggested here, but some of it is contradicted by the discussion here. We hope sufficient detail has been provided to indicate which is which for those who wish to develop deep expertise in this area. We also hope those not concerned with the finer points of these arguments will feel comfortable applying the suggested approach.

11 Evaluate overall implications

'Five to one against and falling ...' she said, 'four to one against and falling ... three to one ... two to one ... probability factor of one to one ... we have normality ... Anything you still can't cope with is therefore your own problem.'— D. Adams, *The Hitchhiker's Guide to the Galaxy*

Introduction

The evaluate phase is central to effective development of insight about the nature of project uncertainty, which is in its turn central to the understanding of effective responses to manage that uncertainty in a risk efficient manner. In this sense the evaluate phase is at the core of understanding uncertainty in order to respond to it. The evaluate phase does not need to be understood at a deep technical level in order to manage uncertainty. However, some very important concepts, like statistical dependence, need to be understood properly at an intuitive level in order to manage uncertainty effectively. An understanding of what is involved when distributions are combined is part of this. This chapter endeavours to provide that understanding without technical detail, which goes beyond this basic need.

The purpose of the evaluate phase is combining the results of the estimate phase in the context of earlier phases and evaluating all relevant decisions and judgements. The evaluate phase includes the synthesis of individual issue estimates, the presentation of results, the interpretation of results, process decisions like 'do we need to refine earlier analysis', and project decisions like 'is plan *A* better than plan *B*'.

The deliverables will depend on the depth of the preceding phases achieved to this point. Looping back to earlier phases before proceeding further is likely to be a key and frequent decision. For example, an important early deliverable might be a prioritized list of issues, while a later deliverable might be a diagnosed potential problem or opportunity associated with a specific aspect of the base plan or contingency plans as well as suggested revisions to these plans to resolve the problem or capture the opportunity. The key deliverable is diagnosis of any and all important opportunities or threats and comparative evaluation of responses to these opportunities or threats.

As indicated in Chapter 10, the evaluate phase should be used to drive and develop the distinction between the two main tasks involved in the estimate phase. A first pass can be used to portray overall uncertainty and the relative size of all contributing factors. A second pass can be used to explore and confirm the importance of the key issues, obtaining additional data and undertaking further analysis of issues where appropriate. Additional passes through the estimate and evaluate phases can further refine our understanding.

In some risk management process (RMP) descriptions, some of these decisions and judgements are viewed as part of other phases. This may not involve any material differences. However, it is important to treat the diagnosis of the need for such decisions and the development of the basis for appropriate judgements as part of the iterative structure that precedes detailed planning for implementation.

It is convenient to consider the specific tasks in the evaluate phase under five headings associated with groups of tasks and a mode of operation:

1. *select an appropriate subset of issues*—as the basis of a process of combining successive subsets of issues, choose an appropriate place to start and each successive issue, using a structure that reflects the causal structure of dependence, the structure of the overall model being used, and/or the most effective storyline to support the case for change;
2. *specify dependence*—specify the level of dependence in an appropriate structure;
3. *integrate the subset of issues*—combine the issues, using addition, multiplication, division, greatest operations, or other operations as appropriate, computing summary parameters as appropriate;
4. *portray the effect*—design a presentation for overall and intermediate results to provide insights for analysts in the first instance and to tell useful stories for analysis users as the plot of these stories emerges;
5. *diagnose the implications*—use the presentation of results to acquire the insight to write the appropriate stories and support associated decision taking.

Figure 11.1 portrays the way these groups of specific tasks relate to the key *assess* tasks. It also portrays starting the evaluate phase in *select an appropriate subset of issues* mode. A step breakdown is not provided. The objectives initially are making sure that the selected issue subset is the most appropriate place to start, for reasons comparable with those discussed in Chapter 10. The rationale becomes more complex later, when dependence becomes a key issue, and developing and telling stories becomes the concern. At this point, grouping issues within the underlying model structure becomes important. For example, if time (duration) uncertainty is the focus of early passes, the project activity structure is the natural and obvious framework and the way activities accumulate delay over the project life defines the storyline sequence. Later passes may extend analysis to the other five Ws, and overall integration in a Net Present Value (NPV) or multiple criteria framework using a balanced scorecard approach (e.g., Kaplan and Norton, 1996) may be crucial at some point. Anticipation of these issues in the estimate phase can be useful.

Specify dependence could be seen as part of the *estimate* phase, but is most

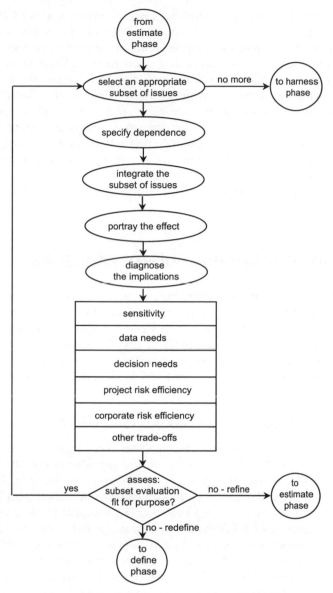

Figure 11.1—Specific tasks of the evaluate phase

conveniently discussed at this point in the *evaluate* phase, and simple
approaches make this an operationally convenient point to address it. Evaluation
then moves into *integrate the subset of issues* mode. This task is not represented
in terms of steps, but a complex range of considerations is involved. The objective is effective and efficient synthesis of all the earlier analysis, with a view to

understanding what matters and what does not. *Portray the effect* follows, again without showing steps. In the subsequent *diagnose the implications* task a number of steps are distinguished, representing an attempt to provide a checklist of the different aspects of diagnosis that need to be addressed in an orderly manner at this stage. Early passes through the process should focus on the early steps, with the focus moving to later steps as the iterative process matures. The final aspect of the evaluate phase is another form of the common *assess* task, with a view to moving on to selecting a wider or different subset of issues, going back to the estimate phase to refine the available information or going back to the define phase for a more fundamental rethink, until proceeding to the plan phase is appropriate.

The structure of this chapter broadly follows the structure of Figure 11.1.

Select an appropriate subset of issues

As indicated in Chapter 10, it may be best to start with one or more subsets of issues that are interesting enough and sufficiently familiar to all those involved, to provide a useful basis for learning. At this point it may be important to throw light on a pressing decision. Alternatively, it may be important to provide those contributing to the RMP with results of immediate use to them, to show them an early return for the effort they have invested in the analysis process.

Example 11.1 Successive evaluation of risks

Early offshore North Sea project risk analyses that Chapman was involved with often started with the core issue in the pipe-laying activity: weather uncertainty. The effect of weather on the pipe-laying schedule was modelled as a semi-Markov process. The calculation started with the state of the system when pipe laying begins (no pipe laid). A progress probability distribution for the first time period was applied to this initial state to define the possible states of the system at the start of the second time period. A progress probability distribution was then applied to this state distribution to define the possible states of the system at the start of the third time period, and so on (Cooper and Chapman, 1987 provides an example).

Only after this central issue had been modelled and understood, and tentative decisions made about the best time of year to start pipe laying for a particular project, did the analysis move on to further issues. Further issues were added one at a time, to test their importance and understand their effect separately. Each successive issue was added in a pairwise structure to the accumulated total effect of earlier issues. Because some

> of these issues (like pipe buckles) were themselves weather-dependent, it was essential to build up the analysis gradually in order to understand the complex dependencies involved.

If semi-Markov processes are not involved and dependence is not an issue, it may be appropriate to treat the subset of time or schedule issues associated with each activity as a base-level issue subset, then move on to other Ws and overall evaluation as indicated earlier.

Specify dependence and integrate the selected subset of issues

Integrating or combining issues together so that their net effect can be portrayed is a central task of the evaluate phase. Typically this integration task is carried out with the aid of computer software based on Monte Carlo simulation (Hertz, 1964; Grey, 1995). This makes it relatively straightforward to add large numbers of probability distributions together in a single operation to assess the overall impact of a set of issues. Unfortunately, this convenience can seduce analysts into a naive approach to issue combination that assumes independence between issues and overlooks the importance of dependency between issues. It also encourages analysts to set up the combination calculations to present the end result and ignore intermediate stages. Also, the mechanics of how individual distributions are combined is not transparent to the user. Together these factors can lead to a failure to appreciate insights from considering intermediate stages of the combination process and dependencies between individual sources of uncertainty.

Below we use a simple form of the simple scenario probability specification introduced in Chapter 10 and an approach based on basic discrete probability arithmetic to demonstrate the nature of dependency and illustrate its potential significance.

Independent addition

The simplest starting point is the addition of two independent distributions, each defined on the same Common Interval (CI) scale, a variant of standard discrete probability calculus (Chapman and Cooper, 1983a).

To keep the example as simple as possible, assume we are combining the costs of two items, A and B, each with the same distribution of costs represented by the three values shown in Table 11.1, defining C_a and C_b.

Table 11.2 shows the calculation of the distribution of $C_i = C_a + C_b$ assuming the costs of A and B are independent.

Table 11.1—Cost distributions for items A and B

cost (£k), C_a or C_b	probability
8	0.2
10	0.5
12	0.3

Table 11.2—Distribution for $C_i = C_a + C_b$ assuming independence

cost (£k), C_i	probability computation	probability
16	0.2×0.2	0.04
18	$0.2 \times 0.5 + 0.5 \times 0.2$	0.20
20	$0.2 \times 0.3 + 0.5 \times 0.5 + 0.3 \times 0.2$	0.37
22	$0.5 \times 0.3 + 0.3 \times 0.5$	0.30
24	0.3×0.3	0.09

The calculation associated with the joint cost of 16 is the product of the probabilities of individual costs of 8, the 0.04 probability reflecting the low chance of both items having a minimum cost. Similarly, the joint cost of 24 reflects the low chance of both items having a maximum cost. In contrast, a joint cost of 20 has a relatively high probability of 0.37 because it is associated with three possible ways of obtaining a cost of 20: $8 + 12$, $10 + 10$, or $12 + 8$. The probabilities associated with joint costs of 18 (via combinations $8 + 10$ and $10 + 8$), or 22 (via combinations $10 + 12$ and $12 + 10$), are closer to the 20 central case than they are to the extremes because of the relatively high probability (0.5) associated with $C_a = 10$ and $C_b = 10$.

Successive additions will make the probability of extreme values smaller and smaller. For example, 10 items with this same distribution will have a minimum value of 80, with a probability of 0.2^{10}: 0 for all practical purposes in the present context. Example 11.2 indicates the misleading effect that a presumption of independence can have.

Example 11.2   Assuming independence can be very misleading

A PERT (Program Evaluation and Review Technique) model of a complex military hardware project involving several hundred activities was used to estimate overall project duration. The model used employed individual activity probability distributions that those involved felt were reasonable. Assuming independence between the duration of individual activities, the PERT model suggested overall project duration would be 12 years ± about

5 weeks. However, the project team believed 12 years ± 5 years was a better reflection of reality. It was recognized that modelling a large number of activities and assuming independence between them effectively assumed away any real variability, making the model detail a dangerous waste of time. The project team's response was to use fewer activities in the model, but this did not directly address the question of dependence and obscured rather than resolved the basic problem.

In practice, assuming independence is always a dangerous assumption if that assumption is unfounded. It becomes obviously foolish if a large number of items or activities is involved. However, it is the apparently plausible understatement of project risk that is the real evaluation risk.

Positive dependence in addition

Positive dependence is the most common kind of statistical dependence, especially in the context of cost items. If item A costs more than expected because of market pressures and B is associated with the same market, the cost of B will be positively correlated with that of A. Similarly, if the same estimator was involved and he or she was optimistic (or pessimistic) about A, the chances are they were also optimistic (or pessimistic) about B.

Table 11.3 portrays the distribution of $C_p = C_a + C_b$ assuming perfect positive correlation. The probabilities shown are the same as for values of C_a and C_b in Table 11.1 because the addition process assumes the low, intermediate, and high values for C_a and C_b occur together (i.e., the only combinations of C_a and C_b possible are $8+8$, $10+10$, and $12+12$). Table 11.3 shows clearly how the overall variability is preserved compared with C_i, the addition of $C_a + C_b$ assuming independence. In this simple special case where A and B have identical cost distributions, C_p has the same distribution with the cost scaled up by a factor of 2. Successive additions assuming perfect positive correlation will have no effect on the probability of extreme values. For example, 10 items with the same distribution will have a minimum scenario value of 80 with a probability of

Table 11.3—Distribution for $C_p = C_a + C_b$ assuming perfect positive correlation

cost (£k), C_p	probability
16	0.2
20	0.5
24	0.3

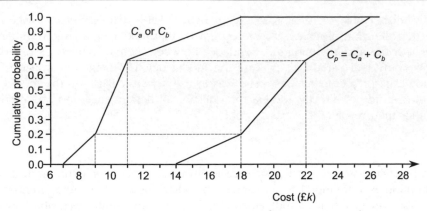

Figure 11.2—$C_p = C_a + C_b$ assuming perfect positive correlation

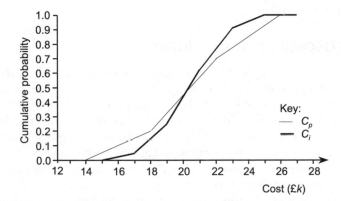

Figure 11.3—Comparison of C_p and C_i cumulative probability curves

0.2. Compare this with the independence case cited earlier, where the probability of the minimum scenario value is 0.2^{10}.

Figure 11.2 portrays the addition of A and B assuming perfect positive correlation using the continuous variable cumulative forms introduced in Chapter 10 and procedures discussed at length elsewhere (Cooper and Chapman, 1987). The two component distributions are added horizontally (i.e., the addition assumes that costs of 7 for A and 7 for B occur together, costs of 8 and 8 occur together, and so on). More generally, all percentile values occur together. Plotting Figure 11.2 directly from Table 11.3 provides the same result.

Figure 11.3 replots the C_p curve of Figure 11.2 in conjunction with a cumulative curve for C_i derived directly from Table 11.2. For C_i the minimum cost of 15 in contrast to the minimum cost of 14 for C_p reflects a small error in the discrete probability calculation of Table 11.2 if it is recognized that the underlying variable is continuous. This error is of no consequence in the present discussion (see Cooper and Chapman, 1987, chap. 3 for a detailed discussion).

In practice, assuming perfect positive correlation for cost items is usually closer to the truth than assuming independence. As indicated in Chapter 8, extensive correlation calibration studies associated with steel fabrication costs for North Sea oil and gas offshore projects in the early 1980s suggested 70–80% dependence on average, defining 'percent dependence' in terms of a linear interpolation between independence (0% dependence) and perfect positive correlation (100% dependence). For most practical purposes, percentage dependence is approximately the same as 'coefficient of correlation' (defined over the range 0–1, with 0.5 corresponding to 50%).

In the absence of good reasons to believe that 100% dependence is not an acceptable assumption, the authors assume about 80% dependence for cost items, a coefficient of correlation of 0.8, representing a slightly conservative stance relative to the 70–80% observed for North Sea projects. For related reasons, 50% is a reasonable working assumption for related project activity duration distributions, unless there is reason to believe otherwise. This avoids the optimism of complete independence when 100% dependence is unduly pessimistic.

Negative dependence in addition

Negative dependence is less common than positive dependence, but it can have very important impacts, especially in the context of successive project activity durations and 'insurance' or 'hedging' arrangements. For example, if A and B are successive activities and B can be speeded up (at a cost) to compensate for delays to A, the duration of B will be negatively correlated with that of A (although their costs will be positively correlated, as discussed in Chapter 8).

In terms of the simple discrete probability example of Table 11.1, perfect negative correlation (-100% dependence) implies that when C_a takes a value of 8, C_b is 12, and vice versa (overlooking for the moment the different probabilities associated with these outcomes). Call the distribution of $C_a + C_b$ under these conditions C_n. In terms of the continuous variable portrayals of Figure 11.2, C_n is a vertical line at a cost of 20 (overlooking the asymmetric distributions for A and B). Negative correlation substantially reduces variability, and perfect negative correlation can eliminate variability completely.

From a risk management point of view, positive correlation should be avoided where possible and negative correlation should be embraced where possible. Negative correlation is the basis of insurance, of 'hedging' bets, of effectively spreading risk. Its value in this context is of central importance to risk management. The point here is that while independence may be a central case between perfect positive and perfect negative correlation, it is important to recognize the significant role that both positive and negative dependence have in specific cases and the fact that positive and negative dependence cannot be assumed to cancel out on average.

Other combining operations

Evaluation of uncertainty in a cost estimate may involve multiplication ('product') and division ('quotient') operations. Evaluation of profit may involve subtraction ('difference') operations. Evaluation of precedence networks can involve 'greatest' operations at a merge event. The mathematics can become more complex. In particular, simple common interval calculations become much more complex than the calculation of Table 11.2. However, the principles remain the same and the effects of positive and negative correlation can become even more important. For example, if costs are perfectly positively correlated with revenues, profit is assured, while perfect negative correlation implies a high gearing up of the risk.

Conditional specifications of dependence

One of the obvious difficulties associated with non-expert use of percentage dependence or coefficient of correlation assessments of dependence is the need for mental calibration of what these measures mean. If this is an issue or if dependence is too complex to be captured adequately by simple measures like percentage dependence, conditional specification of dependence is an effective solution. Table 11.4 provides a simple example, based on the cost of item A with the same C_a distribution as in Table 11.1, but with the distribution C_b of the cost of item B dependent or conditional on the level of C_a.

Table 11.5 shows the calculation of the distribution of the cost $C_c = C_a + C_b$ assuming the conditional specification of Table 11.4 .

The computational effort is not increased by the conditional specification: in this particular example it is actually reduced. However, specification effort is increased and would increase exponentially if we wanted to consider three or more jointly dependent items in this way. It is this specification effort that constrains our use of conditional specifications to occasions when it adds value relative to simple percentage dependence or coefficient of correlation specifications.

Table 11.4—Conditional cost distribution for C_b given C_a

C_a (£k)	probability	C_b (£k)	probability
8	0.2	8	0.7
		10	0.3
10	0.5	8	0.2
		10	0.5
		12	0.3
12	0.3	10	0.3
		12	0.7

Table 11.5—Distribution for $C_c = C_a + C_b$ assuming the specification of Table 11.4

C_c (£k)	probability computation	probability
16	0.2×0.7	0.14
18	$0.2 \times 0.3 + 0.5 \times 0.2$	0.16
20	0.5×0.5	0.25
22	$0.5 \times 0.3 + 0.3 \times 0.3$	0.24
24	0.3×0.7	0.21

Table 11.6—Comparison of the distribution for C_c with C_i and C_p

cost (£k)	probability		
	C_i	C_c	C_p
16	0.04	0.14	0.15
18	0.20	0.16	0.17
20	0.37	0.25	0.25
22	0.30	0.24	0.19
24	0.09	0.21	0.24

Comparison of C_c with C_i and C_p is provided in Table 11.6 and Figure 11.4. Figure 11.4 (and the C_p values in Table 11.6) uses the continuous variable approach developed in Cooper and Chapman (1987) and the C_p bounds of 14 to 26 to correct partially for the errors associated with the discrete probability arithmetic used here because this makes interpretation of the curves easier. Table 11.6 and Figure 11.4 should make it clear that even the simple dependence structure of Table 11.4 does not yield a simple interpolation between C_i and

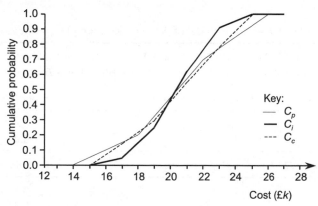

Figure 11.4—Comparison of C_p, C_i, and C_c cumulative probability curves

C_p. However, for most practical purposes 80–90% dependence is a reasonable interpretation of the level of dependence portrayed by Table 11.4, and other levels of dependence could be mentally calibrated in a similar manner. This example should also make it clear that very high levels of dependence are both plausible and common.

Causal model structure for dependence

In addition to the use of conditional specifications like Table 11.4 to calibrate simpler dependence measures, this form of specification is very useful for more complex forms of dependence (Cooper and Chapman, 1987). In this context the use of conditional specifications can become a form of causal structuring of dependence, asking questions about why B ought to vary with A in a particular pattern. Once these questions are raised, it is often more practical to explicitly address the possible need for a causal modelling structure. Indeed, complex models of the SCERT (Synergistic Contingency Planning and Review Technique) variety discussed earlier can be seen as a way of addressing dependence in this spirit.

If, for example, the reason the costs of items A and B are correlated is that they will be the responsibility of either contractor X or contractor Y, X being very efficient and Y being very inefficient, with political pressures determining the outcome, it may be useful to model this choice directly, as indicated in Table 11.7. Table 11.8 computes the associated cost distribution, defined as C_m, the 'm' subscript denoting causally modelled.

Those who do not follow the probability tree calculations embedded in Table 11.8 do not need to worry about the computational detail: what matters is the simplicity and clarity of a format like Table 11.7 relative to a format like Table 11.4, and the quite different results they yield. The result provided in Table 11.8 involves much stronger dependence than even C_p, with very little chance of a value of 20 and 16 or 24 much more likely. That is, the example provided by

Table 11.7—Causal model of dependence example specification

probability X will be responsible for both A and $B = 0.6$	
probability Y will be responsible for both A and $B = 0.4$	

cost (£k) for A or B if X responsible	*probability*
8	0.8
10	0.2

cost (£k) for A or B if Y responsible	*probability*
10	0.1
12	0.9

Table 11.8—Distribution for $C_m = C_a + C_b$ assuming the causal model of Table 11.7

cost (£k)	computation	probability
16	$0.6 \times 0.8 \times 0.8$	0.384
18	$0.6 \times 0.8 \times 0.2 + 0.6 \times 0.2 \times 0.8$	0.192
20	$0.6 \times 0.2 \times 0.2 + 0.4 \times 0.1 \times 0.1$	0.028
22	$0.4 \times 0.1 \times 0.9 + 0.4 \times 0.9 \times 0.1$	0.072
24	$0.4 \times 0.9 \times 0.9$	0.324

Tables 11.7 and 11.8 has been chosen to illustrate a 'bimodal' result that can be so extreme as to virtually eliminate any chance of a central value, one or other of the extremes becoming the likely outcome. This is an even more extreme form of positive dependence than the perfect positive correlation illustrated by C_p, which some people see as a very pessimistic extreme or bound on the impact of positive correlation.

More generally, perfect positive correlation and perfect negative correlation are the most extreme forms of *well-behaved, simple dependence*, but more complex forms of dependence can produce extremes that go significantly beyond the bounds of simple perfect correlation. Cooper and Chapman (1987) develop these ideas in more detail.

More generally still, if a causal structure that can be articulated underlies any complex form of dependence, it is usually efficient and effective to explore that structure using some form of probability or decision tree. An important part of the overall process is defining the structure in a manner that simplifies our understanding of complex issues. Cooper and Chapman (1987) also develop these ideas in more detail. Chapman and Ward (2002) build on this in a less technical and broader context. Other authors taking a compatible line include Spetzler and Stael von Holstein (1975) and Lichtenberg (2000).

Operational sequence

If simple dependence approaches like percentage dependence or correlation are used, often a convenient basis for first-pass analysis, it makes sense to specify dependence after choosing an appropriate subset of issues prior to integrating them as part of the evaluate phase. If a conditional structure for statistical dependencies is used, then it is useful to see dependence specification as part of the *estimate* phase. If a conditional structure is used to portray a causal structure, then it is useful to see dependence specification as part of the define (or structure) phases. Some of the looping back from the *assess* step in Figure 11.1 will reflect these choices.

Portray the effect

Graphs like Figures 11.3 and 11.4 are clearly useful when assessing the nature and importance of dependence and the possible need to reconsider the way dependence might be modelled. Such figures help to develop the story a completed analysis will tell. Even if dependence is not involved, this story needs to be developed a bit at a time, as each successive distribution is combined with the subset considered to date or at intervals as subsets are compiled. Figures 11.5 and 11.6 illustrate other formats that are often useful.

Figure 11.5 portrays the build-up of six issues within a given activity. The curve labelled '6' represents all six issues. The curve labelled '1' represents just the first, the curve labelled '2' is the sum of the first two, and so on. The gaps between the curves indicate the relative importance of each contribution, issue 5 ('industrial disputes') being the most important in this example. This example is based on the 'jacket fabrication' case (Example 8.6) used to illustrate source–response diagrams (Figure 8.2) earlier.

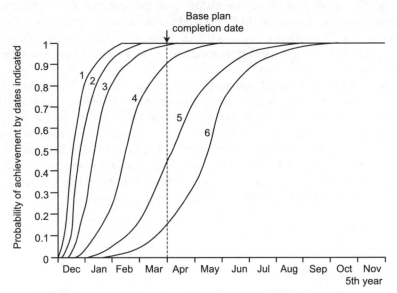

Probability curves show the cumulative effect of the following issues:

1. yard not available, or mobilization delays
2. construction problems / adverse weather
3. subcontracted node delivery delays

4. material delivery delays
5. industrial disputes
6. delayed award of fabrication contract

Notes:
1. the curves assume a minimum fabrication period of 20 months
2. no work is transferred offsite to improve progress
3. no major fire, explosion, or other damage

Figure 11.5—Initial level of output for offshore project

From Chapman et al. (1987), reproduced by permission of John Wiley & Sons

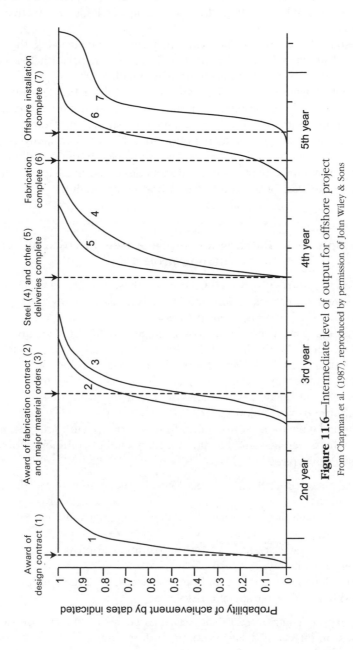

Figure 11.6—Intermediate level of output for offshore project

From Chapman et al. (1987), reproduced by permission of John Wiley & Sons

Each activity in a network can be portrayed using the format of Figure 11.5. Less important sources can be combined to keep the story simple, six separate sources or source subsets being close to the upper limit of effective portrayal in this format.

Relationships between activities can then be portrayed using the format of Figure 11.6. Like Figure 11.5, Figure 11.6 is based on a North Sea oil project case used earlier in several publications (Chapman, 1990).

The format of Figure 11.5 is also extremely useful for building up other performance measures by components. In all cases a nested structure can be used, as illustrated in Example 11.3. The analysis illustrated in Example 11.3 was actually built top-down, rather than bottom-up. The kind of analysis illustrated by Example 11.3 can be undertaken in days or weeks, hours if really pressed, as part of a top-down uncertainty appreciation as discussed in Chapter 6 and can be used to drive the start of a more detailed bottom-up analysis.

Example 11.3   Building a composite view of cost risk for a mining project

A deep mining project for which Chapman advised on RMPs was addressed via top-down uncertainty appreciation analysis as an early part of an integrated set of risk management processes.

The starting point was a 'base cost' estimate already in place and a set of sources of uncertainty defined in terms of conditions or assumptions, mostly explicit, that had been made when producing this 'base cost' estimate. Senior members of the project team provided a subjective estimate of the variability associated with the base estimate given all the conditions held, defining a distribution called B.

Conditions were then grouped into four sets of 'specific sources', the first three of which were assumed to share a high level of common dependence within each group:

- geology sources related to geological uncertainty with direct cost implications;
- geology/design sources related to design changes driven by geology uncertainty;
- geology/planning sources related to planning approval risks driven by geology uncertainty;
- independent sources that could be assumed to be largely independent of each other and other specific risks.

Various experts contributed to subjective estimates of 'direct cost' (ignoring the knock-on effects of delay) probability distributions within each of these four sets, designated: $G_1, G_2, \ldots;$ $GD_1, GD_2, \ldots;$ $GP_1, GP_2, \ldots;$ $IR_1, IR_2, \ldots$
Based on discussions with the experts during the elicitation of these

distributions, Chapman provided initial estimates of a percentage dependence level within and between each set. These were used with the estimates to provide five figures in the Figure 11.5 format. Four defined by:

$$G = G_1 + G_2 + \cdots$$

$$GD = GD_1 + GD_2 + \cdots$$

$$GP = GP_1 + GP_2 + \cdots$$

$$IR = IR_1 + IR_2 + \cdots$$

and the fifth defined by:

$$SR = G + GD + GP + IR$$

In the light of earlier discussions about specific sources, senior members of the project team then provided estimates of the probability of delay to the project (D) and the probability distribution for the indirect cost of delay per unit time (CT). Further graphs in the format of Figure 11.5 showed:

$$CD = CT \times D$$

$$C = B + SR + CD$$

As indicated, the final curve for C was built bottom-up, but the complete set of curves was presented top-down in three levels:

$$1 \quad C = B + SR + CD$$

$$2 \quad CD = CT \times D$$

$$SR = G + GD + GP + IR$$

$$3 \quad G = G_1 + G_2 + \cdots$$

$$GD = GD_1 + GD_2 + \cdots$$

$$GP = GP_1 + GP_2 + \cdots$$

$$IR = IR_1 + IR_2 + \cdots$$

The project team as a whole then discussed these results in relation to the underlying assumptions with the aim of assessing:

- whether it told an overall story that was consistent with their beliefs;
- where the uncertainty was a cause for concern that needed attention (in terms of a clear need for more data and analysis of those data);
- where the uncertainty was a cause for concern that needed attention (in terms of a clear need for exploration of alternative ways of addressing the six Ws).

Diagnose the implications

Diagnosis is central to the risk evaluation process and to providing support for associated decisions. It is discussed here in a layered structure, starting with the most obvious concerns that need early treatment in early passes of the risk management process, then moving on to the more subtle concerns best left until later passes.

Sensitivity

All effective quantitative modelling requires sensitivity analysis, so the analysts and the users of analysis can understand the relative importance of the components that the analysis uses. Figures such as 11.5 provide a direct built-in sensitivity analysis. If partial results are not accumulated and displayed in this way, this sensitivity analysis information is lost.

There are ways of partially recovering such information. For example, a common approach is to hold each parameter at its expected value and let one parameter vary. Another is to use a set of values representing the range for each parameter, letting the others vary. However, a nested structure using the approach illustrated by Figure 11.5 is simpler to compute and use. It requires planning the sequence of the integration operations in advance, but in practice this is a very small price to pay for the convenience and insight that follows such integration operations.

Data needs

A very important aspect of the iterative approach to the overall SHAMPU (Shape, Harness, And Manage Project Uncertainty) process is its use to allocate data acquisition and analysis time efficiently.

> ### Example 11.4   The importance of a source leads to additional analysis
>
> Figure 11.5 reflects the story told by a first-cut analysis based on subjective probability estimates provided by the group responsible for this activity. When the relative importance of 'industrial disputes' was observed, industrial dispute data for all the yards likely to be used for the fabrication of the jacket were gathered and analysed. The analysis confirmed the relative importance of industrial disputes and the sizing of this issue in Figure 11.5. It was worth spending extra time on this issue, but not on comparatively unimportant issues.

Decision needs

Another important aspect of the iterative approach to the overall SHAMPU process is its use to allocate decision analysis time efficiently.

Example 11.5   Analysis identifies the need to smooth work flows

Figure 11.5 suggests a probability of achieving the base plan completion date of about 0.15. This was an unsatisfactory outcome. Once it was confirmed that the picture portrayed by Figure 11.5 was valid, improving the prognosis was in order by changing the base plan or contingency plans with particular reference to key issues. In the process of industrial dispute data acquisition and analysis, the hypothesis that a carefully drafted contract with the yard would be an effective response was explored. Analysis suggested such contracts actually had little effect on these industrial disputes. Such industrial disputes mainly occurred during the last 10% of a contract if no more work was anticipated in that yard on completion. Recognition of this cause led to effective action: smoothing the flow of work to yards to the extent possible by all the oil companies involved. It was recognized that this resolved the particular problem diagnosed by Figure 11.5 and the more general 'industrial disputes' problem. It was also recognized that this smoother work flow reduced jacket fabrication costs by avoiding bidding up the price when demand peaked. These changes contributed to improved risk efficiency, both at the project level and the corporate level.

Further changes motivated by project risk efficiency improvements

Example 3.1 illustrated the risk efficiency concept in the context of a decision to use a 3-m wave height capability barge to perform a hook-up instead of the 1.6-m barge initially chosen. The need to consider an alternative decision was flagged by the analysis results, akin to the Figure 11.5 situation just discussed. However, often improvements in risk efficiency that are possible are not flagged in this way. In such cases we must search for them. Typical examples include: using more capable equipment than the minimum requirements suggest; using more resources initially, then releasing them if rapid progress is made; starting earlier; purchasing insurance; designing out the key threats recognized by this stage in the analysis; writing contracts to allow more flexible responses to possible threats and opportunities. This step is about using the insights gained to search for such changes in an effective manner.

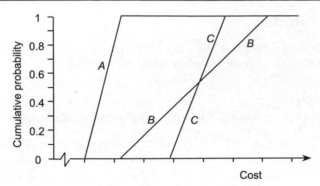

Figure 11.7—Comparison of approaches *A*, *B*, and *C*

Comparison of alternative ways of achieving an activity or a project as a whole can be portrayed in terms of diagrams like Figure 11.7. Figure 11.7 uses simple uniform distributions to clarify the messages discussed here.

Figure 11.7 portrays a comparison between approaches *A*, *B*, and *C* in terms of cost-cumulative probability distributions. It shows that in terms of cost as measured, approach *A* is the risk efficient choice. The expected cost of *A* is less than that of *B* and *C*. In addition, the risk is less, in the sense that the probability of the cost exceeding any given level is higher for *B* and *C* than for *A*. This case involves clear 'stochastic dominance', indicated by the distributions for *B* and *C* being clearly and entirely to the right of the distribution for *A*.

If *A* were not available, *B* would generally be preferable to *C*. It does not 'dominate' completely, indicated by the crossing of the curves. But the increase in potential extreme values associated with *B* relative to *C* is offset by the reduced expected value, and the reduced expected value will make up for the additional variability of *B* relative to *C* in most contexts.

The use of diagrams like Figure 11.7 to portray the comparative implications of alternative approaches is one way to pursue changes in base plans and contingency plans that involve an increase in risk efficiency. In practice, asymmetric 'S' curves like those of Figure 3.3 should be used, but as discussed in Chapter 3 linear curves like those of Figures 11.7 and 3.1 can be useful to clarify what is involved initially.

Further changes motivated by corporate risk efficiency improvements

Example 3.2 illustrated trade-offs between risk and expected cost that may require attention because they can lead to a gain in corporate-level risk efficiency although they may seem to expose the project to a high level of risk. Often these opportunities do not make themselves obvious: they must be searched for. Further, often they reflect opportunities people are not prepared to take if they are not protected from 'bad luck/bad management confusion'. These are key opportunities to address, particularly in the early stages of introducing formal RMPs into an organization.

Typical examples are the flip side of the examples cited in the last subsection context of risk efficiency improvements, if the numbers (probabilities) are different. They include: using less capable equipment than maximum requirements suggest; using fewer resources initially, with fallback plans in place when appropriate; starting later; not purchasing insurance (self-insuring); designing in the possible ability to capture possible opportunities recognized at this stage of the analysis.

Figure 11.7 portrays a comparison between approach *C* and approach *B* in terms of cost cumulative probability distributions. As noted earlier, it shows that in terms of cost as measured neither is more risk efficient. A trade-off is involved. Approach *B* has a lower expected cost, but the tail of the distribution crosses that of approach *C*, implying more risk. In this case most would find this risk worth taking, but the more profound the overlap and the closer the expectations the more difficult the choice.

Using diagrams like Figure 11.7 (in asymmetric 'S' curve form in practice) to portray the comparative implications of alternative approaches is one way to pursue changes in base plans and contingency plans that involve trade-offs between expected values of the key performance measure and associated risk. They provide a way of portraying what the trade-off involves, so that those responsible can make informed choices, considering risk efficiency at a corporate level as well as at a project level.

Further changes motivated by other trade-offs

Further trade-offs may also require consideration at this stage. For example: if an activity was given a less generous time provision, would the direct cost increase be less than the revenue increase?; if the quality specification for a component was decreased, would the related decrease in time or cost be worthwhile?; and so on. The more mature the iterative process the more the focus of analysis will shift toward this final step.

Building up insight on foundations laid earlier

The decreasing amount of space given to successive steps in this section of the process description is inversely proportional to their importance and their impact on project performance improvements. As the iterative nature of the process matures, it will become clearer why the investment in the earlier iterations of the *shaping* phases provides insights that can be used to improve project performance in the later iterations. The focus of attention moves from the strategic at an activity level to the strategic at the level of interfaces between the project as a whole and the corporate strategy it is embedded in, perhaps via an intermediate programme level. We see the forest as a whole in terms of a limited set of trees in clearly defined relationships. The issues are defined in terms of sources that matter and effective response choices within a six Ws and project life cycle (PLC) framework that is holistic and integrated. The depth of understanding that emerges will have to be explained to others top-down, but the insights are built bottom-up within the structure developed in the earlier *shape* phases.

Building up the set of issues and interpreting the complete set

All the above forms of diagnosis require attention as the subset of issues grows. Effective and efficient choices cannot be left until all the issues have been jointly evaluated. Careful attention to partial results as the evaluation process proceeds will suggest changes to those looking for such changes. In particular, conditions or scope assumptions associated with partial aggregation of quantified issues may need careful attention. Such conditions or assumptions can become crucial at the stage when all quantified issues have been aggregated (e.g., when defining a budget for a delivery date). When all quantified issues have been combined, interpretation needs to address the importance of all assumptions, including conditions that have not been quantified. Chapman and Ward (2002) develop a 'cube factor' approach to acknowledging identified conditions, unidentified conditions, and bias, briefly illustrated in Chapter 15. The essence of the matter is the need to interpret any quantification of uncertainty as conditional on a range of assumptions, some unidentified, including assumptions leading to bias.

Assess whether the subset evaluation is fit for the purpose

Sensitivity analysis and subsequent data or decision needs analysis may suggest a need to re-estimate, as indicated in Examples 11.4 and 11.5. Further forms of diagnosis may also indicate a need for a loop back to the estimate phase. More profound loops back to the define phase to restructure may also be suggested, as portrayed in Figure 11.1. Otherwise, a loop back to enlarge the subset of issues may be appropriate, unless all the issues have now been considered and moving on to the plan phase is appropriate. Selecting the next issue to be considered may need to follow a complex nesting structure, like that implicit in Example 11.2. In this case, base-level subsets of issues are combined, then second-level issues, and so on.

Alternative integration procedures

Those not interested in computational issues, computer software selection, or hands-on analysis may be inclined to skip this section. It is arguably the least relevant section in this book for senior managers. However, at least a skim read is advisable for all readers.

The simple controlled interval approach of Table 11.2 involves a systematic error associated with the discrete value approximation of a continuous variable distribution, as explained elsewhere (Cooper and Chapman, 1987, chap. 3). To indicate the size (importance) of the error, note that the Figure 11.2 C_i curve assumes 15 is the absolute minimum, while exact integration indicates that 14 is the absolute minimum, with a probability of 0.05 of a value less than 15. The more intervals used to represent a distribution the smaller this systematic error becomes. Even with only three intervals, this error is not significant for present purposes. To overcome this error a Controlled Interval and Memory (CIM) approach has been developed, as explained elsewhere (Cooper and Chapman, 1987). This approach also overcomes the complications associated with operations other than addition. Software developed to use this approach by BP International (Clark and Chapman, 1987) and K & H (PERK) has been used on a wide range of projects, but it is not currently available. In its original forms it requires pairwise specification of a sequence for combining all distributions. This can raise difficulties (e.g., when irreducible networks are involved: see Soukhakian, 1988). It requires expert use to make effective use of the pairwise structuring and can be tedious to use if pairwise structures are not helpful.

As noted earlier, Monte Carlo simulation is the usual method employed to combine risks in standard risk analysis software packages like @Risk (e.g., Grey, 1995). Monte Carlo simulation is based on sampling. For example, to add the probability distributions for items A and B of Table 11.1 assuming independence to define C_i, we start by taking a sample from the distribution for A. The mechanics of this sample reduce to using a 'pseudorandom number generator' to obtain a random number in the range 0–1, using this sampled value to reference the probability scale of a cumulative distribution for item A like that of Figure 11.2 and reading off the corresponding cost (e.g., a generated random number value of 0.1 would yield a sample cost of 8). Assuming the random numbers are uniformly distributed over the range 0–1, this can be shown to result in costs sampled from the assumed distribution for C_a.

A similar sample for item B can be added to define a sample for $C_a + C_b = C_i$. Repeating this procedure a hundred times results in a frequency distribution for C_i that approximates the true integration with sufficient accuracy for most purposes. However, the 0.05 probability error noted in relation to Figure 11.3 could require 1,000 samples or more to estimate with reasonable precision, a similar number being required for a resulting curve that is smooth, without visible sampling error. Using 10,000 samples gives the same level of precision as a CIM procedure with about 30 classes, the latter being about 1,000 times faster (Yong, 1985).

Non-random sampling procedures (e.g., 'Latin Hypercubes') can be used to speed up the production of smooth curves. In principle, such procedures are a partial move toward the completely systematic sampling procedure that CI (Controlled Interval) or CIM procedures use, partially reducing sampling error while possibly inducing some systematic error. In practice, the systematic error is unlikely to be important, though it can be.

Simple discrete probability methods suitable for manual computations in a decision tree or probability tree context and CIM developments of these methods provide alternatives to Monte Carlo simulation. The key points about the CIM process in the present context are:

1. it requires combining successive pairs of risks for computational reasons;
2. this requirement encourages thinking about a structure for these successive pairs that reflects dependence and the story to be told;
3. a by-product of this computational structure is built-in sensitivity analysis, as discussed in relation to Figure 11.5;
4. for reasons discussed in relation to Figure 11.5 the use of CIM procedures or exposure to the results of their use should persuade any expert analyst or user of analysis without access to CIM software to use Monte Carlo-driven packages as if they were CIM-driven to some extent, if not to the point of always using a pairing structure.

The approach described in this chapter assumes Monte Carlo simulation-driven software will be used, but the lessons from CIM-driven analysis learned by the authors are worth incorporating in the process. In the long term, software that uses expert system technology to select CIM or Monte Carlo processes as appropriate should be practical and forthcoming. In the short term, any sampling software that allows for dependence used with reasonable care should prove effective.

Monte Carlo-driven software can usually accommodate dependence in coefficient of correlation or percentage dependence-equivalent forms. In practice, industry standard packages can cause difficulties when modelling dependence, and care needs to be exercised. Analysts need to understand dependence well enough to realize when results do not make sense.

Earlier industry standard methods based on statistical moments, typically mean variance, as used in the original PERT calculations (Moder and Philips, 1970) and by Lichtenberg (2000) in his 'successive estimation principle', are worth understanding, at least in outline. The mean or expected value of a variable is the sum of all the possible values for the variable weighted by the associated probabilities of each value. This represents a single estimate of what will happen on average. Expected values have the useful property that they are additive (i.e., the expected cost of a sum of costs is equal to the sum of the expected values for each individual cost).

It is important to distinguish between the expected value and other 'measures of central tendency' associated with a distribution, such as the median (the value that has a 50% chance of being exceeded) and the most likely value (most probable, often referred to as the 'best estimate'), which do not have this additive property in general.

For example, the cost of items A and B of Table 11.1 each have an expected value of $(8 \times 0.2) + (10 \times 0.5) + (12 \times 0.3) = 10.2$. This means that the expected cost of 1,000 such items is 10,200 ($\pounds k$). The most likely costs of 10 for each item cannot be added to obtain a most likely value for more than one item. The median cost will lie between the expected cost and the most likely value of total cost. The 2% difference between the expected value of 10.2 and the most likely value of 10.0 is negligible, but it is small only because of the nearly symmetric shape of these distributions. For completely symmetric distributions, this difference would be zero. If 8 were the most likely value, with a probability of 0.5, while 10 and 12 had probabilities of 0.3 and 0.2, respectively, the expected value would be $(8 \times 0.5) + (10 \times 0.3) + (12 \times 0.2) = 9.4$. With this skewed distribution the difference between the most likely value and the expected value is substantial, some 18% of the most likely value. Such a difference in magnitudes is common, arising from much less extreme asymmetry but much longer distribution 'tails'. In general, the more low-probability/high-impact risks a probability distribution embodies the longer the right-hand tail of the distribution and the greater the gap between the expected value and the most likely or median values. Chapman and Ward (1996) provide a plausible nuclear power cost per kWh example where the expected cost is more than double the most likely cost, a context explored in more detail in Chapman and Ward (2002, chap. 11).

The variance of a distribution is a useful single measure of the average amount of dispersion or spread in a distribution. Variances for *independent* random variables are additive (i.e., the variance of a sum of costs is equal to the sum of the variances for each individual cost). For example, the cost of items A and B of Table 11.1 have a variance (in $\pounds^2 k^2$) of $[(8 - 10.2)^2 \times 0.2] + [(10 - 10.2)^2 \times 0.5] + [(12 - 10.2)^2 \times 0.3] = 1.96$. This means that the variance of 1,000 such items is $1.96 \times 1,000 = 1,960$ and the standard deviation (square root of 1960) is about 44 ($\pounds k$). The Central Limit Theorem implies that the sum of n independently distributed random variables of any distribution has a distribution that approximates to the Normal distribution for sufficiently large n. (In practice, quite small n will do. A simple, practical illustration is provided by the distribution of outcomes when rolling dice (n die: $n = 1$ (uniform), 2 (triangular), 3 (already looking roughly Normal), and so on.) Using standard Normal tables, this implies that the expected value of the sum of our 1,000 cost items should fall in the range $10,200 \pm 44$ (i.e., within one standard deviation of the mean) about 68% of the time and almost certainly falls within the range $10,200 \pm 132$, defined by three standard deviations either side of the mean (a 99%

confidence band). This result suggests an extraordinary degree of certainty about the sum of our 1,000 cost items! The absurdity of this result should reinforce Example 11.2 and the importance of dependence. More generally, it illustrates the way independence induces a square root rule reduction in variability as n increases. The standard deviation of the cost of one of our cost items, 1.4 (square root of 1.960), is about 14% of 10.2, but 44 is about 0.43% of 10,200, a reduction by a factor of about 32 (equal to the square root of 1,000). More generally, compared with a single item ($n = 1$), $n = 4$ increases total variability by a factor of 2, $n = 16$ increases total variability by a factor of 4, $n = 64$ increases total variability by a factor of 8, and so on.

Mean variance approaches need not assume independence, and an expert system-driven probability evaluation package could usefully embrace moment-based approaches as well as CIM and Monte Carlo. Moment-based approaches offer speed and precision when appropriate assumptions hold and catastrophic systematic errors (bias) when appropriate assumptions do not hold.

To summarize this section, three types of procedure can be considered, each with their advantages and disadvantages. Current industry standard software based on Monte Carlo simulation is effective if used by experts with adequate understanding of dependence in a manner reflecting the usage of CIM approaches, but it is not a simple, efficient solution to all evaluate phase issues. It needs to be used with care and better software is feasible, even for the simple treatment of dependence discussed in this chapter. The discrete probability approach used in this book is useful at a conceptual level, even if it is replaced by a Monte Carlo simulation approach for operational purposes. Mean variance approaches are also conceptually useful, but need great care when used in practice, especially if they tempt people to assume independence that does not exist.

Conclusion

In a fully developed SHAMPU process, the evaluate phase is the pivotal phase that directs where and how successive iterations develop the analysis. Figure 4.1 indicates two key loops back to other phases, the estimate and define phases, but in practice selective loops back to other phases (like the structure phase) will provide effective short cuts.

The effectiveness and the efficiency of the RMP as a whole depends on how well this iterative process works, in terms of the ability of the analysts to detect what is important and what is not, before spending too much time on the unimportant, without overlooking important threats or opportunities that do not stand out initially. Extensive probabilistic analysis based on carefully researched data can be very useful, but often such analysis is not appropriate. What is usually essential is an initial rough sizing of uncertainty from all the key sources that require management, followed by refinement in some areas where that refinement pays sufficient dividends. With notable exceptions, a focus on sizing uncertainty in order to evaluate the best way to use later passes should be the goal of a first pass through the SHAMPU process. It provides the initial understanding of which areas need the most attention and which can receive less. This assessment is itself prone to risk, which must be managed. But treating all aspects of project uncertainty as equally important in a single-pass process is foolish.

First-pass probabilities used to initiate the evaluate phase should be seen as simple statements of belief by those reasonably able to judge, brought together to provide a basis for discussing what matters and what does not. The numbers should be simple order-of-magnitude assessments, with a clear, overall health warning to the effect that no one will be held accountable for their accuracy. Only when and if it becomes clear where data analysis and objectively estimated probabilities might be useful should the accuracy of such estimates become a concern.

The approach recommended here is based on a need for efficient and effective decision taking, understanding that the probabilities used are a means to an end, not an end in themselves. What matters at the end of the day is the quality of the decisions taken, not the validity of the probability estimates.

The results we get when we combine probability distributions are critically dependent on the dependence assumptions used. Assuming independence when this is not an appropriate assumption renders probabilistic risk analysis misleading and dangerous, not just useless. Those who are not prepared to understand and reflect important dependencies should avoid probabilistic risk analysis. Those using risk analysis results provided by others should pay particular attention to the understanding of dependence displayed by their analysts and totally reject any probabilistic analysis that suggests a failure to deal with dependence in an appropriate manner.

If the range of values associated with an important variable is clearly misjudged by a factor of 10, the associated risk analysis is clearly suspect. If independence is assumed between half a dozen key variables when 50% dependence (or a coefficient of correlation of 0.5 or some equivalent level of dependence) is appropriate, the associated risk analysis is much more misleading. A factor of 10 error on a single variable may be a trivial error in comparison. Understanding dependence and understanding structure are related issues. The most effective way to deal with dependence in a statistical sense is to give it a causal structure that explains it. Statistical dependence is causal dependence we have failed to identify and structure.

Sometimes a causal structure for dependence is not feasible, and other times it is not cost-effective. In such cases experienced analysts can effectively employ measures like percentage dependence or coefficients of correlation. However, to develop that experience, working with causal structures and conditional specifications is an important part of the learning process.

12 Harness the plans

Plans are nothing, planning is everything.—Napoleon Bonaparte

Introduction

The plans produced during the harness phase of the SHAMPU (Shape, Harness, And Manage Project Uncertainty) process may be 'nothing' in Napoleon's implied sense that the one thing we can be sure of is that things will not happen exactly as planned. However, in Napoleon's implied sense the process of developing these plans is essential. In the SHAMPU process the earlier *shaping* phases (Table 4.2) are particularly important, but translating shaped, strategic plans into tactical plans ready for implementation is also important.

Harnessing the plans involves working with several different types of plans, and careful distinction between them and associated terminology is useful.

Project *reference plans* are the starting position for the SHAMPU process as captured in the define phase. They are defined in terms of all six *W*s and over the whole of the project life cycle (PLC), at a level of detail appropriate to a strategic approach to uncertainty management.

Project *strategic plans* are the reference plans with proactive responses to uncertainty and other changes suggested by the *shaping* phases embedded in them. By implication, reference plans are prototype strategic plans, the different terms allowing us to distinguish a starting point from an end point at this level.

Project *tactical plans* are a more detailed version of strategic plans, with added detail to make them appropriate for implementation. They are defined over a tactical planning horizon chosen to facilitate the development of effective plans for implementation purposes. This detail usually includes a much-disaggregated activity structure (20 activities may become 200 or 2,000), more detailed designs, and new detail, like detailed resource allocations and milestones initiating payments and an associated expenditure profile. Producing this detail takes the project out of the plan stage and into the allocate stage of the PLC, as indicated in Figure 4.2.

Project *contingency plans* are the operational form of recommended reactive responses that include trigger points (decision rules) initiating the reactive responses. They reflect anticipated potential departures from targets that deserve planning attention now, whether or not resource commitments are involved now. They may be defined at a tactical level or a strategic level. Both strategic and tactical plans as defined above are *base plans*, incorporating proactive responses but not reactive responses.

Project *action plans* are defined over *action horizons* that accommodate appropriate lead times, but do not go beyond these lead times. Action plans are distinguished from other plans by a commitment to action. By implication other plans remain relatively fluid. This commitment to action may be at a strategic level or at a tactical level and may include commitments needed for contingency plans to remain feasible.

The deliverables the harness phase should provide are in two basic forms: one is clearly stated project plans of all the kinds noted above; the other is documented uncertainty analysis associated with these plans.

It is useful to identify the specific tasks of the harness phase under three headings:

1. *Consolidate and explain the strategy*—Document, verify, assess, and report project strategy and associated uncertainty analysis, completing a current update of the process that has been ongoing since the SHAMPU process began and providing a snapshot of the current state of play.
2. *Formulate the tactics*—Use the project strategic plans and the associated uncertainty analysis to select project management tactics, and develop these into tactical plans and contingency plans that are ready for commitment to implementation within the action horizons, using lower-level risk management processes (RMPs) and intermediate levels of plans as appropriate.
3. *Support and convince*—Explain why the outputs associated with 1 and 2 above are effective and efficient, providing a case that is as convincing as the analysis to date will allow.

Figure 12.1 portrays the way these three specific tasks and associated steps can be used, assuming separate *support and convince* tasks for strategy and tactics, with separate associated *assess for approval* tasks. The structure of this chapter follows that of Figure 12.1.

Figure 12.1 shows no planned iterations apart from those within the harness phase involved in formulating the tactics. In practice, some unplanned iterations back to the SHAMPU define phase may be involved, but they are problems to be managed, not opportunities to be seized. Figure 12.1 shows unplanned iterations back to the define phase after assessing the strategy for approval, best avoided because of the negative aspects of a failed approval process. Figure 12.1 also shows unplanned iterations back to the define phase after assessing the tactics for approval, but unplanned iterations back to earlier SHAMPU phases this late in the PLC suggests earlier SHAMPU process failures that were serious. Stopping the project is a possibility, but stopping a project this late in the PLC suggests earlier process failures that were very serious. The defining difference between the end of the evaluate phase and the start of the harness phase is the desirability (or not) of iterations back to earlier phases, linked to the desirability of going public with the insights generated by the process in some cases.

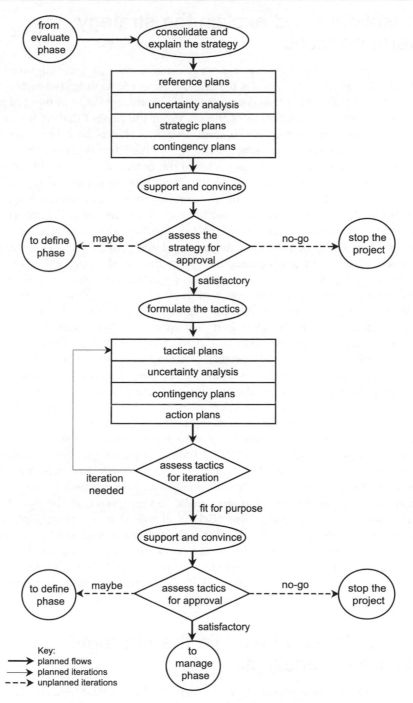

Figure 12.1—Specific tasks of the harness phase

Consolidate and explain the strategy: reference plans

Reference plans reflect the project description at a strategic level captured in the SHAMPU define phase as noted at the end of Chapter 5. As indicated earlier, senior executives and directors often comment on the immense value to them of a carefully crafted, simple explanation of the nature of the project that reference plans should provide. Ensuring an appropriate reference plan is available in an appropriately polished form is the essence of this step of the harness phase, drawing to an effective conclusion a process that started at the outset of the SHAMPU process.

It is important to recognize that to this point reference plans may have been dynamic, with relationships to initial reference plans that may not be worth elaboration. Reference plans can usefully capture some earlier misconceptions: to provide convenient 'straw men' to be knocked down by the uncertainty analysis in order to demonstrate the value of the RMP. Unlike strategic plans, reference plans need not be credible given the latest appreciation of project uncertainty, because they need not embed proactive responses. But if reference plans seriously embarrass any major players, they put the whole RMP at risk. Helping all major players to bury their embarrassing earlier misconceptions by revising reference plans is a key part of a successful RMP. Selective memory is often expedient. A key purpose of the RMP is to uncover aspects of project reference plans or associated project planning processes that need changes. However, provided all necessary changes are made, sometimes some changes are best kept confidential to the analyst and those responsible, to avoid any unnecessary embarrassment. Assuring everyone involved that this will be the case can be an important starting point at the beginning of the analysis. It is comparable with the confidentiality agreement any consultant signs before he or she starts work, except that it is informal and a separate arrangement with each individual player. The operative words here are *avoiding unnecessary embarrassment, provided necessary changes are made.* The practical reason why it is important to adopt this position, and make it very public at the outset in the SHAMPU define phase, should be obvious. If this is not done, people will be inhibited and defensive in a way that is both natural and entirely reasonable given their perspective and to the detriment of the project as a whole from the project owner's perspective. Our ultimate purpose is to help the project's owners succeed. 'Impartial science' operating like a loose cannon will be recognized as a danger by all concerned and properly treated as such.

Consolidate and explain the strategy: uncertainty analysis

An uncertainty analysis report at the strategic level of interest here should include as a minimum a comprehensive list of threats and opportunities, assessed in terms of implications given recommended proactive and reactive responses, along with an assessment of alternative potential proactive and reactive responses.

Uncertainty analysis needs to be documented to back up associated recommendations and to provide an explanation of the need for both proactive and reactive responses. A bottom-up risk analysis process involves a bottom-up documentation process, but it needs to be presented top-down to explain the overall position first, then elaborate on what is driving the uncertainty that matters, using nested sets of diagrams like Figure 11.5.

The process of interpreting uncertainty analysis in top-down terms can be regarded as the essence of this step in the harness phase. This top-down perspective can produce new insights, and it is important to give it the time and space in the overall process that it deserves. Like writing the executive summary for a report, attempting to explain what we understand can be an important process in clarifying and developing that understanding.

Communicating insight to allow decision takers to make choices reflecting *all* relevant issues is the goal. Analysis has serious limitations, and a failure to address these limitations when attempting to offer advice is a very serious mistake, possibly the most serious mistake an analyst can make. Consider a reasonably simple example to illustrate what is involved.

Example 12.1 Highlighting the implications of different bid prices

A major, international computer company wanted a formal system to address bidding for 'systems integration' projects, involving the supply of hardware, new software, revisions to existing software, revamped physical facilities, and retrained staff. The approach developed, often used by the authors as the basis for a case study for teaching purposes, employs a simplified version of the process explained in earlier chapters of this book to making some technical choices and choices between alternative subcontractors in order to derive an estimated expected cost for the project. Suppose the expected cost is estimated at £15 million.

The process then involves assessing a 'probability of winning' curve like that of Figure 12.2 and using it together with the expected cost to define a table like Table 12.1. Figure 12.2 implies that attempting to 'buy the work' with a bid below about £13 million is counterproductive and winning the bid with certainty is not possible. Once the bid is above the expected cost of £15 million, the probability of winning drops rapidly, although the rate of decline of the probability of winning as the bid continues to increase has to drop off as the probability approaches 0.

Table 12.1 implies that bidding at the expected cost involves zero expected profit; each £1 million added to the bid increases the conditional

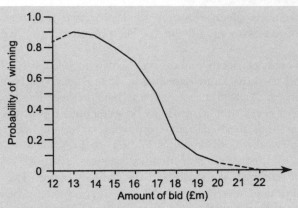

Figure 12.2—Probability of winning against amount bid.

Table 12.1—Profitability of different bids in Example 12.1

bid (£m)	probability of winning	profit if win (£m)	expected profit (£m)
13	0.90	−2.0	−1.80
14	0.88	−1.0	−0.88
15	0.80	0.0	0.00
16	0.70	1.0	0.70
17	0.50	2.0	1.00
18	0.20	3.0	0.60
19	0.10	4.0	0.40
20	0.05	5.0	0.25

expected profit (the expected profit given we win) by £1 million; each £1 million added to the bid increases the unconditional expected profit (profit × probability of winning) by an amount that peaks at a £17 million bid, thereafter declining because of the rate of decline of the probability of winning.

The textbook solution that maximizes expected profit is to bid at £17 million. In practice, what is vitally important is not providing the decision takers with a recommendation 'bid £17 million', but instead giving them Table 12.1 and explaining:

- If the expected cost is of the order of £15 million and if Figure 12.2 is roughly consistent with their beliefs, then bidding at £17 million will maximize short-term expected profit, but: (a) a bid of £16 million increases the chance of winning from 0.50 to 0.70, with an expected profit reduction of £0.3 million; (b) a bid of £15 million increases the chance of winning from 0.50 to 0.80, with an expected profit reduction of £1.0 million.

- These trade-offs will not be significantly affected by minor changes to the expected cost or Figure 12.2, any decision takers' 'what ifs' being amenable to modelling.
- If such analysis is used regularly, recording the probability of winning as forecast by curves like Figure 12.2 will allow feedback to correct any bias in the estimation of such curves.
- Such curves are implicit in any bidding process, as are the trade-offs that lead to departures from the short-run, profit-maximizing bid.
- The use of a table like Table 12.1 allows quantification and data accumulation to test subjective estimates where this is feasible and useful, facilitating the use of this information in conjunction with management judgements about softer issues, such as long-term market advantages associated with winning a bid and the advantages of work to keep otherwise idle or redundant staff busy.

Chapman and Ward (2002, chap. 3) elaborates this analysis.

Consolidate and explain the strategy: strategic plans

It is worth explaining the reference plans and the uncertainty analysis prior to developing an overview of the strategic plans—the focus of this step. The contrast between the reference plans and the strategic plans that this provides can be interpreted as a selling opportunity for risk management, especially if an RMP is being used for the first time in an organization. However, the more substantive reason is a clear demonstration of the quality of thinking that took a plausible reference plan and refined it, or reconstructed it, to produce a risk efficient and robust strategic plan incorporating proactive responses developed by the uncertainty analysis. The strategic plans do not need a separate document. In a report that embodies both the reference plans and the uncertainty analysis, the strategic plans can take the form of a summary of recommended proactive responses and other changes to be embedded in the reference plans. However, in conceptual and operational terms it is useful to see the reference plans and strategic plans as separate entities.

Users of RMPs at the senior executive and director level should see the presence of a sound strategic plan associated with a sound process for its development as a key product of the RMP. A *go* decision for the project should be anticipated at this stage in the RMP, and no significant project management errors of omission or commission should remain. Sometimes it is not feasible to produce such a plan, because of unresolved issues. This is usually a clear sign of impending problems that require immediate management, making a *maybe* decision for the project the prudent choice.

Consolidate and explain the strategy: contingency plans

When seeking approval for a strategy, it may be appropriate to formally elaborate reactive responses in terms of well-developed contingency plans, including trigger points and decision rules, for all significant threats and opportunities that are not fully dealt with via proactive responses. Such contingency plans may be the only effective way to deal with important events that have a low probability and a high impact. However, a separate document for contingency plans is not required, and a summary list of recommended reactive responses may be all that is needed at this point. Even if the latter is the case, it is useful to see contingency plans as separate entities in conceptual and operational terms.

Support and convince at a strategic level

Convincing those responsible for a project *go/no-go/maybe* decision to agree to a *go* can be associated with a change in the mode of operation at this point in the process, from crafted report writing to selling the recommendations of the report. It can be useful to make this change explicit, just to acknowledge the need for going beyond writing a good report. However, once this is done, it becomes obvious that the selling process, more generally defined as taking all key players with us, needs to start much earlier. In precedence relationship terms, this task has a 'finish to finish' relationship with consolidating and explaining the strategy, not a 'finish to start' relationship.

Those experienced with the use of formal analysis to assist with decision taking clearly understand that formal analysis does not make decisions for people, it simply guides decision taking. The support and convince task is concerned with providing an interface between analysis as reported in formal documents and a clear understanding of the issues in holistic terms. It is also concerned with changing people's perceptions in advance of formal reporting when culture change issues are involved, and it may involve important aspects of bargaining to achieve this.

Assess strategy to gain approval

Assessing project strategy ought to focus on uncertainty at a strategic level, not the details, and it ought to start with the difficult issues, not the easy issues. One key reason for separate assessments to gain approval at strategic and tactical levels is to ensure this focus is not lost. It is easier to maintain a strategic focus if detailed tactical plans have yet to be developed.

A failure to achieve a *go* decision for the project at this point should be seen by all concerned as a failure of the project planning process as a whole, which may include a failure of earlier risk management. Chapman and Ward (2002, chaps 2 and 12) address some of these issues.

Assuming a *go* decision is achieved, this triggers transition from the plan stage to the allocate stage of the PLC.

Formulate the tactics: tactical plans

Risk management for some projects requires early consideration of appropriate planning horizons with respect to project reference plans. Often these are captured in the definition of distinct project phases. For example, a project planned to take 15 years may involve a 'phase one', which is effectively the first three or four years, followed by several subsequent phases, in the form of Figure 2.2a. Usually these project phases are defined in terms of deliverables, such as feasibility, development, permission to proceed from a regulator, an operational prototype, production of the 'first of class', and so on.

Sometimes these distinctions are driven by very different types of decisions requiring very different decision processes, an issue that can be very important. For example, deciding what portfolio of sources of electric power an electricity utility ought to aim for at a 25 year horizon, in terms of the mix of nuclear, oil, gas, and other sources, requires a very different form of analysis than that required to make a decision to build plant *A* or *B* over the next 10 years and the timing of the construction of *B* if that is the choice (Chapman and Ward, 2002, chap. 11). However, the general principle is less need for detail and more need for flexibility with respect to strategic choices as we look further into the future. Project management processes that are not integrated with formal risk management tend to use common levels of detail for the whole of each phase, often at two or more levels connected by a hierarchical 'hammocking' structure that tends to be fairly detailed at the most detailed level. The basic idea is to adopt different levels of detail for different purposes.

Planning horizons are important for any kind of plans. Planning horizons may not receive explicit attention in reference plans, but prior to implementation both tactical plans and associated contingency plans require explicit consideration of an appropriate planning horizon—a 'tactical horizon'. A key driver of an appropriate tactical horizon that needs to be identified is the range of associated 'action horizons'—the initial periods of the planning horizon that require detailed action plans and firm commitments. 'Action plans' at a tactical level are the front-end tactical plans and contingency plans that involve a commitment to implementation.

It would be convenient if an action horizon were a single time period, say three months, associated with a regular review and revision of plans as necessary. It is useful to use a single period as a basis for planning. However, different action horizons will be associated with different resources (e.g., ordering critical materials or contracting for critical plant may involve relatively long lead times). Hence, it is usually useful to choose a lowest common denominator review period for tactical plans, like a week or a month, but recognize longer action horizons for specific types of resource.

It would also be convenient if detailed planning could be constrained to the action horizon. However, a longer horizon involving tactical plans and contingency plans is usually required.

Distinguishing action plans from tactical plans and associated contingency plans more generally is desirable because tactical and contingency plans over a reasonable tactical horizon are required to shape action plans and provide a basis for subsequent action plans, but they do not require a commitment to action yet. It may also prove useful to see some strategic plans as action plans (e.g., because commitments are made to end dates), without constraining associated tactical plans.

Experience with RMPs suggests that too much detailed planning beyond a plausible tactical horizon is wasted effort. It usually involves largely deterministic planning effort that would be better spent on uncertainty management, with detailed planning for implementation purposes restricted to a much shorter tactical horizon. Detailed planning of actions beyond a plausible tactical horizon is typically undertaken on the implicit assumption that this plan is what will happen—the one thing we can be fairly sure will not happen.

Effective use of tactical horizons to produce significant saving in detailed planning effort involves a culture change. In the absence of RMPs it is detailed planning that gives people confidence in higher-level plans, or strong nerves. Once people become used to detail being limited to a plausible tactical horizon, they become grateful for the avoidance of what is then seen as unnecessary effort, in addition to seeing the saved time better spent on the RMP.

Effective use of action horizons in terms of increased focus on the flexible nature of plans that are not action plans and more effective change control more generally is a separate but related culture change issue. Once people get used to making the distinction between action plans and other plans, they become more focused on exploiting opportunities associated with flexibility and on resisting costly changes in commitments.

The essence of this task is: choosing an appropriate level of detail for tactical planning; rolling that planning forward within the boundaries provided by the strategic plans; relating these tactical plans to action horizons until all appropriate action horizons are accommodated; and then going a bit farther with the tactical plans to reach a plausible tactical horizon. The plausible nature of the tactical horizon means it is rounded to a convenient span like six months or a year, and it is plausible to assume optimization of the tactical plans over the action horizons.

Formulate the tactics: uncertainty analysis

Uncertainty associated with strategic plans and associated contingency plans will have been shaped by the *shaping* phases, but the additional detail provided by the last step may require lower-level RMPs to refine and develop both proactive and reactive responses. For example, an offshore North Sea project treated in terms of 40 activities in the shaping phases might involve 400 activities at this point. An activity like 'fabricate the modules' (packages of equipment and accommodation installed on top of the offshore platform) that did not distinguish different types of modules earlier can now be decomposed into 10 or so activities to consider each module individually, recognizing different lead times and sources of uncertainty. A lower-level RMP necessarily involves much more detail in terms of the activity structure and the other five Ws, and usually it will involve much less pay-off for effective uncertainty management, so simpler models should be anticipated on average. However, some situations may warrant significant sophistication: a particularly critical module in the above example might warrant very detailed treatment of sources of uncertainty, including attention to contractual issues and particular contractor choices.

Continuing with this illustrative example: for large projects involving a lot of uncertainty, it may be worth seeing the lower-level RMP at this point in the overall SHAMPU process as a 400-activity variant of a 40-activity process used earlier and embedding a largely deterministic 4,000-activity variant in it to reach the level of detail needed for implementation. That is, a single-level RMP is very ineffective, because it does not distinguish strategy and tactics effectively. At least two levels are recommended to increase effectiveness efficiently. Three or more levels might be appropriate in some cases, implying intermediate planning levels that may need a distinguishing label. This is consistent with the notion of hierarchical network structures often used for planning large projects.

Whether or not even a very large project requires more than two levels, with a very decomposed activity level structure at the bottom, will depend on issues like the extent to which work is done in-house or contracted out, the extent to which in-house work is managed centrally or locally, and so on.

Small projects involving modest levels of uncertainty might use only five to ten activities at the reference and strategic planning level and a purely deterministic approach to planning at the tactical level. This two-level approach might accommodate quite a wide range of projects if the number of activities at the strategic level is increased, but a deterministic approach to tactical planning is preserved. When project size and uncertainty makes simple RMPs and then more complex RMPs at the second level desirable is not clearly definable in general terms. However, a minimum of two levels is useful for most projects, and it is important to link the levels in terms of a nested RMP structure. A single level of planning for both strategic and tactical purposes is neither effective nor efficient for any project, always allowing for the rare exception that proves the rule.

A deterministic approach to tactical planning does not mean that the important features of an RMP should not be preserved. For example, deterministic tactical plans in activity terms should still embed proactive responses, identified sources should still be linked to contingency plans, ownership of uncertainty in financial and managerial terms still needs clear definition, and a judgement that this collective uncertainty is effectively captured by the strategic level portrayal of it is essential. The only thing that may be missing is a bottom-up probabilistic analysis to confirm the strategic level's top-down view of what has now been decomposed to clarify the detail for implementation purposes.

These different levels in terms of activity decomposition should be reflected in related treatment of the other five Ws: level of detail in terms of timing, resource definition, resource allocation, design detail, and the management of different party motivation issues.

The level of detail and the tactical/strategic emphasis are drivers that should significantly shape the RMPs used at different levels via the focus phase, along with related issues like the objectives of the analysis. This may have significant modelling implications. For example, at a strategic level, the ambiguity associated with activity precedence relationships may require probabilistic modelling (Cooper and Chapman, 1987) and make some standard network packages inappropriate. However, at a tactical level, reasonably strict precedence relationships may be a viable assumption, and generalized PERT (Program Evaluation and Review Technique) models might be viable if all significant low-probability and high-impact issues are modelled in a SCERT (Synergistic Contingency Planning and Review Technique) structure at the strategic level.

Formulate the tactics: contingency plans

If lower level RMPs are used to develop tactical plans, there may be no need to make a starting point/end point distinction comparable with the reference/strategic plan distinction. The strategic level reference plans may have associated, more detailed plans, but a significant gap between strategic plans and reference plans suggests basing tactical plans directly on strategic plans. This reinforces the long-run case for avoiding detailed planning outside the RMP. Tactical plans can evolve as refinements and restructuring takes place, and proactive responses can be embedded directly. The end point is all that matters unless the process is in question. For simplicity this is assumed to be the case here.

However, developing distinct contingency plans at this level may be very important, assumed to be the case here. That is, reactive responses need to be identified and associated trigger points and other decision rules need to be developed, prior to committing to these tactical plans.

Formulate the tactics: action plans

Whatever form the strategic, tactical, and possible intermediate plans takes, the bottom-line deliverable is *action plans*, including aspects of contingency plans requiring early commitment. This step provides a focus for the development of this deliverable, drawing on all earlier analysis. A comparable step was not required at the end of the strategic level part of the harness phase.

The mechanics are quite straightforward in principle. Refining the 'rules of engagement' provided by triggers and clarifying lead time assumptions usually takes some effort. An effective earlier RMP will have done the hard work, but careful attention to detail at this stage is important.

Formulate the tactics: assess tactics for iterative purposes

Iterations within the RMP used to develop effective and efficient tactical plans and action plans from the strategic plans should be planned for, in the same way as the iterations in the *shaping* phases of the SHAMPU process are planned for. Formulating tactics is a lower level version of shaping strategy. There are important differences, but both need an iterative approach for comparable reasons.

Support and convince with respect to tactics

Supporting and convincing with respect to project tactics should be relatively straightforward and quite different in nature from supporting and convincing with respect to project strategy. But it shares one feature: useful separation from the formal, reported results of a formal process to stress the need for a dialogue that accommodates wider issues. Some of this may involve negotiation about issues like exact boundaries for action plans and plans left open until a later review process: agreeing what should be decided now, what has to be decided by the next review point, and what decisions can be left beyond that point. Such issues can be addressed throughout the process of formulating the tactics, or earlier, but they need addressing before the next step. A possible difference in emphasis is 'managing downward' as opposed to 'managing upward', in the sense that it is particularly important at this stage to ensure that those who are responsible for the tasks at a tactical level are comfortable with the plans (i.e., that top-down and bottom-up plans interface properly). However, to the extent possible managing in both directions simultaneously and holistically is a worthwhile goal throughout the process.

Assess tactics to gain approval

This final assessment before the SHAMPU manage phase and project execute stage begin ought to be straightforward relative to the earlier strategy assessment. However, sometimes 'the devil is in the details'. Adjustments to strategy that are 'refinements' should be expected and accommodated with a minimum of fuss, but they are unwelcome. Adjustments to strategy that require a complete rethink will be seriously unwelcome. 'Better now than later' is a usefully positive frame of mind to adopt, but 'better still if threats or opportunities had been responded to earlier' is the clear message. Stopping the project at this stage will raise questions about the competence of the project team, and threaten careers. It may also raise questions about the RMP and associated project management processes.

Budgets used for financial control purposes are usually part of what is approved at this stage, and associated estimates and controls are related to base plan activity durations and other performance measures. The use of estimates for control purposes requires an understanding of which issues are the responsibilities of which parties and how parties are motivated to behave. Chapman and Ward (2002) explore these concerns in some detail, especially in chaps 4, 5, and 6. Within the SHAMPU process these concerns are addressed in the ownership phase. Final details may receive attention in a lower-level RMP within the harness phase, but strategic issues should have been resolved during the earlier shaping phases.

Conclusion

The purpose of the SHAMPU harness phase is to use all the analysis of the preceding *shaping* phases to develop project plans that pass appropriate assessments and result in a project ready for implementation. Some key messages of this chapter are linked to three specific tasks.

- *Consolidating and explaining the strategy* is the first mode of analysis peculiar to the harness phase. The material this is based on must be produced in the required form from the outset. In a very real sense, 'writing the final report' begins on day 1 of the RMP. However, finishing this report effectively involves a lot of craft, a very clear understanding of why analysis was undertaken, and an ability to explain what was discovered that is important. There is nothing magic about craft. It is based on experience in a learning environment, as understood by craftspeople as far back as one cares to go. The science in terms of a systematic structure provided by modern RMPs does not replace craft skills. It makes them more demanding and more useful and their absence more visible. This enhanced visibility may be perceived as a threat by the incompetent, but it is an opportunity for both the competent and their managers.

- *Formulating the tactics* is the core of the harness phase. It literally provides a bridge between the output of the shaping phases of the SHAMPU process as approved and the action plans needed to implement the project. Again, craft skills and a clear grasp of purposes and possibilities are important. What the formality of the SHAMPU process does is to clarify what is needed.
- *Support and convince* tasks interface the abstraction of analysis with the messy details of reality, accommodating the need for different people with different perspectives and concerns to use the same analysis to reach joint decisions. Finding the most effective manner to interact with people during the process of analysis is a craft, not a science, and it is an important aspect of the craft skills required to achieve a successful RMP.

Separating approval at a strategic level and approval at a tactical level, with separate associated support and convince tasks, is important in conceptual terms and at a practical level. In particular, it helps to separate the plan and allocate stages of the PLC, ensuring a sound strategic plan is in place before detailed planning begins. This makes time that might otherwise be wasted on redundant detailed planning available for risk management at both strategic and tactical levels. In terms of managing an RMP as a programme of projects this is an important opportunity to discover and exploit uncertainty for organizations that currently base their confidence in project plans on detailed deterministic planning. For organizations that use an RMP and currently see no need for this distinction, it may be useful to question the level that their RMP operates at. If it is *de facto* at a tactical level, because of the level of detail used from the outset, the opportunity to address strategic planning issues using RMPs that are appropriate for strategic issues is of considerable importance and should be pursued.

As indicated in Chapter 4, the SCERT process did not involve a harness phase and interpretation of the plan phase equivalent in the Project Risk Analysis and Management (PRAM) framework was not as clear as it might have been. The strategic aspects of the harness phase described in this chapter are based on Chapman's first-hand observations of how successful users of SCERT-based RMPs operated. The tactical aspects of the harness phase described in this chapter are based on second-hand observations of follow-on planning that was significantly beyond Chapman's remit, but their nature is reasonably straightforward.

13 Manage implementation

I have never known a battle plan to survive a first contact with the enemy.—19th century general

Introduction

If project 'management' is decomposed into 'planning' and 'control', a classic binary division, we are now leaving the realm of planning and moving into control, maintaining an ongoing interest in planning. Even the very best of plans need adjusting in the heat of battle, but this chapter is also about the role of initiative and training to bridge the gap between what needs to be done and plans that work.

Planning in this general sense has been decomposed extensively in the earlier chapters of this book. It could be argued that the simple treatment of planning and control offered in this chapter seriously understates the importance of the doing as opposed to the thinking about the doing. For example, leadership, motivating people to 'reach for the sky', and motivating people to work as a team can be more important to project success than anything discussed in this book. However, these issues are also central to the whole of the earlier process. This chapter concentrates on building on the results of the earlier SHAMPU (Shape, Harness, And Manage Project Uncertainty) phases to assist the project Risk Management Process (RMP). There is no intention to play down the importance of other issues.

The basic message of this chapter is that once a project starts there are four quite different, new, specific tasks associated with the SHAMPU manage phase: *manage planned actions, roll action plans forward, monitor and control*, and *manage crises and be prepared to respond to disasters*. These four tasks have to be managed in parallel in conjunction with one basic *assess* common task, as indicated in Figure 13.1. The format of this chapter follows Figure 13.1.

A unique characteristic of Figure 13.1 relative to earlier phase equivalents is the parallel nature of the specific tasks. Effort on all four fronts may not be continuous, but this phase does not involve sequential treatment of these four specific tasks. This has important practical implications. For example, for a large project, if one person is formally responsible for all four specific tasks, problems are almost inevitable if they do not delegate each to a suitable champion and if they do not regularly remind themselves of the need to manage all four simultaneously. Just as earlier phases of the SHAMPU process make extensive use of

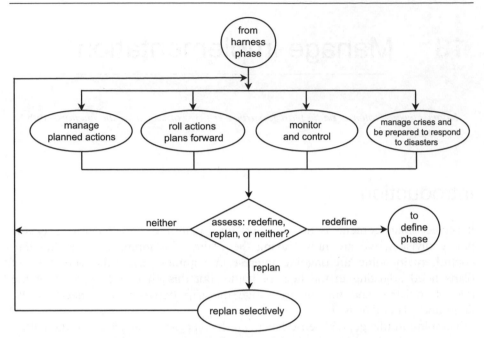

Figure 13.1—Specific tasks of the manage phase

iterations, so iterations are central to the manage phase. However, the four specific tasks require parallel treatment.

Manage planned actions

Operational plans for the immediate 'action horizon' require implementation in the manage phase. This is the basis of progressing the achievement of the project's objectives. Managing this aspect of the project is the basis of project management in the manage phase.

Translating plans into actions is seldom entirely straightforward. Some see the key as planning detail. We see the key as insight about what might happen, as distinct from what we hope will happen, with particular reference to the motivation of the parties involved and a clear vision of what really matters and what does not.

Excessive planning detail in a deterministic framework can be a serious handicap. A simply defined, deterministic base plan embedded in a simple understanding of the uncertainties involved can be much more effective. It can also be much more 'fun' for those involved, 'empowering' them to make decisions, which encourages 'seizing opportunities', providing 'ownership', and generating improved performance through a proper understanding of the project team as a collection of people, with all that implies.

Consider an analogy, based on North American (Canadian or US) football. A distinguishing feature of North American football relative to European football is 'downs'. Leaving aside opening and post-'touchdown' (scoring) 'kick-offs', play starts when the ball is lifted from the ground by the offensive team. Play stops when a forward pass is dropped, the ball carrier is tackled, the ball leaves the field, an offence is committed, or scoring takes place. Each of these 'plays' is separated by a period of reorganization for the next down. This allows detailed planning for the next play in the 'huddle'. When the quarterback says 'number 93' (play number 93), each player knows what he is supposed to do. The plan for a play specifies base plan actions for all players. On most plays, a score is the planned result if everyone does what they are supposed to. The self-evident failure to score with every play does not detract from the value of the planning. Nor does the planning inhibit a skilled running back (ball carrier) or a skilled blocker.

Most project plans are not prespecified plays, and most projects follow their base plans more closely than North American football players. However, the analogy has value in terms of clarifying the distinction between successive action plans and what has to be done to actually move the ball forward. Formal planning in terms of what the play specifies for each play requires additional informal planning by each player. More generally, the higher the skill levels of the players the less players need to be instructed in detail and the more they are able to interpret plans flexibly and effectively in response to what is happening on the ground in real time. Effective use of contingency plans is part of the training, not part of the plan *per se*, although base plans without such contingency plans are of limited use.

Routine project-planning meetings concerned with implementing planned actions should have some of the characteristics of a North American football huddle, including each member of the team being reminded what everyone else is planning to do, how and why they may fail, and reaffirming team bonding. Project activity between meetings should have some of the characteristics of a successful offensive North American football play, including each member of the team doing their best at their own prescribed task, capitalizing on opportunities, and minimizing the impact of teammate failures.

European football (soccer) involves less formal play planning, without the downs structure. This chapter's failure to develop the analogy to include European football should not be seen as a matter of bias. Some time was spent speculating on analogies, but their development is left to the reader.

Roll action plans forward

The 'action horizon' concept developed in Chapter 12 is very important, to avoid wasteful and inhibiting detailed planning. It is part of knowing what is not important and is just as vital as knowing what is important. If the importance of this distinction is grasped, rolling action plans forward becomes a vital ongoing aspect of the manage phase.

In terms of the earlier North American football analogy, we need to call the next play. The formality of calling the next play is perhaps the most appropriate analogy for project RMPs, but a chess analogy also has value. In a chess player's terms, we need to plan moves as far ahead as our capabilities allow, with a view to the next move, but even chess 'masters' do not plan games to 'checkmate' from the outset. A risk management planning horizon needs to be limited for similar reasons. Until we see what happens, some aspects of detailed planning are an inhibiting waste of time. But anticipation in broad strategic terms needs to go beyond the next move or play. A key difference between chess masters and other chess players is the effectiveness of the way they anticipate what will happen without detailed analysis of all possible moves. Devices that can be useful in this context include:

1. updated, detailed plans for all activities to be undertaken during the action horizon, with ownership of issues and responsibility for issues clearly indicated, as well as anticipated progress;
2. a short, prioritized list of issues requiring ongoing management attention, with changes in priority emphasized and trends assessed, and both ownership in financial terms and managerial responsibility clearly defined.

Monitor and control

The North American football example is a useful analogy to carry forward. In the context of the *monitor and control* task it facilitates a clear distinction between formal and informal monitoring and control at different levels of authority.

For example, a running back with the ball under his arm has to monitor play and respond instinctively in fractions of a second. At the end of each play, the quarterback has to monitor progress to choose the next play. The coach will also monitor at this level and may intervene, directly specifying the next play. The manager may get involved at this level and will do so in terms of half-time and end-of-game reviews. End-of-game and end-of-season reviews may involve still higher levels of monitoring and control.

Projects involve very important informal monitoring as well as formal monitoring and change control processes at various levels. As in most other aspects of project risk management, simple devices are usually the best unless there is clear reason for more complex devices. A device that has proven useful for a century is the Gantt chart, indicating planned progress in relation to progress achieved to date in a simple, visual manner.

A useful update on the classical statistical control chart (plotting actual outcomes within preplotted confidence bands) are charts plotting actual outcomes (in cost, duration, or other performance terms) in relation to preplotted target, expected, and commitment values.

Each time the project plan is reviewed, eliminating the issues that have now been realized or avoided, confidence band assessments should contract, unless new issues are envisaged. Plotting how this process is progressing can be useful, especially if some serious setbacks have been experienced but the chance of achieving commitments is stable or improving. However, this is an example of a relatively complex portrayal of the monitoring process, best used infrequently at high levels. The lower the level and the more frequent the monitoring activity the simpler the devices have to be.

It is worth remembering that people directly involved in a project are usually all too well aware when things are going wrong. Usually the concern is not a need for devices to detect when things are going wrong; it is having ways of explaining what is going wrong in order to persuade appropriate people to take appropriate action. More generally, the concern is to ensure that processes are in place that encourage this level of communication to take place in an effective manner.

The distinction between target, expected value, and commitment estimates is of substantial importance in relation to the *monitor and control* task. Managing the process of reconciling what actually happens to these three types of estimates is essential if the monitoring process is to facilitate an understanding of the implications of departures from base plans.

Given a *monitor and control* task that is defined to reflect these links and generate responses using the whole of the RMP outlined earlier, monitoring is not a mechanical reactive task; it is a flexible and creative proactive task, concerned with understanding what is happening in real time in relation to what was planned, anticipating future departures from plans, and initiating all necessary revisions to earlier plans.

Manage crises and be prepared to respond to disasters

Managing planned actions can embrace the variations from base plans that do not warrant contingency plans and the management of variations via contingency plans. A major concern of formal risk management is to avoid nasty surprises that give rise to crises, which then require crisis management. However, it is very unwise to be unprepared for crisis.

Crisis might be defined as 'a time of acute danger or difficulty' or 'a major turning point'. The best responses in general terms are based on insight, effective and efficient information systems, being prepared, being able to respond rapidly, and being decisive. Viewing crisis management as contingency management for

significant unspecified and unanticipated events, a more effective crisis management strategy will make it effective and efficient to devote less time to contingency planning for specified and anticipated events. This view connects with the
concern to develop 'general responses' discussed earlier in Example 8.2.

If we accept crisis in the sense defined above as something we must be
prepared to manage, it follows that a 'disaster' in the sense of a 'crisis we fail
to manage effectively' is something we need to be prepared to respond to. At the
very least there may be legal liability issues.

Assess: redefine, replan, or neither?

Assessment should be initiated by any unplanned significant events, significant
planned events, and the completion of review time cycles. Assessment may
simply confirm that the project can proceed as planned. However, it may indicate a need to go right back to the define (the project) phase or a need for an
intermediate loop back. Figure 4.1 shows only the basic interphase loop back to
the define phase, but judicious use of selective replanning can be effective and
efficient.

Exception or change reporting issues need to be addressed in this context,
'change control' being a thorny issue requiring special care. An adequate grasp of
the importance of this issue at the outset can have a profound effect on the
whole of the project. For example, the nature of all contracts, the nature of the
design, and the basic technologies employed can reflect a need to minimize
changes or to respond effectively to changes that are inevitable.

Conclusion

This is the shortest chapter of the nine addressing each phase of the SHAMPU
process. The manage phase draws on all the earlier phases. This chapter only
addresses new issues. Even so, there is clearly scope for considerable development of the material addressed in this chapter and for further issues to be
addressed in the context of an effective manage phase.

Part III
Closing the loop

Part II made a number of assumptions in order to describe the nine-phase generic framework outlined in Chapter 4. Part III must address relaxation of these assumptions. However, other 'unfinished business' also has to be addressed, concerned with designing and operating efficient and effective risk management processes (RMPs).

Chapter 14 explores the implications of initiating an RMP at different stages in the project life cycle (PLC).

Chapter 15 considers making RMPs *efficient* as well as *effective*, providing two extended examples to illustrate what is involved in practice.

Chapter 16 addresses uncertainty and risk ownership issues, considering a contractor's perspective, and the need to align client and contractor motivation.

Chapter 17 takes a corporate perspective of project RMPs and considers what is involved in establishing and sustaining an organizational project risk management capability.

Risk management initiated at different stages in the project life cycle

14

Experience is not what happens to you, it is what you do with what happens to you.—Aldous Huxley

Introduction

The opportunities for undertaking risk management during the life cycle of a given project are considerable. Table 14.1 gives examples of ways in which risk management could contribute to each stage of the project life cycle (PLC). This acknowledges that risk management could be usefully applied on a separate and different basis in each stage of a PLC without the necessity for risk management in any previous or subsequent stages (e.g., risk analysis could form part of an 'evaluation' step in any stage of the PLC). Alternatively, risk analysis might be used to guide initial progress in each PLC stage. In these circumstances, the focus of risk analysis is likely to reflect immediate project management concerns in the associated project stage (e.g., risk analysis might be undertaken as part of the PLC plan stage primarily to consider the feasibility and development of the work schedule for project execution). There might be no expectation that such risk analysis would or should influence the design, although it might be perceived as a potential influence on subsequent work allocation decisions. In practice, many risk analyses are intentionally limited in scope, as in individual studies to determine the reliability of available equipment, the likely outcome of a particular course of action, or to evaluate alternative decision options within a particular PLC stage. This can be unfortunate if it implies a limited, *ad hoc*, bolted-on, optional extra approach to risk management, rather than undertaking risk management as an integral, built-in part of project management. Wherever it is carried out in a PLC, risk analysis needs to be regarded as a contribution to risk management of the whole project. The opportunities for risk management include looking forward and backward at any stage in the PLC, addressing all the issues indicated by Table 14.1 as appropriate.

This chapter considers the implications of initiating a risk nanagement process (RMP) at various stages of the PLC. The reasons for undertaking risk management of a project can change significantly over the PLC, because the project itself changes and because what is known about the project changes, sometimes in

Table 14.1—Roles for risk analysis in the project life cycle (PLC)

stages of the PLC	roles for risk analysis
conceive the product	identifying stakeholders and their expectations identifying appropriate performance objectives
design the product strategically	testing the reliability of design testing the feasibility of design setting performance criteria assessing the likely cost of a design assessing the likely benefits from a design assessing the effect of changes to a design
plan execution strategically	identifying and allowing for regulatory constraints assessing the feasibility of a plan assessing the likely duration of a plan assessing the likely cost of a plan determining appropriate milestones estimating resources required at a strategic level assessing the effect of changes to the plan determining appropriate levels of contingency funds and resources assessment of contracting strategy at an overview level
allocate resources tactically	estimating resources required at a more detailed level assessment of contracting strategy at a more detailed level evaluating alternative procurement strategies defining contractual terms and conditions determining appropriate risk-sharing arrangements assessing the implications of contract conditions assessing and comparing competitive tenders determining appropriate target costs and bid prices for contracts estimating likely profit following project termination
execute production	identify remaining execution issues assessing implications of changes to design or plan revising estimates of cost on completion revising estimates of the completion time of the execution stage
deliver the product	identifying issues impacting delivery assessing the feasibility of a delivery schedule assessing the feasibility of meeting performance criteria assessing the reliability of testing equipment assessing a requirement for resources to modify a product assessing the availability of commissioning facilities
review the process	assessing the effectiveness of risk management strategies identifying realized sources and effective responses
support the product	identifying the extent of future liabilities assessing appropriate levels of resources required assessing the profitability of the project

quite profound ways. This warrants some modifications and changes of emphasis in any RMP.

Initiating an RMP in the plan stage of a selected project

In Part II it was assumed that an RMP, the SHAMPU (Shape, Harness, And Manage Project Uncertainty) process, is initiated toward the end of a project's plan stage. The rationale behind this was that toward the end of the plan stage is the easiest place to start for first-time users of an RMP, with the best chance of success. By this stage of a project a fair amount of information about the project is available, but scope for significant contributions to project performance by pursuit of formal risk management is likely to remain. If formal risk management is introduced in an organization on a *voluntary* basis, a first-time application to a project at this stage offers the best organizational learning opportunities. It also makes sense to choose a project to learn on that has three characteristics:

1. the project has been very well managed to date;
2. despite the project's successful management to date, uncertainty raises important concerns that need to be addressed to the satisfaction of those granting sanction;
3. there is sufficient time to undertake a comprehensive RMP.

If these three characteristics apply, first-time formal risk management toward the end of the plan stage of a project can be comparatively rewarding and trouble-free. The essence of the argument is 'learn to walk in well-charted terrain before you try to run on difficult, more uncertain terrain', and 'learn about the terrain as a whole before you attempt short cuts under pressure'. This point is discussed in more detail in Chapter 15. We hope the reader interested in direct application of the ideas developed in this book will be able to try them out for the first time in the plan stage of a carefully selected project.

If an RMP is applied for the first time on a *non-voluntary* basis, the plan stage of a project is the most likely point at which it will be required. The requirements of banks and boards motivate many first-time users to employ an RMP, and the plan stage is usually when this requirement can no longer be avoided. Moreover, *prudent* boards and banks will insist on a *comprehensive* RMP if first-time users of RMPs are involved.

Initiating an RMP in other stages of a project

Initiating risk management in a project before the plan stage is in general more difficult, because the project is more fluid and less well defined. A more fluid project means more degrees of freedom, more alternatives to consider, including alternatives that may be eliminated as the project matures, for reasons unrelated to the RMP. A less well-defined project means appropriate documentation is hard to come by and alternative interpretations of what is involved may not be resolvable. Risk management earlier in the PLC is usually less quantitative, less formal, less tactical, more strategic, more creative, and more concerned with the identification and capture of opportunities. Before the plan stage of the PLC it can be particularly important to be very clear about project objectives, in the limit decomposing project objectives and formally mapping their relationships with project activities, because pre-emptive responses to risks need to facilitate lateral thinking that addresses entirely new ways of achieving objectives. Also there is scope for much more fundamental improvements in project plans, perhaps including uncertainty and risk-driven design or redesign of the product of the project. Undertaking formal risk management in an objectives–benefits–design–activities framework clearly demands explicit attention to risk management as early as possible, preferably in the conceive stage. Further, it suggests planning in more formal terms the progression from the conceive stage to later stages in the PLC.

For a given project, initiating any RMP later than the PLC plan stage gives rise to several difficulties, without any significant, worthwhile, compensating benefits. The basic problem is like the one that evokes the response to a request for directions: 'if I were going there, I wouldn't start from here.' After the plan stage, contracts are in place, equipment has been purchased, commitments are in place, reputations are on the line, and managing change is comparatively difficult and unrewarding. That said, even a later RMP can and should encompass routine reappraisal of a project's viability. In this context early warnings are preferable to late recognition that targets are incompatible or unachievable. In general, better late than never.

The next two sections consider the implications of moving the initial application of an RMP on a project back to the design and conceive stages, respectively. Following sections consider the form of an RMP initiated in later PLC stages: first in the allocate stage, then in the execute stage, and so on. In each section the focus of the discussion is moving a first use of an RMP in any given project from the plan stage to another PLC stage, but, where appropriate, comments about building on risk management undertaken in earlier PLC stages are incorporated.

Initiating an RMP in a project's design stage

Initiating an RMP in the design stage involves a significant change in emphasis, but not a totally new process. Initiating a RMP such as the SHAMPU process in a project's plan stage can start with a define phase based on a reasonably complete project design. Shifting initiation from the plan stage back to the design stage of the project necessarily involves more attention to the project *what* and less attention to the project *whichway*, but it still needs to consider the implications of all later stages of the PLC.

The SHAMPU define phase during project design

When addressing the six *W*s in the SHAMPU define phase, the emphasis will switch from the *whichway* and *when* to the *what* (design), but all six *W*s will still require co-ordinated treatment.

The process will be more demanding because the design itself will be more fluid, perhaps with a range of quite different concepts requiring comparison and choices. It will also be more demanding because the six *W* issues associated with later stages in the PLC will usually require more effort. For example, life cycle cost and revenue issues, up to and including final disposal of the product of the project in some cases, are likely to be subject to much greater uncertainty due to more limited clarification to date.

However, this additional effort invested in developing an understanding of whole project life cycle issues will have ongoing benefits in the later stages of the project, as well as direct immediate benefits to the project as a whole. Because there is much more scope to change the project design to reflect whole life issues, it is much more important to understand them properly in order to seize the opportunities provided by the earlier initiation of risk management.

The SHAMPU focus phase during project design

When addressing how best to plan risk management effort, the shift in emphasis to project design choice issues is critical. A very similar process to the generic SHAMPU process may be appropriate, but at the very least significant cosmetic changes may be essential and more fundamental structural changes may be necessary.

> **Example 14.1 Assessing a project design choice**
>
> A client wanted a risk analysis undertaken to confirm (or otherwise) a design decision. The decision was the sizing of storage for Liquefied Natural Gas (LNG) as a buffer between LNG production and shipping. The production and storage facilities being considered were proposed for Melville Island, in the Canadian High Arctic (North West Territories). The proposed shipping involved ice-breaking tankers, taking the LNG to East Coast USA.

One team of consultants addressed variable shipping patterns. Another addressed LNG plant reliability issues. As discussed elsewhere (Chapman et al., 1984), analysis indicated a need for a second compression chain in the LNG production facility, as well as confirming the storage sizing.

Cosmetic changes to the generic RMP were important. For example, 'activities' were replaced by 'components' and 'subsystems', sources of 'activity duration uncertainty' became reasons for 'outages', the probability of a source occurring was couched in terms of 'mean time between failures', and so on (i.e., the activity–source–response–impact structure became a component–outage–response–impact structure). But the change in labels did not affect the models or the computer software used.

The cited paper discussing this example specifically addresses what cosmetic changes were necessary in this case and what aspects of the generic RMP were portable to the different context. For a more general discussion of these issues and other references see Chapman (1992b).

The SHAMPU identify phase during project design

In terms of the identify phase of the SHAMPU process, a shift in emphasis from activity based plans to underlying project design involves a shift in the scope of issues of interest that can be very important. If some of the time typically spent on issue identification in the PLC plan stage is devoted to issue identification in the PLC design stage, considerable benefit can be gained. The operating state of a building or piece of plant may be much more important than its construction and deserving of much more attention. For example, even for comparatively straightforward and routine projects like a speculative office block, making sure there are no design features that will threaten future net rental income (and hence capital value) because of concerns driven by tenants, owners, local authorities, and others may be much more important than construction cost issues that often receive much more attention.

Example 14.2   Pipeline operating risk influences design of a river crossing

A client wanted a risk analysis undertaken to make a design decision in a manner that could be justified with respect to a number of interested parties. The decision was how to get a proposed, very large gas pipeline (1.2 m) across the Yukon River in Alaska. The gas pipeline was following the route of a very large oil pipeline. The obvious choice was putting the gas pipeline in an empty, spare pipe rack on a road bridge built to carry the oil pipeline. Concerned parties included the owners of the oil line, the State of Alaska Transport Department as owners of the bridge (which had generated considerable road traffic), the local indigenous people (who were particularly concerned about the possible pollution impacts of any oil spills caused by bridge failure), and the US Federal Government Department of Energy (who were concerned about a significant portion of the US energy supply being exposed to potential sabotage on a single bridge).

An early issue of concern was which parts of the pipeline's life cycle should be the focus for the risk analysis. Construction, operation, and maintenance were addressed, but the emphasis was on the operation of the pipeline. 'Sources' in the project construction plan sense were replaced by 'failure' sources. In this case catastrophic failures were the concern, not minor operating difficulties.

The RMP had to reflect more significant changes in this case than in the Example 14.1 case, including the need to explicitly demonstrate the relative merits of alternative structures to different groups of people with quite different concerns, as discussed elsewhere (Chapman et al., 1985a). For example, the project manager (Debelius) was a very experienced and pragmatic former senior officer in the US Army Corps of Engineers. He made it clear at the outset that the insights gained during the course of the study must be summarized by a clear defence of a recommended choice on one side of a single sheet of A4 paper. The study was a large and complex one, involving about 30 people working full-time for about three months at its peak. The challenge of summarizing its results on one page in this way was formidable, but its value has been remembered for all subsequent studies, a lesson worth learning well. The purpose of the analysis was gaining the insight required to write very simple stories. The main story in this case was a surprising story for many. The recommended approach, a separate aerial crossing, was the least likely option as perceived by all parties involved at the outset. Moreover, it was not difficult to explain the rationale for the preferred approach, in terms of effective rapid recovery from loss of the separate aerial crossing by temporary use of the bridge pipe rack if the bridge survived and a reasonable degree of independence between threats to the aerial crossing and threats to the bridge. Complex source–response dependencies that were not anticipated could be reduced to a simple story once their impact was understood.

The SHAMPU structure phase during project design

The design of the SHAMPU structure phase requires an understanding of those aspects of project uncertainty that need explicit attention and those that do not. All the concerns addressed in Chapter 8 are relevant, but the extent to which structural issues can be anticipated in the focus phase may be significantly reduced. This makes the structure phase more important and more demanding. Chapman et al. (1985a) develop this issue.

The SHAMPU ownership phase during project design

Ownership issues of special interest as a consequence of the shift in emphasis from project plans to project design include the impact of design–build–operate concepts. Source and response ownership discussions develop a distinctive new flavour when project whole life issues involve designers directly. More generally, ownership issues can become much more complex in the project design stage, because all the other PLC stages require clear recognition and attention.

The SHAMPU estimate, evaluate, harness, and manage phases during project design

Subsequent estimate, evaluate, harness and manage phases of the SHAMPU process implemented in the project design stage follow on in a way largely determined by earlier SHAMPU phases and the general principles discussed in Chapters 10 to 13. However, it is worth emphasizing that if the SHAMPU process embraces the design stage from the outset, project change control issues right back to design become part of an integrated and ongoing evaluate, harness, and manage process. For example, the distinction between 'target', 'expected' and 'commitment' values becomes an essential part of the language of design, with the management of expectations about design achievement linked to the management of expectations about time, cost and performance achievement. One obvious and important benefit of this is ensuring a reasonable chance of regular delivery of good news. If a messenger *always* brings bad news, it could be argued he or she may not deserve to be shot, but this is the likely outcome!

Initiating an RMP in a project's conception stage

Taking the initiation of an RMP back into the conceive stage of the PLC intensifies all the issues discussed in the previous section.

The SHAMPU define phase during project conception

The distinctions between project design stage and conceive stage approaches to the SHAMPU define phase can be relatively unimportant, because of the overlapping nature of these stages. For instance, Example 14.1 relates to a project that was quite explicitly a concept-proving exercise, part of the conceive stage of a broader project. This context did not significantly affect the approach taken to the define phase. Example 14.2 could also be viewed as an example of a conceive stage approach.

However, if the emphasis switches to the project *who* (parties) and the *why* (objectives), the resulting distinction between approaches to the SHAMPU define phase in the design and conceive stages of the PLC can be very important, and the impact of this difference can be extreme. For example, most textbooks on decision analysis emphasize examples that involve conceive stage choices between alternative project strategies, basic decision tree models being useful for simple representations of such choices. But addressing uncertainty and *who* and *why* leads to an alternative process view of such decisions, which opens up a whole new view of the role of decision analysis in strategy formulation (Chapman and Ward, 2002, chap. 9).

Following SHAMPU phases during project conception

The focus of any RMP may change dramatically as a consequence of initiating the RMP during the project conceive stage rather than the design stage. In particular, change control issues right back to setting project objectives become part of the ongoing RMP process. For example, the uncertainty associated with opportunity cost or value associated with delayed availability of a finished capital investment item becomes an essential aspect of the whole decision process, including concept and design development. For instance, the basic design of a speculative office block may be heavily influenced by assessed uncertainty about construction cost escalation and rent increases. The basic design of an electric power station may become heavily influenced by assessed uncertainty about construction cost escalation and growth in the demand for electric power. In both cases the approach to basic design concept development may be driven by the wish to minimize the period between committing to construction and completing construction, in order to facilitate management of cost escalation uncertainty as well as demand and revenue uncertainty. Chapman and Ward (2002, chap. 11) develop linkages between strategic planning and individual project decisions of this kind.

Changes in approach may not be significant, but when they are the shift is away from an elaborate, predesigned RMP like those of Examples 14.1 and 14.2 toward the use of simple decision tree models as in Example 14.3, parametric approaches as in Examples 14.4 and 14.5, and 'soft' situation structuring methods (Rosenhead, 1989). Examples 14.3, 14.4, 14.5, 14.1, and 14.2 (in that order) can be seen as an ordered set illustrating the range of complexity of appropriate approaches to uncertainty evaluation when an RMP is initiated in the conception stage of a project.

Example 14.3   Risk analysis for new product introduction

In 1979, Maritime Engines and Motors (MEM), a medium-sized British firm manufacturing outboard engines and motors for pleasure craft, was considering the introduction of a new product based on modifications to one of its best-selling models.

Recently, this model had been banned in the USA because it did not meet federal emission standards. Fortunately this was not an important market for MEM, but the managing director was concerned that similar emission controls might be introduced in Britain. Consequently, MEM was considering introducing a new motor with a redesigned carburation system using conventional but up-to-date technology. However, the existing model was so well established that any change to its design might cause a loss of market share, and in any event the new product might soon be overtaken by motors using microchip technology produced by a German competitor.

A decision tree showing different possible scenarios was developed and supported by a financial model that calculated the Net Present Value (NPV) of each scenario over a 10-year planning horizon. The first part of the decision tree developed is shown in Figure 14.1.

The tree starts with a decision node representing the choice between going for the new, redesigned product or staying with the old one. If the new product option were chosen it was estimated that there was a 0.4 probability of various significant possible sources of trouble in introducing the new product. Nodes *A–E* were followed by further branches showing possible scenarios relating to sales levels and the penetration into the market of products using microchip technology. The numbers above each node correspond to the expected NPV in millions of pounds of all scenarios to the right of the node in the tree. It will be noticed that the expected values (in £m) at nodes *C*, *D*, and *E*—75, 74, and 78, respectively—are not very different. Whatever the probability assignments, the expected value for the old product cannot be less than 74 or more than 78 and is always less than the expected value with the new product. Sensitivity analysis tended to support this conclusion. Thus the uncertainty that had motivated the analysis initially turned out to be unimportant because the decision was insensitive to the entire range of possible probability assignments for the 'banned' event. This insensitivity arose because developing the decision tree had forced the managing director to think strategically about the consequences of a ban in the light of the microchip threat, and the expected NPVs at nodes *C*, *D*, *E* reflected responses that had been developed to cope effectively with a ban.

While the difference between the expected NPV for the new product and the old product (82 − 77 = 5) is small, the expected NPV following an 'untroubled introduction' is £12 million more than the expected NPV for

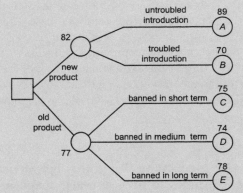

Figure 14.1—First part of decision tree in Example 14.3

Reproduced by permission of the Operational Research Society

the old product. This highlighted the value of developing responses to increase the probability of an 'untroubled introduction'. Eventually, the managing director called in an outside design consultant to redesign the new product so it would look as good as the old product, and several thousand pounds were spent to ensure that the marketing of the new product was done as well as possible.

Summarized from Phillips (1982)

Example 14.4 Choosing between alternative power-generating approaches

The State of Alaska Electric Power Authority had to choose between a major hydroelectric power project or incremental development of coal-fired power units. RMP developed to assist with this decision (Chapman and Cooper, 1983b) avoided direct probabilistic modelling of any of the parameters of the standard NPV decision framework, because the key parameter uncertainties involved issues such as the rate of inflation of fuel prices relative to general inflation and the terminal value (at a 50-year planning horizon) of a hydroelectric power unit, which are by nature only amenable to subjective probability distribution estimates and highly correlated. This approach was 'parametric' in that it systematically identified how far parameters had to move from their expected values to change ('flip') the decision, comparing that movement with plausible ranges of values to identify the relative importance of risks. It facilitates a simple story in a framework most suited to the key parameter risk. For example, instead of NPV as a framework for discussing the hydro/coal choice, it suggests a Terminal Value (TV) approach. TV = 0 is a standard assumption many would insist on, but a terminal value for the hydroelectric project in money of today before discounting greater than the cost of construction was a plausible possibility in this case (90% of the capital cost was roads, dams, and other civil works that might be more valuable in 50 years than their cost today, if properly maintained, given inflation in construction costs and further relative escalation in fuel costs). It was useful to indicate what minimum TV would indicate hydro was the preferred choice under various expected value assumptions for other parameters.

Example 14.5   Identifying flip points between alternative approaches to nuclear waste disposal

A more recent study, which used the parametric discounting framework of Example 14.4 as a starting point, addressed the question 'should the UK defer the disposal of intermediate-level nuclear waste for 50 years, or not?' In the process of the analysis a number of the parameters received probabilistic treatment within the parametric framework (Chapman and Howden, 1995; Chapman and Ward, 2002, chap. 8). For example, costs associated with temporary surface storage of nuclear waste were assessed probabilistically because the engineers responsible for the estimated costs felt much more comfortable with estimates structured around a formal representation of what reprocessing and other safety measures might and might not be required. Also, the chance of losing the proposed site as a consequence of delay was accepted as high (above 80%), and this was considered to be a key issue that could greatly increase costs.

Of particular importance in this decision is the discount rate. The UK Treasury saw the discount rate as a policy variable. The cited paper suggests this was a very high risk strategy. If the appropriate discount rate as economists would measure it with hindsight is slightly less than the Treasury policy rate at the time of the decision, the decision flips from 'deferral' to 'non-deferral'. The scope for actual appropriate discount outcomes below the policy rate is substantial, relative to the scope for actual appropriate discount rates above the policy rate. This gives rise to an asymmetric risk, with very serious implications associated with deferral being selected and proving non-optimal, relative to the implications if non-deferral is selected and proves non-optimal. That is, if the UK does not defer disposal and in 50 years' time history suggests deferral would have been the best choice the opportunity loss will probably be small, relative to the opportunity loss if the UK does defer disposal and in 50 years' time history suggests non-deferral would have been the best choice. Current Treasury views (HMT, 2002) may involve a major change in the discount rate, which would flip the decision taken.

Some projects may require different styles of analysis from those illustrated in Examples 14.3, 14.4, and 14.5, particularly in the conception stage. For example, the absence of both detail and structure can make 'soft' or situation-structuring methods particularly useful and a focus on issue identification may make a 'soft' approach preferable. Skills needed in the conception stage can raise difficulties even in the context of more traditional approaches (Uher and Toakley, 1999).

Initiating an RMP in a project's allocate stage

Delaying the initiation of an RMP in a given project from the end of the project's plan stage, as assumed in Part II, until the allocate stage is well under way or complete, should have a profound impact. We move from project planning with a strategic planning tone toward project planning with a tactical planning tone. Our project may or may not resemble the 'Charge of the Light Brigade', but the tone of appropriate thinking moves sharply from 'the reason why' toward 'do or die', and the RMP must accommodate this shift. That said, the allocate stage is the last of three stages (design, plan, and allocate) often referred to together as the 'planning phase' (see Table 2.1); so, without our refined PLC stage structure this delay is not detectable. Further, the allocate stage still precedes the execute stage when the project is well and truly under way (see Table 2.1). It is still not too late to go back to 'square one' if major potential difficulties are identified, although it is a very good idea not to be responsible for having earlier overlooked these potential difficulties.

As Table 2.1 and the associated discussion in Chapter 2 indicate, we are now concerned with the allocation of resources to implement our plans. Within the relevant 'action horizons' we have to put contracts in place, get ready to make commitments, and define appropriate 'action plans'.

If initiating an RMP on a project has been left until this stage of the PLC, the lack of any risk management based project strategy can be a major problem. It can mean that RMP tactical plans are largely a waste of time at a general overall level, because they will be based on a wide range of assumptions that in general may not hold, with no clear understanding of the implications of the failure of these assumptions. Generally speaking, to add value effectively, effort needs to be focused on specific tactical areas and decisions or fairly massive effort applied to readdress plan, design, and even conceive stage issues, which should have been addressed earlier in the PLC in risk management terms.

By way of contrast, if an RMP has been previously employed in the conceive, design, and plan stages of a project, risk management in the allocate stage can use the framework that this earlier risk management effort provides to assist with tactical planning for the action horizon within a strategy that is already well developed. Indeed, where earlier strategic choices required an understanding of subsequent tactical issues, as modelled in conventional decision tree analysis, tactical choices may simply require refining at an operational level.

The SHAMPU define phase during the project allocate stage

When addressing the six *W*s in SHAMPU process terms for the first time in the allocate stage, the emphasis will be on the *wherewithal* (resources), but all six *W*s will still require co-ordinated treatment.

Project manager expectations of the RMP introduced at this stage of a project may be assistance with pressing tactical issues, or it may be confirmation that previous planning has been properly done and 'release of funds' is appropriate, or some combination of these. Most project team members will have similar expectations, although a board or banks about to give approvals will have quite different concerns. Questioning earlier strategic assumptions at this stage is rarely welcome, but it is an inevitable part of a proper RMP initiated at this late stage of a project. An audit of the quality and effectiveness of project management to date is a key part of the SHAMPU process at this stage, and considerable tact and strength of character are key prerequisites for the risk analysts. External (to the project) guidance for the RMP that is resistant to project team coercion is vital. When banks or other external funders are involved, authority and independence in relation to the client organization can also be important.

If an RMP has been introduced at an earlier stage in the project and our concern is revisiting an ongoing RMP in the allocate stage, some revisiting of strategic decisions in the light of new information will be essential, but the SHAMPU define phase could concentrate on filling in detail in relation to action plans in preparation for tactical risk management. In the absence of this earlier analysis serious problems can arise. Getting ready for 'the off' is the focus. Looking in more detail at the implication of plans over the 'action horizon' may reveal new insights that include unwelcome surprises. We have to look for such surprises and remain sensitive to the possible need for a rethink. But such surprises should be the exception, not the rule, if earlier risk management has been effective.

The SHAMPU focus phase during the project allocate stage

The nature of the focus phase of a SHAMPU process introduced for the first time in a project at the allocate stage is shaped by the concerns discussed in the last subsection. The 'quality audit' tone of the process becomes much more of a concern than for a process introduced at an earlier stage in the project. However, it remains very important to provide useful feedback to the whole project team as soon as possible. If those responsible for implementing the RMP are not accepted by the project team as part of the team, serious problems will follow. Risk management on the whole project may be aborted as a consequence.

Empowerment from the top and experienced analysts are essential if purely cosmetic analysis is to be avoided. Purely cosmetic analysis at this stage is not just a waste of time; it is dangerously misleading and the basis of some well-founded mistrust of risk management. Most people who are seriously suspicious of RMPs have been 'burned' by ineffective RMPs at this stage of a project and have not understood that it was the particular RMP practitioners who were at fault, or those who hired and directed them, not the basic idea of such a process. There are RMPs and there are RMPs. Each needs to be used in an appropriate way at an appropriate time. Further, there are RMP practitioners and RMP practitioners. Some are very good with specific familiar problems, but are not flexible enough in terms of conceptual education or experience to deal effectively with situations they have not encountered before. It is important to see RMP design skills as part of a craft that requires serious attention. It is not an activity that provides something useful to do for people who are otherwise unengaged who have attended a two-day intensive course. We do not want to put people off who wish to have a go, but we are particularly anxious that mistakes, and the ongoing consequences of those mistakes, are avoided if the uninitiated tackle the infeasible or inappropriate.

In effect, the SHAMPU define phase properly done needs to cover all the important issues that should have been addressed earlier, if this is feasible. If this is not feasible, detailed bottom-up analysis of the whole project is a dangerous waste of time. Time is much better spent on two alternative forms of analysis, with an emphasis dependent on relative priorities:

1. bottom-up risk analysis of specific tactical issues;
2. top-down risk analysis of the project and its context as a whole.

For example, a decision to spend the time and resources available for a last minute RMP on strategic top-down risk analysis with a view to a possible decision to delay release of funds and the start of the execute stage must be made very early in the RMP, because it involves a profoundly different approach to the define phase than a focus on selected tactical decisions. In practice, the feasibility of undertaking a SHAMPU process shapes the focus phase, which in turn shapes the define phase, breaking down both the separability and the previously assumed sequence of the define and focus phases.

When an RMP has been initiated in an earlier stage of the project, revisiting risk management in the allocate stage involves quite different considerations in the focus phase. In this case, a choice between fundamentally different approaches may not be the issue. However, desirable changes in approach can be much more than refinement in detail. For example, an earlier RMP may have more of the flavour of Examples 14.1 to 14.5 than the SHAMPU process described in Part II, with a focus on the project's design stage, which was not fully transformed during the plan stage. Ensuring a full transformation in relation to all strategic issues as well as due attention to 'action plans' may be necessary. A major change in analysis style is not necessarily an indication of earlier RMP failures. It is to be expected, given the change in focus and concerns. In principle, a smooth transition in the style of analysis used at successive stages in the PLC might seem desirable. In practice, more radical steps are easier to manage, and the exact timing of the changes need not follow the PLC stage structure exactly.

Following SHAMPU phases during the project allocate stage

The nature of the following SHAMPU phases (identify, structure, ownership, estimate, evaluate, harness, and manage) will be shaped by the earlier phases and the general principles discussed in Part II. The details are not worth developing here. However, it is worth emphasizing that if the define phase and the focus phase do not resolve the problems posed by late introduction of risk management in the allocate stage, risk management will remain crippled for the rest of the PLC. Further, successful adaptation of RMPs in earlier PLC stages to the needs of the allocate stage will provide the necessary foundation for ongoing effective and efficient risk management.

Initiating an RMP in a project's execution stage

Delaying the initiation of risk management from a project's plan stage until the execute stage will have a profound impact on the role of risk management. It is too late to stop the project without a loss of face that will necessitate some changes in the faces present. The project manager who asks for risk management to be introduced at this stage because his or her project is out of control should be looking for another employer at the same time. That said, all the issues raised in the previous section remain relevant. The changes are a matter of degree. For example, in the SHAMPU define phase, all six *W*s will still require integrated treatment, but the emphasis may swing toward *whichway* (how), to the extent that *whichway* is a matter of detail without fundamental implications requiring much earlier focus. We have gone beyond planning over an 'action horizon', although such planning must be rolled forward as part of the project management process. We are into the details of doing it, executing the action plans. At this level, planning may not be a centralized function any more, other than on an exception basis. Planning may be undertaken very locally, perhaps even to the level of each person planning their next step with no consultation required unless there is a major glitch or difficulty. In the limit, it does not make economic sense to plan how every nut and bolt is put into a piece of machinery, how every weld goes into a bridge, or how every element of software code will be written. Where the line is drawn is very important in terms of the efficiency of the management process, and inefficiency can degrade effectiveness.

In the authors' experience, a lack of detailed consideration of the consequences of uncertainty via an appropriate RMP tends to go hand-in-hand with excessive detail in a deterministic planning process. One of the very important results of an effective RMP is what might be viewed as 'empowerment' of those at the coalface or sharp end by a reduced amount of centralized and formalized detailed planning and by an increased degree to which goals and objectives and 'rules of engagement' are specified, with the details left to those in charge of implementing particular tasks. Hence, if an RMP is ongoing from previous stages of a project, reviewing the nature of that process in the execute stage of the PLC can involve substantial savings in effort in subsequent risk management, as well as much more effective use of both formal and informal processes. Battle commanders have understood this for hundreds of years. Professional sports coaches have also understood it for as long as they have been around—Roman gladiator coaches included. At this level people need to react the appropriate way by instinct. It is too late for any kind of planning. Part of the purpose of training is building in the appropriate instincts.

Initiating an RMP in a project's deliver stage

The deliver stage is the first of three PLC stages sometimes associated with the project 'termination phase' indicated in Table 2.1. As for earlier PLC stages, the PLC decomposition provided by Chapter 2 is useful in terms of discussing how risk management should adapt to being introduced very late in the PLC.

The deliver stage involves commissioning and handover. The 'basic deliverable verification' step of Table 2.1 involves verifying what the product of the project will do in practice (i.e., its actual performance as a whole system, as distinct from its design performance or its performance on a component-by-component basis during the execute stage). It is too late for 'co-ordinate and control' in the execute stage sense.

If the product of the project does not meet a contract performance specification, it is usually too late to introduce a meaningful RMP for the first time, unless most of the project's senior staff are first relieved of their posts. Corporate sacred cows and individual reputations can get in the way of the radical thinking that will be required if an RMP is initiated at this stage because serious problems are becoming self-evident.

There are exceptions that prove the rule. For example, if most of the problems were caused by the client or third parties, a contractor who has not previously used risk management may find it very useful to introduce a 'forensic RMP' at this stage to demonstrate why they should be paid very much more than the obvious direct cost increases that have been generated by feedback loops within the project environment (see Examples 8.4, 8.5, and 8.7). For example, a late design change for Channel Tunnel rolling stock due to the goal posts being moved by government safety inspectors, together with no delay in the required delivery date by the client, induced an increase in parallel working. This in turn made the cost of subsequent redesign even more expensive and required an increase in staffing, which in turn meant that staff on average were less experienced and more likely to make mistakes, and so on. The methodology for this kind of 'forensic RMP' is quite different to the SHAMPU process discussed in Part II in terms of its emphasis. In terms of the SHAMPU focus phase, the risk analysis at this late stage in the PLC has to be designed to serve quite different purposes. It is not concerned with making effective decisions. It is concerned with explaining why effective decisions on the part of the contractor were not enough, given the behaviour of the client and third parties.

If project abort or not is the issue in a project's deliver stage, a quite different approach to the SHAMPU focus phase is appropriate, akin to those discussed earlier in the design and conceive stage contexts. However, prevention is better than cure. In particular, if risk management was introduced back in the define or design stage, performance will be defined in terms of 'targets', 'expected values', and 'commitments'. Modification of product performance achievement may be possible and effective, but modification of performance criteria can also be addressed within a framework that facilitates trade-offs because it was used to establish commitments in the first place. In particular, client/contractor negotiations may involve 'user groups' within the client organization in useful dialogues that go well beyond which 'commitments' to relax, considering where ambitious 'targets' might be approached or exceeded to capture opportunities. For example, it may not be possible to achieve a maximum weight specification for a weapon system, but given the extra weight, it may be possible to make it so much more effective that a smaller number of weapons on the same platform offers much better overall performance than the client expected. In such a case the defence procurement executive involved should want to encourage the capture of such opportunities, even if the contract involves a fixed price, high-performance penalty approach.

Initiating an RMP in a project's review stage

The review stage of a project involves a documental audit after delivery of the product, including a full audit of the RMP employed during the project. If an RMP was not in place early in the PLC, *effective* review is impossible: it is not just difficult, it is impossible. In the absence of an earlier RMP the review will involve ambiguities that will be difficult to resolve owing to:

1. an inability to distinguish between targets, expectations, and commitments;

2. inevitable differences of opinion about which issues were predictable and which were not;
3. arguments about who owned which issues;
4. confusion about what the project was supposed to achieve in terms of basic objectives;
5. the natural wish to avoid witch-hunts and get on with the next project.

Perhaps not quite so obvious is the lack of a framework to allow effective and efficient capturing of corporate experience. For example, in the bidding context of Example 12.1, once an RMP is in place, explicit estimates of the probability of winning each bid allow feedback on bids actually won to refine future estimates. Without the explicit prior estimates, this feedback is inefficient and ineffective. In a similar way, a decomposition of sources and responses as discussed in Part II allows efficient development of databases for common sources of uncertainty and responses that could not be developed without the structure to build on that an effective RMP provides. More generally, effective database construction has to follow effective risk analysis that in the first instance may have to work without adequate data. In theory, it would be nice to have all the data for the first application of an RMP, but in practice RMPs have to be developed and used before we know what data we really want and how we want them stored for effective retrieval. Trying to build databases in advance of the associated RMP application is inefficient and ineffective, although a degree of simultaneous development is usually possible. In a broad sense we must have some informal data gathering to postulate an approach to RMP design and available data will directly affect our RMP process design, but detailed, formal data gathering and capturing of related corporate experience in terms of how best to handle risks and responses depends on the structuring of those issues adopted by the RMP. To some extent this is counterintuitive for most people who have not been directly involved in RMPs. This makes it all the more important for everyone to understand that effective review must be built on the back of effective RMPs and effective data and corporate experience capture must be built on the back of an effective review stage. No RMP means no review, which means no effective experience or data capture. This is an expensive and debilitating shortcoming for any organization.

Initiating an RMP in a project's support stage

The support stage of a project involves living with the ongoing legacy of apparent project completion, possibly in a passive 'endure' mode. Product liability issues may originate right back in the conceive or design stage. Reliability, maintainability, and availability issues may have arisen in the design stage, but they may relate to plan, allocate, execute, or deliver stages. All these issues were sources of uncertainty earlier in the PLC that may not 'come home to roost' until the support stage. They can be crisis managed in the support stage and earlier risk management planning can be developed, but it is too late for an RMP to be initiated without a fairly catastrophic rethink.

Product withdrawal is an obvious classic example, as in the case of pharmaceutical products that are found to have dangerous side effects only after significant numbers of people have suffered these side effects. However, pharmaceutical companies are so obviously in the risk management game that most of them should be managing this kind of potential liability issue from the outset. Product withdrawal associated with 'dangerous' car designs in the USA some time ago is perhaps a more useful example. What makes this example particularly instructive is the more recent practice of European car manufacturers to design cars for recycling at the end of their life, a movement toward a true whole life cycle view of basic design issues. In this sense the international automobile industry is a 'model' others might usefully learn from.

Those responsible for decommissioning nuclear facilities, particularly in the former Soviet Bloc, no doubt wish their current concerns had received more attention in the PLC conceive and design stages. However, it would be unfair to be too heavily critical of the nuclear industry, in the sense that their approach was in general understandable, even if in some particular instances it may not be forgivable. At the time nuclear reactors currently being decommissioned were designed and built, very few organizations or industries had an effective RMP that embodied PLC support stage issues and the change in political attitudes to such issues was not readily predictable. Some very reputable standard approaches left considerable room for further development (Anderson et al., 1975).

Twenty years from now this defence will not be available, even to the builders of routine office blocks or highways. Designers of today's products who fail to give adequate consideration to support stage issues and who plead ignorance of the law or good practice will be held accountable for their errors of omission or commission, in moral if not in legal terms. To avoid a potential guilty verdict and associated damaging commercial consequences, they need to address these issues now. Further, the industries responsible for projects in specific areas need to lead the development of appropriate definitions of good practice for their industries, drawing on the experience of all other industries that can teach them something useful. Collective sharing of good practice across industries is an important aspect of the evolution of good risk management practice.

Conclusion

This chapter provides a discussion of the impact of initiating an RMP at stages in the PLC other than toward the end of the plan stage, as assumed in Part II. It also gives modest attention to the impact of revising an ongoing RMP at different stages in the PLC. The analysis offered is necessarily incomplete, but the authors hope it indicates the nature of the issues and some useful ways to deal with them.

An initial observation was that there is some merit in initially developing effective RMPs introduced toward the end of the plan stage of the PLC on the 'learn to walk before you can run' principle. However, there are several benefits from adopting an RMP earlier in the PLC, including:

- it stimulates effective integration of design–plan–cost considerations;
- it facilitates consideration of parties–objectives–design–activities linkages;
- it allows more focus on later PLC stages and related product performance issues;
- the distinction between targets, expected values, and commitments becomes part of the language of design, with benefits in later stages, particularly the delivery stage;
- it facilitates consideration of change control processes and associated management of expectations.

At present, soft systems and soft operational research methods are perhaps the most useful tools for formalization of these early RMPs (Rosenhead, 1989), but experience should yield more specific methods and processes in time. In particular, data- and broader experience-gathering systems are most effectively designed following successful design and implementation of RMP, rather than the other way around.

If an RMP is adopted for the first time after the plan stage of a project, it becomes progressively more difficult to obtain benefits from risk management. In the PLC allocate stage effort needs to be focused on specific tactical areas and decisions, although an audit of the quality and effectiveness of project management data should be a key part of any RMP initiated at this stage. This implies that empowerment from senior management and the use of experienced risk analysts are important prerequisites for effective RMP. Beyond the allocate stage it is generally too late to initiate an RMP. Once in the execute stage risk management becomes more decentralized to those empowered to act. An effective RMP commenced at an earlier stage of the PLC encourages the empowerment of those directly implementing plans, with more attention to communicating objectives and 'rules of engagement', less attention to the details of *whichway*, and more attention to developing effective instincts.

Effective and efficient risk management

15

The art of being wise is the art of knowing what to overlook.—William James

Introduction

Effective risk management involves *doing the right things* with respect to the risk management process (RMP) so that the *project* is risk efficient in the corporate sense and all other project objectives are achieved. To understand the full extent of what is involved in achieving *effective* risk management, it is essential to understand the nature of a comprehensive RMP. This was one reason why Part II assumed circumstances that warranted a comprehensive SHAMPU (Shape, Harness, And Manage Project Uncertainty) process, addressing all relevant sources of uncertainty, taking a whole project life cycle perspective, and undertaking detailed analysis of issues as appropriate. Chapter 14 took the development of a comprehensive approach to risk management a step further, extending application of the SHAMPU process late in the project plan stage to include repeated application from the earliest stages of the PLC.

However, undertaking any RMP is not without costs, and a key concern is ensuring an appropriate trade-off between these costs and the effectiveness of the RMP. In practice, the comprehensive approach of Part II will often need simplification to meet the practical needs of a particular context, to provide *efficient* risk management. Efficient in this context means *doing things right* with respect to the RMP so that the *process* is efficient as well as effective. Simplification merely to economize on resources and time spent on risk management is *never* appropriate. What is *always* appropriate is ensuring that the available resources are used to operate an RMP that is as effective and efficient as possible within the time available. What is *always desirable* is adjusting the time and resources available to an appropriate level, but sometimes this is not feasible.

To some extent what is required was addressed in the discussion of the focus phase (Chapter 6). Ensuring effectiveness and efficiency involves designing an approach within the SHAMPU framework that is most appropriate for the given context on a case-by-case basis, via the focus phase. Chapter 6 provided a normative discussion of what factors need to be considered using a six *W*s framework. However, no specific suggestions were made because much depends on the nature and status of the subject project, in six *W*s and project life cycle (PLC)-stage terms, and on other project characteristics like complexity and novelty. The possibilities for varying approaches are so numerous a general treatment is not feasible.

Stepping back from a comprehensive approach could involve limiting the extent of application, making the RMP less formal, restricting its focus, or reducing the scope of analysis in a given context.

Limiting the extent of application could involve employing an RMP only on particular kinds of projects or only at specific, selected stages of the PLC. The implications of this will be clear from the discussion in Chapter 14.

The degree of formality sought in using a given RMP framework can be a key influence in achieving an effective and efficient approach. At one extreme a purely informal, intuitive approach could be adopted. At the other, a very high level of formality could be adopted, involving more cost but more benefits. Making the RMP less formal involves less explicit structure, less formal documentation, less explicit articulation of objectives, deliverables, phases, and steps within a phase, and fewer explicit phases. Informal risk management processes tend to produce RMPs with a limited focus. Part of the role of formality is clarifying the need for a richer set of motives, as well as helping the pursuit of that richer set of motives.

Restricting the focus of an RMP involves limiting the objectives that are sought. An obvious way of doing this is to consider only significant threats to project performance, rather than all significant sources of certainty and their implications. Another way of restricting focus is to limit the degree of anticipation sought in the RMP. At one extreme a purely reactive approach to project uncertainty could be adopted. At the other, an exhaustive, proactive approach to managing uncertainty could be adopted. Key issues here are the extent to which decisions are irreversible and the seriousness of the consequences of inappropriate decisions as judged after the fact. In the limit, a very flexible approach to a project involving no costs associated with changes requires no proactive risk management. However, there are usually practical limits on the level of flexibility possible and efficiency gains associated with giving up some feasible flexibility. Hence, choosing an appropriate level of flexibility for the project should be related to choosing an appropriate level of sophistication for proactive risk management. The choices about the approach to the project itself are the primary choices, while the RMP choices are secondary. In general it is worth adopting a deliberately excessively flexible approach to the project as well as a deliberately excessively proactive approach to planning, particularly while going down a learning curve, because the penalties for adopting too little flexibility are greater than the costs of too much flexibility and there are learning benefits associated with a degree of overkill.

Reducing the scope of analysis in a given context can be achieved in several ways, including:

- utilizing standard, pro forma documentation such as checklists;

- prespecifying the form of qualitative and quantitative analysis to be under-taken;
- limiting the depth of analysis undertaken;
- adopting single-pass processes that preclude revisiting earlier phases of the process;
- limiting the time and resources available for undertaking risk management.

In general all the above simplifications reduce the effectiveness of risk manage-ment and the benefits that can be obtained. A common reason for RMPs that are neither effective nor efficient is lack of appreciation of the benefits obtainable from comprehensive approaches, which is usually linked to a lack of organiza-tional capability or investment in risk management. If comprehensive approaches are never used, those responsible for RMPs will never fully appreciate what they are missing or how to take effective short cuts. And if benefits are not appre-ciated, there will be limited investment in developing an organizational capability to obtain these benefits. Vicious or virtuous circles are involved. Likely benefits for undertaking risk management need to be assessed in terms of the motives discussed in Chapter 3, the full set of relevant performance criteria and concerns discussed in Chapter 5 (the SHAMPU define phase), and in relation to the nature of the target projects. Such an assessment can be demanding in terms of skill and experience, and associated learning curves are significant.

Rephrasing key points made earlier, organizations need an RMP that is both effective in terms of what it does for each project and efficient (cost-effective) in terms of the delivery of this effectiveness. Just providing a net benefit is not enough. To remain competitive, organizations need the maximum benefit for a given level of resource invested in the time available. Ideally they need to be able to adjust the resource and the time available in an optimal manner as well. Rather than ill-considered short cuts, which merely seek to economize on risk management effort, the concern should be to apply risk management effort where the benefits are particularly obvious and significant, or to adopt efficient, streamlined processes designed for particular contexts. For example, if risk management is required for a series of projects with similar features in terms of the six Ws, then it can be both effective and efficient to devise a standardized approach, based on a prototype process developed from a comprehensive approach to the first project.

Determining what can be simplified and what it is appropriate to simplify is not a simple matter. To address this problem, organizations might adopt generic simplifications to RMP applications by using common guiding principles or by making policy decisions that constrain the nature and scope of formal RMPs. Such generic simplifications are most likely to be made when an RMP is first established in an organization. They need to be made with a full knowledge of what is involved in a comprehensive RMP. In particular, simply adopting a very specific, rigidly designed, 'off-the-shelf' RMP touted by a consultancy or 'borrowed' from another organization is not advisable. Such RMPs often involve quite specific (and simplistic) 'tools' or prescribed methods of analysis that encourage a mechanistic, 'paint by numbers' approach to risk management. The very closely defined tried-and-tested nature of these processes can make them very attractive and amenable to rapid implementation. However, they represent a serious risk to the ongoing development of an organization's risk management capability. In particular, they can prematurely constrain employees' perceptions of what risk management is all about and what can be achieved with it. They can be comparable with patent medicines sold at a fair to cure all ills without the need for any kind of professional diagnosis of the patient.

In this respect it is important to remember that the SHAMPU process framework (or variants tailored to specific organizations) is not intended as a step-by-step procedure to be followed literally, except possibly by inexperienced users in a carefully selected learning process. It is an illustrative formal process framework, to be simplified as appropriate, based on the user's experience. However, the most effective way to refine judgements about how to simplify involves starting with some practice, using a formalized process as close to that of Part II as possible.

Learning from early applications

When the introduction of formal RMPs into an organization is part of a long-term change in project management and organizational culture, usually a desirable position to adopt, it is very important to see early applications as part of a corporate learning process. Viewed in this light, the effectiveness of an RMP relates to benefits derived from subsequent application of risk management in later projects, as well as benefits for the project of immediate concern. Over time, an understanding of both the costs and the benefits of alternative approaches can be developed that will inform choices about short cuts in subsequent applications. This implies that the first project an organization subjects to the kind of RMP discussed in this book should be carefully selected to facilitate these longer-term benefits. As an example of taking this to the limit, the very first application of the SCERT (Synergistic Contingency Planning and Review Technique) approach (Chapman, 1979) with BP International was a 'passive' and retrospective analysis of a project just completed, to polish the process before its first test on a 'live' project. Most organizations do not need a 'passive' test, but it is very useful to see the first application as a test and as a learning experience, an approach the authors have taken with a number of clients who successfully introduced their own variants of a SHAMPU-like process.

As a simple analogy, consider planning to sail a yacht across the English Channel from Southampton to Cherbourg for the first time. Reading a few sailing magazines will soon make it clear that it is a good idea to make the first crossing in daylight, in spring (when days are longest), starting at dawn, with stable weather conditions forecast for several days ahead. Given this starting position, project planning and an associated RMP based on a simplistic approach to navigation would suffice: assuming you take the Isle of Wight on your left, head due south from the Needles until you hit the French coast, then turn right. However, such easy crossings allow time for refining navigation skills, making course corrections that are designed to enhance knowledge rather than minimize crossing time, making frequent checks with positioning instruments, and using visual checks where feasible. Developing effective and efficient navigating skills for other conditions requires practice using formalized methods with ample time to compare and contrast alternative ways of determining the position (location) of the yacht. This learning process should be fun. Most people who go into project management as a career need a measure of fun to keep them on the job, as well as the stimulation of challenges to meet. A bit more fun and a bit less challenge than the norm can be a useful bias for early learning experiences. The saying 'there are old pilots and bold pilots, but no bold old pilots' does not apply directly to project staff, but some of the bolder young project staff need to be explicitly taken on a few Channel crossings with a pleasurable learning experience before letting them attempt more challenging crossings like the Atlantic Ocean. Navigating through a high-risk project can be much more difficult than crossing the Channel in a yacht and in general warrants more attention to formality, not less.

The above ideas apply to choosing an appropriate level of sophistication in the first attempt at an RMP of the kind discussed in this book, as well as choosing an appropriate project. As most people who have acquired some of their wisdom via the 'school of hard knocks' know, making mistakes is the only way to learn some of life's more important lessons, but it is important not to make mistakes that kill or cripple future opportunities. If mistakes are inevitable, we need to make mistakes we can live with. Continuing the Southampton to Cherbourg sailing analogy, it is advisable to aim to hit the French coast several miles uptide and/or upwind of the destination, because it is comparatively easy to alter course at the last minute in a downwind and downtide direction, but comparatively difficult to do so upwind against the tide. We know we will get it wrong to some extent, and the error is not symmetric in its effect, so we aim for low-cost errors. The magnitude of error assumed should reflect our proven navigation skill. Choosing a low level of sophistication for a first RMP and observing the results is like hitting the French coast in the dark with no position-finding instruments and no knowledge of the coast. If you can safely assume you are uptide and upwind you can drift downwind and downtide until what looks like a major harbour comes into view. This is comparable with choosing a high level of sophistication for a first RMP with a view to adjusting toward simpler RMPs as experience is gained. If you don't know which side of Cherbourg you are, you have a potential major problem on your hands. If you start with sophisticated RMPs, then simplify as experience is gained, you will be clear 'which side of Cherbourg you are on' in RMP terms.

An excessively sophisticated RMP will be a handicap, as will an excessively difficult project. But learning requires a challenge, and only by using a bit more sophistication than we need can we recognize when and where it is safe to take short cuts. As experience is gained, the emphasis can move from RMPs as a general risk management learning experience in the context of effective use from the outset for all projects considered, to RMPs as an effective *and efficient* way to deal with immediate concerns. Short cuts can be taken in the light of an understanding of how much effort will be saved by the short cuts and what the likely impact will be on the effectiveness of the project management process as a whole.

Most organizations first use a formal RMP because of an organizational imperative: sometimes imposed by 'nature', sometimes imposed by regulators, bankers, or other interested parties. However, once formal RMPs are in place, most organizations have expanded their motives as an appreciation of the benefits has been acquired. In the past organizations have tended to 'learn the hard way', as have the authors. There is now no need for organizations to 'learn the hard way' to such an extent. The pioneers took a decade to learn what first-time users can now learn in a year. This doesn't mean there will be no learning curve. But to use the Southampton to Cherbourg sailing analogy yet again, other people have now made the crossing lots of times and written about their experiences, in some cases with guidance about specific crossings. The *International Journal of Project Management,* particularly since 1990, is one good source of project risk management experience that may provide cases relevant to the reader's circumstances.

Model complexity

As noted in Chapter 6, the degree of model complexity employed in analysis is a key aspect of designing effective RMPs and other management science intervention processes. An interesting survey of failures and successes of quantitative methods in management by Tilanus (1985) supports the widely held view that successful modelling requires approaches that are 'simple', flexible, easily understood, appropriate to the situation, and able to cope with low-quality data. A detailed discussion of the effectiveness of 'simple' analysis is provided by Ward (1989), employing a 'constructive simplicity' concept that describes the form and level of detail in a model. Chapman and Ward (2002) further develop this 'constructive simplicity' concept and its application to various aspects of project uncertainty. Usual arguments for constructive simplicity focus on model-building considerations such as model clarity, flexibility, and convenience, but constructively simple models can also provide an efficient way of learning about decision situations. The basic idea is to start with effective, simple analysis that is then elaborated in useful directions as understanding develops. A key theme here is that additional model complexity should be introduced only if it is useful. In this respect, a constructively simple approach is fundamentally different from a *simplistic* approach that involves adopting simplicity naively and precludes any further model development.

Note that this approach to modelling in a particular instance is the reverse of the overall approach just discussed. This reversing of directions is not inconsistent. The craft skills required to use the process effectively in a particular instance are developed within the overall approach outlined earlier in this chapter.

Usually additional model complexity proves useful (constructive) because it:

- makes estimation easier;
- allows the integration of estimation expertise involving different people or databases;
- clarifies what estimates measure and what they do not measure;
- provides richer insights about decision alternatives;
- provides more confidence that issues are properly understood.

As indicated earlier, the simplest formal quantitative model of uncertainty for project duration analysis is the basic PERT (Program Evaluation and Review Technique) model; the most complex the authors are aware of in a source–response–impact dimension is the basic SCERT model (Chapman, 1979). An earlier publication (Chapman et al., 1985b) addresses making choices along the PERT–SCERT axis, and subsequent publications have discussed these choices in more detail (e.g., Chapman, 1990). Other modelling complexity dimensions include systems dynamics models to capture feedback and feedforward loops (Forrester, 1961; Richardson and Pugh, 1981; Senge, 1990), cognitive mapping to capture other interdependencies in a qualitative manner (Eden, 1988), and more general 'soft' methods (Rosenhead, 1989; Checkland and Scholes, 1990), as mentioned in Chapter 8. Such modelling complexity dimensions are worth exploring by the reader with a view to more effective modelling of uncertainty, and further approaches may prove worthy of development.

The more modelling choices become available the more difficult it is to make the most appropriate choices, unless we clearly understand what each model feature costs and what benefits it is likely to yield. Only some very general guidelines can be offered here in terms of where to start with basic model development:

- make sure all key issues are identified and associated with appropriate responses, whether or not formal quantitative modelling is feasible;
- don't attempt implementation or interpretation of quantitative analysis unless you understand prior, underlying qualitative analysis;
- if project activities involve repetitive component processes, consider the use of Markov process models to show the combined effect of these processes;

- if feedback or feedforward loops are important, consider the use of system dynamics models.

A 'constructively simple' approach to estimating parameters for any given model structure will facilitate starting with a very simple but 'conservative' (safe) approach to filtering out what matters and what does not, in order to spend the available analysis effort as effectively as possible. Two extended examples illustrate what is involved in the next two sections. Both are heavily based on recent papers: Chapman and Ward (2000) in the case of the next section and Chapman and Ward (2003) in the following section. Both examples are treated jointly and somewhat differently in Chapman and Ward (2002, chap. 4).

An extended example: estimating the cost of a pipe-laying contract

The extended example that follows illustrates a 'minimalist', first-pass approach to estimation and evaluation of uncertainty that is aimed at achieving an efficient and effective approach to uncertainty assessment. The minimalist approach defines uncertainty ranges for impact *and probability* associated with each source of uncertainty. Subsequent calculations preserve expected value and measures of variability, while explicitly managing associated optimistic bias.

The minimalist approach departs from the first-pass use of probability density histograms or convenient probability distribution assumptions that the authors and many others have used for years in similar contexts. It is a further simplification of the simple scenario approach developed in Chapter 10. Readers used to first-pass approaches that attempt considerable precision may feel uncomfortable with the deliberate lack of precision incorporated in the minimalist approach. However, more precise modelling is frequently accompanied by questionable underlying assumptions like independence and lack of attention to the uncertainty in original estimates. The minimalist approach forces explicit consideration of these issues. It may be step back, taking a simple view of the 'big picture', but it should facilitate more precise modelling of uncertainty where it matters and confidence that the level of precision employed is not spurious.

Example context

A cost estimator with an offshore oil and gas pipe-laying contractor is given a 'request for tender' for a 200-km pipeline to be constructed on a fixed-price basis and asked to report back in a few hours with a preliminary view of the cost. Modifications to the estimator's preliminary view can be negotiated when he or she reports and refinement of the analysis will be feasible prior to bidding. The estimator's initial analysis should provide a framework for identifying what the thrust of such refinements should be. The estimator has access to company experts and data, but the organization has no experience of formal risk management.

A minimalist approach

This subsection outlines the mechanics of the proposed approach step by step using the example situation to illustrate the methodology. For ease of exposition, some aspects of the rationale related to specific parts of the proposed approach are explained in this subsection, but development of the rationale as a whole and exploration of alternatives is left until following subsections.

A minimalist approach involves the following six steps in a first-pass attempt to estimate and evaluate uncertainty:

1. identify the parameters to be quantified;
2. estimate crude but credible ranges for probability of occurrence and impact;
3. recast the estimates of probability and impact ranges;
4. calculate expected values and ranges for composite parameters;
5. present the results graphically (optional);
6. summarize the results.

During these steps there is an underlying concern to avoid optimistic bias in the assessment of uncertainty and a concern to retain simplicity with enough complexity to provide clarity and insight to guide uncertainty management.

Step 1   Identify the parameters to be quantified

Step 1 involves preliminaries that include setting out the basic parameters of the situation, the composite parameter structure, and associated sources of uncertainty. Table 15.1 illustrates the format applied to our example context.

The first section of Table 15.1 identifies the proposed parameter structure of the cost estimate, in a top-down sequence. 'Cost' might be estimated directly as a basic parameter, as might associated uncertainty. However, if cost uncertainty is primarily driven by other factors, such as time in this case, a 'duration × cost rate' composite parameter structure is appropriate, to separate the driving factors. Further, it is often useful to break 'duration' down into 'length/progress rate', to address more basic parameters and drivers of uncertainty within specific time frames. In this case it is also useful to break 'progress rate' down into 'lay rate × productive days per month', where 'lay rate' reflects uncertainty about the number of km of pipe that can be laid per day given pipe laying is feasible, and 'productive days per month', the number of days in a month when pipe laying is feasible, reflects a different set of uncertainties. Finally, it is convenient in this case to express 'productive days per month' in terms of days lost per month.

Table 15.1—Relationships, base values, issues, and assessment modes

composite parameter relationships		units
cost = duration × cost rate		£m
duration = length/progress rate		months
progress rate = lay rate × productive days per month		km/month
productive days per month = 30 − days lost rate		days/month

basic parameters	base values	
length	200 km	
lay rate	2 km/productive day	
days lost rate	0 productive days/month	
cost rate	2.5 £m/month	

basic parameters	issues	probabilistic treatment?
length	client route change	no
	other (length)	no
lay rate	barge choice	no
	personnel	yes
	other (lay rate)	yes
days lost rate	weather	yes
	supplies	yes
	equipment	yes
	buckles	yes
	lay barge sinks	no
	other (days lost rate)	no
cost rate	market	yes
	other (cost rate)	no

The second section of Table 15.1 provides base values for all the basic parameters. The 2 km per productive day 'lay rate' and the £2.5m per month 'cost rate' assume a particular choice of lay barge that the estimator might regard as a conservative first choice. The estimator might anticipate later consideration of less capable barges with lower nominal 'lay rate' and 'cost rate'.

The third section of Table 15.1 identifies sources of uncertainty associated with each of the basic parameters, referred to as 'issues' in the source–response sense introduced earlier because each source will be associated with an assumed response. This section asks in relation to each issue whether or not probabilistic treatment would be useful.

'Length' has 'client route change' identified as a key issue, which might be defined in terms of client-induced route changes associated with potential collector systems. 'Other (length)' might refer to any other reasons for pipeline length changes (e.g., unsuitable sea bed conditions might force route changes).

These are examples of issues that it is not sensible to quantify in probability terms because they are more usefully treated as basic assumptions or conditions that need to be addressed contractually (i.e., the contract should ensure that responsibility for such changes is not born by the contractor, so they are not relevant to assessment of the contractor's cost). Ensuring that this happens makes listing such issues essential, even if in its simplest terms a standardized list of generic exclusions is the response used.

'Lay rate' identifies 'barge choice' as an issue not suitable for quantification. This is an example of an issue not suitable for probabilistic treatment because it involves a decision parameter usefully associated with assumed values and determined via separate comparative analysis.

'Lay rate' is also influenced by two issues that might be deemed appropriate for probabilistic treatment because the contractor must manage them and bear financial responsibility within the contract price. 'Personnel' might reflect the impact on the 'lay rate' of the experience, skill, and motivation of the barge crew, with potential to either increase or decrease 'lay rate' with respect to the base value. 'Other (lay rate)' might reflect minor equipment, supply, and other operating problems that are part of the pipe laying daily routine.

'Days lost rate' identifies four issues usefully treated probabilistically because the operator must own and deal with them within the contract price. 'Weather' might result in days when attempting pipe laying is not feasible because the waves are too high. 'Supplies' and 'equipment' might involve further days lost because of serious supply failures or equipment failures, which are the contractor's responsibility. 'Buckles' might be associated with 'wet buckles', when the pipe kinks and fractures allowing water to fill it, necessitating dropping it, with very serious repair implications. 'Dry buckles', a comparatively minor problem, might be part of 'other (lay rate)'. In all four cases the financial ownership of these effects might be limited to direct cost implications for the contractor, with an assumption that any of the client's knock-on costs are not covered by financial penalties in the contract at this stage.

'Days lost rate' also identifies two issues best treated as conditions or assumptions. 'Lay barge sinks' might be deemed not suitable for probabilistic treatment because it is a *force majeure* event responsibility for which the contractor would pass on to the lay barge supplier in the assumed subcontract for bid purposes at this stage, avoiding responsibility for its effects on the client in the main contract. 'Other (days lost rate)' might be associated with catastrophic equipment failures (passed on to the subcontractor), catastrophic supply failures (passed back to the client), or any other sources of days lost that the contractor could reasonably avoid responsibility for.

'Cost rate' might involve a 'market' issue associated with normal market force variations that must be born by the contractor and usefully quantified.

'Cost rate' might also involve an 'other (cost rate)' issue placing financial responsibility for the implications of abnormal market conditions with the client and therefore not quantified.

In this example most of the issues treated as assumptions or conditions are associated with financial ownership of the consequences for contractual purposes. The exception is the barge choice decision variable. In general, there may be a number of such 'barge choice' decisions to be made in a project. Where and why we draw the lines between probabilistic treatment or not is a key risk management process issue, developed with further examples in Chapman and Ward (2002).

Step 1 corresponds to a first pass through the SHAMPU process of Part II to the end of the first part of the *estimate* phase in the context of the beginning of the PLC from a potential contractor's perspective. Step 2 carries on with the *estimate* phase.   ·

Step 2   *Estimate crude but credible estimates of probabilities and impacts*

Step 2 involves estimating crude but credible ranges for the probability of occurrence and the size of impact of the issues that indicate 'yes' to probabilistic treatment in Table 15.1. Table 15.2 illustrates the format applied to our example context. Table 15.2 is in three parts, each part corresponding to a basic parameter. All estimates are to a minimal number of significant figures to maintain simplicity, which is important in practice as well as for example purposes.

The 'impact' columns show estimated pessimistic and optimistic scenario values. They are approximate 90 and 10 percentile values rather than absolute maximum and minimum values. Extensive analysis (Moder and Philips, 1970) suggests the lack of an absolute maximum, and confusion about what might or might not be considered in relation to an absolute minimum, makes 95–5 or 90–10 confidence band estimates much easier to obtain and more robust to use. A 90–10 confidence band approach is chosen rather than 95–5 because it better reflects the minimalist style and lends itself to simple refinement in subsequent iterations. This is consistent with the simple scenario approach of Chapter 10 in a direct manner.

For each 'issue' there are two 'event probability' columns showing the estimated range (also assumed to be a 90–10 percentile range) for the probability of some level of impact occurring. A probability of 1 indicates an ever-present impact, as in the case of personnel and weather or market conditions.

The 'probability × impact', 'pessimistic' and 'optimistic' columns indicate the possible range for unconditional expected impact values given the estimates for event probability and conditional impact. The 'midpoint' column shows the midpoint of the range of possible values for unconditional expected impact.

For the 'lay rate' section of Table 15.2, impacts are defined in terms of percentage decrease (for estimating convenience) to the nearest 10%. The 'combined' uncertainty factor estimate involves an expected decrease of 5% in the

Table 15.2—Crude but credible estimates of probabilities and impacts

lay rate		*impact scenarios: percentage decrease*					
	event probability		*impact*		*probability × impact*		
issues	*pessimistic* p_p	*optimistic* p_o	*pessimistic* i_p	*optimistic* i_o	*pessimistic* $p_p \times i_p$	*optimistic* $p_o \times i_o$	*midpoint*
personnel	1	1	10	−20	10	−20	−5
other	1	1	20	0	20	0	10
combined			30	−20			5

days lost rate		*impact scenarios: days lost per month*					
	event probability		*impact*		*probability × impact*		
issues	*pessimistic* p_p	*optimistic* p_o	*pessimistic* i_p	*optimistic* i_o	*pessimistic* $p_p \times i_p$	*optimistic* $p_o \times i_o$	*midpoint*
weather	1	1	10	2	10	2	6
supplies	0.3	0.1	3	1	0.9	0.1	0.5
equipment	0.1	0.01	6	2	0.6	0.02	0.31
buckles	0.01	0.001	60	20	0.6	0.02	0.31
combined			79	2			7.12

cost rate		*impact scenarios: percentage increase*					
	event probability		*impact*		*probability × impact*		
issues	*pessimistic* p_p	*optimistic* p_o	*pessimistic* i_p	*optimistic* i_o	*pessimistic* $p_p \times i_p$	*optimistic* $p_o \times i_o$	*midpoint*
market	1	1	30	−20	30	−20	5
combined			30	−20			5

nominal lay rate, defined by the 'midpoint' column, and ±25% bands, defined by the i_p and i_o values.

The 'days lost rate' section treats 'weather' as ever present in the context of an average month, but other factors have associated probabilities over the range 0 to 1, estimated to one significant figure. Impact estimates are also to one significant figure in terms of days lost per month.

The 'combined' uncertainty factor estimate provided in the final row shows an expected impact 'midpoint' of 7.12 days lost per month and a corresponding optimistic estimate of 2 days lost per month, but 79 days might be lost if a buckle occurs together with equipment, supplies, and weather 'pessimistic' values. The pipe-laying process could finish the month well behind where it started in progress terms. The bounds here are clearly not obtainable by adding $p_p \times i_p$ and $p_o \times i_o$ values.

The 'cost rate' section is a simplified version of the 'lay rate' section.

Step 3   Recast the estimates of probability and impact ranges

The next step is to recast the estimates in Table 15.2 to reflect more extreme values of probability and impact ranges and associated distribution assumptions. This step can also convert units from those convenient for estimation to those needed for combinations, if necessary. Further, it can simplify the issue structure. Table 15.3 illustrates what is involved, building on Table 15.2. Apart from changes in units, 10% has been added to each $(p_p–p_o)$ and $(i_p–i_o)$ range at either end. This approximates to assuming a uniform probability distribution for both the Table 15.2 probability and impact ranges and the extended Table 15.3 ranges. Strictly, given 10 and 90 percentile figures in Table 15.2, ranges ought to be extended by 12.5% at each end so the extensions are 10% of the extended range. However, using 10% extensions is computationally more convenient and emphasizes the approximate nature of the whole approach. It also

Table 15.3—Recast estimates

lay rate	impact scenarios: km/day						
	event probability		impact		probability × impact		
issues	very pessimistic p_{vp}	very optimistic p_{vo}	very pessimistic i_{vp}	very optimistic i_{vo}	very pessimistic $p_{vp} \times i_{vp}$	very optimistic $p_{vo} \times i_{vo}$	midpoint
Combined	1	1	1.3	2.5			1.9

days lost rate	impact scenarios: days lost per month						
	event probability		impact		probability × impact		
issues	very pessimistic p_{vp}	very optimistic p_{vo}	very pessimistic i_{vp}	very optimistic i_{vo}	very pessimistic $p_{vp} \times i_{vp}$	very optimistic $p_{vo} \times i_{vo}$	midpoint
weather	1	1	11	1	11	1	6
supplies	0.32	0.08	3.2	0.8	1.02	0.06	0.54
equipment	0.11	0	6.4	1.6	0.70	0	0.35
buckles	0.011	0	64	16	0.70	0	0.35
combined			84.6	1			7.25

cost rate	impact scenarios: £m/month						
	event probability		impact		probability × impact		
issues	very pessimistic p_{vp}	very optimistic p_{vo}	very pessimistic i_{vp}	very optimistic i_{vo}	very pessimistic $p_{vp} \times i_{vp}$	very optimistic $p_{vo} \times i_{vo}$	midpoint
combined	1	1	3.38	1.87			2.63

helps to avoid any illusion of spurious accuracy and offers one simple conces-
sion to optimism, whose effect is both limited and clear.

The 'lay rate' section combines the 'personnel' and 'other' entries of Table 15.2
directly (using the combined entries from Table 15.2 as its basis), on the grounds
that Table 15.2 revealed no serious concerns. It first converts the 30% 'pessimistic' impact estimate of Table 15.2 to a 'very pessimistic' estimate of
$[30 + 0.1(30 - (-20))] = 35\%$, adding 10% of the $(i_p - i_o)$ range. It then applies
this percentage decrease to the base lay rate to obtain a 'very pessimistic' lay rate
of $[2 \times (100 - 35)/100] = 1.3$ km per day, to move from units convenient for
estimation purposes to units required for analysis. Table 15.3 converts the i_o
estimate of a 20% increase in a similar way. Converting from percentage
change figures to km/day figures is convenient here for computational reasons
(it must be done somewhere).

The 'days lost rate' section retains a breakdown of individual issues directly,
on the grounds that Table 15.2 reveals some concerns. Event probability values
less than 1 are converted to 'very pessimistic–very optimistic' $(p_{vp} - p_{vo})$ ranges in
the same way as impact ranges. In this case the 'combined' entries mirror the
'combined' entries of Table 15.2 on a 'very pessimistic' and 'very optimistic' basis.

The 'cost rate' section is obtained in a similar way to the 'lay rate' section. The
impact range in Table 15.2 is extended by 10% at either end and these extreme
values for percentage increase are applied to the base cost rate of £2.5m per
month.

An obvious question is why do we need 'very pessimistic' and 'very optimistic'
values as well as the 'pessimistic' and 'optimistic' values of Table 15.2? The
answer is to make graphical presentation feasible in Step 5. If graphical presentation is not required and a simple spreadsheet model conversion from Table 15.2
to Table 15.3 is not available, we could skip the 'very pessimistic' and 'very
optimistic' conversions, but in practice the time saved will be negligible. The
term 'minimalist' was chosen to imply minimal effort appropriate to context,
ensuring that sophistication and generality to deal effectively with all contexts
is preserved. Graphs are often useful, if not essential.

Step 3 can be seen as part of the *estimate* phase or the *evaluate* phase of the
SHAMPU process, but Step 4 takes us clearly into the *evaluate* phase.

Step 4 *Calculate expected values and ranges for composite parameters*

The next step is to calculate the expected values and ranges for the composite
parameters of Table 1 using the range and midpoint values in Table 15.3. The
calculations are shown in Table 15.4. They work through the 'composite parameter' relationships in the first section of Table 15.1 in reverse (bottom-up) order.
The 'midpoint' columns use midpoint values from Table 15.3. The 'very optimistic' columns use i_{vo} values from Table 15.3. Because a 'very pessimistic' or even a

Table 15.4—Results

composite parameters	computation			results		
	plausibly pessimistic	*very optimistic*	*midpoint*	*plausibly pessimistic*	*very optimistic*	*midpoint*
productive days per month	30–20	30–1	30–7.25	10	29	22.75
progress rate (productive days × Lay rate)	10 × 1.3	29 × 2.4	22.75 × 1.9	13	72.5	43.23
duration (months) (length/progress rate)	200/13	200/72.3	200/43.23	15.38	2.76	4.63
cost (£m) (duration × cost rate)	15.38 × 3.38	2.76 × 1.87	4.63 × 2.63	52.0	5.2	12.18

current estimate of expected cost is £12m in the range 5 to 50.

'pessimistic' calculation on the same basis would involve never finishing the pipeline, a 'plausibly pessimistic' column uses i_{vp} values except in the case of 'days lost rate', when 20 days replaces the i_{vp} value of 84.6 days. The source of this 20-day figure might be a simple rule of thumb like:

$$3(\text{midpoint} - i_{vo}) + \text{midpoint}$$

rounded to one significant figure. Later evaluation passes might call for more effective but more time-consuming approaches to estimating a plausibly pessimistic value.

The final section of Table 15.4 summarizes the results, rounding the 'current estimate' based on the midpoint to the nearest £m, its 'very optimistic' lower limit to the nearest £m, and its 'plausibly pessimistic' upper limit to reflect an order of magnitude relationship with the lower limit.

Step 5   Present the results graphically (optional)

For key areas of concern, additional graphical representation of assessments may be worthwhile, using formats like Figure 15.1 and Figure 15.2.

Figure 15.1 illustrates a Probability Impact Picture (PIP), which can be produced directly from Table 15.3. The estimator in our example context might produce Figure 15.1 because 'days lost rate' is a key area of concern, the estimator anticipates discussion of assumptions in this area, and the person the estimator reports to likes a Probability Impact Matrix (PIM) format.

The PIM approach typically defines 'low', 'medium', and 'high' bands for possible probabilities and impacts associated with identified issues (usually 'risks' involving adverse impacts). These bands may be defined as quantified ranges or left wholly subjective. In either case assessment of probabilities and

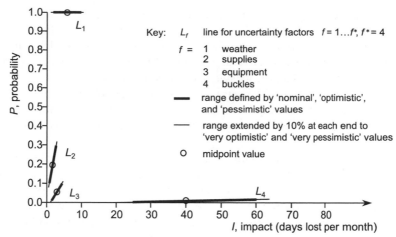

Figure 15.1—Probability Impact Picture (PIP): 'days lost rate' example

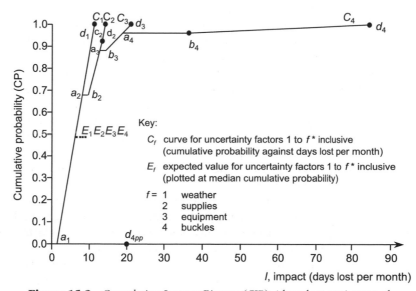

Figure 15.2—Cumulative Impact Picture (CIP): 'days lost rate' example

impacts is a relatively crude process whereby each issue is assigned to a particular box defined by probability bands and impact bands. This limited information about each issue is then usually diluted by using 'risk indices' with common values for different probability band and impact band combinations. Information about uncertainty is often still further obscured by the practice of adding individual risk indices together to calculate spurious 'project risk indices'. The PIM approach seems to offer a rapid, first-pass assessment of the relative importance of identified issues, but it delivers very little useful information and even less real insight. Figure 15.1 can be related directly to a PIM approach because a PIM approach uses the same dimensions to define low, medium, and high boxes. In effect, each issue in the PIP format is represented by the diagonal of a PIM box defined to suit that particular issue.

Figure 15.1 can be a useful portrayal of Table 15.3 information in terms of confirming estimation assumptions. It captures the key probability density function information of all the issues in both event probability and impact dimensions.

Each L_j line plotted corresponds to an issue that contributes to the 'days lost rate'. If the L_j lines are interpreted as diagonals of associated boxes defining the set of possible combinations of probability and impact, the absence of the rest of these boxes can be interpreted as a perfect correlation assumption between event probability and impact for each uncertainty factor j, but nothing can be inferred about correlation between the uncertainty factors.

A horizontal L_j, like L_1, implies some impact uncertainty but no event probability uncertainty. A vertical L_j would imply the converse. A steep slope, like L_2, implies more uncertainty about the event probability than impact uncertainty. Slope measures necessarily reflect the choice of units for impact, so they are relative and must be interpreted with care. For example, L_3 and L_4 involve the same expected impact midpoint, but order-of-magnitude differences with respect to event probability and impact, a relationship that is not captured by Figure 15.1 (although non-linear, isoproduct midpoint values could be plotted).

Figure 15.1 is a useful way to picture the implications of the 'days lost rate' part of Table 15.3 for those who are used to using the PIM approach. However, in the context of the minimalist approach it is redundant as an operational tool unless the use of computer graphics input make it an alternative way to specify the data in Tables 15.2 and 15.3.

The authors hope that Figure 15.1 in the context of the minimalist approach will help to end the use of conventional PIM approaches, illustrating the inherent and fatal flaws in these approaches from a somewhat different angle than that used earlier (Chapman and Ward, 1997; Ward, 1999). That is, those who use PIM approaches typically take (or should take) longer to assess uncertainty in this framework than it would take in a Figure 15.1 format for those used to this PIP format, and the minimalist approach can put the information content of Figure 15.1 specifications to simple and much more effective use than a conventional PIM approach.

For evaluation purposes a CIP (Cumulative Impact Probability) diagram like Figure 15.2 is a more useful view of the information in Table 15.3 than that portrayed by Figure 15.1. The estimator might produce Figure 15.2 with or without Figure 15.1. Figure 15.2 shows the potential cumulative effect of each of the issues contributing to days lost. For convenience the issues are considered in order of decreasing event probability values.

In Figure 15.2 the C_1 curve depicts the potential impact of weather on days lost. It is plotted linearly between point a_1 ($i_{vo} = 1$, Cumulative Probability (CP) = 0.0) and point d_1 ($i_{vp} = 11$, CP = 1.0), as for any unconditional, uniform probability density function transformation into a cumulative distribution form.

The C_2 curve depicts the potential additional impact on days lost of supply failures in a manner that assumes a degree of positive correlation with impacts from the weather. The idea is to incorporate a degree of plausible pessimism reflecting Son of Sod's law. Sod's law is well known: 'if anything can go wrong it will.' Son of Sod's law is a simple extension: 'if things can go wrong at the same time they will.'

C_2 is plotted in three linear segments via four points, generalizing the C_1 curve procedure to accommodate a conditional uniform probability density function with a 'Minimalist Son of Sod' (MSS) form of correlation:

1. $p_{vp} = 0.32$ is used in the transformation $1 - 0.32 = 0.68$ to plot point a_2 on C_1;
2. $i_{vo} = 0.8$ is used to move from point a_2 horizontally to the right 0.8 days to plot point b_2;
3. $p_{vo} = 0.08$ is used in the transformation $1 - 0.08 = 0.92$ along with $i_{vp} = 3.2$ to move from a point on C_1 at CP $= 0.92$ horizontally to the right 3.2 days to plot point c_2;
4. $i_{vp} = 3.2$ is used to move from point d_1 to the right 3.2 days to plot point d_2;
5. points a_2, b_2, c_2, and d_2 are joined by linear segments.

This implies the following correlations between weather and supply failure:

- if weather impact is in the range 0 to 7.8 days (the 0 to 68 percentile values of weather occur, defined by p_{vp} for the 'supplies event'), the 'supplies event' does not occur;
- if weather impact is in the range 10 to 11 days (the 92 to 100 percentile values of weather occur, defined by the p_{vo} value for 'supplies event'), the 'supplies event' occurs with impact i_{vp};
- if weather impact is in the range 7.8 to 10 (between 68 and 92 percentile values of 'weather'), the 'supplies event' occurs with a magnitude rising from i_{vo} to i_{vp} in a linear manner.

A similar procedure is used for curves C_3 and C_4 associated with equipment failures and buckles, but with $c_3 d_3$ and $c_4 d_4$ coinciding since $p_{vo} = 0$ in each case.

Figure 15.2 plots E_i values defined by midpoint values along the median (0.5 CP) line. Given the uniform probability density distribution assumption for the unconditional 'weather' distribution, E_1 lies on C_1 and no new assumptions are involved. Given the conditional nature ('event probability' less than 1) of the other three uncertainty factors, interpreting Table 15.3 midpoint values as E_j is an additional assumption, and plotting them off the C_j curves resists employing the optimistic nature of these curves in the 0–68 percentile range.

The 'combined very optimistic' value $= 1$ is plotted as point a_1, the 'combined very pessimistic' value $= 84.6$, is plotted as point d_4. Figure 15.2 also shows the 'plausibly pessimistic' impact value (20), plotted on the impact axis (CP $= 0$) as point d_{4pp}, to avoid a prescriptive probabilistic interpretation in CP terms. The plausibly pessimistic value should not be associated with a CP $= 0.99$ or 99% confidence level in general because it is conditional on the MSS correlation assumption, although that interpretation is invited by Figure 15.2.

Step 6   Summarize the results

Whether or not the estimator produces Figures 15.1 and 15.2, the thrust of a summary of analysis results might be as follows:

1. A £12m expected cost should be used as the basis for bidding purposes at present.
2. This £12m expected value should be interpreted as a conservative estimate because it assumes a more capable barge than may be necessary. Given weather data and time to test alternative barges, it may be possible to justify a lower expected cost based on a less capable barge. If this contract were obtained it would certainly be worth doing this kind of analysis. If a bid is submitted without doing it, committing to a particular barge should be avoided, if possible, to preserve flexibility.
3. A cost outcome of the order of £50m is as plausible as £5m. This range of uncertainty is inherent in the fixed-price-contract, offshore pipe-laying business: *no abnormal risks are involved*. The organization should be able to live with this risk, or it should get out of the fixed-price, offshore pipe-laying business. On this particular contract a £50m outcome could be associated with no buckles, but most other things going very badly (e.g., associating a 'plausibly pessimistic' impact with d_3 on Figure 15.2, or a buckle and a more modest number of other problems). Further analysis will clarify these scenarios, but it is not going to make this possibility go away. Further analysis of uncertainty should be primarily directed at refining expected value estimates for bidding purposes or for making choices (which barge to use, when to start, and so on) if the contract is obtained. Further analysis may reduce the plausible cost range as a spin-off, but this should not be its primary aim.

Completing this summary of results corresponds to reaching the end of the SHAMPU *evaluate* phase on a first pass.

First-pass interpretation and anticipation of further passes

A key driver behind the shape of the minimalist approach of the last subsection is the need for a simple first-pass sizing of uncertainties that are usefully quantified.

Table 15.2 (or 15.3) should make it clear that 'days lost rate' is the major source of uncertainty. The 5% decrease implied by the midpoint value of the 'lay rate' distribution relative to the base value is important, as is the 5% increase in the midpoint value of the 'cost rate' distribution. However, refining the basis of these adjustments is a low priority relative to refining the basis of the 7.12 (7.25) days lost per month adjustment, because of the size of that adjustment and its associated variability. In any refinement of the first pass of the last section, 'days lost rate' is the place to start.

Within 'days lost rate' uncertainty, Table 15.2 (or 15.3 or Figure 15.2) should make it clear that 'weather' is the dominant source of uncertainty in terms of the six-day increase in the midpoint value relative to the base value (E_j contribution). In E_j terms 'weather' is an order of magnitude more important than 'supplies', the next most important issue. To refine the $E_1 = 6$ estimate there is no point in simply refining the shape of the assumed distribution (with or without attempting to obtain data for direct use in refining the shape of the assumed distribution). Implicit in the Table 15.2 estimate is pipe laying taking place in an 'average month', perhaps associated with the summer season plus a modest proportion in shoulder seasons. This 'average month' should be roughly consistent with the Table 15.4 duration midpoint of just 4.63 months. However, the range of 2.76 months to 15.38 months makes the 'average month' concept inherently unreliable because this range must involve 'non-average' winter months. To refine the $E_1 = 6$ estimate it is sensible to refine the 'average month' concept. The first step is to estimate an empirical 'days lost' distribution for each month of the year, using readily available wave height exceedence data for the relevant sea area and the assumed barge's nominal wave height capability. The second step is to transform these distributions into corresponding 'productive days' distributions. A Markov process model can then be used to derive a completion date distribution given any assumed start date (Chapman and Cooper, 1983a), with or without the other 'days lost rate' issues and the 'lay rate' issues of Table 15.2 (Table 15.3). Standard Monte Carlo simulation methods, discrete probability, or CIM (Controlled Interval and Memory) arithmetic (Cooper and Chapman, 1987) can be used.

An understanding of Markov processes should make it clear that over the number of months necessary to lay the pipeline the variability associated with 'weather', 'supplies', and 'equipment' will largely cancel out on a 'swings and roundabouts' basis despite significant dependence (expected value effects will not cancel out). This should reduce the residual variability associated with these issues to the same order of magnitude as 'lay rate' and 'cost rate' uncertainty. However, 'buckles' involves an extreme event that has to be averaged out over contracts, not months on a given contract. A provision must be made for 'buckles' in each contract, but when one happens its cost is not likely to be recovered on that contract, and it would endanger winning appropriate bids if attempts were made to avoid making a loss if a buckle occurs.

It is important to ensure that issues like buckles are identified and expected value provisions are made at an appropriate organizational level. It is also important to ensure that the risk they pose is acceptable. However, it should be clear that one 'buckle' could happen and two or more are possible: whether the appropriate provision is 0.35 days lost per month, twice or half that figure, is a relatively minor issue. In the present context the first pass would not suggest second-pass attention should be given to buckles as a priority relative to other 'days lost' issues or their dependence.

If the equivalent of C_1 on Figure 15.2 is available for each relevant month, it makes sense to model the C_1 to C_4 relationships illustrated by Figure 15.2 plus the 'lay rate' uncertainty via a standard Monte Carlo simulation (sampling) process for each month, prior to running the Markov process. Further, it makes sense to then model, via a sampling process, the 'cost' = 'duration' × 'cost rate' relationship. This means layered cumulative representations of the CIP form of Figure 15.2 can be used to show a top level cumulative probability distribution for cost, including confidence bands, and this can be decomposed to provide built-in sensitivity analysis for all components of the overall uncertainty. A second-pass approach might seek to do this as simply as possible. A tempting assumption to achieve this is assuming that all the Table 15.2 distributions other than 'weather' still apply and that independence is appropriate. However, in-dependence on its own is not a reasonable default option. For example, if the 'lay rate' distribution has a low value in the first month (because the barge is not working properly) it is very likely to be low for the next, and so on. The simplest acceptable default option short of perfect positive correlation is to assume in-dependence for one run, a form of perfect positive correlation comparable with MSS for a second run, and interpolate between the two for expected values at an overall level of dependence that seems conservative but appropriate. This will size the effect of dependence at an overall level as well as the uncertainty associated with component issues. The next simplest default option, which the authors strongly recommend, involves some level of decomposition of this approach. For example, the four issues associated with 'lost days' might be associated with one pair of bounds and interpolation, but the lay days distribu-tion might be associated with another level of dependence between periods in the Markov process analysis, and the 'duration' and 'cost rate' dependence interpolation assumption might be different again.

In general, a second pass might refine the estimation of a small set of key issues (just 'weather' in our example), using a sampling process (Monte Carlo simulation) and some degree of decomposition of issues. This second pass might involve consideration of all the first-pass issues in terms of both indepen-dence and strong or perfect positive correlation bounds with an interpolated intermediate level of dependence defining expected values, some level of decomposition generally being advisable for this approach to dependence. Default correlation assumptions of the kind used in Figure 15.2 should suffice as plausible correlation bounds in this context.

A third pass is likely to address and refine dependence assumptions and associated variability assumptions in the context of particularly important issues, further passes adding to the refinement of the analysis as and where issues are identified as important relative to the attention paid them to date.

The number of passes required to reach any given level of understanding of uncertainty will be a function of a number of considerations, including the level of computer software support.

Scope for automation

The minimalist approach was deliberately designed for simple manual processing and no supporting software requirements. A pertinent question is whether software could provide useful support.

The Table 15.1 specification input to a generic package could be used to present the user with Table 15.2 formats and a request for the necessary information in Table 15.2 format. The analysis could then proceed automatically to Figure 15.2 formats with or without Figure 15.1 portrayals (as pure outputs) in the same manner. The Figure 15.2 format diagrams might be provided assuming independence as well as a variant of MSS, with a request to use these results to select an appropriate intermediate dependence level. As discussed in the context of a second-pass approach, this 'sizes' dependence as well as associated parameter variability and could (and should) be decomposed. Relatively simple hardware and inexpensive, commercially available software (like @Risk) could be used to make the input demands of such analysis minimal, the outputs easy to interpret and rich, and the movement on to second and further passes relatively straightforward.

In general such application-specific software should be developed once it is clear what analysis is required, after significant experience of the most appropriate forms of analysis for first and subsequent passes has been acquired. If such software and associated development experience is available, a key benefit is analysis on the first pass at the level described here as second or third pass, with no more effort or time required.

In our example context, a firm operating lay barges on a regular basis would be well advised to develop a computer software package, or a set of macros within a standard package, to automate the aspects of uncertainty evaluation that are common to all offshore pipe-laying operations, including drawing on the relevant background data as needed. Following the example of BP (Clark and Chapman, 1987), software could allow the selection of a sea area and a wave height capability and automatically produce the equivalent of all relevant Figure 15.2 C_1 diagrams for all relevant months using appropriate weather data. Given a start date and the Table 15.1 base parameters, it could then run the Markov process calculations (with or without other 'days lost' uncertainty factors), to derive completion date (duration) probability distributions.

In the context of bidding for information systems projects (Chapman et al., 2000), very similar considerations apply, although the context and the details are very different.

Managing and shaping expectations

The minimalist approach uses ranges primarily to obtain an estimate of expected impact in terms of cost or time that is simple, plausible, and free of bias on the low side. The estimator and those the estimator reports to should be confident that more work on refining the analysis is at least as likely to decrease the expected value estimate as to increase it. A tendency for cost estimates to drift upward as more analysis is undertaken indicates a failure of earlier analysis. The minimalist approach has been designed to help manage the expectations of the estimator and those the estimator reports to in terms of expected values. Preserving credibility should be an important concern.

The minimalist approach provides a lower bound on impacts that is plausible and free of bias. However, in the current example, the approach does not provide a directly comparable upper bound (in simpler contexts it will, see Chapman et al., 2000, for example) and resorts to a very simple rule of thumb in a first pass to define a plausible upper bound. The resulting ranges are wide. This should reflect the estimator's secondary interest in variability and associated downside risk at this stage, unless major unbearable risks are involved. It should also reflect a wish to manage the expectations of those reported to in terms of variability. Those reported to should expect variability to decline as more analysis is undertaken.

In the example context, the extent to which the organization accepts the estimator's view that no abnormal risks are involved should have been tested by the plausible upper bound of £50m in Table 15.4. As noted earlier (Step 6), one implication of this plausible upper bound is that a pipe-laying company in the business of bidding for firm fixed-price contracts with a base cost estimate of the order of £12m must be prepared for a very low probability extreme project to cost four times this amount. A 4.63 month expected duration and Figure 15.2 should suggest a one season project is the most likely outcome (say, probability = 0.90 to 0.99), but being unable to complete before winter weather forces a second season is an outcome with a significant probability (say, 0.01 to 0.1), and a third season is unlikely but possible. The £50m upper bound could be viewed as a scenario associated with three moderately expensive seasons or two very expensive seasons, without taking the time to clarify the complex paths that might lead to such outcomes at this stage.

Regarding this risk as 'bearable' does not mean realizing it cannot be disastrous. It means either:

(a) accepting this level of risk is not a problem in terms of swings and round-abouts that are acceptable; or

(b) not accepting this risk would put the firm at an even higher risk of going out of business, because competitors would bid on the basis of accepting such risks.

Firms working on the basis of (b) can balance the risk of going out of business on the basis of one project or a series of projects, but they cannot eliminate the risk of going out of business. Being sure you will never make a loss on any project is a sure way to go out of business. A firm operating in mode (b) should have some idea what both probabilities are if a balance is to be achieved consistently. The pipe-laying contractor may approach this issue operationally by preparing each bid using the barge that is believed to be the highest capability/cost rate option likely to win the bid (a conservative, lowest possible risk approach) and then testing the attractiveness of successive, lower capability/cost rate options. Consideration of such options will focus attention on the question of what level of risk defines the limit of bearability for the contractor. This limit can then be assessed in relation to the need to take risk to stay in business, which may have merger implications. In this sense the estimator can help the organization to shape expectations.

Robustness of the minimalist approach

How might the estimator defend and explain the minimalist first-pass approach from all the substantive criticisms others might put? The issue of interest here is not robustness in terms of the sensitivity of specific parameter assumptions, but robustness in a more fundamental process sense, as explored in the SHAMPU *structure* phase, glossed over in the Step 1 portrayal of the minimalist process.

This subsection addresses aspects of robustness of the approach in a sequence chosen to facilitate further clarification of the rationale for the approach. The concern is more with clarifying the rationale for the general form of the approach rather than with defending the details of each step, and the authors have no wish to defend example parameter values or associated rules of thumb.

The parameter structure

The example used to illustrate the approach employed four basic parameters and four composite parameters. This may seem excessively complex, and in many contexts it would be. However, in the present example this detail offers a decomposition structure for the estimation process that is extremely useful. The combinations that it makes formal and explicit in Table 15.4 would have to be dealt with intuitively and implicitly in Tables 15.1 to 15.3 if they were not broken out in the first section of Table 15.1. Saving time by using a simpler structure is possible, but it would not be a cost-effective short cut in the authors' view.

If eight parameters is better than six or seven, what about nine or ten? The answer here is less clear-cut. For example, 'cost rate' might be decomposed into a 'lay day cost rate' (associated with days when the weather is good and pipe laying takes place) and an 'idle day cost rate' (associated with bad weather), the £2.5m being an average linked to about 7 idle days and 23 lay days per month, consistent with Table 15.2. Uncertainty as to which rate applies might be explicitly negatively correlated with weather uncertainty, reducing variability considerably. This might be useful. Certainly it would be useful to decompose in this way if a subcontract defined the cost this way.

However, the spirit of the minimalist approach is to avoid introducing complications that don't have a clear benefit provided the simple assumptions are conservative (biased on the pessimistic side). Deliberate bias on the conservative side is justified on the grounds that by and large people underestimate variability, so a failure to build in appropriate conservative bias will lead to inevitable optimistic bias. How far this conservatism needs to be taken can only be determined empirically. When more projects come in under cost and ahead of time than the original estimates suggest is statistically valid, a less conservative approach is warranted. BP achieved this using the SCERT approach (Chapman, 1979), their label for the process being Probabilistic Project Planning (PPP), but they are unique in the authors' experience. Few organizations have this 'problem', and it is relatively easy to deal with if they do.

The issue structure

It might be tempting to use a composite single issue for some or even all basic parameters that are to be given a quantitative treatment. However, in the present example wide-ranging experience suggests that this would produce a much lower estimate of potential variations, since estimators tend to underestimate variability consistently. Accordingly, decomposition into identified contributing issues should yield wider ranges that are closer to reality. Further, and much more important in general, different contributing issues lend themselves to: different sources of expertise and data; different responses including different ownership; and a better understanding of the whole via clear definition of the parts. It is difficult to see what would be gained by recombining any of the issues associated with probabilistic treatment in Table 15.1. The most attractive possible simplification would seem to be combining 'supplies' and 'equipment', but apart from different sources of data and expertise it might be possible to transfer the 'supplies' risk to the client if 'pipe supplies' is the key component, and 'equipment' might raise different issue ownership concerns.

Combining issues that are not treated probabilistically saves minimal analysis effort, but it is worth considering in terms of interpretation effort. A collection of non-quantified 'other' categories is the risk analyst's last refuge when issues occur that have not been explicitly identified. However, this should not make it a 'last refuge for scoundrels', and examples not worth separate identification should be provided.

Pushing the argument the other way, there is a declining benefit as more issues are individually identified. There is no suggestion that the set of 13 issues in Table 15.1 is optimal, but 10 is the order of magnitude (in a range 5–50) that might be expected to capture the optimum benefit most of the time for a case involving the level of uncertainty illustrated by the example.

Treatment of low probability/high impact events

In our example context, suppose 'catastrophic equipment failure' has a probability of occurring of about 0.001 per month, with consequences comparable with a buckle. It might be tempting to identify and quantify this issue, but doing so would lead to a variant of Figure 15.2 where the additional curve cannot be distinguished from the CP = 1.0 bound and an expected value impact observable on Table 15.3 of the order of 0.035 days lost per month. The minimalist approach will communicate the spurious nature of such sophistication very clearly, to support the learning process for inexperienced estimators. This is extremely important, because making mistakes is inevitable, but making the same mistakes over and over is not. Nevertheless, it may be very useful to identify 'catastrophic equipment failure' as an issue not to be quantified, or to be combined with other low-probability/high-impact issues like buckles.

Now suppose some other issue has a probability of occurring of about 0.01 per month, directly comparable with a buckle, with consequences comparable with a buckle. The expected value impact is small (0.35 days per month, about a day and a half over the project), but the additional downside risk is significant and clearly visible on the equivalent of Figure 15.2. It is important not to overlook any genuine buckle equivalents, while studiously avoiding spurious sophistication.

There is no suggestion that the one buckle issue equivalent of Table 15.1 is optimal, but 1 is the order of magnitude (in a range 0–5) we might expect to capture the optimum benefit most of the time for cases involving the level of uncertainty illustrated by the example.

In our example context, the event 'lay barge sinks' might have a probability of the order one-tenth of that of a buckle and implications a factor of 10 worse, giving an expected value of the same order as a buckle, but with a much more catastrophic implication when it happens. In expected value terms quantification is of very modest importance, but recognizing the risk exposure when bidding if insurance or contractual measures are not in place is of great importance. The minimalist approach recognizes the need to list such issues, but it clarifies the limited advantages of attempting quantification for present purposes.

Less than perfect positive correlation

Less than perfect positive correlation would affect the expected value interpretation of midpoint values of Tables 15.2–15.4 and Figure 15.2, and the Figure 15.2 curves C_2–C_4 would develop 'S' shapes.

For example, in Table 15.2 the 'supplies' event probability midpoint is $(0.3 + 0.1)/2 = 0.2$ and the impact midpoint is $(3 - 1)/2 = 2$. If these two distributions are combined assuming independence, the expected impact of supplies should be $(0.2 \times 2) = 0.4$ (and the product distribution will not be symmetric). However, the supplies midpoint expected impact is 5, rising to 5.4 in Table 15.3.

There are several reasons for avoiding the sophistication of less than perfect positive correlation for a first-pass approach, although more refined assessments later may focus on statistical dependence structures:

1. It is important to emphasize that some form of perfect positive correlation should be the default option rather than independence, because perfect positive correlation is usually closer to the truth and any first-order approximation should be inherently conservative.
2. Successive attempts to estimate uncertainty tend to uncover more and more uncertainty. This is part of the general tendency for people to underestimate uncertainty. It makes sense to counterbalance this with assumptions that err on the side of building in additional uncertainty. If this is done to a sufficient level, successive attempts to estimate uncertainty ought to be able to reduce the perceived uncertainty. Failure to achieve this clearly signals failure of earlier analysis, throwing obvious shadows over current efforts. The perfect positive correlation assumption is a key element in the overall strategy to control bias in the minimalist approach.
3. It is particularly important to have a first-pass approach that is biased on the pessimistic side if one possible outcome of the first pass is subsequently ignoring variability or expected values associated with uncertainty.
4. Perfect positive correlation is the simplest assumption to implement and to interpret, and a minimalist approach should keep processes and interpretations as simple as possible. This simplicity may be less important than the first two reasons, but it is still very important.
5. Perfect positive correlation clearly proclaims itself as an approximation that can be refined, avoiding any illusions of truth or unwarranted precision and inviting refinement where it matters.

The assumption of uniform probability density functions

An assumption of uniform probability density functions involves a relatively crude specification of uncertainty. Other forms of distribution would assign lower probabilities to extreme values and higher probabilities to central values and allow a degree of asymmetry to be incorporated.

Dropping the uniform probability distribution assumption is likely to affect expected value estimates of both cost and duration because such distributions are usually considered asymmetric. Typically cost and duration distributions are perceived to be left-skewed, implying a reduction in expected values compared with an assumption of a uniform distribution over the same range of values. However, employing uniform distributions in a first pass is useful for a number of reasons that are similar to the reasons for assuming perfect positive correlation:

1. The first pass is a first-order approximation that should be inherently conservative.
2. It is useful to build in enough uncertainty and bias in expected values to overcome inherent tendencies to underestimate risk and make successive measurement of uncertainty diminish the perceived uncertainty.
3. Linearity in density and cumulative probability functions has the elegance of simplicity that works. It clarifies issues that smooth curves can hide.
4. A uniform distribution clearly proclaims itself as an approximation that can be readily modified if later analysis warrants more sophisticated distribution shapes.

Objectives of the minimalist approach

The SHAMPU focus phase was glossed over in the Step 1 discussion, but the minimalist approach is usefully characterized by seven objectives that the focus phase addresses when assessing the cost-effectiveness of RMP choices.

Objective 1   Understanding uncertainty in general terms

Understanding uncertainty needs to go beyond variability and available data. It needs to address ambiguity and incorporate structure and knowledge, with a focus on making the best decisions possible given available data, information, knowledge, and understanding of structure.

Objective 2   Understanding sources of uncertainty and responses (issues)

One important aspect of structure is the need to understand uncertainty in terms of sources of uncertainty and associated responses (issues), because some (not all) appropriate ways of managing uncertainty are specific to its source and the implications of responses have to be understood to assess impacts.

Objective 3   Determining what to quantify appropriately

Distinguishing between what is usefully quantified and what is best treated as a condition or assumption in terms of decision-making effectiveness is very important. Knight's (1921) classical distinction between risk and uncertainty based on the availability of objective probabilities is not appropriate. Subjective probabilities are the starting point for all quantification in terms of probabilities, in the 'decision analysis' tradition (Raiffa, 1968). At best 'objective' probabilities based on data will address only part of the uncertainty of interest with a less than perfect fit between source and application, and a subjective view of the quality of coverage and fit is required. Knowledge gaps and the role of organizational learning need direct explicit treatment.

Objective 4   Managing iterative processes effectively
and efficiently

To facilitate insight and learning, uncertainty has to be addressed in terms of an iterative process, with process objectives that change on successive passes. An iterative approach is essential to optimize the use of time and other resources during the risk management process, because initially where uncertainty lies, whether or not it matters, or how best to respond to it are unknown. At the outset the process is concerned with sizing uncertainty to discover what matters. Subsequent passes are concerned with refining assessments in order to effectively manage what matters. Final passes may be concerned with convincing others that what matters is being properly managed. The way successive iterations are used needs to be addressed in a systematic manner. A simple, one-shot, linear approach is hopelessly inefficient.

Objective 5   A minimalist first pass at estimation and evaluation

A minimalist approach to the first pass at estimation and evaluation in order to 'optimize' the overall process is critical. A minimalist first-pass approach to estimation should be so easy to use that the usual resistance to appropriate quantification based on lack of data and lack of comfort with subjective probabilities is overcome and the use of simplistic PIMs is eliminated.

Objective 6   Avoiding optimistic bias to manage
expectations effectively

The optimistic bias of most approaches to estimation and evaluation needs direct and explicit attention to manage expectations in an effective manner. If successive estimates associated with managing uncertainty do not narrow the perceived variability and improve the perceived expected cost or profit on average, then the earlier analysis process is flawed. Very few organizations have processes that meet this test. They are failing to manage expectations. The more sophisticated the process used the more optimistic bias damages the credibility of risk management in the organization. If this leads to a failure to apply risk management, it can precipitate failure of the organization.

Objective 7   Simplicity with constructive complexity

Simplicity is an important virtue in its own right, not just with respect to the efficiency of a minimalist first-pass approach, but because it can amplify clarity and deepen insight. However, an appropriate level of complexity, or 'constructive complexity', is also important, for the same reasons. Getting the best balance is partly a question of structure and process, partly a question of skills that can be learned via a process that is engineered to enhance learning.

No current approaches the authors are aware of explicitly address this set of objectives as a whole, with the exception of the 'simple scenario' approach discussed in Chapter 10. The minimalist approach discussed here is a special case of the simple scenario approach, developed to make further progress with respect to Objective 5. Evidence of a need to further address Objective 5 is provided by the sustained, widespread promotion and use of first-pass approaches to estimation and evaluation employing a PIM. This was deliberately accommodated, although not promoted in the *PRAM Guide* (Simon et al., 1997) because of differences of opinion among the working group. It is promoted in the *PMBOK Guide* (PMI, 2000). Even with the availability of proprietary software products such as @Risk for quantifying, displaying, and combining uncertain parameters, use of PIMs has persisted (further encouraged by PIM software). This is surprising, but it suggests a gap between simple direct prioritization of issues and quantification requiring the use of specialist software. This may be caused, at least in part, by the considerations addressed by the extended example in the next section In any event none of these PIM approaches deals directly with the complete set of objectives set out above for estimation and evaluation.

This section makes use of a particular example context to illustrate the minimalist approach. The focus is important generic assessment issues, but context-specific issues cannot be avoided, and there is considerable scope for addressing the relevance of the specific techniques and the philosophy behind the minimalist approach in other contexts. The next section complements the example of this section with this in mind. It also complements it by simplifying some aspects, making others more sophisticated, and in other ways.

An extended example: estimating and rational subjectivity

The extended example of the last section illustrated a number of considerations, but it involved a *contractor* perspective on a *reasonably complex context*. The extended example considered now provides a *client* perspective on *relatively simple context*, to provide balance with a complementary set of new concerns linked to those developed earlier.

Example context

A project manager wants to estimate how long it will take to obtain 'corporate centre' approval for a particular potential design change with expenditure approval implications in the context of planning the associated project as a whole. The example's origins are a weapons system project, but a wide range of projects will involve similar concerns, and the example is very generic in this sense. The project manager is aware that there is a 'corporate standard time' for such approvals of 3 weeks. The corporate culture places a high value on professional competence, objectivity in estimating and analysis, and there is a strong 'can do' ethos. How should the project manager proceed?

The project manager has recorded how long similar approvals have taken on earlier projects he was involved with, as shown in Table 15.5. These various outcomes suggest that the standard time of 3 weeks ought to be interpreted as a target, something sensible to aim for given no problems. But 3 weeks is not a sensible estimate of what is likely to happen, on average. If data were not available, the project manager might just use a 3-week duration estimate. However, this would not be rational if such data were available to the organization as a whole, using the term 'rational' in Simon's (1979) 'procedural rationality' sense. It is never rational to use objective numbers that are known to be inconsistent with reasonable expectations.

Table 15.5—Example data for design change approval

project	duration of approval (weeks)
1	3
2	7
3	6
4	4
5	15

Conventional approaches

A basic objective probability textbook approach would assume $(3 + 7 + 6 + 4 + 15)/5 = 7$ weeks is the best estimate of the expected duration, the simple mean or average of all the observations in Table 15.5.

Some people with a classical statistical training (e.g., Waters, 2001) might be tempted to associate this mean with a Normal (Gaussian) distribution, to estimate an associated spread (confidence bound) via the variance. The 15 week observation clearly makes this dubious, which may lead some to reject the 15 weeks as an outlier, especially if it involved very unusual circumstances that the project manager is confident will not occur this time. Presuming that this is legitimate is dubious, but it leads to a mean of $(3 + 7 + 6 + 4)/4 = 5$ associated with a probability distribution that looks Normal, and mean and variance estimates look objectively determined in the sense that the observation of 15 can be rejected as an outlier relative to the 'normal' variability reflected by the other four observations using classical statistical tests.

In a project planning context, some seasoned users of PERT (Moder and Philips, 1970) might prefer to start by assuming a standard Beta distribution approximation. Then the mean value is approximated by $(b + 4m + h)6$ where b is a plausible pessimistic value, m the most likely value, and h is a plausible optimistic value. Table 15.5 raises the obvious problem 'what is the most likely value?' If the value 6 is assumed, b is estimated by 3 and h by 15, and the estimate of mean duration is $(3 + 4 \times 6 + 15)/6 = 7$. The corresponding standard deviation estimate is $(h - b)/6 = (15 - 3)/6 = 2$. This Beta distribution approximation accommodates the obvious skew in the data and makes use of all the data. It is somewhat rough and ready and does not encourage examination of the pessimistic tail, but it is clearly more robust than a Normal distribution approach with or without outlier rejection.

Some people who are particularly partial to a Bayesian approach (e.g., Waters, 2001) may argue that the 'corporate standard time' for approval of 3 weeks is a form of 'prior' distribution with zero variance and the data of Table 15.5 define 'posterior' information: the two need to be combined. The key effect of this perspective is to bring the mean of 7 (or 5) closer to 3 and tighten the distribution, whatever assumptions are made for the posterior distribution.

Some people with a classical statistical training (whether or not they are Bayesians) might treat the $(3 + 7 + 6 + 4)/4 = 5$ estimate of the mean and an associated variance as Normally distributed uncertainty related to 'normal variability', which occurs approximately four times out of five, while associating the 15 week observation with 'abnormal variability', which occurs approximately one time out of five. This perspective would recognize that normal variability may be important, but that abnormal variability may be *much more* important and may need to be understood, incorporated in estimates, and *managed*, if it is cost-effective to do so. This immediately raises the need to model abnormal variability in subjective terms, *if* it matters, in a manner that facilitates its management. We have only one observation, which may or may not reflect issues associated with the current potential design change and which may or may not matter.

Some people, who may or may not understand the preceding perspectives, may take the view that the project manager's best course of action is to assume that approval for the design change will take 3 weeks, since this is the corporate standard time for approvals, implying that the risk of exceeding this estimate belongs to the corporate centre, not the project manager. This approach, known as a 'conditional estimate cop-out', is widespread practice in a wide variety of related forms. Such conditions are usually subsequently forgotten. They involve particularly dangerous practice when the assumed conditions for the estimate are ambiguous and allocation of responsibility for the conditions is unclear. Such practice is likely to flourish in organizations whose culture includes strong management pressures to avoid revealing bad news, appearing pessimistic, or lacking in confidence. In these situations, the conditional estimate cop-out is a useful defensive mechanism, but one that reinforces the culture and can result in a 'conspiracy of optimism'. Estimates based on this kind of corporate standard may appear rational and objective, but they are actually 'irrational', because they do not reflect estimators' rationally held beliefs.

To the authors, all these issues mean that a 'rational subjective' approach to estimating is essential. One priority issue is stamping out conditional estimate cop-outs and picking up related effects. Another priority issue is to determine whether the uncertainty matters. If it matters, it needs to receive further attention proportionate to how much it matters and the extent to which it can be managed given available estimation resources. This implies an approach to estimating that is iterative, starting out with a perspective that is transparent and simple, and goes into more detail in later passes to the extent that this is useful.

A constructively simple approach

Based on the Table 15.5 data, consider a first-pass estimate for design approval of 9 weeks using Table 15.6. The key working assumption is a uniform distribution that is deliberately conservative (biased on the pessimistic side) with respect to the expected value estimate and deliberately conservative and crude with respect to variability. This is a 'rational' approach to take because we know people are usually too optimistic when estimating variability (e.g., Kahneman et al., 1982). We also wish to use a simple process to identify what clearly does not matter, so it can be dismissed. The residual sources of variability that are not dismissed on a first pass may or may not matter, and more effort may be needed to clarify what is involved in a second-pass analysis. If both the 9 week expected value and the ±6-week plausible variation are not problems in the context of planning the project as a whole, then no further estimating effort is necessary and the first-pass estimate is 'fit for the purpose'. If either is a potential problem, further analysis to refine the estimates will be required. Assume that the

Table 15.6—Estimating the duration of design change approval—first pass

estimates	duration	comments
optimistic estimate	3 weeks	lowest observed value, a plausible minimum
pessimistic estimate	15 weeks	highest observed value, a plausible maximum
expected value	9 weeks	central value, $(3 + 15)/2$

Working assumptions: the data come from a uniform probability distribution, 3 and 15 corresponding very approximately to 10 and 90 percentile values.

9 week expected duration is a potential problem and that a 15 week outcome would be a significant problem for the project manager.

A second pass at estimating the time taken to obtain approval for a design change might start by questioning a possible trend associated with the 15 week observation. In broad terms this might involve looking at the reasons for variability within what normally happens, developing an understanding of reasons for possible outliers from what normally happens, and developing an understanding of what defines abnormal events. It might be observed that the reason for the previously observed 15 week outcome was a critical review of the project as a whole at the time approval was sought for the design change. However, similar lengthy delays might be associated with a number of other identified reasons for abnormal variation, such as: bad timing in relation to extended leave taken by key approvals staff, perhaps due to illness; serious defects in the project's management or approval request; and general funding reviews. It might be observed that the 7, 6, and 4 week observation are all normal variations, associated with, for example, pressure on staff from other projects, or routine shortcomings in the approval requests involving a need for further information. The 3 week standard, achieved once, might have involved no problems of any kind, a situation that occurred once in five observations.

These second-pass deliberations might lead to the specification of a stochastic model of the form outlined in Table 15.7. This particular model involves subjective estimates related to both the duration of an 'abnormal situation' and the 'probability that an abnormal situation is involved', in the latter case using the range 0.1 to 0.5 with an expected value of 0.3. The one observation of an abnormal situation in Table 15.5 suggests a probability of 0.2 (a 1 in 5 chance), but a rational response to only one observation requires a degree of conservatism if the outcome may be a decision to accept this potential variability and take the analysis no further. Given the limited data about a normal situation, which may not be representative, even the normal situation estimates of 3 to 7 weeks with an expected value of 5 weeks are best viewed as plausible subjective estimates, in a manner consistent with the first-pass approach.

Even if no data were available, the Table 15.7 approach would still be a sound rational subjective approach if the numbers seemed sensible in the context of a project team brainstorm of relevant experience and changes in circumstances.

Table 15.7—Estimating the duration of design change approval—second pass

situation	duration	comments
normal situation		
optimistic estimate	3 weeks	lowest observed value, plausible minimum
pessimistic estimate	7 weeks	highest observed values, plausible maximum
expected value	5 weeks	central value, $(3 + 7)/2$
abnormal situation		
optimistic estimate	10 weeks	plausible minimum, given observed 15
pessimistic estimate	20 weeks	plausible maximum, given observed 15
expected value	15 weeks	$(10 + 20)/2$, equal to observed 15 by design
probability that an abnormal situation is involved		
optimistic estimate	0.1	plausible minimum, given observed 0.2
pessimistic estimate	0.5	plausible maximum, given observed 0.2
expected value	0.3	$(0.1 + 0.5)/2$, greater than 0.2 by design
combined view		
optimistic estimate	3 weeks	normal minimum
pessimistic estimate	20 weeks	abnormal maximum
expected value	8 weeks	$(5 \times (1 - 0.3) + 15 \times 0.3)$

Working assumptions: the 'normal' data come from a uniform probability distribution, 3 and 7 corresponding very approximately to 10 and 90 percentile values. The 'abnormal' data come from uniform probability distributions. Probabilities of 0.1 and 0.5 and durations of 10 and 20 weeks both correspond very approximately to 10 and 90 percentile values, defined subjectively (based on unquantified experience) in this case in relation to an observed 1 in 5 chance (probability 0.2) of an observed 15-week outcome, a sample of one.

However, it is worth noting that *project managers* may tend to focus on reasons for delay attributable to *approvals staff*, while *approvals staff* will understandably take a different view. Everyone is naturally inclined to look for reasons for variability that do not reflect badly on themselves. Assumptions about how well (or badly) this particular project will manage its approvals request is an issue that should significantly affect the estimates, whether or not data are available. And who is preparing the estimates will inevitably colour their nature.

The second-pass estimation model produces an 8 week expected value that is less than the 9 week expected value from the first pass. The ±6 week, crude 10 to 90 percentile value associated with the first pass remains plausible, but the distribution shape is considerably refined by the second-pass estimate. A third pass might now be required, to explore the abnormal 10 to 20 week possibility, or its 0.1 to 0.5 probability range, and to refine understanding of abnormal events. This could employ well-established project risk modelling and process practices, building on the minimalist basis as outlined earlier, if the importance and complexity of the issues makes it worthwhile. A very rich set of model structures can be drawn on. The basic PERT model implicit in our first two passes is the simplest model available and may not be an appropriate choice. Other estimation contexts offer similar choices.

A cube factor to evaluate and interpret estimates

If any estimate involves assumptions that may not be true, the conditional nature of the estimate, in terms of its dependence on those assumptions being true, may be very important. Treating such an estimate as if it were unconditional (i.e., not dependent on any assumptions being true) may involve a serious misrepresentation of reality. Unfortunately, there is a common tendency for assumptions underpinning estimates to be subsequently overlooked or not made explicit in the first place. This tendency is reinforced in the context of evaluating the combined effect of uncertainty about all activities in a project. Often this tendency is condoned and further reinforced by bias driven by a 'conspiracy of optimism'. Such treatment of assumptions is especially likely where people do not like uncertainty and they prefer not to see it. The presence of a conspiracy of optimism is more than enough to make this issue crucial in the formulation of estimates. If messengers get shot for telling the truth, people will be motivated to be economical with the truth.

Understanding the conditional nature of estimates is particularly important when estimates prepared by one party are used by another party, especially when contractual issues are involved. By way of a simple example, suppose the project manager concerned with estimating the approval duration used a second-pass estimate of 8 weeks and similar kinds of estimates for all activity durations in the project as a whole. How should the 'customer', 'the head office', or any other party who is a 'user' of the project manager's estimates interpret the project manager's estimate of project duration?

The user would be wise to adjust the project manager's estimate to allow for residual uncertainty due to three basic sources:

- *known unknowns*—*explicit* assumptions or conditions that, if not valid, could have uncertain, significant consequences;
- *unknown unknowns*—*implicit* assumptions or conditions that, if not valid, could have uncertain, significant consequences;
- *bias*—systematic estimation errors that have significant consequences.

A problem is that adjusting estimates to allow for these sources of uncertainty often involves greater subjectivity than that involved in producing the estimates in question. This is an especially acute problem if 'objective estimates' are used that are irrational. User response to this problem varies. One approach is to collude and make no adjustments since there is no objective way to do so. Such a response may reinforce and encourage any 'conspiracy of optimism' or requirement for the appearance of objectivity in future estimating. Another response is to demand more explicit, detailed information about assumptions and potential limitations in estimates. However, unless this leads to more detailed scrutiny of estimates and further analysis, it does not in itself lead to changes in estimates. Indeed it may encourage the previously mentioned practice of conditional estimate cop-outs, especially if proffered assumptions become numerous and are less likely to be scrutinized and their implications explored. A third response, which is very common, is for users of estimates to make informal adjustments to estimates, although the reasons for these adjustments may not be clearly articulated. For example, forecasts from sales staff may be regarded as conservative by managers using the data to develop next year's incentive scheme, and project managers may treat cost or duration estimates as pessimistic and set deliberately tight performance targets to compensate. A well-known consequence of this is the development of a vicious circle in the production of estimates, whereby the estimator attempts to compensate for the user's anticipated adjustments, while suspicion of this practice encourages the estimate user to make increased adjustments to estimates. If several estimators are involved and estimates combined in a nested fashion, the scope for uncertainty about how realistic aggregated estimates are can be considerable. A current controversy, centred on this issue, is the use of data-based adjustments to cost estimates as tentatively proposed by the UK Treasury (HMT, 2002). To adjust for the historically observed bias in project cost estimates, statistical estimates of bias by project type have been produced. It is argued that these estimates of bias should be used directly as a scaling factor on future cost estimates unless the process used to produce the estimate warrants lower adjustment. All those concerned with following the advice that emerged (www.greenbook.treasury. gov.uk/) can use the approach outlined here.

Taking a constructively simple approach involves attempting to roughly size adjustments for known unknowns, unknown unknowns and bias explicitly, in an effort to size the underlying uncertainty. The need to relate these adjustments to the base estimate implies the use of three scaling factors, F_k, F_u, and F_b, corresponding, respectively, to known unknowns, unknown unknowns and bias, that ought to be applied to an expected value estimate E.

F_k, F_u, or $F_b < 1$ signifies a downward adjustment to an estimate E, while F_k, F_u, or $F_b > 1$ signifies an upward adjustment. Each scaling factor will itself be uncertain in size. Each adjustment factor is 1 ± 0 if a negligible adjustment effect is involved, but expected values different from 1 for each factor and an associated rational subjective probability distribution for each factor with a non-zero spread will often be involved. For conservative estimates of performance measures, like cost or time, expected values for F_k and $F_u > 1$ will usually be appropriate, while the expected value of F_b might be greater or less than 1 depending on the circumstances.

To test the validity of the project manager's estimate of project duration as a whole and to maintain simplicity, suppose the user of this estimate takes a sample of one activity estimate and selects the estimated duration of design approval for this purpose.

Consider first the adjustment factor F_k for known unknowns: any *explicit* assumptions that matter. If the project manager has identified a list of sources of uncertainty embodied in the normal situation and another list of sources of uncertainty embodied in the abnormal situation, and if these lists look appropriate and the quantification of associated uncertainty looks appropriate, then a negligible adjustment for known unknowns is involved and an $F_k = 1 \pm 0$ is reasonable. However, if the estimator does not use rational, subjective probabilities, then the user of those estimates ought to do so to make a suitable adjustment. For example, if the project manager has recorded a conditional estimate cop-out for the approval duration of 3 weeks, this should suggest an expected value for F_k greater than 2 with an anticipated outcome range 1 to 10 if the user is familiar with data like those of Table 15.5 and analysis like that of Table 15.7. It would not be rational for the user to fail to make such an adjustment.

Similarly, an $F_u = 1 \pm 0$ may be reasonable if the project manager made a provision for unknown unknowns when quantifying approval duration estimates in a Table 15.7 format that the user deems suitably conservative in the light of the quality of the identification of explicit assumptions. In contrast, an expected $F_k > 2$ with an anticipated outcome range 1 to 10 may suggest comparable values for F_u, depending on the user's confidence about F_k estimation and the quality of the project manager's estimate more generally.

In respect of any adjustment for systematic estimation errors or bias, setting $F_b = 1 \pm 0$ may be reasonable if $F_k = 1 \pm 0$ and $F_u = 1 \pm 0$ seem sensible, conservative estimates and the organization involved has a history of no bias. However, if estimates of design approval duration are thought to be understated relative to recent organizational history, a suitably large F_b expected value and associated spread is warranted.

Estimating scaling factors should depend to some extent on how they will be combined. The expected values of the scale factors might be applied to the conditional expected value of an estimate E to obtain an adjusted expected value E_a in a number of ways, including the following:

$$\text{Additive approach} \quad E_a = E[(F_k - 1) + (F_u - 1) + (F_b - 1) + 1]$$

$$\text{Mixed approach} \quad E_a = EF_b[(F_k - 1) + (F_u - 1) + 1]$$

$$\text{Multiplicative approach} \quad E_a = EF_bF_kF_u$$

The additive approach implies separate adjustments are made to the estimate E and merely added together to obtain E_a. The mixed approach implies separate adjustments via F_k and F_u are applied to the base estimate E after it has been scaled for bias. The multiplicative approach is the most conservative, assuming the adjustments should operate in a cumulative fashion, and is operationally the simplest. This combination of characteristics makes it the preferred choice for the authors.

The product $F_kF_uF_b$ constitutes a single 'cube' factor, short for Known Unknowns, Unknown Unknowns, and Bias (KUUUB), conveniently designated F^3 and usefully portrayed graphically by the cube shown in Figure 15.3 provided

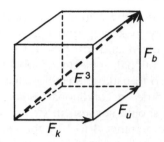

F_k is a factor reflecting 'known unknowns':
        conditions, including scope assumptions
F_u is a factor reflecting 'unknown unknowns':
        unidentified conditions
F_b is a factor reflecting 'bias': likely systematic error

F^3 reflects all three: for example $F^3 = F_k \times F_u \times F_b$

Figure 15.3—A visual representation of the cube factor F^3

this does not stimulate a desire for a geometric reinterpretation of F^3. Given the tendency for perceived uncertainty to grow as it is decomposed, estimating three separate factors and then combining them using the multiplicative approach may be especially appropriate in the first-pass estimating process. A composite scale factor incorporating adjustments for KUUUB could be estimated in probability terms directly, but considering the three components separately helps to clarify the rather different issues involved.

Large F^3 values will seem worryingly subjective to those who cling to an irrational objectivity perspective. However, explicit attention to F^3 factors is an essential part of a rational subjectivity approach. It is seriously irrational to assume $F^3 = 1 + 0$ without sound grounds for doing so. At present, most organizations fail this rationality test.

The key value of explicit quantification of F^3 is forcing those involved to think about the implications of the factors that drive the expected size and variability of F^3. Such factors may be far more important than the factors captured in a prior conventional estimation process where there is a natural tendency to forget about conditions and assumptions and focus on the numbers. Not considering an F^3 factor explicitly can be seen as overlooking Heisenberg's principle: 'we have to remember that what we observe is not nature itself, but nature exposed to our method of questioning.' Attempting to explicitly size F^3 makes it possible to *try* to avoid this omission. Different parties may emerge with different views about an appropriate F^3, but the process of discussion should be beneficial. *If an organization refuses to acknowledge and estimate F^3 explicitly, the issues involved do not go away: they simply become unmanaged and the realization of associated downside risk will be a betting certainty.*

The size of appropriate F^3 factors is not just a simple function of objective data availability and the use of statistical estimation techniques; it is a function of the quality of the whole process of estimation and interpretation. In a project management context it will include issues driven by factors like the nature of the intended contracts.

In practice, a sample of one estimate yielding an F_k significantly different from 1 ought to lead to wider scrutiny of other estimates and other aspects of the process as a whole. In a project planning context, if one sampled activity duration estimate, such as duration of design change approval, yields an F_k significantly greater than 1, this ought to prompt scrutiny of other activity estimates and the role of the estimates in a wider context. Conversely, if no sample activity estimates are examined, this ought to lead to a large F^3 value for a whole project estimate, given the track record of most organizations. Project teams *and all users of their estimates* need to negotiate a jointly optimal approach to producing original estimates and associated F^3 factors. Any aspect of uncertainty that is left out by an estimate producer and is of interest to an estimate user should be addressed in the user's F^3.

Interpreting another party's subjective or objective probability distributions requires explicit consideration of an F^3 factor. The quality of the modelling as well as the associated parameter estimates need to be assessed to estimate F^3. This includes issues like attention to dependence. Estimators and users of estimates who do not have an agreed approach to F^3 factors are communicating in an ambiguous fashion, which is bound to generate mistrust. Trust is an important driver of the size of F^3 factors.

As described here, the F^3 factor concept is very simple and clearly involves a high level of subjectivity. Nevertheless, on the basis of 'what gets measured gets managed', it is necessary to highlight important sources of uncertainty and prompt consideration of underlying management implications. For the most part, high levels of precision in F^3 factors and component factors is not practicable or needed. The reason for sizing F^3 factors is 'insight not numbers'. However, more developed versions explicitly recognizing subjective probability distributions for F^3 and its components are feasible (Chapman and Ward, 2002) and may be appropriate in estimation or modelling iterations where this is constructive.

This extended example makes use of a particular context to illustrate the rational subjectivity and cube factor aspects of a constructively simple approach to estimating. The focus is on important generic assessment issues and is less context-dependent than the first extended example, but some context-specific considerations cannot be avoided. There is considerable scope for addressing the relevance of the specific techniques and the philosophy behind the constructively simple estimating approach in other contexts, some examples being addressed elsewhere (Chapman and Ward, 2002).

A further objective

Estimation and evaluation of uncertainty are core tasks in any decision support process. The constructively simple estimating approach to these core tasks demonstrated by this example involves all seven important objectives that contribute to cost-effective uncertainty assessment discussed in the last section, plus one more.

Objective 8   *Avoiding irrational objectivity*

Corporate culture can drive people to displaying irrational objectivity. An important objective is neutralizing this pressure, via 'rational subjectivity'. In particular, it is very easy to make assumptions, then lose sight of them, between the basic analysis and the ultimate use of that analysis: the F_k factor forces integration of the implications of such explicit assumptions; the F_u factor picks up the implicit assumptions; and the F_b factor integrates any residual bias. Ensuring this is done is an important objective.

Simplicity efficiency

In addition to a further objective, Objective 7 (simplicity with constructive complexity) is developed further in this example. In particular, it provides a useful direct illustration of the notion of 'simplicity efficiency'. If we see the probability structures that estimates are based on as models, with a wide range of feasible choices, a first-pass, constructively simple choice involves targeting a point on $b–c$ in Figure 15.4. Choices on $a–b$ are too simplistic to give enough insight. Later-pass choices should target a point on $c–d$. Choices like e are inefficient on any pass and should not be used. We start with an effective, constructively simple approach. We add 'constructive complexity' where it pays, when it pays, using earlier passes to help manage the choice process with respect to ongoing iterative analysis. Simplicity efficiency is the basis of risk management

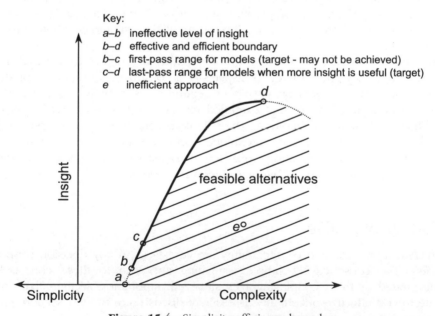

Figure 15.4—Simplicity efficiency boundary

that is both *effective* and *efficient*. Chapman and Ward (2002) develop this simplicity efficiency concept further, in terms of concepts and processes as well as models.

Simplicity efficiency might be termed simplicity–insight efficiency (SI efficiency for short), especially if the term risk–reward efficiency (RR efficiency) is adopted instead of risk efficiency. The term SI efficiency emphasizes the nature of the trade-off between simplicity and insight along an efficient frontier or boundary that is directly comparable with the RR trade-off associated with risk efficiency. This book will stick to the term simplicity efficiency. But it is important to see the conceptual link between simplicity efficiency and risk efficiency. Risk efficiency is a property of projects that we try to achieve as a basic objective common to all projects. Simplicity efficiency is a property of RMPs that we try to achieve with respect to all RMPs. Simplicity efficiency is a necessary condition for risk efficiency. Both effectiveness and efficiency in project terms requires simplicity efficiency.

Ambiguity and a holistic view of uncertainty

A holistic view of uncertainty (see Objective 1 as discussed in the last section) must embrace ambiguity as well as variability. Ambiguity is associated with lack of clarity because of lack of data, lack of detail, lack of structure to consider the issues, assumptions employed, sources of bias, and ignorance about how much effort it is worth expending to clarify the situation. This ambiguity warrants attention in all parts of the decision support process, including estimation and evaluation. However, consideration of uncertainty in the form of ambiguity is not facilitated in estimation by the commonly used probability models that focus on variability, especially when variability is associated with objective probabilities.

The implications of uncertainty in simple, deterministic model parameters and associated model outputs are commonly explored by sensitivity analysis, and complex probabilistic models commonly use techniques like Monte Carlo simulation to explore uncertainty modelled directly. However, neither of these evaluation approaches explicitly addresses ambiguity issues concerning the structure of the modelling of core issues, choices about the nature of the specific process being used, and the wider characterization of the context being addressed.

The SHAMPU process recognizes that estimating expected values and the variability of decision support parameters cannot be decoupled from understanding the context, choosing a specific process for this analysis, specifying the model structure, and evaluating and interpreting the consequences of this uncertainty. However, the presence of ambiguity increases the need for data acquisition, estimation, and model development to proceed in a closely coupled process. Failure to recognize this can lead to decision support processes that are irrational as well as ineffective and inefficient.

This weakness is sometimes reinforced by a 'hard science' view of the desirability of rigorous theory and objective data. An obvious general concern in estimating is the basis of estimates. In principle, we would like all estimates to be entirely objective, based on an unambiguous interpretation of underlying data. However, in attempting to estimate variability in model parameters or any other decision parameters, this is virtually impossible. In particular, for all practical purposes there is no such thing as a completely objective estimate of any probability distribution model that is suitable for rational decision making. Assumptions are always involved in the estimating process, even when lots of relevant data are available, and any assumptions that are not *strictly* true make associated estimates subjective. If we wish to make decisions that are consistent with our beliefs, we must use subjective estimates. This means our decisions will be non-optimal to the extent that our beliefs are misguided. However, assuming our beliefs have some rational basis, if we make decisions that are inconsistent with our beliefs, the chances of non-optimal decisions will be much higher. This is rational subjectivity in its simplest form, now widely understood and subscribed to, and the basis of most modern decision analysis textbooks. Given that objectivity is not feasible, it should not be an issue. What is always an issue is the rationality of estimates used. Subjective estimates that are rational are what is needed, and irrational objective estimates have to be avoided.

Failure to recognize the significance of ambiguity is also reinforced by a reluctance to take subjective probabilities to their logical conclusion in a pragmatic framework that emphasizes the importance of being 'approximately right' in terms of a broad view of the right question. Being 'precisely wrong' in the sense of having a precisely correct answer to the wrong question is a standing joke, but there are clear pressures driving many people in this direction. A constructively simple approach is designed to neutralize these pressures.

Conclusion

In summary, some of the key messages of this chapter as a whole include:

1. The central issue when considering RMP short cuts is the trade-off between the effectiveness of the RMP and the cost of the RMP.
2. Simplicity efficiency, as portrayed in Figure 15.4, is central to managing these trade-offs. It is part of the concept of risk efficiency defined in the general sense used by this book.
3. RMP effectiveness is a complex concept to assess and requires an understanding of risk efficiency in terms of all relevant criteria and a rich set of motives that include creating a learning organization that people want to be a part of.

4. The high opportunity cost of time in a crisis is also part of the argument for much more proactive learning based on formal processes than might seem obvious. Time spent training, developing skills, developing judgement, so everyone is effective, efficient, and cool in a crisis has advantages well understood by military commanders for millennia.

Ownership issues:
16 a contractor perspective

We must indeed all hang together, or most assuredly we shall all hang separately.—
Benjamin Franklin, a remark to John Hancock at signing of the *Declaration of Independence*, 4 July 1776

Introduction

The ownership phase of the SHAMPU (Shape, Harness, And Manage Project Uncertainty) process (Chapter 9) is concerned with allocating responsibility for managing project uncertainty to appropriate project parties. As noted previously, the issues involved are of fundamental importance, because allocations can strongly influence the motivation of parties and the extent to which project uncertainty is assessed and managed by each party.

In so far as individual parties perceive risks differently and have different abilities and motivations to manage uncertainty, then their approach to risk management will be different. In particular, any one party is likely to try to manage risk primarily for his or her own benefit, perhaps to the disadvantage of other parties. If one party, typically the client (project owner), is in a position to allocate risks, then this party may regard allocating all risks to other parties as a perfectly acceptable allocation, even if the other parties are not happy about this. The fundamental weakness in this simple but extreme strategy is that it may not produce risk management that is in the interests of the client. For example, the use of exculpatory contract clauses by the client to unfairly transfer risk to the contractor can cause contractors to increase their prices and destroy the contractor's trust (DeMaere et al., 2001). This can increase defensive behaviour and conflict, reduce the potential for establishing long-term or partnering relationships, and jeopardize project success. In most situations, a more considered allocation strategy can produce a situation where uncertainty is managed more effectively, to the benefit of all parties concerned.

Effective risk management requires that there is:

1. a clear specification of the required activities and associated issues;
2. a clear perception of the issues being borne by each party;

3. sufficient capability to manage the issues;
4. appropriate motivation to manage the issues.

The rationale for allocating risk between the client and other parties ought to be based on meeting these conditions as far as possible. If condition 1 is not met, then effective risk management is impossible because not all issues that need to be managed will have been identified. If condition 2 is not met, parties may not be aware of their responsibilities, or what the client and other parties are expecting from them in terms of issues management. In respect of condition 3, as any manager knows, assigning a task to an individual, team, or organization unit is only appropriate if the assignee has the skills and capacity to carry out the task. A high and appropriate combination of skills and capacity is necessary for effective (and efficient) performance. Condition 3 captures the frequently touted maxim that 'risk should be allocated to the party best able to control and manage the risk', with our preferred term 'issue' replacing 'risk'.

Condition 4 is about ensuring appropriate motivation of project parties (i.e., motivation to manage issues in the *client*'s interests). Basic motivation theory tells us that parties will be motivated to do this to the extent that this serves their own interests and to the extent that the expected rewards are commensurate with the effort expended. This calls for a significant degree of alignment of a party's objectives with those of the client, and difficulties arise when project parties have different objectives that are not congruent. Unless a shared perception of project success criteria is possible, these different, conflicting criteria may imply very different perceptions of project-related risk and different priorities in project risk management.

Differences in perception of project success arise most obviously in client–contractor relationships. The question of 'success from whose point of view?' matters to even the most egocentric party. For example, in a simple, single client and single contractor context, if the client or the contractor pushes his or her luck, mutual trust and co-operation may be early casualties, as noted above, but in the limit the other party may walk away, or go broke and cease to exist. Thus, in making allocations, it is important to distinguish between responsibility for managing an issue and responsibility for bearing the consequences of the issue. In particular, as noted in Chapter 9, it may be desirable to allocate these responsibilities to different parties, recognizing that the party best able to physically manage an issue may not be the party best able to bear the financial consequences of that issue.

Different people within the same client or contractor organization can give rise to essentially the same problems, as can multiple clients or multiple contractors. Equally, agreements about issue allocation in a hierarchical structure or between different units in the same organization can be viewed as 'contracts' for present purposes (Chapman and Ward, 2002, chap. 6).

This chapter addresses these concerns, using the context of a simple, two party situation involving a client and contractor to illustrate the basic issues.

Consequences of two simple contract payment terms

Two basic forms of risk allocation via contract payment terms are the fixed price contract and the Cost Plus Fixed Fee (CPFF) or 'reimbursement' contract. In the fixed price contract the contractor theoretically carries all the risk. In the CPFF contract the client theoretically carries all the risk. From a risk management perspective, neither is entirely satisfactory under all circumstances. Fixed price contracts are by far the most common and are frequently used inappropriately.

CPFF contracts

With a CPFF contract the client pays the contractor a fixed fee and reimburses the contractor for all costs associated with the project: labour, plant, and materials actually consumed are charged at rates that are checked and approved by open book accounting. The cost of overcoming errors, omissions, and other charges is borne by the client.

Advantages for the client include the following: costs are limited to what is actually needed, the contractor cannot earn excessive profits, and the possibility that a potential loss for a contractor will lead to adverse effects is avoided.

However, CPFF contracts have a serious disadvantage as far as most clients are concerned, in that there is an uncertain cost commitment coupled with an absence of any incentive on contractors to control costs. Under a CPFF contract, the contractor's motivation to carry out work efficiently and cost-effectively is considerably weakened. Moreover, contractors may be tempted to pad costs in ways that bring benefits to other work they are undertaking. Examples include expanded purchases of equipment, excessive testing and experimentation, generous arrangements with suppliers, and overmanning to avoid non-reimbursable lay-off costs, a problem that is more pronounced when the fee is based on a percentage of actual project costs.

A further difficulty is that of agreeing and documenting in the contract what are allowable costs on a given project. However, it is important that all project-related costs are correctly identified and included at appropriate charging rates in the contract. Particular areas of difficulty are overhead costs and managerial time. To the extent that costs are not specifically reimbursed, they will be paid for out of the fixed fee and contractors will be motivated to minimize such costs.

The use of a CPFF contract also presents problems in selecting a contractor who can perform the work for the lowest cost. Selecting a contractor on the basis of the lowest fixed fee tendered in a competitive bidding situation does not guarantee a least cost outcome. It could be argued that it encourages a maximum cost outcome.

Fixed price contracts

Common practice is for clients to aim to transfer all risk to contractors via fixed price contracts. Typically, a contract is awarded to the lowest fixed price bid in a competitive tender, on the assumption that *all* other things are equal, including the expertise of the tendering organizations. Competitive tendering is perceived as an efficient way of obtaining value for money, whether or not the client is relatively ignorant of the underlying project costs compared with potential contractors.

With a fixed price contract, the client pays a fixed price to the contractor regardless of what the contract actually costs the contractor to perform. The contractor carries all the risk of loss associated with higher than expected costs, but benefits if costs turn out to be less than expected.

Under a fixed price contract, the contractor is motivated to manage project costs downward. For example, by increasing efficiency or using the most cost-effective approaches the contractor can increase profit. Hopefully this is without prejudice to the quality of the completed work, but the client is directly exposed to quality degradation risk to the extent that quality is not completely specified or verifiable. The difficulty of completely specifying requirements or performance in a contract is well known. This difficulty is perhaps greatest in the procurement of services as compared with construction or product procurement. For example, it is very difficult to define unambiguously terms like 'co-operate', 'advise', 'co-ordinate', 'supervise', 'best endeavours', or 'ensure economic and expeditious execution', and it is unrealistic to assume that contractors have priced work under the most costly conditions in a competitive bidding situation.

In the case of a high risk project, where uncertainty demands explicit attention and policy or behaviour modification, a fixed price contract may appear initially attractive to the client. However, contractors may prefer a cost reimbursement contract and require what the client regards as an excessive price to take on cost risk within a fixed price contract. More seriously, even a carefully specified fixed price contract may not remove all uncertainty about the final price the client has to pay. For some sources of uncertainty, such as variation in quantity or unfore-seen ground conditions, the contractor will be entitled to additional payments via a claims procedure. If the fixed price is too low, additional risks are introduced (e.g., the contractor may be unable to fulfil contractual conditions and go into liquidation, or use every means to generate claims). The nature of uncertainty and claims, coupled with the confidentiality of the contractor's costs, introduce an element of chance into the adequacy of the payment, from whichever side of the contract it is viewed (Perry, 1986). This undermines the concept of a fixed price contract and at the same time may cause the client to pay a higher than necessary risk premium because risks effectively being carried by the client are not explicitly so indicated. In effect, a cost reimbursement contract is agreed by default for risks that are not controllable by the contractor or the client. This allocation of uncontrollable risk may not be efficient. Client insistence on placing fixed price contracts with the lowest bidder may only serve to aggravate this problem.

The following example illustrates the way the rationale for a particular risk allocation policy can change within a given organization, over the dimension 'hands-on' to 'hands-off eyes-on' (as the use of fixed price contracts is referred to in the UK Ministry of Defence).

Example 16.1   A changing rationale for risk allocation

Oil majors with North Sea projects in the 1970s typically took a very hands-on approach to risk management (e.g., they paid their contractors on a piece or day rate basis for pipe laying). Some risks, like bad weather, they left to their contractors to manage, but they took on the cost consequences of unexpected bad weather and all other external risks of this kind (like buckles). The rationale was based on the size and unpredictability of risks like buckles, the ability of the oil companies to bear such risks relative to the ability of the contractors to bear them, and the charges contractors would have insisted on if they had to bear them.

By the late 1980s, many similar projects involved fixed price contracts for laying a pipeline. The rationale was based on contractor experience of the problems and lower charges because of this experience and market pressures.

The above observations suggest that fixed price contracts should be avoided in the early stages of a project when specifications may be incomplete and realistic performance objectives difficult to set (Sadeh et al., 2000). A more appropriate strategy might be to break the project into a number of stages and to move from cost based contracts for early stages (negotiated with contractors that the client trusts), through to fixed price competitively tendered contracts in later stages as project objectives and specifications become better defined.

Normally, the client will have to pay a premium to the contractor for bearing the cost uncertainty as part of the contract price. From the client's perspective, this premium may be excessive unless moderated by competitive forces. However, the client will not know how much of a given bid is for estimated project costs and how much is for the bidder's risk premium unless these elements are clearly distinguished. In the face of competition, tendering contractors (in any industry) will be under continuous temptation to pare prices and profits in an attempt to win work. Faced with the difficulty of earning an adequate return, such contractors may seek to recover costs and increase earnings by cutting back on the quality of materials and services supplied in ways that are not visible to the client, or by a determined and systematic pursuit of claims, a practice common in the construction industry. This situation is most likely to occur where the supply of goods or services exceeds demand, clients are price-conscious, and clients find suppliers difficult to differentiate. Even with prior or post-bidding screening out of any contractors not deemed capable, reliable, and sound, the lowest bidder will have to be that member of the viable set of contractors who scores highest overall in the following categories:

1. Most optimistic in relation to cost uncertainties. This may reflect expertise, but it may reflect a willingness to depart from implicit and explicit specification of the project, or ignorance of what is required.
2. Most optimistic in relation to claims for additional revenue.
3. Least concerned with considerations such as the impact on reputation or the chance of bankruptcy.
4. Most desperate for work.

Selecting the lowest fixed price bid is an approach that should be used with caution, particularly when:

1. Uncertainty is significant.
2. Performance specifications are not comprehensive, clear, and legally enforceable.
3. The expertise, reputation, and financial security of the contractor are not beyond question.

The situation has been summed up by Barnes (1984):

> *The problem is that when conditions of contract placing large total risk upon the contractor are used, and work is awarded by competitive tender, the contractor who accidentally or deliberately underestimated the risks is most likely to get the work. When the risks materialize with full force he must then either struggle to extract compensation from the client or suffer the loss. This stimulates the growth of the claims problem.*
>
> *The remedy seems to be to take factors other than lowest price into account when appointing contractors. In particular, a reputation gained for finishing fast and on time without aggressive pursuit of extra payment for the unexpected should be given very great weight and should be seen to do so.*

An underlying issue is the extent to which clients and contractors wish to co-operate with an attitude of mutual gain from trade, seeing each other as partners. Unfortunately, the all-too-common approach is inherently confrontational, based on trying to gain most at the other party's expense, or at least seeking to demonstrate that one has not been 'beaten' by the other party. This confrontational attitude can breed an atmosphere of wariness and mistrust. It appears to matter greatly whether the client is entering a one-off, non-repeating, contractual relationship, or a relationship that may be repeated in the future. To the extent that the client is not a regular customer, the client can be concerned only with the present project and may have limited expertise in distinguishing the quality of potential contractors and bids. Competition is then used to 'get the best deal'. This is often manifested as seeking the lowest fixed price on the naive and rash assumption that all other things are equal. As indicated above, this practice brings its own risks, often in large quantities.

Well-founded willingness to bear risk

Many of the problems with claims and arbitration arise because of contractual parties' preoccupation with transferring risk to other parties, generally under fixed price contracts. To the extent that either clients or contractors believe that risks can be transferred or offloaded onto the other, or some third party, such as a subcontractor, then any assessment or management of project risks on their part is likely to be half-hearted. Consequently, many contracting parties do not assess risks or share information about risks in any systematic way. As we have seen in the previous section, this behaviour may not be in the best interests of either party.

Abrahamson (1973) has commented on the problem in the following way:

> *The strangest thing is that the pricing of risk ... is resisted by both sides. Some contractors prefer a contentious right to their extra costs to a chance to price a risk, and indeed rely on the increase in their final account from claims to make up for low tenders. On the other hand, some clients and engineers prefer to refer to risks generally or as obliquely as possible, presumably in the hope of finding a contractor who will not allow for them fully in his price.*
>
> *These two attitudes are equally reprehensible and short sighted. What a sorry start to a project when they encounter each other!*

Such behaviour is often encouraged by legal advisers concerned to put their client's legal interests first. In legal circles debate about risk allocation is usually about clarifying and ensuring the effectiveness of allocation arrangements in the contract. Lawyers are not concerned with the principles that should guide appropriate allocation of risk between contracting parties. It could be argued that they are pursuing their own future interests by maximizing conflict, implicitly if not explicitly.

At first sight, appropriate allocation might be based on the willingness of parties to take on a risk (Ward et al., 1991). However, willingness to bear risk will only result in conscientious management of project risks to the extent that it is based on:

1. an adequate perception of project risks;
2. a reasoned assessment of risk/reward trade-offs;
3. a real ability to bear the consequences of a risk eventuating;
4. a real ability to manage the associated uncertainty and thereby mitigate risks.

Willingness to bear risk should not be a criterion for risk allocation to the extent that it is based on:

1. an inadequate perception of project risks;
2. a false perception of ability to bear the consequences of a risk eventuating;
3. a need to obtain work;
4. perceptions of the risk/return trade-offs of transferring risks to another party.

As noted earlier, these latter conditions can be an underlying reason for low tender prices on fixed price contracts.

To ensure that willingness to bear risk is well founded, explicit consideration of risks allocated between the contracting parties is desirable, preferably at an early stage in negotiations or the tendering process. In particular, contractors ought to be given an adequate opportunity to price for risks they will be expected to carry. Unfortunately, the following scenario for a construction project is often typical.

Example 16.2   The effects of limited time to prepare a bid

A project that has taken several years to justify and prepare is parcelled up and handed to tendering contractors who are given just a few weeks to evaluate it from scratch and commit themselves to a price for building it. The tenderers have been through an extensive and costly prequalification exercise that is designed to determine their capacity to undertake the work. Having the gratification of being considered acceptable, they would like to be allowed the time to study the tender documents in detail and to consider carefully their approach to the work. Instead they are faced with a tender submission deadline that only permits a scanty appraisal of the complex construction problems and risks that are often involved. Consequently, each tenderer proceeds along the following lines.

A site assessment team, which may include a project manager, estimator, planner, geologist, and representatives of specialist subcontractors, is assembled and dispatched to the site with instructions to gather in all method- and cost-related information needed for preparing the bid. This information, together with quotations from materials suppliers, subcontractors, and plant companies, and advice on the legal, insurance, financial, and taxation implications, is assessed by the estimating team working under great pressure to meet the deadline. Various construction techniques have to be investigated and compared and temporary works proposals considered and designed. Lack of information on ground conditions, plant availability, materials supply, subcontractor capacity and many other important factors have to be overcome by further investigation and inspired guesswork. The contractual terms have to be explored to elicit the imposed risk strategy of the client. An assessment has to be made of the client's reaction to any qualifications in the bid. Possible claims opportunities are evaluated.

In the absence of adequate time and information, any evaluation and pricing of potential risk exposure is on an *ad hoc* basis. Evaluation of risks begins by questioning experienced managers in the contractor's organization and arriving at a consensus of the 'gut feelings' expressed. The overall level of risk is assessed by looking at the overall programme, checking if it is very 'tight', considering the effects of delays by suppliers, and checking the basic conditions for any extension of time. Few, if any, calculations or references to specific results on previous contracts are made, the rationale being that any such references are unlikely to be applicable to the circumstances of the contract in question, even if any relevant data existed. The chairman ends up by pulling a figure out of the air based on his feelings about the advice obtained.

Even if the contractor is prepared to undertake appropriate analysis of project risks, lack of information about project uncertainties coupled with lack of time to prepare a tender may preclude proper evaluation of project risks.

Joint identification of risks by client and tendering contractors is desirable on efficiency grounds, in terms of cost-effective identification of a comprehensive list, and to ensure that both parties are fully aware of the risks involved. If tendering contractors were simply given more time to tender without client involvement, they might undertake adequate analysis of project risks. However, while many project risks may be best assessed by knowledgeable contractors, it may be more efficient for the client to undertake analysis of certain project risks to expedite the tendering process and to ensure that all tenderers have similar information. For example, contractors should not be expected to bear risks that cannot be cost-effectively quantified with sufficient certainty, such as variable ground on a tunnelling project. In such cases the price ought to be related to what is actually encountered (Barber, 1989). If clients are unduly concerned about bearing such risks, then it will be appropriate for them to undertake the necessary in-depth risk analysis themselves and require tendering contracts to price for the risk on the basis of the client's risk analysis. Sharing such risks is always an option, as discussed later. Obviously, the greater the detail provided by the client in relation to risks that are to be borne in whole or in part by the contractor the less the contractor has to price for risk related to the contractor's uncertainty about what the project involves.

In determining a final bid figure, contractors need to consider several other factors besides estimates of the prime cost of performing the contract (Ward and Chapman, 1988). The intensity of the competition from other contractors, the costs of financing, insurance, and bonding, the financial status of the client, terms of payment and project cash flow, and the level of the contingency allowance to cover risks all affect the mark-up that is added to the prime cost of construction. Tendering contractors' risk analysis will have additional dimensions to the client's risk analysis. Each contractor requires a bid that gives an appropriate balance between the risk of not getting the contract and the risk associated with possible profits or losses if the contract is obtained, as illustrated in Example 12.1.

Transparent pricing

Aside from allowing contractors sufficient time to properly consider the pricing of risk, clients need to be able to assess the extent to which contractors' tender prices are based on well-founded willingness to take on project risk. A useful 'transparent pricing' strategy is for the client to require fixed price bids to be broken down into a price for expected project costs and risk premia for various risks. Supporting documentation could also show the contractors' perceptions of risk on which the risk premia were based. As in insurance contracts, pricing based on broad categories of risk rather than related to small details is a realistic approach. An important consideration in performing risk analysis is the identification of factors that can have a major impact on project performance. However, detailed risk analysis may be necessary to determine the relative significance of project risks. Pricing need not consider all project risks in detail, but it does need to be related to major sources.

An important benefit of a transparent pricing strategy to both client and contractor is clarification of categories of risk remaining with the client despite a fixed price contract. For example, there may be project risks associated with exogenous factors, such as changes in regulatory requirements during the project, that are not identified or allocated by the contract. Such factors are unlikely to be allowed for in bids, because tenderers will consider such factors outside of their control and the responsibility of the client.

A further benefit of transparent pricing is that it helps to address an important, potential 'adverse selection' problem. Contractors who can provide honestly stated, good-quality risk pricing may price themselves out of the market in relation to those who provide dishonestly stated, poor-quality risk pricing at low prices, if sufficient clients are unable to distinguish between good and poor quality, honesty and dishonesty. As Akerlof (1970) argues in a paper entitled 'The market for "lemons": quality uncertainty and the market mechanism', poor quality and dishonesty can drive good quality and honesty out of the market. Clients can address this problem by requiring transparent pricing of risk in tenders and by requiring tender submissions to include plans for managing risk. In this way comparisons between tenderers in terms of the extent of well-founded willingness to bear risk can be made on a more informed basis.

In practice, tenderers experienced in risk management may be able to demonstrate well-founded willingness to bear risk *and* submit lower tender prices than competitors. In such cases transparent pricing should help to consolidate their advantage over less experienced contractors.

Efficient allocation of risk

It is often suggested that cost risk should be allocated to the party best able to anticipate and control that risk. On this basis, a tentative conclusion is that fixed price contracts are appropriate when risks are controllable by the contractor, while CPFF contracts are appropriate when risks are controllable by the client. However, this conclusion ignores the relative willingness and ability of each party to bear risk. In particular, it ignores the pricing of risks, the client's attitude to trade-offs between expected cost and carrying risk, and the contractor's attitude to trade-offs between expected profit and carrying risk. Further, it fails to address questions about how risk that is not controllable by either party should be allocated.

In principle, decisions about the allocation of risk ought to be motivated by a search for risk efficiency and favourable trade-offs between risk and expected performance as described in Chapter 3. Given the opportunity, a client should favour risk efficient allocation of risk between parties to a project that simultaneously reduces risk and improves project performance for the client, be it in terms of lower expected cost or higher expected profits or some other measure of performance. An obvious example is decisions about purchasing insurance cover. Insurance is best regarded as one way of developing contingency plans (one of the nine types of risk response listed in Table 7.3), where payment of insurance premia ensures the ability to make some level of restitution in the event that an insured risk eventuates. The basic maxim for risk efficient insurance purchase is only insure risks that you cannot afford to take, because an uncovered event would cause serious financial distress that would distort other basic operations, or because dealing with an uncovered event would cause other forms of distress it is worth paying to avoid. For example, employment injury liability insurance may be worthwhile on both counts. A project may not be able to meet large claims without financial distress, but it may be just as important to avoid a position of conflict with employees over claims. The insured party may take steps to reduce the possibility of loss or mitigate the impact of any insured risk, and reasonable efforts to do this may be required by the insurer. Insurers are third parties who take on specific risks with a view to making a profit. Therefore, if the premium they can charge is not greater than the expected cost of the risk, giving them a positive expected profit, they will not take on the risk. In this sense they are subcontractors, competing for risks that might be better left with other contractors or the client.

Elsewhere (Chapman and Ward, 1994), we show in detail how the allocation of risk might be guided by consideration of the risk efficiency of alternative forms of contract payment terms. In choosing between a fixed price or CPFF contract, the criterion of risk efficiency implies choosing the contract with the preferred combination of expected cost and risk. As explained in Chapter 3, if one option offers both lower cost and lower risk, then this is a risk efficient choice.

The approach in Chapman and Ward (1994) distinguishes three basic types of project cost uncertainty or risk: contractor-controllable uncertainty, client-controllable uncertainty, and uncontrolled uncertainty. The analysis suggests that different contractual arrangements may be appropriate for each type of uncertainty, in each case dependent on the relative willingness of the client and contractor to accept project related risk. If a project involves all three types of uncertainty, the contract should involve different payment terms for each set of risks. To the extent that individual sources of cost uncertainty independently contribute to each of the three categories, it may be appropriate to subdivide categories and negotiate different payment terms for each major, independent risk source. One simple, practical example of this approach is where a client undertakes to pay a lower fixed price if the client agrees to carry a designated risk via cost reimbursement in respect of that risk.

The analysis highlights the need for clients to consider project cost uncertainty explicitly in the form of a 'PC curve' (Probability distribution of Costs) and to identify the client's 'equivalent' certain cost T, corresponding to the maximum fixed price the client is prepared to pay. In the envisaged procedure, the client first identifies appropriate constituent groupings of project risks, constructing associated PC curves and identifying T values for each. The PC curve for the project as a whole is then obtained by combining the component PC curves. The total project PC curve together with the associated T value is used later for checking the consistency and completeness of submitted bids rather than to determine a single payment method for the whole project. Tenderers are asked to submit for each group of project risks designated by the client:

1. fixed price bids R (the contractor's 'equivalent' certain cost);
2. the contribution to profit, or fee, K (a constant), required if a CPFF contract is agreed.

In addition, tenderers might be required or choose to submit their perceptions of constituent risk PC curves (which need not match the client's perceptions), to demonstrate the depth of their understanding of the project risks and to justify the level of bids, should these be regarded by the client as unusually low or high. Equally, a client might provide tenderers with the client's perceptions of constituent risk PC curves to encourage and facilitate appropriate attention to project cost uncertainties. If a spirit of co-operation and willingness to negotiate mutually beneficial, risk sharing arrangements prevailed, the client and individual tenderers could exchange perceptions about constituent risk PC curves with a view to developing a consensus view of project risks. Such views expressed as PC curves would facilitate the negotiation of mutually beneficial, risk sharing agreements without the necessity for the PC curves themselves to have any legal status in the contract.

In assessing bids, the client would be concerned about the relative sizes of R and T values for each constituent risk PC curve. The contractor bidding with the lowest total sum of R values would not necessarily be the contractor with the most preferred pattern of R values.

Our analysis (Chapman and Ward, 1994) concludes the following about the risk efficiency of fixed price and CPFF contracts:

1. a fixed price contract is usually risk efficient in allocating contractor-controllable risk;
2. a CPFF contract is usually risk efficient in allocating client-controllable risk;
3. in respect of uncontrollable risk, a fixed price contract is risk efficient if the contractor is more willing to accept risk ($R < T$), but a CPFF contract is risk efficient if the client is more willing to accept risk ($T < R$).

An important conclusion is that, even where client and contractor share similar perceptions of project cost uncertainty, a fixed price contract may be inefficient for the client, if the contractor is more risk averse than the client. In this situation the contractor will require a higher premium to bear the risk than the client would be prepared to pay for avoiding the risk. This situation can arise where the client is a relatively large organization, for whom the project is one of many, but the contractor is a relatively small organization, for whom the project is a major proportion of the contractor's business, a fairly common scenario.

We believe the results this analysis suggests are robust. These are not abstract arguments that will not withstand the impact of practical considerations. However, some clients have appeared to be willing to enter into CPFF contracts only as a last resort. For example, Thorn (1986, p. 229) notes experience in the UK Ministry of Defence in which the desire to avoid non-risk contracts has frequently led to non-competitive contracts being placed on a fixed price basis, even when the specification has been insufficiently defined for a firm estimate to be agreed:

> *In such cases, the contractor is unwilling to commit to a fixed price without a substantial contingency to cover any unknown risks, and the Authority is unable to accept the high level of contingency required by the contractor. The result is that prices have been agreed at such a late stage in the contract that the amount of risk eventually accepted by the contractor is substantially reduced and, in some cases, removed altogether. The Review Board has frequently expressed concern at delays in price fixing,*

and has advocated the use of incentive contracts. These are intended to be used when the risks are too great to enable fixed prices to be negotiated, but not so great as to justify the use of cost plus contracts.

Risk sharing and incentive contracts

Incentive contracts, often referred to as target cost or cost-plus-incentive-fee contracts, offer the possibility of sharing risk between the client and contractor and take an intermediary position between fixed price and CPFF contracts. This is potentially a more risk efficient alternative for both client and contractor.

In the simplest form of incentive contract, where:

C = the actual project cost (which is uncertain at the start of the project)

E = target cost

b = the sharing rate, $0 < b < 1$

F = the target profit level

and E, b, and F are fixed at the commencement of the contract, payment by the client to the contractor is:

$$C_T = F + bE + C(1 - b) \qquad (16.1)$$

and the profit to the contractor is:

$$P = F + b(E - C) \qquad (16.2)$$

When $b = 1$ the contract corresponds to a fixed price contract and when $b = 0$ the contract corresponds to a CPFF contract.

Note that in Equation (16.2), if the cost C exceeds E by more than F/b, then the profit to the contractor becomes negative and the contractor makes a loss.

In the situation described by Equation (16.2), which is sometimes referred to as a budget-based scheme, tendering firms select a budget (target cost) and incentive profit is proportional to budget variance (Reichelstein, 1992). Three parameters are required to specify the contract: the sharing rate b, the target cost level E, and the target profit level F. In theory, the target cost level should correspond to the expected value of project costs. In practice, it is very important that this is understood, lest misunderstandings about the status of this figure arise. Instead of specifying F, a target profit rate r may be specified, where $F = rE$. With this specification the client must decide which (if any) values to preset for E, b, and F or r prior to inviting tenders.

An alternative form of Equation (16.2) is:

$$P = d - bC \qquad (16.3)$$

where d is a fixed profit fee, with:

$$d = F + bE \qquad (16.4)$$

In Equation (16.3) only two parameters are required to specify the contract: the sharing rate b and the fixed profit fee d. Tenders may be invited in the form of d if b is prespecified by the client, or for both b and d. Typically, if a 'uniform' value for b is prespecified by the client, the contract is awarded to the contractor submitting the lowest fixed profit fee d.

The economic literature focuses on linear incentive contracts in the form of Equation (16.1), but in practice incentive contracts often involve more than one sharing rate over the range of possible project costs and may incorporate minimum and maximum levels of allowable profit. Two main types of incentive contract are usually distinguished: the Fixed Price Incentive (FPI) contract and the Cost Plus Incentive Fee (CPIF) contract. These differ mainly in the treatment of cost overruns beyond some ceiling. In both forms of contract the contractor's profit from cost underruns is subject to a ceiling value, but risk sharing takes place for costs in some range around the target or expected cost. With an FPI contract the contractor assumes a higher share of risk for cost overruns outside this range and may carry all risk above some set cost level. With a CPIF contract the client takes all cost risk above some cost level and the contractor receives a minimum level of profit.

Selection of an appropriate sharing rate

Risk sharing arrangements may be risk efficient from the client's point of view when contractors are risk averse, have superior precontractual information, or limited liability under the proposed contract. The desirability of risk sharing will also depend on whether the cost risks are controllable by the contractor, controllable by the client, or controllable by neither. In the latter case, the party bearing the risk acts as a quasi-insurer (Ward et al., 1991), and the desirability of risk sharing is related to the relative levels of risk aversion of the contractor and client. In the case of cost risks that are controllable to some extent by either party, risk sharing influences incentives to manage those risks.

An inherent problem with risk sharing is the reduction in a contractor's sensitivity to adverse outcomes as the proportion of cost risk borne by the client increases. In the case of contractor-controllable risk, the contractor's motivation to limit cost overruns and seek cost savings will be reduced as the client takes on more risk. It follows that different levels of risk sharing may be appropriate for categories of risk that are (a) controllable by the contractor, (b) controllable by the client, and (c) not controllable by either.

Samuelson (1986) shows that under 'general conditions', *some* level of risk sharing, with $0 < b < 1$, should be preferred by the client to either CPFF or fixed price contracts. The general nature of Samuelson's analysis does not lead to any specific optimal values for b, but the optimum value of b increases the more risk averse the client and the more costs are controllable by the contractor. A further complication is that contractor risk aversion affects the actual level of contractor effort on controlling costs once the sharing rate b has been negotiated. The greater the perceived risk of loss in a contracting situation the more vigorously contractors strive to reduce costs for the sake of avoiding loss as well as for the sake of gaining increments of profit (Scherer, 1964). A similar difficulty exists in considering the efficiency of sharing client-controllable risk. However, in specific situations, the client may be able to identify and cost various options available and evaluate these under different risk sharing arrangements.

In the case of risk that is not controllable by either client or contractor, a plausible variation to the risk sharing arrangement in (16.1) and (16.2) is to set $F = K + b^2(V - E)$, where K is the fee required by the contractor if a cost reimbursement CPFF contract were to be agreed and V is set to the value R or T referred to in the previous section. Assuming variance (Var) is an appropriate measure of risk, this risk sharing arrangement reduces the contractor's risk from $\text{Var}(E - C)$ to $\text{Var}\,b(E - C) = b^2\,\text{Var}(E - C)$. Therefore the contractor's risk premium should be reduced from $(V - E)$ to $b^2(V - E)$ under this risk sharing arrangement. With agreement between client and contractor on the value of the expected cost E, this arrangement is risk efficient for both client and contractor for a wide range of circumstances (Chapman and Ward, 1994).

Of course, difficulties in specifying an optimum, risk efficient level for the sharing rate need not preclude the use of incentive contracts and pragmatic definition of sharing rates by the client. In practice, incentive contracts, or target cost contracts, often specify different sharing rates for costs above, below, and close to the target cost, as in the case of FPI and CPIF contracts noted earlier. This provides substantial flexibility to design incentive contracts that can reflect the particular project context and the relative willingness and ability of client and contractor to bear financial risk. Broome and Perry (2002) describe several examples of incentive contracts and the different rationales underlying each one, usefully illustrating many of the considerations involved in effective and efficient allocation of risk. The underlying principle, as Broome and Perry put it, is:

> *the alignment of the motivations of the parties so as to maximize the likelihood of project objectives being achieved, taking into account the constraints and risks that act on the project and the strengths and weaknesses of the parties to it.*

Determining an appropriate target cost

A further problem in ensuring a risk efficient incentive contract is determining an appropriate value for the target cost E. Ideally, the client would like the target cost to correspond to the contractor's true estimate of expected cost. Obviously, the benefit to the client of an incentive element in the contractor's remuneration will be undermined if the target cost is higher than the contractor's true estimate of expected cost.

Suppose firms are invited to tender values for b and E. A disadvantage of this invitation is that it can encourage a generally high level of tender values for E. But the client would like to encourage truthful, unbiased estimates of the expected costs from tenderers. In principle, the client could achieve this by offering higher values of b for lower estimates of E. Then submitting an overestimate of expected cost will be less appealing to the contractor because the associated lower sharing rate limits the contractor's ability to earn large profits when costs turn out to be low. Conversely, if a contractor truly believes costs will be high, the threat of low profits if costs turn out to be high will dissuade the contractor from submitting an underestimate of expected cost.

Thus, the client could offer a menu of contracts, in terms of values of F and b for different values of E. By submitting a cost estimate, a tendering firm chooses one particular incentive contract given by the corresponding F and b values. Provided F and b are suitably defined, such a menu of contracts can induce firms to provide unbiased estimates of project cost.

A practical application of this menu approach for rewarding sales personnel in IBM Brazil is described by Gonik (1978). Gonik describes an incentive system that gears rewards to how close staff forecasts of territory sales and actual results are to the company's objectives. A sales forecast S is made by each salesperson for a given period and sales region, and this is used to determine each person's level of bonus P. If the company quota is Q, actual sales achieved are A, and a base level of bonus payment preset by the company is B, then each person's level of bonus payment P is given by:

$$P = BS/Q \quad \text{where } S = A \tag{16.5}$$

$$P = B(A + S)/2Q \quad \text{where } S < A \tag{16.6}$$

$$P = B(3A - S)/2Q \quad \text{where } S > A \tag{16.7}$$

In general, for a given sales forecast S, bonuses increase as A increases, but for a given A, payments are maximized if $A = S$. Thus, sales personnel receive more for higher sales but are also better off if they succeed in forecasting actual sales as closely as possible. In principle, a similar system could be adopted in contracting to encourage contractors to provide unbiased estimates of project costs and control these costs to the best of their ability (e.g., Reichelstein, 1992).

Selection of efficient contractors

If the client presets b and F (or r where $F = rE$), the selection of the contractor who bids the lowest value for E (or d) is not guaranteed to minimize procurement costs for the client. There may still be difficulties in selecting the most efficient contractor. For example, McCall (1970) has argued that incentive contracts awarded on the basis of the lowest bid leads to inefficient firms being selected. McCall's analysis implies that relatively inefficient firms, whose actual costs are high, tend to submit estimated costs (bids E) that are lower than actual costs, because they can share some of their losses with the client. Conversely, relatively efficient firms, whose actual costs of production are low, tend to submit estimated costs (bids) that are higher than actual costs. With the client sharing in any cost underrun, the less an efficient firm's expected cost the more it must bid to secure a profit equal to that obtainable elsewhere. Hence, if the client chooses among firms on the basis of the lowest bid, then it is possible that it will select relatively inefficient firms (high actual costs) instead of relatively efficient ones (low actual costs). The probability of selecting a high cost instead of a low cost firm increases as the declared sharing rate decreases.

In addition, where F and b are fixed by the client, Baron (1972) shows that if two firms are bidding for a contract, other things being equal, the more risk averse firm will submit the lower bid (in effect the lower estimate of E from Equation (16.4)) and the probability of a cost overrun will be greater if that firm is selected. Thus a low bid for d may reflect a contractor's wish to reduce the risk of not winning the contract rather than ability to perform the contract at low cost. This possibility is generally recognized in both fixed price and CPFF contract situations.

However, the above arguments by Baron and McCall are of limited relevance where clients do not preset the sharing rate b. More usually, it might be expected that the fixed profit fee d and sharing rates would be determined together, so that clients would bargain simultaneously for both low cost targets *and* high contractor share rates. Thus, in general, the tighter the negotiated cost target the higher the sharing proportion desired by the client. In these circumstances, Canes (1975) showed that there is a systematic tendency toward cost overruns, because contractors tend to submit bids below their actual estimate of expected costs. According to Canes only a subset of efficient firms will be willing to compete by simultaneously increasing the share rate they will accept and reducing their target cost bid. Inefficient firms and the remainder of efficient firms will prefer to charge for higher share rates by raising target cost bids, and in Canes' analysis these firms correspond to the set of firms that submit bids below their expected costs. To the extent that tendering contractors are observed to charge for higher share rates in this way, cost overruns can be expected from such contractors. As a contract-letting strategy, Canes suggests setting the target profit rate r (and hence the target profit level F) at 0 while allowing firms to choose share rates subject to some minimum rate greater than 0. Canes argues that this policy should minimize clients' costs of procurement while inducing firms to reveal their true opportunity costs of production.

However, an important assumption in the analysis of Canes (1975) and McCall (1970) is that the contracting firms are assumed to be risk neutral (maximizers of expected profit). In situations where contractors are significantly risk averse, their conclusions need to be treated with caution.

Conclusion

Addressing ownership issues in this chapter has been focused on the client–contractor relationships because this is one of the most common and clear-cut contexts in which ownership issues arise. It is also a useful context to illustrate basic ownership issues that apply in most multiparty situations, including intra-organizational contexts where legal contracts are replaced by various forms of agreement ranging from formal terms of reference, written undertakings, informal 'understandings', to traditional working practices. Even with limited client–contractor focus, ownership issues are not simple, and only an overview has been provided. Those seriously touched by these issues need to follow up the references provided.

Despite the risks inherent in the fixed price contract this is still a very common form of contract. CPFF contracts have weaknesses for the client/project owner that severely limit its use by risk averse client organizations. Incentive contracts offer a variety of middle ground positions, but do not appear to be as widely used as they might be. This may be because of a lack of awareness of the shortcomings of typical fixed price contracts or because of a lack of appreciation of the value of incentive contracts in motivating contractors. However, the additional complexity of incentive contracts may make them difficult and time-consuming to negotiate. In particular, there are problems in selecting the lowest cost contractor and appropriate values for the sharing rate b and the target cost E. Unless firms can be motivated to provide unbiased estimates of costs (perhaps by arrangements such as those described above), client organizations may be wary of incentive contracts when they are unable to formulate realistic project cost targets for themselves. Incentive contracts may be confined to procurement projects where the client has a sound basis to estimate contract costs, there are uncertainties that make a fixed price contract impractical, but the uncertainties are not so great as to justify the use of cost plus contracts (Thorn, 1986). A further problem with incentive contracts is that the evaluation of the conse-quences of a particular incentive contract is not straightforward when project costs are uncertain. This can make it difficult to carry out negotiations on a fully informed basis, but such difficulties are not insurmountable (Ward and Chapman, 1995a; Chapman and Ward, 2002, chaps 5 and 6). In particular, the Balanced Incentive And Risk Sharing (BIARS) contract approach developed in

Chapman and Ward (2002) provides an operational approach to resolving all the issues the authors are aware of, provided the client is prepared to assess preferred trade-offs between attributes of interest, like cost, duration, and various measures of 'quality'. Perhaps the most significant obstacle to greater use of incentive contracts and risk sharing is the still widespread unwillingness of parties entering into procurement contracts to explore the effects of project risk and the possibilities for effective risk management.

Negotiating a fixed price contract with a trusted or previously employed contractor may be a preferred alternative for knowledgeable clients and perhaps also worth pursuing by less knowledgeable clients. Also, a move away from 'adversarial' contracting towards 'obligational' contracting (Morris and Imrie, 1993) may be mutually beneficial for both clients and contractors and may give rise to an atmosphere of increased trust and sharing of information. In these circumstances there will be opportunities for increased mutual understanding and management of contract risks.

The flexibility of incentive contract forms of payment is attractive here, but more widespread use of such contracts may depend on the development of more 'obligational' contracting rather than 'adversarial' contracting. However, their use is essential for the achievement of effective risk management.

17 Organizing for risk management

All men are equal—all men, that is to say, who possess umbrellas.—E. M. Forster

Introduction

This book has been largely about how to achieve effective and efficient risk management in the context of a single project. In order to fully exploit the benefits of risk management, we have argued for the use of a formal process framework, the SHAMPU (Shape, Harness, And Manage Project Uncertainty) process framework in particular. Part II has discussed what is involved in each phase of this process framework, and Chapters 14–16 of Part III have considered modifications to the content of each phase to reflect application context.

In this chapter a corporate perspective on project risk management processes (RMPs) is adopted. We consider briefly what is involved in establishing and sustaining an organizational project risk management capability (PRMC).

The issues involved can be explored more systematically if we consider the setting up and operation of a PRMC as a project in its own right and examine this project in terms of the six *W*s framework of Chapter 1 and the eight stage project life cycle (PLC) framework of Chapter 2. This approach shapes the structure of this chapter.

A six *W*s perspective

In considering the development of a PRMC *de novo*, or even from a limited pre-existing capability, it is useful to review the six *W*s and the project definition process depicted in Figure 1.1.

1 *Who*: who are the parties ultimately involved?

The parties involved in establishing an organization's PRMC include those who might champion the initiative, the individual or project team responsible for making it happen, those who use the associated risk management systems and procedures, and those who subsequently support and maintain the PRMC. Outside parties may also be influential, such as banks or major customers. The experience, seniority, and role of the PRMC project manager is obviously of critical importance. That such a manager is appointed with these responsibilities is a basic tenet of effective project management.

Effective development of PRMC requires a recognition of where and how risk management processes already occur in the organization, decisions about where attempts to develop PRMC should be made, and further decisions about who should be involved. Such decisions might adopt a 'logical incrementalist' approach (Quinn, 1978), first targeting areas of the organization where the benefits from risk management will be greatest, and using this experience as a learning process before attempting more widespread deployment. For example, in a project based organization, an obvious starting place is at project manager level, working down into project components and then teams. Further development of risk management might be targeted at the function based units that provide support to projects.

Example 17.1 An example of evolution in risk management support

In the late 1970s an oil major began the development of its PRMC with a single risk analyst undertaking analysis late in the plan stage of the PLC. Initially he had extensive and almost continuous external consulting support (from Chapman), but over time consulting support became less intense and was largely concerned with generic methodology for new considerations. Very soon a group of analysts were working in the same way, to cover all projects, often earlier in the PLC. This group of analysts reported direct to the project managers for the most part, as a service function for project managers independent of the design, planning, and costing functions. After a few years, a more senior person was made head of the risk analysis function and the planning function, effectively integrating planning and risk management formally. Then a still more senior person was made responsible for risk management, planning, and costing, extending the integration. As time went on analysis was undertaken earlier and earlier in the PLC, although to our knowledge it did not get back to the design stage, which had separate risk analysis support, with a somewhat different (safety, reliability, and availability based) focus.

Developing PRMC for many organizations should include facilitating and monitoring PRMC in other 'partner' or 'agent' organizations. For example, an organization contracting with suppliers on an extensive and regular basis ought to be concerned with the potential for risk transfer between the contracting parties. The nature and extent of RMPs operated by suppliers should have some influence on the nature and extent of risk management undertaken by their business partners. In particular, a client organization might seek to manage risks by implicitly transferring them to a contractor via a firm, fixed price contract, but this implicit transfer might be no guarantee that the contractor will identify all relevant risks or accept responsibility for managing them. This is one reason why some client organizations, such as the UK Ministry of Defence, require offering contractors to demonstrate PRMC by requiring them to submit risk management plans along with their fixed price tenders.

2 *Why*: what do the parties want to achieve?

As Figure 1.1 shows, project parties (the project *who*) can drive the objectives of a project (in this case of PRMC development). The danger is that objectives are inappropriately restricted by particular parties. What is needed is a project champion who is aware of the potential benefits that can accrue from an effective PRMC and who has the will and the influence to maintain an ambitious view of what can and should be achieved.

The benefits of formal RMPs, as described in Chapter 3 and elsewhere, have tended to focus on the manner in which improvements in performance of individual projects can be obtained. In the present context a more long-term corporate view of potential benefits is appropriate. Put simply, the benefits of effective RMPs are in terms of improved project performance in a stream of projects across the range of project performance objectives. But part of the role of a formal risk management is clarifying the need for a richer set of motives, as well as helping pursuit of that richer set.

To illustrate this, Figure 17.1 offers a view of corporate benefits that the application of formal RMP for all projects might bring in a contracting organization. The diagram incorporates the benefits of documentation and corporate learning in a direct manner, with all other aspects of Chapter 3 working through 'ability to manage risks'. Assuming a contracting organization undertakes risk management prior to and after tendering, then a number of interrelated benefits can accrue, all driving up profitability, through lower level benefits such as:

- keener pricing, better design, and stronger risk management abilities provide competitive advantage and improve chances of winning contracts;
- better appreciation of uncertainty means more realistic pricing and the avoidance of potential loss-making 'disaster' contracts where uncertainty is too great;
- ability to manage risks means lower project costs with direct profit implications;
- reduced tendering costs mean higher profits.

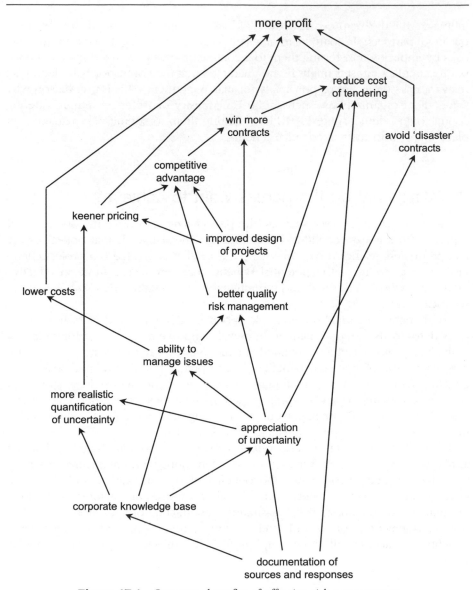

Figure 17.1—Corporate benefits of effective risk management

Figure 17.1 does not explicitly address the very valuable culture changes that can be an important part of the process of building a PRMC. Making 'enlightened caution', 'enlightened gambles', and 'enlightened controls' part of an organization's culture (as discussed in Chapter 3) can be central to killing a risk averse culture based on 'uncertainty and risk are negative issues, and what you don't know won't hurt you', generating a new risk management culture based on

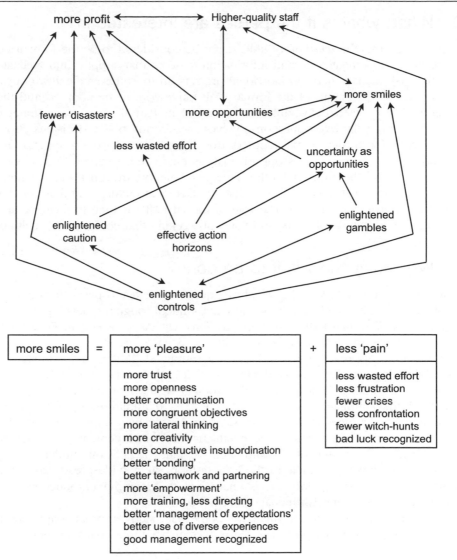

Figure 17.2—Corporate benefits of a risk management culture

'uncertainty is the source of our opportunities, and we need to understand our opportunities to capture them effectively'. Effective use of action horizons and other visible reductions in wasted effort and frustration can also be important. This kind of culture change can make an organization more exciting to work for and make going to work more enjoyable. This in turn can lead to higher quality staff wanting to join (and stay with) the organization, with obvious general benefits. Figure 17.2 portrays the spirit of this aspect of the impact of RMP. Figures 17.1 and 17.2 may be useful alongside a rereading of Chapter 3.

3   *What*: what is it the parties are interested in?

In physical terms the *what* of a PRMC might be considered to be the formalized procedures, documentation, and information systems that support and facilitate effective risk management on individual projects. In these terms the *what* question relates to the nature of the formal RMP framework to be adopted and the resulting documented deliverables as discussed in Part II. At a more strategic level, answering the *what* question involves considering policy decisions about the degree of formality to be adopted, the degree of anticipation sought, and potential restrictions on the scope of analysis envisaged. Chapter 15 discussed these issues and their impact on the benefits obtainable from risk management. Ultimately, the target *what* may be a 'risk management culture' with the benefits noted in the previous section. The role of formal RMPs is then to facilitate and encourage the attitudes, beliefs, and ways of working that comprise this culture.

4   *Whichway*: how is it to be done?

In terms of building PRMC, the *whichway* question relates to plans for the tasks involved in initial implementation and subsequent ongoing development of applications of formal RMPs on individual projects. As indicated in Figure 1.1, the *what* drives the *whichway* to a significant extent.

A common approach is to begin with a simplified RMP, perhaps limited to probability impact diagrams and checklists, introduced fairly rapidly with a minimum of piloting. Following rapid introduction, the intention is to continue operating the simplified process in a well defined administrative framework, without major changes in format. In Chapter 15 we have argued against this approach, contending that to achieve effective risk management it is essential to understand the nature of a comprehensive RMP. Ideally this understanding needs to be developed in a methodical fashion on a widespread basis, not confined to one or two individuals charged with the rapid introduction of a limited, new, corporate risk management policy.

The approach advocated in this book is the pilot study approach, applying a comprehensive RMP to a project to learn on that has three characteristics:

1. it has been very well managed to date;
2. despite its successful management to date, important sources of uncertainty raise concerns that need to be addressed to the satisfaction to those granting sanction;
3. there is sufficient time to undertake a comprehensive risk management process.

A pilot study approach of this kind should ultimately lead to relatively effective risk management procedures, but it may be relatively slow as a learning process. In contracting organizations, retrospective analysis of recently completed projects may provide more time for the necessary analysis and learning, divorced from tight time schedules associated with tender formulation.

As noted in Chapter 6, the application of an RMP to a given project can be a high-risk project in its own right, warranting particular attention to the process *who* question in the focus phase of the RMP. The process of instituting formal risk management procedures as a standard corporate policy is also not without risk. The essential threat is that the policy fails to bring sufficient benefits, perhaps because procedures are inappropriate, not properly implemented, or only partially adopted. Once difficulties are encountered the credibility of the initiative may suffer, making it very difficult to revive a PRMC initiative at a later date. Such threats and their underlying causes need to be recognized and managed in much the same way as any significant organizational change.

Walsham (1992) has suggested a management framework that views organizational change as a jointly analytical, educational and political process where important interacting dimensions are the context, content, and process of the change. Significant aspects of context include: stakeholders' perspectives and relationships between those affected by a particular project, the history of existing procedures and systems, informal networks and procedures, and infrastructure needs (e.g., skills and resources required). The process of change involves the dynamics of interaction between participants in a project and others who are affected by it or who can affect it. Significant aspects of process include power politics and organizational culture. Implementing a significant change, like the introduction of RMP, needs to take these dimensions into account. Other writers on the management of change have related the implementation process to Lewin's (1947) model of planned change, which involves three phases: unfreezing–changing–refreezing. Each phase is concerned with changes in the balance of (psychological) forces in the organization and the degree to which they restrain or drive change. Unfreezing involves disturbing the equilibrium of the status quo by increasing the balance of driving forces over restraining forces, decreasing restraining forces, or a combination of these. Effective unfreezing generally involves increasing driving forces while managing a reduction in restraining forces to reduce resistance to change. Refreezing involves the systematic replacement of the temporary change inducing forces that more permanent forces, which can maintain the new status quo.

Forces for change in terms of building PRMC are likely to be derived from a senior management recognition of the potential benefits as noted earlier. Resistance to change coming from other parties may be due to some or all of the following:

1. parochial self-interest in maintaining the status quo;
2. inability to perceive a need for change;
3. pressure of other work;
4. concern about the costs of introducing new procedures;

5. individuals concerned that they will be unable to carry out the new procedures;
6. uncertainty and suspicion about the nature of the change.

Suggested strategies for reducing resistance to change often include education, communication, participation and involvement, facilitation and support, and offering incentives. Discussing the introduction of strategic planning processes as a significant organizational change, Ansoff (1984) has argued that maximum resistance is produced by a change process that seeks to impose administrative systems before addressing sources of behavioural resistance to change. In contrast, Ansoff argues that minimum resistance is created when a change process builds acceptance of change before introducing administrative systems. In the context of introducing formal RMPs, the minimum resistance route implies a process that first clarifies the need for and relevance of formal risk management, seeks to improve stakeholders' understanding of what is involved, and provides motivation for individuals to use the new formal processes. Additionally, there is a need to ensure that risk management skills are developed and that individuals have sufficient time and resources to operate the RMP on individual projects. Subsequently, administrative systems for co-ordinating and monitoring the application and effectiveness of RMP applications can be introduced. The pilot study approach advocated above and the learning perspective discussed in Chapter 15 are entirely consistent with this minimum resistance route for implementation.

5   *Wherewithal*: what resources are required?

The *wherewithal* question concerns the extent of resources formally invested in developing and maintaining a PRMC. Such resources include personnel in terms of both numbers and expertise, the time allocated to risk management, and the provision of supporting infrastructure such as information systems and appropriate software. The greater the investment in such resources the easier it will be to move toward more effective risk management in terms of the other five Ws and choices made in respect of the other five W questions may be influenced by the resources available.

In terms of personnel, resourcing choices include decisions about the number, expertise, and location of dedicated risk management personnel deployed, the resources available to them, and the extent of training to develop the expertise of other employees. An obvious issue is the location and size of any corporate risk management support unit. In a project based contractor organization, alternative modes of support include:

• no specific risk management support for project managers, but limited training in risk management techniques;

- the provision of a central risk analysis support unit that project managers can call on as necessary; or
- project managers provided with risk management support in the form of a full-time, dedicated risk analyst.

Formal allocation and resourcing of time dedicated to risk management is another important aspect of *wherewithal* choices. For example, a senior management directive that formal project review meetings should also consider risk management issues may not result in much additional risk management if it has to be squeezed into already busy, one day meetings. A directive accompanied by an expectation that risk management deliberations should involve an additional full day's consideration is a rather more substantial resource commitment. Similar observations apply to the establishment and maintenance of information systems to support risk management.

6   *When*: when does it have to be done?

In a PRMC context, the *when* question concerns the timing of initiatives to establish the PRMC. As indicated in Figure 1.1, the *what* drives the *when* to a significant extent in terms of the timing of implementation across particular or all kinds of projects. A pilot approach fostering learning can be very effective, but assumes time is available for this. A situation to be avoided is an external *who* such as a bank or a major customer, driving the PRMC *why* and *what*, and forcing a rushed programme to establish and operate formal RMPs

A PLC perspective

The six *W*s framework points to a number of important aspects for consideration in establishing a PRMC. Taking a PLC perspective of the project 'establish a PRMC' provides a complementary, chronological perspective and additional insights into what issues need to be addressed.

PRMC: conception

As noted in Table 2.1, the conceive stage involves an outline specification of the deliverable to be produced and clarifying the purpose of the project. In respect of establishing PRMC this stage should be reasonably straightforward in that the purpose and deliverable are readily identifiable. The purpose is to obtain the benefits described in the *why* section above and in Chapter 3. The deliverable is the application of a formal RMP in various projects, with the SHAMPU process as a recommended framework.

As with any corporate initiative, senior management support is crucial to empower the project and to ensure it reflects the needs and concerns of senior management. All relevant managers, but especially project managers as future users of formal RMPs, need to become involved at this early stage, to ensure that their concerns are addressed at an early stage.

Ideally, a manager for the PRMC project should be appointed in this stage so that he or she can actively participate in elaborating the PRMC concept and clarify its purpose before the more detailed design and plan stages. It can be useful to involve a wider group of parties, including individuals in functional departments in the organization, key customers, key contractors or subcontractors, potential partners, and external consultants to facilitate the design and introduction of associated procedures and infrastructure.

PRMC: design

As noted in Chapter 2, the focus of the design stage is giving substance to the *what* of the PRMC as discussed earlier, although some consideration of the other five *W*s will be involved. It is assumed that the SHAMPU process framework can form the basis of the formal RMP ultimately needed. The aim is to build an effective PRMC that can pursue flexible tactics within the scope of a comprehensive process framework. If administrative processes for a simplified RMP that is limited in scope are introduced, this may delay and even discourage development of risk analysis and risk management expertise, as noted in Chapter 15.

Another design consideration is the range of projects that will be subject to a formal RMP. A simple answer, adopted by the UK Ministry of Defence, is 'all projects'. We support this approach. However, it implies that different levels of RMP will be cost-effective for different sizes and types of projects, which transforms the question into 'what kind of RMP should be used over the range of projects of interest?' In general, comprehensive risk management will tend to be most useful when projects involve one or more of the following:

1. substantial resources;
2. significant novelty (technological, geographical, environmental, or organizational);
3. long planning horizons;
4. large size;
5. complexity;
6. several organizations;
7. significant political issues.

In time, organizations institutionalizing project risk management may apply different guidelines for applying RMPs to projects, dependent on the degree of presence of the factors listed above. However, such sophistication needs to wait on the development of experience with a comprehensive RMP on selected projects.

A further design consideration is at what stage of a PLC an RMP will be applied. Chapter 14 discussed this issue in detail, making the observation that in general RMP was best applied as early as possible in a PLC. This is a significant issue for contracting organizations. As indicated in Example 9.1, contractors may usefully undertake risk analysis in respect of a given contract: first, as part of tender development, to help determine whether to bid or not and at what price; and, second, as ongoing risk management of a contract that is actually won. Contracting organizations ought to institute RMPs that incorporate risk analysis and management at each of these stages. As indicated in Figure 17.1, this may lead to strategic decisions about the amount of effort to be applied to submission of tenders, the level of profits expected on individual contracts, and an appropriate target success rate for submitted tenders.

PRMC: plan

The plan stage of establishing a PRMC involves determining how the design will be executed, what steps to take in what order, what resources are required in broad terms, and how long it will take. This involves determining specific targets for establishing an operative RMP, particularly in terms of the scope of the projects to be covered and the timescale in which this is to be achieved. To a large degree these targets will depend on the impetus behind the initiative, related to the parties involved and perceived need.

Plan development needs to include arrangements for capturing existing risk management expertise and disseminating it as part of developing risk management thinking and expertise in individual personnel. This may include in-house training courses and special interest group seminars (as a form of 'quality circle').

PRMC: allocation

As noted in Chapter 2, the allocate stage involves decisions about project organization, identification of appropriate participants, and allocation of tasks between them. From a corporate perspective, responsibility needs to be clearly allocated for:

- development of RMP documentation and guidelines;
- implementation of RMPs;
- monitoring compliance with guidelines and the effectiveness of RMPs.

A key aspect is the choice of roles allocated to corporate and business unit 'risk officers', project managers, support function managers, risk analysts, internal audit, and other specific functional areas.

Most organizations introduce project RMPs using a 'risk analyst' ('riskateer' is a term some prefer) who may be an external consultant, an internal consultant, or a member of the project team who has undertaken some form of training or self-study programme on risk management. A sizeable team of analysts may be involved, or the part-time efforts of a single individual. Most organizations with mature RMPs maintain a risk analysis team. In large organizations this team may be dedicated to project risk management. In small organizations this 'team' may be a single individual with other responsibilities. Even a very small organization needs somebody to act as the repository of risk management skills and facilitate formal risk management.

This team or individual may undertake risk analysis for individual project managers. However, they should not be regarded as risk *managers*, since proper integration of project risk management and project management more generally requires that the project manager take personal responsibility for all risk not explicitly delegated to managers of components of the project.

The provision of analytical support, while useful, is only part of institutionalizing RMPs. There is an additional need to ensure widespread, effective application of risk management guidelines, to monitor the quality of RMP applications, and to ensure that risk management experience is captured and used to improve risk management in subsequent projects.

PRMC: execution

The steps in the execute stage of the PLC shown in Table 2.1 are:

1. co-ordinate and control;
2. monitor progress;
3. modification of targets and milestones;
4. allocation modification;
5. control evaluation.

These steps carried out in a continuous iterative process are part of the ongoing management of RMP applications. From this perspective the PRMC project never terminates and the deliver, review, and support stages become part of the execute stage. However, a first pass through the execute stage might usefully involve a pilot exercise applying the proposed, formal, RMP framework to a suitable project, as indicated earlier. Lessons from this experience may influence the design of the RMP in a subsequent pass back through the design, plan, and allocate stages before application of the RMP on another project. This experience might also provide data in respect of sources of risk and efficacy of responses of direct relevance to other concurrent and subsequent projects. Such feedback clearly need not wait for termination of the subject project. As a general principle the institutionalizing of a formal RMP framework should include arrangements to disseminate the latest experience in managing uncertainty as rapidly as possible. In this context it may be useful to see the PRMC project as a programme of projects, in the sense of Figure 2.3.

PRMC: delivery

As indicated in Chapter 2 the deliver stage of a project involves commissioning and handover, with the steps shown in Table 2.1:

1. basic deliverable verification;
2. deliverable modification;
3. modification of performance criteria;
4. deliver evaluation.

In the context of completion of a pilot RMP application, such steps look very much like tasks that form a necessary part of a loop back through the design, plan, and allocate stages prior to further applications of the chosen RMP framework on a wider scale. Subsequently, these steps are worth addressing periodically to check and appraise the effectiveness of RMP procedures. Over time this can lead to significant changes in the way RMPs are co-ordinated and controlled.

PRMC: review

Following each application of the chosen RMP framework to a project, a systematic appraisal of the RMP application is appropriate to evaluate the likely relevance and usefulness of both project specific results and process specific results, to inform both future projects and future risk management practice.

Periodically, a broadly based review of RMP procedures and supporting infrastructure is appropriate to draw out lessons from the operation of RMP procedures across the organization.

PRMC: support

As indicated in Table 2.1, the support stage of a project involves the following steps:

1. basic maintenance and liability perception;
2. development of support criteria;
3. support perception development;
4. support evaluation.

There is a need to provide continuing support for risk management in future projects in both a facilitating and supervisory sense. Aside from analytical expertise that may be called on by project management teams, there may well be a need for corporate management involvement in scrutinizing individual RMPs to ensure an appropriately rigorous approach, to facilitate improvements in risk management practice and to monitor the effectiveness of RMPs. The level of such support will need to be reassessed periodically to ensure it remains cost-effective. As noted in Example 17.1, the level of analytical support may need to be increased over time and may need to change qualitatively, depending on the expertise and resources available within the project teams. Policy decisions may need to be made about the composition of project teams if the need for risk analysis increases. Apart from analytical support, senior management scrutiny of risk analyses and risk management plans may be well worth maintaining indefinitely as part of standard project appraisal procedures. This will help to maintain and improve standards of risk management, particularly through changes in personnel at all levels.

Benchmarking

Benchmarking PRMC deserves attention because any organization that starts a process of development for its PRMC will want to monitor progress, and organizations that want comfort or need a shock may seek external comparisons. Two 'risk maturity model' approaches to PRMC benchmarking are directly relevant (Hillson, 1997; DeLoach, 2000). Both attempt to simplify the benchmarking process by defining a limited number of 'maturity levels', ranging from organizations with no formal RMP to those with highly developed and fully integrated processes. Table 17.1 summarizes these two examples.

Example 1 (DeLoach, 2000) is an adaptation of a capability maturity model for software engineering organizations developed by the Software Engineering Institute (SEI) of Carnegie-Mellon University (Paulk et al., 1993, 1995). It identifies five levels of maturity: initial, repeatable, defined, managed, and optimizing. Example 2 (Hillson, 1997) is also influenced by the SEI maturity model, but it identifies just four levels of maturity: naive, novice, normalized, and natural. Hillson argues that some organizations may not fit neatly into specific maturity categories, but his four levels are 'sufficiently different to accommodate most organizations unambiguously ... more than four levels would increase ambiguity without giving sufficient additional refinement to aid use of the model.' Ward (2003) elaborates on the very brief summary provided by Table 17.1 and then provides a critique. But the essence of the problem is illuminated by the Hillson quote above. Ambiguity arises because both examples are one dimensional—a vector of possibilities in one dimension. Hillson addresses four attributes (culture, process, experience, and application) alongside his maturity level 'definitions', to define a matrix instead of the vector shown above, but each level involves only one possibility for each attribute. His attributes are not independent dimensions

Table 17.1—Two examples of risk management maturity models

Example 1 (DeLoach, 2000)

description	maturity level				
	1 initial	2 repeatable	3 defined	4 managed	5 optimizing
capability	(ad hoc/chaotic) No institutionalized processes Reliance on competence of individual	(intuitive) Processes established and repeating Reliance on individuals reduced	(qualitative/quantitative) Policies, processes, and standards defined and uniformly applied across the organization	(quantitative) Risks measured and managed quantitatively and aggregated enterprise-wide Risk/Reward trade-offs considered	(continuous feedback) Emphasis on taking and exploiting risk Knowledge accumulated and shared

Example 2 (Hillson, 1997)

description	maturity level			
	1 naive	2 novice	3 normalized	4 natural
definition	No structured approaches for dealing with uncertainty Reactive crisis management Reliance on competence of individuals	Experimentation via nominated individuals and specific projects No effectively -implemented, organization-wide process	Generic risk policies and procedures formalized and widespread	Proactive approach required to risk management in all aspects of the organization Common organization-wide understanding of activities, roles, and responsibilities for risk management Standard processes and tools tailored to specific applications Formal assignment of responsibility for risk management Organization-wide training

of a multi-dimensional model. They are additional features assumed to vary in a perfectly correlated manner, elaborations within a single dimension. The maturity model implicit in the analysis earlier in this chapter involves a separate dimension for each W and the PLC, and it should be obvious that more progress may be achieved in some dimensions than others, perhaps for very good reasons related to the organizational context. This six Ws and PLC model may be too simple, but to try to make it simpler still, by assuming maturity in all relevant dimensions will be correlated so that a one dimensional model can capture maturity, necessarily introduces ambiguity. This ambiguity shows less if only four levels are used, but it is inherent in any model that does not allow for two or more independent dimensions. The authors believe the Hillson model is an important step in the right direction, but the ambiguous nature of the level definitions in only one dimension may prove confusing.

Some concluding speculations

The evolution of RMP frameworks has been very rapid in the past decade. For those interested in project risk management in general terms, the most productive big issue to address is getting those organizations and institutions that lag well behind the leading edge up to best practice standards. How this is best done is not an easy question to address. The authors are keen to do what we can in this respect and we are very hopeful, but our expectations are not overly optimistic. For the past three decades some organizations have maintained PRMC at very high levels. But they have been the exception rather than the rule. This situation is unlikely to change quickly in the short run. It is a major threat for some areas of industry, a clear opportunity for those who achieve PRMC their competitors lack.

Further advancing the leading edge is a big issue for those already there, and three further speculations may be useful to lend the leading edge a sense of direction.

First, there is a clear need to develop the benchmarking ideas touched on in the last section into a generally usable operational form. Hillson's approach has a number of enthusiastic advocates and users, including slightly different forms developed by Hopkinson (HVR Consulting Services) for a range of clients. The need for sound benchmarking models that are simple when appropriate, without being simplistic, is clear. This chapter should make it clear why they need to be multi-dimensional to avoid ambiguity. What it does not resolve is how to do this. Those who do so successfully will be making a major contribution to the field and may enjoy associated commercial success.

Second, understanding the links between concerns about organizational culture and RMPs, models, and concepts used by the organization is a broader 'next frontier' for project risk management that can be construed to embrace the benchmarking issue as a special case. RMPs drive culture and vice versa and they are critically dependent on the models and concepts that they build on. Understanding how this works, and how to manage it, is a key big issue for the authors. Some aspects of what is involved are briefly explored in Chapman and Ward (2002, chap. 12) and touched on in this book, but these efforts just scratch the surface.

Third, formal contract structures between buyers and suppliers that are different organizations, and buyers and suppliers within the same organization, are the focus of several chapters in Chapman and Ward (2002). This is another important 'next frontier' that needs a lot more work in our view.

Most project risk is generated by the way different people perceive issues and react to them, shaped by 'the way we do things around here'. Culture and contracts, including informal contracts, and their interaction with operational RMPs and background corporate learning processes, take us into territory far removed from the technology uncertainty that drove early project risk management efforts, but this seems to be the favoured direction for developments over the next decade.

References

Abrahamson, M. (1973). Contractual risks in tunnelling: How they should be shared. *Tunnels and Tunnelling*, November, 587–598.

Adams, D. (1979). *The Hitchhiker's Guide to the Galaxy*. London: Pan Books.

Adams, D. (1980). *The Restaurant at the End of the Universe*. London: Pan Books.

Adams, J. R. and Barndt, S. E. (1988). Behavioral implications of the project life cycle. In: D. I. Cleland and W. R. King (eds), *Project Management Handbook* (2nd edn). New York: Von Nostrand Reinhold.

AIRMIC/ALARM/IRM (2002). *A Risk Management Standard*. London: Association of Insurance and Risk Managers, Association of Local Authority Risk Managers, Institute of Risk Management.

Akerlof, G. A. (1970). The market for 'lemons': Quality uncertainty and the market mechanism. *Quarterly Journal of Economics*, **84**, 488–500.

Alpert, M. and Raiffa, H. (1982). A progress report on the training of probability assessors. In: D. Kahneman, P. Slovic, and A. Tversky (eds), *Judgment Under Uncertainty: Heuristics and Biases*. New York: Cambridge University Press.

Anderson, D. L., Charlwood, R. G., and Chapman, C. B. (1975). On seismic risk analysis of nuclear plants safety systems. *Canadian Journal of Civil Engineering*, December.

Ansoff, H. I. (1984). *Implanting Strategic Management*. Englewood Cliffs, NJ: Prentice Hall International.

APM (1997). *PRAM Project Risk Analysis and Management Guide*. Association for Project Management, Norwich, UK.

Armstrong, J. S., Denniston, W. B., and Gordon, M. M. (1975). The use of the decomposition principle in making judgments. *Organisation Behaviour and Human Performance*, **14**, 257–263.

AS/NZS 4360 (1999). *Risk Management*. Strathfield, Standards Association of Australia. www.standards.com.au

Baccarini, D. and Archer, R. (2001). The risk ranking of projects: A methodology, *International Journal of Project Management*, **19**(3), 139–145.

Barber, J. N. (1989). Risks in the method of construction. In J. Uff and P. Capper (eds), *Construction Contract Policy: Improved Procedures and Practice*. London: Centre of Construction Law and Management, King's College.

Barnes, M. (1984). Effective project organisation. *Building Technology and Management*, December, 21–23.

Barnes, N. M. L. (1988). Construction project management. *International Journal of Project Management*, **6**(2), 60–79.

Baron, D. P. (1972). Incentive contracts and competitive bidding. *American Economic Review*, **62**, 384–394.

Berny, J. (1989). A new distribution function for risk analysis. *Journal of the Operational Research Society*, **40**(12), 1121–1127.

Bonnai, P., Gourc, D., and Lacosta, G. (2002). The life cycle of technical projects. *Project Management Journal*, **33**(1), 12–19.

Brooks, F. P. (1975). *The Mythical Man-month: Essays on Software Engineering*. Reading, MA: Addison-Wesley.

Broome, J. and Perry, J. (2002). How practitioners set share fractions in target cost contracts. *International Journal of Project Management*, **20**, 59–66.

BS6079 (2000). British Standard BS6079-3:2000. *Project Management—Part 3: Guide to the Management of Business Related Project Risk*. London: British Standards Institute.

CAN/CSA–Q850-97 (1997). *Risk Management: Guidelines for Decision Makers* (ISSN 0317-5609). Ontario: National Standards of Canada, Canadian Standards Association.

Canes, M. E. (1975). The simple economics of incentive contracting: Note. *American Economic Review*, **65**, 478–483.

CCTA (1995a). *Management of Project Risk* (Central Computer and Telecommunications Agency). London: HMSO.

CCTA (1995b). *Management of Programme Risk* (Central Computer and Telecommunications Agency, chapter 2). London: HMSO.

CCTA (1999). *Managing Successful Programmes* (Central Computer and Telecommunications Agency). London: HMSO.

Chapman, C. B. (1979). Large engineering project risk analysis. *IEEE Transactions on Engineering Management*, **EM-26**, 78–86.

Chapman, C. B. (1988). Science, engineering and economics: OR at the interface. *Journal of the Operational Research Society*, **39**(1), 1–6.

Chapman, C. B. (1990). A risk engineering approach to project management. *International Journal of Project Management*, **8**(1), 5–16.

Chapman, C. B. (1992a). *Risk Management: Predicting and Dealing with an Uncertain Future* (Exhibit #748, Province of Ontario Environmental Assessment Board Hearings on Ontario Hydro's demand/supply plan). Ontario: Independent Power Producers Society.

Chapman, C. B. (1992b). My two cents worth on how OR should develop. *Journal of the Operational Research Society*, **43**(7), 647–664.

Chapman, C. B. and Cooper, D. F. (1983a). Risk engineering: Basic controlled interval and memory models. *Journal of the Operational Research Society*, **34**(1), 51–60.

Chapman, C. B. and Cooper, D. F. (1983b). Parametric discounting. *Omega—International Journal of Management Science*, **11**(3), 303–310.

Chapman, V. B. and El Hoyo, J. (1972). Progressive basic decision CPM. *Operational Research Quarterly*, **23**(3), 345–359.

Chapman, C. B. and Howden, M. (1997). Two phase parametric and probabilistic NPV calculations, with possible deferral of disposal of UK Nuclear Waste as an example. *Omega, International Journal of Management Science*, **25**(6), 707–714.

Chapman, C. B. and Ward, S. C. (1994). The efficient allocation of risk in contracts. *Omega—The International Journal of Management Science*, **22**(6), 537–552.

Chapman, C. B. and Ward, S. C. (1996). Valuing the flexibility of alternative sources of power generation. *Energy Policy*, **24**(2), 129–136.

Chapman, C. and Ward, S. (1997). *Project Risk Management—Processes, Techniques and Insights* (1st edn). Chichester, UK: John Wiley & Sons.

Chapman, C. and Ward, S. (2002). *Managing Project Risk and Uncertainty—A Constructively Simple Approach to Decision Making.* Chichester, UK: John Wiley & Sons.

Chapman, C. and Ward, S. (2003). Constructively simple estimating. *Journal of the Operational Research Society.* Forthcoming.

Chapman, C. B., Cooper, D. F., and Cammaert, A. B. (1984). Model and situation specific OR methods: Risk engineering reliability analysis of an L.N.G. facility. *Journal of the Operational Research Society,* **35**, 27–35.

Chapman, C. B., Cooper, D. F., Debelius, C. A., and Pecora, A. G. (1985a). Problem solving methodology design on the run. *Journal of the Operational Research Society,* **36**(9), 769–778.

Chapman, C. B., Phillips, E. D., Cooper, D. F., and Lightfoot, L. (1985b). Selecting an approach to project time and cost planning. *International Journal of Project Management,* **3**(1), 19–26.

Chapman, C. B., Cooper, D. F., and Page, M. J. (1987). *Management for Engineers.* Chichester, UK: John Wiley & Sons.

Chapman, C. B., Ward, S. C., and Bennell, J. A. (2000). Incorporating uncertainty in competitive bidding. *International Journal of Project Management,* **18**, 337–347

Charette, R. N. (1989). *Software Engineering Risk Analysis and Management.* New York: McGraw-Hill.

Charette, R. N. (1993). Essential risk management: Note from the front. *Second SEI Conference on Risk Management, Pittsburg, Pennsylvania.*

Checkland, P. B. and Scholes, J. (1990). *Soft Systems Methodology in Action.* Chichester, UK: John Wiley & Sons.

Clark, P. and Chapman, C. B. (1987). The development of computer software for risk analysis: A decision support system development case study. *European Journal of Operational Research,* **29**(3), 252–261.

Cooper, D. F. and Chapman, C. B. (1987). *Risk Analysis for Large Projects—Models, Methods and Cases.* Chichester, UK: John Wiley & Sons.

Cooper, K. G. (1980). Naval ship production: A claim settled and a framework built. *Interfaces,* **10**(6), 20–36.

Crosby, A. (1968). *Creativity and Performance in Industrial Organisation.* London: Tavistock Publications.

Curtis, B., Ward, S. C., and Chapman, C. B. (1991). *Roles, Responsibilities and Risks in Management Contracting* (Special Publication No. 81). London: Construction Industry Research and Information Association.

DeLoach, J. W. (2000). *Enterprise Wide Risk Management: Strategies for Linking Risk with Opportunity.* London: Financial Times/Prentice Hall.

DeMaere, R., Skulmoski, G., Zaghloul, R., and Hartman, F. (2001) Contracting and the flying trapeze: The trust factor. *Project Management,* **7**(1), 32–35.

Dennison, M. and Morgan, T. (1994). Decision conferencing as a management process—A development programme at Dudley MBC. *OR Insight,* **7**(2), 16–22.

Diffenbach, J. (1982). Influence diagrams for complex strategic issues. *Strategic Management Journal,* **3**, 133–146.

Eden, C. (1988). Cognitive mapping: A review. *European Journal of Operational Research,* **36**, 1–13.

Eden, C., Williams, T., Ackermann, F., and Howick, S. (2000). The role of feedback dynamics in disruption and delay (D&D) in major projects. *Journal of the Operational Research Society*, **51**, 291–300.

Eisenhardt, K. M. (1989). Agency theory: An assessment and review. *Academy of Management Review*, **8**(1), 57–74.

Finlay, P. and Marples, C. (1991). A review of group decision support systems. *OR Insight*, **4**(4), 3–7.

Fischoff, B. (1982). For those condemned to study the past: Heuristics and biases in hindsight. In: D. Kahneman, P. Slovic, and A. Tversky (eds), *Judgment Under Uncertainty: Heuristics and Biases*. New York: Cambridge University Press.

Fischoff, B., Slovic, P., and Lichtenstein, S. (1978). Fault trees: Sensitivity of estimated failure probabilistics to problem representation. *Journal of Experimental Psychology: Human Perception and Performance*, **4**, 330–334.

Forrester, J. (1958). Industrial dynamics: A major breakthrough for decision making. *Harvard Business Review*, **36**(4), 37–66.

Forrester, J. (1961). *Industrial Dynamics*. Cambridge, MA: MIT Press.

Furnham, A. (2000) The brainstorming myth. *Business Strategy Review*, **11**(4), 21–28.

Godfrey, P. (1996). *Control of Risk: A Guide to the Systematic Management of Risk from Construction* (ISBN 0-86017-441-7). London: Construction Industry Research and Information Association.

Goldratt, E. M. (1997). *Critical Chain*. Great Barrington, MA: The North River Press.

Golenko-Ginzburg, D. (1988). On the distribution of activity time in PERT [Program Evaluation and Review Technique]. *Journal of the Operational Research Society*, **39**(8), 767–771.

Gonik, J. (1978). Tie salesmen's bonuses to their forecasts. *Harvard Business Review*, May–June, 116–123.

Gordon, G. and Pressman, I. (1978). *Quantitative Decision Making for Business*. Englewood Cliffs, NJ: Prentice Hall International.

Gordon, W. J. J. (1956). Operational approach to creativity. *Harvard Business Review*, **34**(6), pp. 41–51.

Gordon, W. J. J. (1968). *Creativity and Performance in Industrial Organisation*. London: Tavistock Publications.

Green, S. D. (1994). Beyond value engineering: SMART value management for building projects. *International Journal of Project Management*, **12**(1), 49–56.

Green, S. D. (2001). Towards an integrated script for risk and value management. *Project Management*, **7**(1), 52–58.

Grey, S. (1995). *Practical Risk Assessment for Project Management*. Chichester, UK: John Wiley & Sons.

Hall, W. K. (1975). Why risk analysis isn't working. *Long Range Planning*, December, 25–29.

Hartman, F. and Snelgrove, P. (1996). Risk allocation in lump sum contracts—concept of latent dispute. *Journal of Construction Engineering and Management*, September, 291–296.

Hartman, F., Snelgrove, P., and Ashrafi, R. (1997). Effective wording to improve risk allocation in lump sum contracts. *Journal of Construction Engineering and Management*, December, 379–387.

Hertz, D. B. (1964). Risk analysis in capital investment. *Harvard Business Review*, **42**(1), 95–106.

Hillson, D. A. (1997). Towards a risk maturity model. *The International Journal of Project and Business Risk Management*, Spring **1**(1), 35–45.

Hillson, D. (2002a). What is risk?—Towards a common definition. *InfoRM*, April, 11–12.

Hillson, D. (2002b). Extending the risk process to manage opportunities. *International Journal of Project Management*, **20**(3), 235–240.

Hook, C. D. (2003). The role of restaurant entrepreneurs' social competencies in the success of their businesses. BSc Management Sciences Dissertation, School of Management, University of Southampton.

HMT (2002). *The Green Book—Consultation Paper* (Public Service Delivery Analysis). London: HM Treasury.

Howick, S. (2003). Using systems dynamics to analyze disruption and delay in complex projects for litigation—Can modeling purposes be met? *Journal of the Operational Research Society*, **54**, 222–229.

ICE (Institution of Civil Engineers) (1995). *The New Engineering Contract* (2nd edn). London: Thomas Telford.

ICAEW (1999). *Internal Control; Guidance for Directors on the Combined Code: Turnbill Report*. London: Institute of Chartered Accountants in England and Wales.

Ishikawa, K. (1986). *Guide to Quality Control* (2nd edn). White Plains, NY: Asia Productivity Organization/Quality Resources.

Jordanger, I. (1998). Value-oriented management of project uncertainties. *Proceedings of the 14th World Congress on Project Management, 10–13 June, Ljubljana, Slovenia* (Vol. 2).

Kahneman, D., Slovic, P., and Tversky, A. (eds) (1982). *Judgment under Uncertainty: Heuristics and Biases*. New York: Cambridge University Press.

Kaplan, R. S. and Norton, D. P. (1996). *The Balanced Scorecard: Translating Strategy into Action*. Boston: Harvard Business School Press.

Keeney, R. L. and van Winterfeldt, D. (1991). Eliciting probabilities from experts in complex technical problems. *IEEE Transactions on Engineering Management*, **38**(3), August, 191–201.

Klein, J. H. (1993). Modelling risk trade-off. *Journal of the Operational Research Society*, **44**, 445–460.

Klein, J. H. and Cork, R. B. (1998) An approach to technical risk assessment. *International Journal of Project Management*, **16**(6), 345–351.

Kletz, T. A. (1985). *An Engineer's View of Human Error*. Rugby, UK: The Institution of Chemical Engineers.

Knight, F. (1921). *Risk, Uncertainty and Profit*. Boston: Houghton Mifflin.

Lam, P. T. I. (1999). A sectoral review of risks associated with major infrastructure projects. *International Journal of Project Management*, **17**, 77–87.

Lemaitre, N. and Stenier, B. (1988). Stimulating innovation in large companies: Observations and recommendations from Belgium. *R & D Management*, **18**(2), 141–158.

Lewin, C. (2002). *RAMP Risk Analysis and Management for Projects*. London: Institution of Civil Engineers and the Faculty and Institute of Actuaries in association with Thomas Telford.

Lewin, K. (1947). Frontiers in group dynamics. *Human Relations*, **1**(1), 5–41.

Lichtenberg, S. (2000). *Proactive Management of Uncertainty Using the Successive Principle*. Copenhagen: Polyteknisk Press.

Lichtenstein, S., Fischoff, B., and Phillips, L. D. (1982). Calibration of probabilities: The state of the art to 1980. In: D. Kahneman, P. Slovic, and A. Tversky (eds), *Judgment under Uncertainty: Heuristics and Biases*. New York: Cambridge University Press.

Lyles, M. A. (1981). Formulating strategic problems: Empirical analysis and model development. *Strategic Management Journal*, **2**, 61–75.

Markowitz, H. (1959) *Portfolio Selection: Efficient Diversification of Investments*. New York: John Wiley and Sons.

Marples, C. and Riddle, D. (1992). Formulating strategy in the Pod—An application of Decision Conferencing with Welwyn Hatfield District Council. *OR Insight*, **5**(2), 12–15.

McCall, J. J. (1970). The simple economics of incentive contracting. *American Economic Review*, **60**, 837–846.

Merkhofer, M. W. (1987). Quantifying judgmental uncertainty: Methodology, experiences and insights. *IEEE Transactions on Systems, Man and Cybernetics*, **SMC-17**(5), 741–752.

Miller, R. and Lessard, D. (2000). *The Strategic Management of Large Engineering Projects: Shaping Risks, Institutions and Governance*. Cambridge, MA: MIT Press.

Miller, R. and Lessard, D. (2001). Understanding and managing risks in large engineering projects. *International Journal of Project Management*, **19**, 437–443.

Mintzberg, H. (1978). Patterns in strategy formation. *Management Science*, **24**(9), 934–948.

MoD (1991). *Risk Management in Defence Procurement* (reference D/DPP(PM)/2/1/12). London: Ministry of Defence, Procurement Executive, Directorate of Procurement Policy (Project Management).

Moder, J. J. and Philips, C. R. (1970). *Project Management with CPM [Clinical Path Method] and PERT [Program Evaluation and Review Technique]*. New York: Van Nostrand.

Moore, P. G. and Thomas, H. (1976). *Anatomy of Decisions*. London: Penguin Books.

Morgan, M. G. and Herion, M. (1990). *Uncertainty—A Guide to Dealing with Uncertainty in Quantitative Risk and Policy Analysis*. New York: Cambridge University Press.

Morris, J. and Imrie, R. (1993). Japanese style subcontracting—Its impact on European industries. *Long Range Planning*, **26**(4), 53–58.

Mould, G. (1993). Depending on the weather—Assessing weather risk in North Sea oil production. *OR Insight*, **6**(4), 13–17.

NUREG (1975). *An Assessment of Accident Risks in US Commercial Nuclear Power Plants* (Reactor Safety Study, WASH-1400 (NUREG—75/014). Washington, DC: US Nuclear Regulatory Commission.

OGC (2002). *Management of Risk: Guidance for Practitioners* (Office of Government Commerce). London: The Stationery Office.

Paulk, M. C., Curtis, W., Chrissis, M., and Weber, C. B. (1993). Capability maturity model, Version 1.1. *IEEE Software*, **10**(4), 18–27.

Paulk, M. C., Weber, C. B., Curtis, W., and Chrissis, M. (eds) (1995). *Capability Maturity Model: Guidelines for Improving the Software Process*. Reading, MA: Addison-Wesley.

Perry, J. G. (1986). Dealing with risk in contracts. *Building Technology and Management*, April, 23–26.

Phillips, L. D. (1982). Requisite decision modelling: A case study. *Journal of the Operational Research Society*, **33**, 303–311.

PMI (2000). *A Guide to the Project Management Book of Knowledge: PMBOK [Project Management Book of Knowledge] Guide* (2000 edn). Upper Darby, PA: Project Management Institute.

Quinn, J. B. (1978). Strategic change: Logical incrementalism. *Sloan Management Review*, **20**(1), 7–21.

Raiffa, H. (1968). *Decision Analysis: Introductory Lectures on Choices under Uncertainty.* Reading, MA: Addison-Wesley.

Reichelstein, S. (1992). Constructing incentive schemes for government contracts: An application of agency theory. *The Accounting Review,* 67(4), 712–731.

Richardson, G. P. and Pugh, A. L. (1981). *Introduction to Systems Dynamics Modeling with DYNAMO.* Portland, OR: Productivity Press.

Rodrigues, A. G. and Williams, T. M. (1998). Systems dynamics in project management: Assessing the impacts of client behaviour on project performance. *Journal of the Operational Research Society,* **49**, 2–15.

Rosenhead, J. (1989). *Rational Analysis for a Problematic World: Problem Structuring Methods for Complexity, Uncertainty and Conflict.* Chichester, UK: John Wiley & Sons.

Sadeh, A., Dvir, D., and Shenhar, A. (2000). The role of contract type in the success of R&D defence projects under increasing uncertainty. *Project Management Journal,* 31(3), 14–22.

Samuelson, W. (1986). Bidding for contracts. *Management Science,* 32(12), 1533–1550.

Scherer, F. M. (1964). The theory of contractual incentives for cost reduction. *Quarterly Journal of Economics,* **78**, 257–280.

Senge, P. M. (1990). *The Fifth Discipline: The Art and Practice of the Learning Organization.* New York: Doubleday.

Simon, H. A. (1979). Rational decision-making in business organizations. *American Economic Review,* **69**, 493–513.

Simon, O. (1998). *RAMP Risk Analysis and Management for Projects: RAMP Guide.* London: Institution of Civil Engineers and the Faculty and Institute of Actuaries in association with Thomas Telford.

Simon, P., Hillson, D., and Newland, K. (1997). *PRAM Project Risk Analysis and Management Guide.* Norwich, UK: Association for Project Management.

Slovic, P., Fischoff, B., and Lichtenstein, S. (1982). Facts versus fears: Understanding perceived risk. In: D. Kahneman, P. Slovic, and A. Tversky (eds), *Judgment under Uncertainty: Heuristics and Biases.* New York: Cambridge University Press.

Soukhakian, M. A. (1988). Project completion times and criticality indices. PhD dissertation, Department of Management, University of Southampton.

Spetzler, C. S. and Stael von Holstein, C. S. (1975). Probability encoding in decision analysis. *Management Science,* 22(3), 340–358.

Taylor, A. (1991). Four inch set back for 30 miles of Channel tunnel. *Financial Times,* Tuesday, 9 April.

Thamhain, H. J. and Wileman, D. L. (1975). Conflict management in project life cycles. *Sloan Management Review,* 26(3), summer.

Thorn, D. G. (1986). *Pricing and Negotiating Defence Contracts.* London: Longman.

Tilanus, C. B. (1985). Failures and successes of quantitative methods in management. *European Journal of Operational Research,* **19**, 170–175.

Tummala, V. M. R. and Burchett, J. F. (1999). Applying a risk management process (RMP) to manage cost risk for an EHV transmission line project. *International Journal of Project Management,* 17(4), 223–235.

Turner, J. R. (1992). *The Handbook of Project Based Management: Improving Processes for Achieving Your Strategic Objectives.* New York: McGraw-Hill.

Turner, J. R. and Cochrane, R. A. (1993). Goals-and-methods matrix: Coping with projects with ill-defined goals and/or methods of achieving them. *International Journal of Project Management,* **11**, 93–102.

Tversky, A. and Kahneman, D. (1974). Judgment under uncertainty: Heuristics and biases. *Science*, **185**, 1124–1131 (reprinted in Kahneman, D., Slovic, P., and Tversky, A. (eds) (1982). *Judgment under Uncertainty: Heuristics and Biases*. New York: Cambridge University Press).

Uher, T. E. and Toakley, A. R. (1999). Risk management in the conceptual phase of a project. *International Journal of Project Management*, **17**(3), 161–169.

Walsham, G. (1992). Management science and organizational change: A framework for analysis. *Omega—The International Journal of Management Science*, **20**(1), 1–9.

Ward, S. C. (1989). Arguments for constructively simple models. *Journal of the Operational Research Society*, **40**(2), 141–153.

Ward, S. C. (1999). Requirements for an effective project risk management process. *Project Management Journal*, September, 37–43.

Ward, S. C. (2003) Approaches to integrative risk management—A multi-dimensional framework. *Risk Management—An International Journal* (forthcoming).

Ward, S. C. and Chapman, C. B. (1988). Developing competitive bids: A framework for information processing. *Journal of the Operational Research Society*, **39**(2), 123–134.

Ward, S. C. and Chapman, C. B. (1994). Choosing contractor payment terms. *International Journal of Project Management*, **12**(4), 216–221.

Ward, S. C. and Chapman, C. B. (1995a). Evaluating fixed price incentive contracts. *Omega—The International Journal of Management Science*, **23**(1), 49–62.

Ward, S. C. and Chapman, C. B. (1995b). Risk management and the project life cycle. *International Journal of Project Management*, **13**(3), 145–149.

Ward, S. C. and Chapman, C. B. (2003). Transforming project risk management into project uncertainty management. *International Journal of Project Management*, **21**(2), 97–105.

Ward, S. C., Chapman, C. B., and Curtis, B. (1991). On the allocation of risk in construction projects. *International Journal of Project Management*, **9**(3), 140–147.

Waters, D. (2001). *Quantitative Methods for Business* (3rd edn). London: Pearson Education.

Wheelwright, S. C. (1978). Reflecting corporate strategy in manufacturing decisions. *Business Horizons*, February, 57–66.

Whiting, C. S. (1958). *Creative Thinking*. New York: Reinhold.

Williams, T. M. (1992). Practical use of distributions in network analysis. *Journal of the Operational Research Society*, **43**(3), 265–270.

Williams, T. (1995). A classified bibliography of recent research relating to project risk management. *European Journal of Operational Research*, **85**, 18–38.

Williams, T. (2003). Learning from projects. *Journal of the Operational Research Society*, **54**(5), 443–451.

Williams, T., Eden, C., Ackermann, F., and Tait, A. (1995a). The effects of design changes and delays on project costs. *Journal of the Operational Research Society*, **46**, 809–818.

Williams, T., Eden, C., Ackermann, F., and Tait, A. (1995b). Vicious circles of parallelism. *International Journal of Project Management*, **13**, 151–155.

Woodhouse, J. (1993). *Managing Industrial Risk—Getting Value for Money in Your Business*. London: Chapman & Hall.

Yong, D. H. H. (1985). Risk analysis software computation error balancing for British Petroleum International Limited. MSc dissertation, Department of Management, University of Southampton.

Index